The Adventures of Franky Fabs

Volume One

Frank John Trousdell

FriesenPress

One Printers Way
Altona, MB R0G 0B0
Canada

www.friesenpress.com

Copyright © 2022 by Frank John Trousdell
First Edition — 2022

All rights reserved.

No part of this publication may be reproduced in any form, or by any means, electronic or mechanical, including photocopying, recording, or any information browsing, storage, or retrieval system, without permission in writing from FriesenPress.

Scripture quotations taken from the 21st Century King James Version®, copyright © 1994. Used by permission of Deuel Enterprises, Inc., Gary, SD 57237. All rights reserved.

www.franktrousdell.net

ISBN
978-1-03-913825-4 (Hardcover)
978-1-03-913824-7 (Paperback)
978-1-03-913826-1 (eBook)

1. BIOGRAPHY & AUTOBIOGRAPHY, PERSONAL MEMOIRS

Distributed to the trade by The Ingram Book Company

To my youngest son, Michael Alexander Trousdell
January 30, 1981–June 2, 2019

"Life is not worth it since you left,
but for your memory I will stay."

Dave,
  Thank you for your advice, direction & friendship. Proud to know you.
     Frank Trousdell
      Dec 19, 2022

Contents

Preface VII
Chapter 2 18
Chapter 3 23
Chapter 4 38
Chapter 5 57
Chapter 6 69
Chapter 7 83
Chapter 8 93
Chapter 9 115
Chapter 10 138
Chapter 11 149
Chapter 12 166
Chapter 13 178
Chapter 14 198
Chapter 15 216
Chapter 16 235
Chapter 17 267
Chapter 18 290
Chapter 19 316
Chapter 20 322
Chapter 21 330
Chapter 22 335

PREFACE

I started writing this book in 2002, with the intent to try to understand why I'd made the life choices that guided me here today. As I tried to creatively place the words just right to make sense of my life, I eventually realized that while my memories drew me back, way on back, I was challenged with more important issues and questions that compelled me to find answers.

Why would I even think that my life would make a difference to someone I probably will never meet? What makes me think that what I have experienced over the last sixty-seven years would intrigue masses of people to want to read about me? I find my questions almost self-indulgent with a dose of arrogance and narcissism. Yet I am driven quietly to complete this task chronologically and to the best of my memory, to put pen to paper, documenting my life's journey, looking through the scratched glass of alcoholism.

From the get-go, I want to make it known that I have been blessed throughout my controversial life. The road I walked was riddled with failure and heartache, a lot of which I take full responsibility for. An accountant once commented that I was living my life like a motorboat travelling too close to the shore, and my wake was wiping out anyone and everything situated before and lying on the beach. My response was, "At least I'm in the boat and not on the beach."

My true blessings are my children and grandchildren. I can only hope they make a point to learn from my mistakes and not follow the many choices that led to my failures and indiscretions. I often wonder if that was my purpose, to pave the way for them to live a better and more righteous life. I cannot complain. When I look back over the years, I find that I was truly a social junkie, looking to be something better than I was the day before. I walked with only one fear, that of not trying. Yes, not trying anything that was available for me to access and give it my best shot. Over the decades from the sixties, seventies, eighties, and even the nineties, my drive to succeed was based on the effort, not necessarily the knowledge. The knowledge would come through the attempt.

Today, I believe that with the overbearing government controls and regulations, the old theory "You can do anything you put your mind to" has been vetted out of the formula and slowly eliminated. If you've got the money, the training, and the support from the right influential people or person, you will have a chance. Back in my day, you networked your way into the right crowd. Then you set out to sell your way into getting the money and the influence, and when you accessed enough money, you bought your professional support. An old business mentor once said to me, "First you get the money. Then you own the power . . . finally, the women will want you." I found out the hard way that he was so right. He did, however, miss one very important element: "Then the lawyers will begin to try to take it all away."

I am blessed because I have a son, who, through his own efforts, built his fortunes in eight years. He is now a multi-millionaire. He is also a very devoted father and husband. My son once said to me, "When I am about to make a very important and critical business decision, I think of what you would have done. Then I do the opposite."

At first, I was hurt by what he said. Then, after careful thought, I realized he had just complimented me. He took the advice from the results of my actions and made the right choices. What better thank you can a father get from his son than to learn from his mistakes and do better because of it?

I remember a story of a father with two sons. The father was concerned about making sure both sons were well balanced. The older son was extremely optimistic, and the younger was desperately pessimistic. So, the father put the younger into a room filled with the most beautiful toys and said to him, "Have a blast for the next few days and we'll see what happens." Then he put his oldest son in a room full of nothing but horse shit, leaving enough room at the top to have air to breathe.

Two days go by, and then the father visited the son with the toys. He opened the door to find his younger son curled up in a corner, crying. "What's wrong, son? Didn't you have fun?"

"No," he said. "That toy is broken, the other doesn't work right, and there just isn't anything that I like."

The father, in total dismay, replied, "Oh well, I tried."

He then went to his older son with a great deal of reservation and opened the door. All he could see was horse shit flying everywhere and his son in the middle of the pile, digging as hard as he could. "What the hell are you doing?" the father asked in complete shock and surprise.

The older son popped up his shit-covered head and replied with great confidence, "I know you, Dad! There's got to be a pony in here somewhere!"

Life is full of surprises. Sometimes you get nothing but crap, and that's how you end up feeling. But no matter what, if you just keep trying, sooner or later that pony might come prancing up and allow you to go for one hell of a ride. Ride on, my sons . . . ride on!

Most people jump-start their adult life with a highly motivated, optimistic vision of how they will travel along their life's path. Get an education, specialize in some profession or trade, start making money, get married, have kids, buy a house, and enjoy every waking minute each day. Some of us start out with the full intent to fulfill our childhood dreams, possibly as an athlete, blending in the fundamental lifestyles, as I previously stated.

But as we all know now, things change for unexplainable reasons. Some for the good, and for most, we experience life-altering turns of events that curse and haunt us for the rest of our lives.

We all try to make sense of it along the way. But most of us desperately fight each day to stay off the gravel roads and get on to the paved main thoroughfares. We find ourselves, at times, walking barefoot on that gravel road, hoping and praying to find relief. Maybe a pair of shoes might be left off the side of the road. Or better yet, someone might come along and show us the way back to the main highway, affording us a new pair of shoes and even a vehicle, granting us the luxury to travel farther and faster.

I think about all the people who sit on their couches and watch TV, looking for answers to soothe their self-inflicted mediocrity. They are mesmerized by Jerry Springer and Maury Povich, who do nothing more than immortalize and enable the lowest common denominator of society, suggesting to the viewer how to relate to the demonic lifestyle these participants live and portray as everyday life.

I think about the big picture and how saturated our minds are due to the world's media preaching self-help and you-can theories. I am behooved while I realize the true reality of what we believe to be good and helpful and what motivates us to reach out and achieve our goals as human beings. There is not a minute that goes by without our TV or radio selling products and services that will better our lives if we only take the time to buy it. We will instantly change for the good. All you have to do is watch Oprah or Dr. Phil. They promote that they have the answers, or someone else does who it just so happens has recently released a book with all the right steps to complete success, but *only if you buy it.*

The reality is they (the icons) make mega-money every time you watch their show through contractual arrangements called residuals, reach and awareness ratings, and syndication ownership. How do you think Oprah makes billions of dollars? I'll tell you. She and her colleagues have capitalized on sensationalizing our hurt, our shortcomings, and our weaknesses. They call this *focus hammering* and *draw clawing*. Dr. Phil has done the same under the guise of his PhD in psychology, and promotes his many self-help books, which really just re-edify what has been said and written over the past one hundred years. All you have to do is go to the library for free and read Norman Vincent Peel's *The Peter Principle* or Napoleon Hill's *Think and Grow Rich,* or better yet, Dale Carnegie's many books on the topic of self-help. I do, however, agree that the TV icons are reaching out to millions of potential *lonely walkers*, aimlessly wandering through life, only needing a nudge to change their lives positively. So, in the end, someone benefits.

So, they say Anthony Robbins sat in a bathtub every day for months, reading all of the many motivational books with full intent to find his so-needed answers to pave the way to success. Imagine this seven-foot-tall, twenty-something, naked man sitting for days, weeks, and months in a five-foot-long bathtub, struggling to write his first manuscript.

Then he had his epiphany. "I am going to get rich by writing my theories on how to get out of the pits of life and become wealthy, famous, and healthy. All I have to do is sensationalize all that has been published on the power of positive thinking for the past one hundred years and make it so exciting that millions of people will think my theories are all new-found methodologies."

"But that's okay," Tony might have said to himself, "because I have interpreted their work in my own way, which allows me to take licence with these age-old ideas." These same ideologies are found laced throughout the Bible. Needless to say, Tony made his fortune by selling millions of books and lecturing hungry people in need of answers as to how to get their lives on track and make money.

I bet Bernie Madoff read every book Tony Robbins wrote, as well as all the ones that came before Tony. You can be sure that Bernie found a way to twist the message to suit his deviant $50 billion Ponzi plan. Isn't it amazing how righteous the powerful people present themselves? And we buy into it, especially the ones in the public eye, in the courts, and in the financial world. It is truly amazing how they personify their purpose and ideologies, but in the end, they usually get exposed for the weak and suspect actions that they have allowed to dominate their true existence.

Their answer to the question "Why did you do it?" is always trailed by, "But I'm only human.Consider the US governors eliciting affairs, the statesmen receiving bribes, the high-profile pro-straight clergyman gone gay or caught soliciting prostitution. How about Canada's Prime Minister Trudeau and the ministers caught three times in ethics violations in 2020? Trudeau's team is under investigation for a $912 million scam, moving that money to a WE International group; Trudeau, his wife, brother, mother, and Minister Morneau's daughter were paid for their involvement. This is evil and fraudulent.

Their elusive so-called transparent messages and overconfidence, presiding over life itself, make us all stand back and ask: How vulnerable and stupid do these cons really think we are? What gave them the right and ability to stand in self-judgment and pass off their actions as being only a blip on life's radar, one that will be forgotten in a year? Who gave them the right?

We did. We decided to believe in them. We, society, are as much to blame, don't you think? According to most victims, they and the law are at fault, denying any responsibility for their own actions. Again, the bottom feeders and talking heads feast on the victim, sensationalizing and embellishing the vulnerability and heartfelt mistakes they made while in the clutches of these evildoers. The truth is, greed took over the victim and blinded their sense of judgment—"Don't ya think?" as Sara Palin might say.

But my ultimate question is: What are the media moguls, TV, movie industry, online advertising, and communications businesses concerning themselves with? The devastation that these serial programs, demographic-specific, preplanned, subliminal messages are creating in our society as a whole? Do they care that for every action, there is an equal and opposite reaction? Just look at our children and how they have become so demanding to have it all before they reach puberty. They expect the clothes, the cell phone, and the car on their sixteenth birthday. They expect to be movie stars or at least live the lifestyle of the rock stars because they must be current in fashion and technology, let alone stand out amongst their peer groups.

Where do they get these mores from? They are programmed by media of all forms and factions. Their parents enable this behaviour because they have no time or need to confront their children. The parents are just as guilty, not only because of the reasons most psychologists tend to interpret, but also because the family unit has evolved into demanding both parents to work just to make ends meet. The multimedia industries are promoting at any given time and to any slotted demographic group to buy . . . buy . . . buy all the new forms of cell phones, iPhones, PlayStations, and the newest and best laptops.

The parents experience the same problems of self-indulgence as their children do because of the pressures and ever-increasing costs of living, such as heat, hydro, and property taxes, which are constantly increasing to provide more and better services to our community. Yet some parents don't pay their bills and put them off to afford these insignificant multimedia feel-good toys. Parents will forgo their mortgage payments just to feel like a millionaire for the moment instead of keeping their long-range plan in place. Today's parents are giving up on what is right for the family and wanting what is attractive for them today. We must watch out for the paradigm shift from *selfless* to *selfish*; the moment young adults become parents, they must give up being selfish and take the role of the selfless.

We are seeing too much of this discretionary, self-fulfilling, self-indulgent attitude in the young parents of today. They raise their kids during the day and demand a form of single life away from their family at night. What's wrong with having a life with the family 24/7? When you couldn't wait to have sex, you immediately bought into learning how to raise children and live the family life.

I see the opposite all the time. The wife or mother is burnt out by supper time; the husband or father figure gets home from ten hours of work and is left with the kids while Mommy goes out with her girlfriends. It's okay once in a while, but to go out three to four times a week? Something is wrong with this picture. You think I am stereotyping? Just watch Jerry, Maury, Dr. Phil, and Oprah. The family unit then breaks down, and off to divorce court they go. Welcome to child custody hearings and the parents' new little friend—the blood-sucking lawyer.

Our school system is failing to teach our children how to prepare to make the right choices before it's too late. An ever-increasing number of children under the age of eighteen are consciously choosing to have babies before they graduate from high school. The first reason is to qualify for the government mother's allowance they receive as a single mother. This benefit is too attractive to avoid and allows them the excuse not to graduate because they do not have the work ethic to stay in school. They now have the ultimate excuse to quit school. Second, they're counting on their family and their mate's family to support them. They learn the words "family inner-circle support group," which means a money source and built-in babysitters to the single kid mom.

The *coup de grâce* of the whole issue of this element of social failure is that single moms are dropping their kids off with their parents and expecting the grandparents to raise these kids because the single moms are not ready to or capable of taking full responsibility for child care. Who pays? Who suffers in the end besides all of these helpless little babies? The baby boomers. They're the weight carriers of our society. In my parents' day, my generation was expected to get an education, get a job while in school, and carry ourselves through it all. It was a bonus or a gift if your parents financially supported you along the way. Mom and Dad's help was not expected, not like it is with today's generation, who assume their parents' money is their God-given right . . . and they want it now.

I believe it's time to quit enabling these kids to continue their dysfunctional lives. Young women end up living in low rent, bug-infested dwellings, trying to raise kids on the "no-daddy alleys" found in every city. Yes, we are at fault. But we cannot keep bailing them out. We must stop hand-feeding them and start to teach them how to feed themselves. We must show them the bigger picture. Money is needed to self-sustain, but to earn the money yourself is more gratifying than spending all your time creating a story that will convince your family to lend or hand out your parents' hard-earned savings whenever you run out. We must teach our children to stand on their own and to be proud that they are able—capable of not only surviving, but succeeding—as their forefathers and generations before them did.

What's wrong with striving to understand what your own reality is and what your true limitations might be? Maybe it's okay to be part of the crowd and not the show. Maybe it's okay to live in the same house for thirty years and not buy and sell houses every two years and eat up the equity you have built just to have that larger, more expensive house. Maybe it's okay to make twenty, thirty, or forty thousand a year sweeping floors or working in the field and stop doing the 100-yard dash every day in order to earn $150,000+. Maybe you just might be happy every day of your life and find you are not always searching for that great monetary high and excitement that only lasts until the cash runs out and you are again in need of another money fix.

I have come to the realization that chasing the American dream is bittersweet. One in a million can legally and properly sustain monetary success and sustain its value for a lifetime. All you have to do is watch CNN, contrasted with Fox News, and see the countless fraud and criminal cases that plague courts all over the world. The desperation that has encompassed the financial world has destroyed and is destroying the very fibre of all societies worldwide. Murders, suicides, mass assassinations, and dysfunctional family breakdowns are at an all-time high. Everyone has to have bigger and better—the faster and more expensive cars, the bigger house, the faster computers—and become the better hockey or football player, the singing star child—and it goes on and on. NASA has to go farther in space than anyone before. I ask, why? To date, scientists have not been able to prove anything more than what we already know. No one can prove that there is no God or how the galaxy was truly formed.

Does it make you wonder what truth really is? I am at peace knowing, after all these years, by believing and striving to live by two cardinal laws of faith and humanity that are found in the greatest book ever written, the Bible. The first is: "Thou shalt love the Lord thy God with all thy heart, and with all thy soul, and with all they mind, and with all they strength" (Mark 12:30). This is belief in a higher power. The second is: "Thou shalt love thy neighbour as thyself" (Mark 12:31). This is acceptance of who or what you accept to be real in this life, but care for your neighbours when needed.

If I can simply fulfill those two commandments, then I have done something that I can be proud of while I have taken up space on this earth. All I really am sure of after sixty-seven years of living each and every day, somewhere, from time to time on this globe and learning through personal experience is that God loves you, and it's up to us to capture the real power of faith. We must learn to live by design!

So, let me take you for a long walk through my life's journey and, who knows, you just might see a little of yourself in what I have experienced, or maybe you might see something that will create interest for you and trigger a positive change in your life. Who knows, maybe you will get a good laugh, cry, or even feel the emotions that I did living out this autobiography? I hope you will learn that, "It's all good in the end," and that as life-standing members of humanity, we are meant to be friends, no matter what lifestyle we choose, no matter what type of communities or walks of life and social groupings we find ourselves among. Live each day as if it counts because the true, hard fact of our reality on earth is that you will never ever get that day back again. So, make the next twenty-four hours everything because that is all we have. You cannot get yesterday back, and tomorrow has not come. This is the moment you have been waiting for. Make it the greatest ever!

Chapter 1

This story really starts back in May 1972, in Grand Forks, North Dakota, US. I was attending university on a hockey scholarship and studying sociology. I remember how beautiful the spring weather felt after my first experience of the cold Midwest winters. The campus couldn't have been prettier. The trees were budding leaves, and the plants had begun their blooming season. The fresh air of the Midwest was so distinct that I almost forgot about my home in Chatham, Ontario, Canada. I got out of bed early; it was a Saturday. I had worked the late shift at MacDonald's the night before and was tired of mopping floors and cooking hamburgers. I was ready to quit the job. My friend Yosemite came over to help me work on the 1968 Volkswagen Beetle I had bought the week before. We had planned on changing the generator brushes. Volkswagens were so easy to work on in those days. You could do most repairs yourself.

Yosemite arrived not long after I had started on the engine. "Hey Frank," he grunted as he walked over,

"Don't be so fucking cheerful. It's too early," I said in response.

He could tell I was somewhat angsty about something. "So, who peed in your Corn Flakes this morning?"

"Oh, I'm just tired of the same old thing, classes, hockey, you know, the grind. I need a change of things. I think it'd work for me just to try something new."

Yosemite knelt down beside me and asked, "Is it Monica? Aren't you getting enough? Or is she just busting your balls as usual?" He started to laugh.

Yosemite looked, talked, and lived just like the cartoon character Yosemite Sam. He was a third-year geology major and was at total bliss sleeping in a cave with rocks, snakes, and bats.

"No, it's not Monica; it's me. I can't get excited about anything. I've lost the drive I had when I came here. I can't seem to get it back. Got any ideas?"

We puttered at the generator, then Yosemite dropped the wrench and turned toward me with his steely eyes and responded. "My brother's in town. You ought to meet him. He may have some crazy ideas for you."

"Anything might help at this point! What does he do?" I asked without really thinking seriously.

"Oh, he's a Green Beret. He's a Marine."

"Right!" I said, thinking, *All I need now is to enlist and end up in Vietnam and get shot.*

Yosemite rambled on about how he was shipped off every three months and back again. He couldn't talk about what he really did over there, except that he spent most of his time busting US Army grunt balls.

I began thinking about my friend from Detroit, Danny Motherfucker. Obviously, that was his nickname. During my last year of junior hockey in Canada, I was playing for the Blenheim Golden Blades. Danny's father was the financial partner of the team. Danny played for the first month of the season before he was drafted to the US Army. Within two months, he was shipped off to Vietnam, right to the front lines. His second week there was his last. His squad was sent into a wildfire in the jungle, someplace near Laos.

He was second man in and ran headfirst into a .50-calibre gun spraying the path he was on. Danny took five slugs, which miraculously missed all vital parts of his body. They carried him out, keeping him alive by pouring gunpowder in his wounds and lighting them on fire, as well as injecting him with morphine. He spent a month convalescing in Singapore, then two weeks in Tokyo.

He arrived back in the States late February 1971, just when we were about to start the playoffs. Ironically, I had broken my collarbone two weeks before and was sidelined for eight weeks. I arrived at the opening game just as it started. Standing in the top row of seats was this very thin man, dressed in full parade uniform, propped up with a cane.

In total surprise, I yelled, "Danny, you old motherfucker!"

He didn't even flinch.

I walked up to him and without even turning his head to look at me, he quietly responded in a low monotone voice, "Hi, Frank." He just stared off onto the ice.

I then realized he was not the same Danny, who had been fun, full of energy, and loved to joke with everyone. He was short but very well built for an eighteen-year-old before he went to Vietnam. But there he was, looking twenty years older, crippled, and even worse, his youthful life had been ripped away.

Danny said, "Let's go sit down." He started by saying, "It was hell. Every day got worse. Every time we entered the kill zone, somebody got it. I knew it was going to happen to me. I knew that morning. My lieutenant walked up to us and said, 'This one's routine.' Bullshit! My gut said this was no regular recon. I started to get the shakes like never before.

"Not even an hour out, it happened. I was so close to that bastard I could see his eyes. I'll never forget the look in his eyes. Die, die, die, as he pulled the trigger. That's all I remember.

"Everything from that point was in slow motion. I felt nothing. No pain. The medic was hovering over me screaming. I didn't know what he was saying, except the fear in his eyes was real. It's amazing how all I saw was those eyes.

"You know, Frank, I think it was the first time I can think of that I remember the look in someone's eyes. I can hardly sleep each night. I can't shake it. Faces and eyes, full of fear."

"So, now what are you going to do? You're going to start working out and get back on the ice, aren't you? If you don't, I'll kick your ass!" I said, and laughed, trying to lighten him up.

He turned and said right to my face, so serious and non-forgiving, "I'll never play again, nor do I want to." He set me back; he was so cold, so definite.

My stomach tightened like I had said the wrong thing, or I was about to lose my dear old friend for life.

The game went on and so did my first lesson in the real world of the unforgiving. At the end, his dad came over, and I could see the strain and self-guilt in his father's face.

"Danny, did Frank spark you to get back in the saddle?" He laughed nervously.

Danny just looked away.

"Well, we've got to head back State-side. See you next week, Frank," Danny's dad said with timid hope and sad optimism, hoping Danny would say, "Yeah, you motherfucker," like he used to.

Danny began to slowly move toward the exit. Then he turned, and with a look so dark and distant, he said to me, "The first lesson you'll learn is nothin' really matters. The second lesson is you only go around this mud ball once, and it ain't nothing but a ball of shit. And third and final is the first lesson is everything."

I didn't see him again after that night. Yet almost every day since that night, I think of him and the words he said to me. That look in his eyes, how a young vibrant man with everything going for him could lose it all so quickly. It was like he died and came back to hell on earth, even with the safety and comfort of family and friends. What happened to him? How could anything take his soul like that?

"I know what you need; you need the taste of reality," Yosemite coyly blurted.

I replied, "I don't need three days in a cave with you telling me crazy camping stories all night."

Yosemite carried on, "Let me tell you something. Dean—you know Dean Hyack?—was telling me of a program the sociology department was quietly talking to some of the grad students about. The US Army was looking for a group to conduct a study in Vietnam."

"Oh yeah, just what I need, to go over and get my ass shot off. My dad would kill me if I even thought of the idea," I said.

Yosemite replied, "Come on, and where's your sense of adventure? You Canadians are so chicken shit when it comes to facing shit. You think your mouth and a hockey stick is good enough to get you anything you want. Be a man. Take a shot of reality.

"My brother is a Green Beret and is doing three-month tours back and forth from the States. He's having a blast. Go for it. You never know; you might like it."

Just as soon as Yosemite said the last words, I heard a yell about twenty yards from me. I looked up, and there was a gang of upper-classmen running toward me. It was the varsity hockey team members. Within seconds, I remembered it was freshman varsity hockey week. They were going to initiate me, it being the end of my first year as a junior varsity player. This was nothing to take lightly, for in their hands were hair clippers and spray paint, and there were ghoulish looks on their faces. I knew I was in trouble, so my instinct was to get the hell out of there. I dropped my wrench and started running. It seemed like I ran for miles, but when I looked back, I saw they were right on my tail. Something came over me, and I quit. I just stopped dead in my tracks. At that point, I didn't care what was going to happen to me, for I sensed that no matter where I might hide, they would find me.

"We got you!" Scott yelled as he and two others caught up to me. Ron Smith, Jim Wilson, and Dennis Johnson—all three stood six-foot-two or better—lifted me over their heads and carried me back to Walsh Hall, to the quad's courtyard, where the rest of the varsity squad was waiting. Within seconds, the three dorms emptied into the yard and surrounded me. I was grabbed, stripped of my clothes, and put to the ground.

Dave Burr leaned over me and with that subtle but suspicious smile, whispered in my ear. "Do as I tell you, and you'll get through this with no pain!"

Someone barked, "Grab his head and don't let go!"

Buzz, buzz, was all I heard, and then my hair started falling all over me. They were cutting my hair off? They were shaving my damned hair off! All I could think was, *It's too late to fight. What the hell. I've got to let it happen to belong to this elite group of athletes, the University of North Dakota hockey program.* To belong, you must go through this hazing process. It was so serious that two of our freshmen left campus to avoid it. They eventually left for another university, having quietly been asked to leave.

Loud screams and laughing could be heard like a lynch mob, feeling great pleasure as the executioner pulled the lever. "Cut it all off! Get it all! You're a bald-headed bastard now!"

Then Dave was standing over me with a container of something. He reached inside the jar, and then started to apply this gooey substance to my scrotum. He was kind enough, I thought at the time, to suggest, "Run to the shower, and it'll come off and it won't hurt!"

"Are you sure?" I asked in a nervous trusting voice.

Dave replied with concern for my well-being, a look in his eyes, "Trust me, Frank, it's the only way."

As he disappeared into the crowd, Scott jumped on top of me with a decal cut out of cardboard in the shape of an Indian head, our team logo. He then began spray-painting it on my chest. All the while, I was being held down by four teammates. The crowds were dancing around me like they were performing a war dance before they offered me to the gods and boiled me for dinner.

It seemed like my teammates and the crowd were satisfied with their sadism, at least for that moment. I jumped up and began walking toward the dorm when a burning sensation began to creep up from my inner thighs to my family jewels. *Holy shit!* I yelled, "My balls are on fire!" I began to run.

"Run, you motherfucker, run!"

I was crying out. I reached the shower and without any forethought, turned on the water and vigorously rubbed as fast as I could to try to get the rest of the ointment off. But the more that I tried to get rid of it, the more it inflamed. "What the hell is this stuff?" I was in tears yelling and half crying.

By this time, Dennis Johnson and a couple of other team members were standing outside my bathroom door, watching like cheetah cats at their prey. "Oh, does it hurt, Hammer?"

My nickname was Hammer due to one night earlier that year, when I'd had the pleasure of a co-ed bed partner, who walked out the next morning and into Dennis' room, reporting to him I had a dick the size of a ball-peen hammer.

He then, with great glee, sent a photocopied, hand-drawn picture of a cartoon version of me in my hockey gear with a hammer protruding from my crotch. Hence, the whole campus joined in and adopted the name. It became rather embarrassing when some gorgeous freshman would walk up and ask, "Why do they call you the Hammer?" Or they would ask quietly, "Can I see your hammer?"

"Yeah, it hurts, you fuckers! Oh man, what the hell is this stuff?" I asked and pleaded. "What am I going to do?"

Dennis replied, "You shouldn't have showered. It only makes it worse. Rub it off with a towel. You won't be getting it tonight. Ha, ha, ha! Don't forget the party's in your room tonight. We've got a keg, so clear your shit out to make room."

Monica arrived as I was lying on my bed, soothing my very tender love muscle. "What happened to you?" she asked with surprise and shock. "What are we going to do now? Can you still get it up? This is serious. I need that hammer. Do you want me to do something? I can lick it, maybe rub it, you know, like I did last night, baby. Let me kiss it better."

"No, no," I pleaded. "Don't touch it. Please! I was initiated. In front of the whole school! It wasn't pretty."

"I know," she said. "I heard. Actually, Nicki and Carol saw the whole thing. They were very impressed with what they saw. Ha. I was kind of proud of you, showing off my boy toy and your tool kit! No one but me gets to use it, though," she said with a sense of demand and control.

I liked her possessive tone. "Give me a kiss, baby," I said as she cuddled up next to me.

"Are you sure you don't want me to . . ." She reached down and gently clutched my penis.

"Oh God . . . does that hurt!" I whimpered like a sick dog after a beating.

Monica and I had met on campus the first month I arrived. It was a late September afternoon. A bunch of the freshman hockey team members and I were playing catch with a football out in front of Walsh Hall. In a window overlooking the courtyard was this girl sitting there, with long brown hair and a smile that would stop a train at full speed. As I stood there looking at her, I got hit with the ball in the back of my head, intentionally thrown by one of the guys.

"Come on, Trousdell. Leave the girls alone."

Monica looked down at me and said, "I hope you can play hockey better than you can catch!"

I then threw the ball to her, and she caught it.

"If you want it, you have to come and get it!"

I turned around to the boys and smiled with that cocky guy thing, and sauntered into the girl's dorm. Of course, the head dorm master yelled at me to remove myself from the girls dorm, which was off-limits to men. I was not going to let anyone stop this opportunity and continued up the stairs.

"Well, I like that in a man."

"What's that?" I asked coyly.

"Nothing gets in your way if you want something badly enough," Monica answered. "Here's your ball, Frank," she said, as she turned and walked toward her door.

"Ah, wait, ah, what's your name?" I asked without questioning how she knew mine.

Halfway through the door, she quickly replied, "Monica. The rest is for you to find out."

And so I did. It took me a month to finally get to her again, asking her classmates and friends, showing up at her dorm and leaving notes with my telephone number, and finally, delivering flowers with an invite to go out to a pub night. Since that first date, we had become inseparable. Ironically, we had no sex for the first three months.

My first Christmas break had arrived. I was flying back to Canada for the holidays. The night before, Monica and I decided to do laundry together. As I was putting my clothes in the washer, she grabbed me and said, "You had better not fuck around with your old high-school sweeties, or I'll cut your balls off." Monica then pushed me against the dryers and began to take my penis out of my pants. Then, with great passion, she began to blow me.

Half shocked, a quarter pleased, I was left in wonderment.

When she finished, she rose back to eye level, kissed me ever so tightly, like never wanting to let me go and said, "When you come back, you will be mine and only mine. You are in me now. You will always be mine. Come back to me, and you will have all of me."

That night, we slept together and held each other almost frightfully, clutching, not wanting ever to let go. The sun came up too quickly that morning, and for the first time in my life, the sun was not inviting . . . for either of us.

Monica drove me to the airport, and as we waited for me to board, very little was said. "Call me, Frank. Oh, I was going to get you a Christmas present," she said apologetically.

"You just be here for me when I come back. That will be the biggest present I could ever hope for," I replied.

While on the plane flying back to Chatham for Christmas, I felt a total oneness with Monica, and all through my time at home, we both comforted the distance between our hearts through letters and the telephone. When going back to university after Christmas, I arrived with a clear determination never to be without Monica again. We were together from that moment on.

Well, later the night of initiation day, the freshman squad and their dates started showing up at my room. Dennis had set the keg up in the bathroom and made a makeshift bar. By eleven o'clock that evening, the room was full of people, and the hallways were wall-to-wall co-eds from all over campus. Everyone on our floor synchronized their stereo so the same music could be heard throughout the dorm. It was the party of the year.

I was standing at the end of my room on top of my bed, taking pictures, when it occurred to me: most of the guys in the room were shaven bald. It was quite a sight. It was so exciting, and I felt proud that I was one of the school's elite.

We partied pretty well all night. I had so much to drink that Dennis and Monica had to carry me to the showers, for I was vomiting all over the floor. I had passed out on my bed, and people just sat on me like I wasn't even there. Someone tapped me on the head, and as I lifted it and looked, I spewed like a sewer hose pumping raw sewage from an outdoor toilet all over them.

Needless to say, they all moved me to the showers for a second time and thought it was a big joke.

Dennis turned the shower on cold and left me there.

I sobered up real quick from the cold water. Not realizing where I was or what I was doing, I proceeded to take my wet clothes off and walked back into the party.

Everyone cheered and began to disrobe. Within minutes, everyone was naked. Beer was flowing, and people were dancing throughout the dorm. It seemed like hours had gone by when the campus police arrived. Girls were running out through the quad, naked being chased by guys, and some were on the lawn having sex. It turned out to be a giant orgy.

I woke up the next day only to see bodies in bed sleeping with me, on my chairs, in my closet, on the floor, in the shower, on my toilet, all passed out. Everywhere I walked, I was wading through pools of beer. The hallway was like a murky river carrying the stale stench of barley and hops. As I got to the end of the hall, three dorm officials from the university met me. They had these disgusted frowns on their faces as they quickly determined that I was the ringleader.

"Mr. Trousdell, I don't care if you are varsity, the Prince of Wales, or even a member of the Kennedy family. You are responsible. If you want to stay here, you will rectify the situation. You know where the mops and buckets are. You've got to the end of the day to clean the whole building up and bring it back to order."

As they turned and left, the dorm floor rep turned, smiled, and said with a smirk, "That was the best party we've ever seen."

Dennis came out about an hour later as I was mopping the hallways. "They got you? Who squealed?"

"I don't know, but you better get about ten guys helping me; I really don't feel like doing this for the rest of the day."

It did take all of us till about seven that night to finish, but we felt real good about our effort. We all agreed that it was only right that we cleaned up the place, for we'd caused the damage. I didn't know it at the time, nor did I even fathom that there would be many more events like this in the future.

The rest of that month was filled with last-minute events and free-for-all parties, which slowly dwindled as the final days of the semester came to a close. Not only was everyone mentally exhausted, but we were emotionally drained from the year's growing pains and coming-of-age awakenings.

I felt like I had just gotten off a roller-coaster ride that lasted eight months. I arrived on campus eighteen years of age and was going home for the summer a whole lot older.

There was something nagging at me throughout that first year, like a taunting voice inside of me to look further than what seemed in front of me. This calling would never define itself as being good or evil but definitely would not let go. Every day I felt more uneasy, more tempted to search and try. Whatever it was, it frightened me. The voice would hit at the most unsuspecting times.

I remember, after a night of drinking with John Mackay and Sheldon Joperue, varsity NCAA football players having a good time in their room, when, without warning, I felt the need to go up to the roof of the dorm. It was about 12:30 a.m., and no one was around, so I climbed the ladder leading to the roof. As I got onto the roof, I could feel the breeze off the open fields. It felt so reaffirming, laced with a subtle sense of being suspended from everything that mattered.

I sat on the edge of the building and absorbed the feeling all around me. For a while, it seemed free and expansive. Then, without warning, I felt like the darkness was closing in on me. *What is wrong with me? Why do I feel so alone and useless?* I kept asking myself. I then started to think about some of the guys I'd met who were just back from Vietnam, and how they were struggling, trying to fit back into society, especially on campus. I repeated over and over, "You poor guys. You poor guys. What's wrong with everybody? Why can't they see you're one of us?"

Yet I felt just as guilty, for when talking to them, I would feel this sense of curiosity, holding myself back from continuously asking them, "What was it like? Tell me the worst parts of it all. What was it like killing or fearing being killed every day of your time there? I knew they could see it in my eyes; I tried so hard not to let them see.

I started crying. I couldn't stop. Their faces wouldn't leave my mind. Danny's image kept flashing in front of my eyes. Then, one at a time, they would all take over; I would visualize them all together running into battle, screaming, dodging bullets, and seeing them fall as they got hit. I clutched my head, trying to stop the vision. It wouldn't go away. I then started to ask myself, *Why them, and what makes me so lucky, not having to go?*

At this point, I heard someone climb down the roof to the edge. A hand was on my shoulder.

"So, what do you think, high enough to do the job? You'd really make quite a fashion statement; your head would smash just like a pumpkin on that concrete."

I turned around, and sitting behind me was John Mackay. John was from Winnipeg. He was a senior on a football scholarship, an education major with aspirations of playing professional football. He weighed in at 250-pounds, six-foot-one of pure muscle. John and I got along fairly well, and for some reason, he had an insight into me that sometimes spooked me. He somehow sensed I might be in trouble that night.

"Are you coming unglued, Frank? Want to talk about it?"

"I'm lost, John. I never seem totally together. I see all these people focused, and they got these clear plans. I can't seem to stay on track."

"I felt like that my first year," John said. "Everything is hitting you at a hundred miles an hour. You're constantly trying to absorb and understand and all the while thinking everyone expects you to be able to take it all in. Well, the good news is everyone can't and won't. The bad news is it just gets worse. Did you hear about the two accounting majors that committed suicide last week?"

"No?" I answered in slight shock. "What happened?"

"They finished their finals, which everything was riding on for them to graduate, and the pressure got so bad that they both lost it one night and hung themselves in their closet, together."

"They were found a couple of days later, and in the mail not long ago, their final marks came out; they both passed with a three-point grade average. Come on, Frank, let's get out of here before I have to throw you over. You're making me sick just thinking about you wimping out."

The next day, after the big party, I had to meet up with Monica. We were going to Tioga, North Dakota, for the weekend to visit her parents. She came over to my room and began packing my bags for me.

At the same time, Dean Hyack came in and said, "What's your plan this summer?"

"I don't know," I replied.

"I've got an offer for you. Stay for the summer and work with me. This way, you and Monica can get a place; maybe all of us can live together—Janet, you, and Monica and me."

I thought for a moment and asked Monica what she thought. "Do you think our parents would approve?"

"Shit, we're over eighteen, we are living on our own anyway. We sleep together most nights, and when we do go to my parents', well, it's pretty obvious how involved we are, don't you think, Frank?"

"Yeah, you're right. My mom couldn't handle it. I don't know. I'll let you know, Dean."

Monica took offence to my response; she actually thought I would immediately say yes. I respected my parents so much that I didn't even shit, let alone go to the bathroom without asking permission. I was raised to respect my parents no matter what. Plus, our family was a very close clan as I was growing up.

I was born on a farm north of Chatham, Ontario, forty-five minutes from Windsor, the most southern border town to the United States. This farm was my father's dream come true and my mother's worst nightmare. You see, when my father met my mother, it was at the beginning of World War Two. He was stationed at RCAF Station Brandon, a Manitoba airbase. Dad was a sergeant in the engineering division in charge of mechanics repairing the Lancaster bombers and other large aircraft.

As the story goes, one weekend, my mother and other fellow teachers, all women, went up to Clear Lake just north of Brandon for a girls' weekend. They rented a cottage by the lake and planned three days of fun in the sun.

They arrived on the Saturday morning, got set up, and unpacked. A car drove up carrying five air force men, one being my father.

Now, this is where the story gets twisted. I think my mom and dad had a wild weekend at the lake. My mom got pregnant. They had to get married.

My mother's version goes like this. As the five airmen arrived at their cottage, which was situated next door to the teachers' cabin, Mother, sitting in the open bedroom window upstairs, noticed this handsome gentleman standing by a well in the backyard. He then saw her, and they began to talk. Supposedly, this talking process took all weekend, back and forth from the window to the yard, etc., till they felt comfortable to exchange numbers and addresses. Later, my father contacted Mom, and they dated for some time.

My dad was transferred to Brantford, Ontario, so my mother agreed to marry my dad when she was able to travel. This union took approximately two or three months. They were married, and then the Immaculate Conception happened, as an unexpected shock but a happy, joyous surprise: Mom's pregnant! Winifred was born, my oldest sister. Now, one must remember that my mother was raised a strict Roman Catholic and was born a French Canadian. My father was born on a farm outside of Oshawa, Ontario and raised a White, Angelo Saxon Protestant. Back in those days, especially in Ontario, this union of a French Canadian and an Angelo Saxon was not socially accepted in general terms, let alone for the couple living in Ontario.

Then again, this was my mother's interpretation. She blamed Ontario, in the beginning, for her not teaching when she reached the farm. They wanted her to go to one year of teacher's college before granting her an Ontario certificate. She blatantly refused. "Why should I go back and complete one year when I have been teaching in Manitoba for the last two years?" So, she didn't teach but complained constantly. The school board was hit with her wrath over everything and anything.

Then when I began school, it felt like the teacher was waiting for me to arrive. Here I was, the son of this rebel queen of the French Canadians, who just so happened to own the schoolhouse (situated on our farmland) and wanted every teacher who taught in that school to suffer her pain and to bear her burden. I walked into the class and was met by Mrs. White. This was typical—eight grades in a one-room country school with one teacher. She had scraggly white hair, eyes of steel, and always had a willow whip in hand, just in case someone got out of line.

"What do you think you're doing, young man? Do you know who I am? Have your sisters warned you of the rules? We have very strict rules, you know, and you must follow them to the letter, or you will meet Mr. Willow. You do not want to meet Mr. Willow, now do you? I know your mother, and she can't stop me now, can she, Mr. Trousdell? You had better toe the mark in this classroom, sir."

Well, all that year, I spent three-quarters of all recesses in class, up at the blackboard, writing lines with my right hand. You see, I was left-handed, and in those days, left-hand writing was considered unacceptable and less intelligent. So, my teacher would make me stand there at the blackboard and write over and over again.

One day, in front of the whole eight grades, she made a spectacle out of me. She made me stand in front of everyone and recite some lines from a book. I didn't even know how to read; I began to pee my pants in front of everyone. My one sister, Jackie—I had five sisters, by the way. Jackie was sister number four. She was three years older than me—she mouthed the lines to me, and somehow, I got through it. The teacher let me sit down.

It seemed for that whole year, I was under the scurrilous eyes of not only this teacher but also my sisters, my friends, and the community. I felt in constant fear. I hated school because of this. I couldn't wait to end the day, and I would run as fast as I could home and not stop running until I was deep inside the main barn up in the hayloft. I had built a fort in the loft where I would tuck myself away from the world as I knew it and dreamed of faraway places and stories that I'd had told to me, seen on the TV, or heard on the radio.

My close friends during that time were the cows in the field, grazing. They never seemed to mind me. I would walk with them, pet them, talk to them. They seemed to understand me for some reason. One day, I got in between some cows in the pasture next to the schoolhouse. The cows began to rub up against me. They liked to do that when they got comfortable with a human. The only problem was that I was only six years old, and there I was, four foot nothing, in the middle of half a dozen twelve-hundred-pound mobile meat trucks, rubbing up against me. From the schoolhouse windows, Cheryll, my third-oldest sister, saw what was happening and began to scream at me to run. I couldn't hear her, nor could I move.

Finally, Mrs. White ran out over to the fence and started whipping the cows with Mr. Willow. I saw an opening and began to run. I ran to the barn and wouldn't come out for hours. Again, I was the hamlet's topic of discussion for weeks to come.

I guess I should have expected everyone's concern, for when I was two-and-a-half years old, I almost died. My mother was pregnant with my youngest sister Vickie, and I was told that I didn't understand what my mother was going through, so I gave her a bit of a rough time. One day, my mother was cutting the lawn at the side of the house, when I walked into the lawn mower's path and my foot slid under the front of it. Needless to say, my foot was cut up pretty badly. My mother fainted, and my oldest sister, Winnie, and second oldest, Marie, carried me into the kitchen, blood spewing everywhere. It took two double bed sheets to contain the bleeding before the doctor arrived from town. Marie took charge, and between Winnie and Marie, they were able to tourniquet my leg at the ankle, saving me from bleeding to death. My father arrived at the same time the doc was placing me into the front seat of his car and commencing to fly down the dirt roads to the hospital. En route, he injected me with a needle while driving. I guess, in those days, you didn't think about legal stuff, just life. I'm glad he did, for I doubt very much if he hadn't gotten there and did what he did, I would have died, according to my sisters.

There was always something happening on the farm: tragedy, excitement, challenges, life, and death. I guess that's why farm life was so intense. You had to be strong to face each day and what it gave you. My father, Fred Trousdell, was born on a farm, as was my mother. Their lives started similarly yet were different ancestrally. My dad's parents were of Irish and English descent. My grandfather was a jack-of-all-trades, loving to paint on canvas. He carried this gift throughout his whole life. My grandmother was the typical farm wife, cooking and cleaning, loving her children and her children's children. As did my mother's mother; she couldn't say no to her children.

My mother's father was known to us as a hard-working farmer but somewhat of a drunk. I remember the stories my mother would tell us about him and some of his antics. One Christmas Eve morning, my grandfather set out to town in horse and buggy to get food and presents for the seven children. He didn't arrive back until 11:30 that night, just in time to drive the family to midnight mass, totally drunk and with no food or presents in hand. To my mother, this was a devastating event in her life, and so it should have been; she never let us forget it for a moment.

My dad's dad had a wandering heart, according to my mother. My dad never said anything about my granddad. He just wouldn't talk about it.

My dad was a fun-loving, good old boy while growing up, always being in the wrong place at the wrong time. He was lucky most times and didn't get in too much trouble, so they say. I might never know. He was always working, be it in the field or later on, he was on the road most of the time when he started with the Union Gas Company. That job came about after we went through the worst winter ever. The bank shut Dad down, and we had no food or heat in the house. My mother had to walk one mile to the corner store up a dirt road covered in snow, pulling a small wagon full of fresh produce. She went to trade with the store to get staples and dry goods.

My dad knew he had no choice but to become a weekend farmer and get a new job. That was so defeating to him. I remember when Mom and Dad made the decision one night in the kitchen to sell the farm. Dad got up from the table, walked back into the shed, and started beating the wall with his fist, crying out loud so hard. I held on to his leg ever so tight, trying to comfort him. He refused to show defeat to anyone. He was my pillar of strength then, and he always will be, now in spirit.

Not long after that evening, we had the auction, selling off all the equipment. I saw the strain in my father's eyes as each piece of machinery left the yard. The accountant sat in the kitchen with his large manual calculator, punching and cranking in each sale number. I didn't quite understand what was going on but knew there was a major change about to happen in all of our lives.

Chapter 2

The drive to Tioga, North Dakota, was a long and arduous event. I had traded the Volkswagen for a 1968 MGB GT, a forest-green, hardtop fastback. I had bought the car a week before from a twenty-eight-year-old divorcee flower child. She was standing by her car when I drove up. The sun was shining on her long blonde hair, accentuating her big blue eyes and beautiful smile. Protruding with perfection were her large, voluptuous, bra-less breasts, skimpily covered with a flower child, tie-dyed T-shirt. She stood there, subliminally saying, "You can have me if you buy my car."

I was so taken by her sexuality and beauty. she could have asked for anything and I would have said yes. She invited me into her house and offered a drag off her joint. To be cool, I sat and smoked it with her. We sat next to each other on the couch; the more we toked, the more amorous she became, to the point I found myself hard just looking at her.

She noticed and quietly commented, "So, you like me, Frank..."

I answered, "How could I not? You're very attractive."

"Well," she replied, "if my friend wasn't in the bedroom, well maybe, ah, and are you interested in the car?"

"Oh yeah, oh, ah, how much do you want?"

"$800."

"What are you going to do for wheels when you sell it?"

"I don't know," she answered. "I have to buy another one."

"Why are you selling?" I asked.

"I got the MGB from my divorce settlement, and it has too many bad memories."

I thought for a moment. "Why don't we just swap vehicles? We just trade ownerships. I bought my car for $1,200 just a few weeks ago, and I want your car. What do you think?"

"I like that. I've always wanted a Volkswagen," she said, with a very happy smile.

So, we parted with a plan to meet the next day and trade for one dollar. She gave me the most suggestive hug and a kiss that even today I can't forget.

"Until tomorrow morning. We'll meet at your place?" she suggested with pleasure.

When she arrived, I couldn't wait. I psychologically prepared myself to cheat on Monica. *I just can't pass this up*, I thought. I told Dean the night before, and he said the same.

"Do it . . . do it, or you'll regret it for the rest of your life!"

When she arrived, she looked even better than before. "So, are you ready?" she asked

"More than you'll ever know. Do you want to come up to my place?" I asked coyly.

She sat back in her seat and nicely said, "Let's get the deal done first."

Something came over me at that moment. A sense of morality set in, and a whole lot of guilt took over.

We did the paperwork, and when we were done, I said to her, "I know I'll probably regret this for the rest of my life, but it would be best to let what might have been be . . . just that."

She looked at me with those eyes, leaned over, and kissed me so passionately, letting me know it was okay. Yet she left me with a fantasy that would stay locked away in my mind forever. "Are you there?" Monica yelled. "Hello, is anybody in there?" *Slap!*

"Oh, I'm sorry, sweetie," I quickly responded. "I got lost on the road. You know, the humming of the tires and the radio. Well, you've been gone for about an hour! Let's stop for a coffee and get some smokes."

"Okay," I responded.

A Husky truck stop came up not far down the road, just before the last stretch of highway to Tioga. We went in and sat for about twenty minutes. On the way out, Monica suggested I go to the car and wait while she got the supplies.

A few minutes later, she came running out and jumped into the car. "Get going!" she yelled.

"Why?"

"Just do it, okay? I shoplifted the supplies," Monica confessed.

"What?" I screamed

"I stole the supplies."

"How could you do that?" I asked in total disgust.

"What? Are you telling me you never stole from a store before?" Monica responded sarcastically.

I screamed. "Never in my life, nor will I ever! Why would you do such a thing? We have money. Why?"

"I don't know, maybe for the rush. Shit . . . I'll never do that again," Monica begrudgingly replied.

"I hope not!" I said.

It was kind of quiet until we reached Monica's parents' place. We got settled and had dinner with them.

Monica suggested we go to a bar about twenty miles west of Montana's border. I had never been to this bar before and was looking forward to it. The way Monica described the place, it seemed to be the ultimate, old-time, redneck honky-tonk.

As we crossed over a very large ridge and a bunch of rolling hills, down in a valley, miles away, we could see a group of flickering lights that kept getting closer and brighter. There it was, this gigantic, flat-metal-roofed, barn-like building with pickup trucks and cars parked as far as you could see. JR's was the name of the bar and quite befitting for, as I expected, they were all rednecks with brush cuts, and drove pickups with .303s in the back window with a .357 Magnum hidden in the glove compartment. Everyone had cowboy boots and hats; I wore bib overalls and running shoes. I was totally out of place, and everyone seemed to be staring at me.

"We got hippies! Looks like a fag, don't he?" they all jeered as we walked by.

I looked at Monica, and she was laughing at me as if it were funny.

"I want to leave," I said to her.

"Oh, come on, they won't hurt you," Monica replied. "You're with me. I'm considered a local."

"Uh, I don't think that's gonna matter," I replied.

Just then, David and Mindie came running up, both freshmen from campus.

"What the hell are you guys doing here?"

"We live not far from here," David replied, "and come almost every weekend. Just wait till you hear the band. They're real cool! Do you like country music, Frank?"

"Oh, a little bit, like Waylon Jennings and Willie Nelson?"

"These guys do all their stuff and more. I know you'll get into it, or the locals might make you." Both started to laugh at me.

We finally relaxed a bit and were feeling pretty good when this six-foot local cowpoke decided to dance with Monica. He grabbed her arm and swung her out on the dance floor. I wasn't sure whether to interfere or see how Monica would handle the situation. Just as my worst fear predicted, he hit on her and wanted to leave with her. She screamed at me, and with huge reservations, I stepped in front of this giant redneck, cowboy, hippie-eating thug, half-tanked and ready for anything.

"Listen, this is my girlfriend, and we're together. Could you let her go?"

"Or what," he said sarcastically.

"Look, I don't think it's a good idea for us to make a big thing out of this, so just let her go," I asked him nicely.

By this time, it seemed the whole room surrounded us, just like back in the schoolyard when two kids were squaring off. I wasn't very good at barroom fighting, except on the ice in a hockey game, where your adrenalin is running, and you have lots of protective gear on. Back at the bar, all I had was my wits and, hopefully, only one man to deal with, not 500 drooling rednecks, all wanting a piece of this eighteen-year-old hippie-type freak.

At that moment, as I was waiting for the first blow, a very painful expression came over his face, like something had grabbed him by the balls. I was right. A very large, tall waitress, with red hair and hands the size of a basketball player's, had come up behind him and grabbed his most vulnerable appendage. "Now get your skinny ass and drunken face out of my bar, or you'll be singing Patsy Cline falsetto. You got it?"

The whole crowd started to laugh, whoop, and holler while "Billy Bob Bone Head" skulked out of the bar and off into the night.

We had a great weekend, partying out at the Missouri River with all of Monica's school friends. We swam, drank beer, smoked a little grass, rode motorbikes through the sandhills, and just had good old fun.

Sunday, we did the big drive back to campus.

Chapter 3

The last week of school was uneventful except for finding a place to live in Grand Forks, North Dakota. Yosemite, Dean, and I went in together on a rental house, and Monica moved in with a friend not far away. Yosemite found the house, and wouldn't you expect it? The house had to be 200 years old and leaned to the left quite noticeably. As we entered the place the day we moved in, we all chose rooms. Dean got the big room, and I took the small one. It was so tiny that my bed touched all four walls. There was no door, just an opening. All I had to do was fall through the door, and I was in bed. It was great when coming home after a drunk. I would drop my clothes, fall backward through the door, and pass out.

Now, Yosemite was in his glory. He took the basement. The only entrance was through a trap door in the bathroom floor. There was no concrete or wood in this basement. It was the old dugout with tree beam posts, with only footings holding the foundation together. Yosemite dug into the wall to create a cave-like room. There he hung a hammock with a light and a plug for an alarm clock. He was in heaven, for he loved caves and holes. As I stated earlier, he was a geologist and spent most of his time studying bats, caves, crevasses, and rock formations.

Not long after we moved in, I got up about six in the morning after a drunken Sunday and went to the bathroom. Half in a daze, I committed the most cardinal sin in the house. I accidentally unplugged the extension cord leading down to the cave and left the door open to the bathroom, blocking the trap door to the basement. Of course, I went to bed and forgot about Yosemite.

Tuesday, at about five in the afternoon, I had just got back from work and was sitting on the toilet, humming a song and wondering about very little when in front of me, the trap door opened. All I saw were two beady eyes peering through round-rimmed glasses and a thick, handlebar-moustached miner-type face appearing in front of me, almost between my legs.

"What time is it?" Yosemite asked, half asleep.

"It's about five," I answered without concern.

"Great! I didn't miss work," Yosemite replied in relief.

"What . . . are you on night shift?" I asked.

"Night shift? What do you mean night shift? It's five in the morning, Monday morning. Fuck!" he retorted.

"You slept for two fucking days, Yosemite!" We both looked at the wall plug and then at each other, his eyes in anger and mine in fright.

"You fucking assholes! You unplugged the alarm clock, and I slept for two fucking days! I'm gonna get you varmint fuckers if it's the last thing I do!"

I couldn't stop laughing, for the event reminded me of the cartoon of Yosemite Sam, always getting screwed unsuspectingly.

The summer of 72 went on like most would expect—working, partying, and travelling—till the inevitable month of August emerged as the ghost of reality. Back to school and fall training camp demanded the ultimate lifestyle adjustment that led to pain, diet, and social change.

The fall has always had a startling effect on me for as long as I can remember. My emotions ran wild. One would think spring caused the same roller-coaster ride, but September foliage and its colours reminded me of the paintings hung on the walls in my home. There were two portraits that were painted by my mother, who once had a technique session with A.Y. Jackson, one of the Group of Seven.

I accepted the preparation of going back to school, meeting new faces, and experiencing new beginnings with great anticipation. I can still smell the crispness in the air as well as the fragrance of burning leaves, wet sod, and clean laundry hanging on the line. Cigarettes always tasted and smelled fresher, more inviting than at any other time of the year, yet I had to quit this luxury in order to get ready for hockey season. What masochistic psychological torture I would put myself through.

Somehow, I adjusted to the rest of the team's pace and to campus life as a sophomore.

I sensed within myself a depleting interest in Monica from the get-go of that third semester. My focus on doing well for the last term as a freshman was not a difficult challenge, to say the least. Especially after taking courses like fundamentals of basketball, fundamentals of football, fundamentals of volleyball, and everyone's favourite, tests and measurements, which were no test for my scholastic depth. There was another reason of concern because I switched majors from Physical Education to Sociology. This would mean more intense subjects like criminology, economics, political science, and a rash of many more brain busters.

Monica had decided to leave university to work. As soon as classes started, I felt an immediate distance cloud my priorities. I started focusing on studying and met new friends. Unfortunately, along with new acquaintances came new dating opportunities. I was only nineteen and still green to university life. I eventually took the bait.

Dating seemed to be so foreign. One year with one girl, practically living together and not without her by my side for more than a day, seemed very strange. In fact, for the most part, I felt like a junkie trying to kick the habit, yet jonesing for the fix every five minutes. I found myself spending more time with my teammates and new friends. I would try to study but could not sustain concentration. By the second month, I gave up on two required courses and changed to easier subjects.

I started dating a girl from town but found we were not compatible. In fact, the night of our first date ended by running into Monica coming down the dorm stairs just as I gave this girl a good-night kiss. I immediately felt guilty and ashamed. I ran out after Monica and tried to apologize. She seemed to understand, yet I could tell that I had hurt her.

For days, I wandered around campus depressed, for I could not get myself to go back to Monica and try to straighten things out. Yet I yearned for her to at least talk to me. Finally, after about a week, I was able to reach her by phone. She allowed me to come over, and after about fifteen minutes of grovelling, she took me back. I learned very quickly how sweet making up could be.

Every day and week went by faster and faster. My studies diminished to nothing. I began skipping class, missing hockey practice, and finally, in late November of that year I had to make a very difficult decision: cram after having done absolutely no studying, leave school and quit, or leave school and marry Monica. I have no idea, even to this day, why the latter issue was such a critical choice. If I crammed, I could have gotten help and probably squeezed through, and I definitely would've had to eat crow with the hockey coach. But as they say, hindsight is 20/20. My decision was to quit university and marry Monica.

It's one thing to make such a definitive change, but it's another to get everyone involved to agree with it. First, Monica had not said yes to my proposal quite yet. I was running out of time, so every waking hour was spent convincing Monica that our life together would be great. She finally agreed and accepted me as her fiancé. Then I had to convince my mother and father. They were devastated that I wanted to quit university. Then I told them I was going to marry Monica. They almost disowned me long distance.

"You're only nineteen years old, and you have no job or career. How are you going to make this work?"

I started to suggest we would come home to Chatham and live with them until we got jobs.

"Just wait a minute! If you think the two of you are planning on shacking up in my basement, you've got another think coming, young man. No child of mine has ever done it, nor will they ever do it in my home!" My mother sternly spat this response out like an M16 spraying through the telephone lines from Ontario to Grand Forks.

"Okay, Mom. I'll let you know what we're going to do," I nervously replied. "I need a little time to plan."

"Monica, it looks like the only way we're going to move to Chatham is if we get jobs first."

"We can't do that until we get there. How are we going to apply for these jobs? By mail? That'll take weeks and months. We don't have that kind of time," Monica questioned.

"I'll talk it out with Dad. He'll find a way," I assured her.

Soon after, we had made an arrangement with my mother and father, allowing us to stay at their home but with a clear understanding that we had to get jobs and an apartment as soon as possible.

There was one more condition from my parents that almost finished the whole event: they wanted us to marry immediately in a Catholic Church. Monica was Lutheran, which meant she would have to attend pre-marital classes before the Church would accept us. The course went on for three weekends in a row, analyzing us alone, then as a couple, and finally, our families as a whole. By the time we finished the sessions, we were exhausted and somewhat unsure as to what we really wanted then and in the future. Were we doing this for us or for the families? That was the biggest question for us to answer.

We set the date. December 16, 1972. Monica began to rally friends and her family, delegating roles, responsibilities, and as well, who was paying what expenses. Like all weddings, Monica, the bride, was beside herself, determining who was to be bridesmaids and the maid of honour. I had already picked my best man and ushers.

During all this time of planning and organizing, a very important piece of business was hovering in the wings. The issue of my dropping out of university and leaving the hockey program still had to be completed. My lifelong dream had been pushed to the back of my mind. Like so many personal issues I had cherished and protected for so long, it seemed to have lost its value and priority during the planning, collaboration, and compromising in the name of young love.

I remembered the week before I'd left Chatham for university, how I had been so determined to think of nothing but proving my high-school guidance teacher wrong about my scholastic abilities. I could handle the demands and regimentation of higher education. Mr. Mariontette was hell-bound to keep me from attaining a hockey scholarship. He purposely submitted a very bad report to the admissions department of Boston University, who had nurtured me during my last high-school year. The hockey program had plans for me to be a very important contributor to their 1971 to 1975 program.

I was flown to Boston to visit the campus and sign my tenure during March break, and as well to see the legendary Bean Pot Tournament, in which all the great eastern state universities battled for the coveted eastern conference title. I was amazed by the size of the campus when I first arrived; buildings that looked like office towers and the stadium . . . a huge complex housing all the great football and hockey facilities in one block in downtown Boston. The home of the Boston Bruins enveloped my very being as I was driven to my temporary residence. I felt overwhelmed and extremely confident as each day passed, for I had never been treated with such first-class status before in my life. I had only read about such an experience and heard similar stories from my other friends already playing at Providence College.

The day I visited admissions was even greater. I sat in the head coaches' office. Don Crocker, the assistant coach who had scouted me, was outlining my potential and importance to the upcoming season. Don then quoted stats from my three years playing in the Ontario Junior B Hockey League from a hardcover book he had pulled down from a very large bookshelf. I had no idea such records were kept, and to think I was listed twentieth out of all eligible Junior B players across Canada. Later that day, Don made it very clear to me that I was invited to Boston University as a student and very much a candidate to play varsity hockey.

The parties were endless; girls and booze flowed like rain . . . I thought that my future had begun right at the top of the heap. Going home seemed to be a short stopover before the grand Boston adventure would begin in the fall.

Two months went by, and I was starting to wonder why I had not received any confirmation or admittance updates. June was closing in, and everyone that was going from my group had already received their documents. One day, while attending a gym class, I was called to the high-school office. Mr. Mariontette was waiting for me at the desk.

"Come in to my office, Frank. We have to talk."

As I sat down, I felt a cold shiver overcome my body as if a ghost had crossed my path.

"I was requested two months ago to report to the Boston University concerning your standing and grades, etc.," he began in a very formal tone. "As well, I was requested to personally support your ability to achieve acceptable standards while attending the university. I want you to know from me that I could not do that, for I do not believe you could ever last a day in any university. I believe you will even find community college a challenge. If you think I would stretch the truth about how I feel just for you to live out this fantasy, then you are sorely mistaken. Do you understand my position, Frank?"

I was shocked as if a train had hit me dead on; the stunning effect of his words paralyzed my body and my mind. It seemed like hours rolled by before I could respond. Then, finally, I heard myself ask nervously, as if I were a third person listening to our conversation. "Does this mean I didn't get accepted at BU, sir?"

"That's quite correct!" he responded, his tone one of self-gratification and dominance.

"How could you? What did I ever do to you?" I queried, almost in tears and feeling helpless.

He smiled like he had just eaten the last bite of a very delicious yet decedent meal. "I am very sorry, but your case is final. Do not try to run another college by me again, do you understand? Now, get back to class."

He was right, I kept thinking as I walked to the dean's office to file my termination of classes and sign off as an active student at the University of North Dakota at Grand Forks. *UND will no longer be my home. I am no longer a student after this day. I'm twenty years old, and I'm about to be married and embark on a real life. A job . . . a real job*, my inner voice was saying as I walked slower and slower toward that Gothic hall. *Mr. Marionette was so right. I didn't last more than two years. I couldn't cut the mustard.* The coldness of defeat slowly drenched my soul, to the point that I didn't care what I was going say to the dean's office.

"Mr. Trousdell, here are all the necessary papers for you to fill out and when you are done, the dean of admissions wants to see you," the secretary stated.

"The dean? Why?" I asked.

"He requested that you talk to him before you leave."

Well, I guess this is just the beginning of a long line of explanations I'm going to be confronted with, so best start at the top and work my way down the line, I said to myself.

"Here are the papers, ma'am."

"Fine . . . follow me, Frank," the secretary replied almost sympathetically as we walked down the hallway to the dean's office.

"Sit down, son, and let's take a look at these ah . . . papers," the dean said quietly. After a few moments, he looked up over his half-moon glasses. "You started out here with great promise. Your grade-point average was slightly above average, not to mention your social acceptance amongst the students and the professors are without any occurrence of devious or negative behaviour. You are a very strong athlete with the potential to be a great hockey player.

"Frank, what went wrong? Normally I wouldn't question a student leaving here. We expect a certain retention factor each year, but you stand out in my eyes. You had a bad semester; everyone goes through it, especially at your age. We can correct this if you're willing to apply yourself."

He sounded so convincing, and he truly made sense, but I felt so let down by the hockey coach and his reluctance to give me a real shot after he led me to believe at the beginning of the season that I would be given a full opportunity to play varsity.

I began thanking the dean for allowing me to attend UND and told him that I was very proud to be a part of the hockey team. I then stopped and looked at him as if he were a relative and I needed help. I had to hold my tears back, for I was about to shut the final door at UND.

"Sir, my decision was not easy but very complicated. I came to your extraordinary institution with full intention to do great things and, most of all, to obtain a degree. I came here wanting to become a Physical Education teacher. But most of all, I came here to play varsity hockey for the Fighting Sioux. I believed in Coach Rube Bjorkman and assistant coach Gino Gasparini. They led me to believe they believed in me. I came here with the full understanding that I would have to make the team, that there were no gravy walk-ons. My first season, I set out to achieve my place, and by the end of my first semester, I led the junior varsity team in scoring. The university student body paper even put a story in my hometown paper as to my first year's success. Coach spent a lot of time first year letting me know I would get a fair shot this season.

"Well, I have not to this date been given one game as a test. Again, I was leading the junior varsity scoring, and the games were so inferior. I got real frustrated. The coaching staff would shun me and tell me I couldn't meet the standard, so back off with the request to get a game tryout. Last month I went to Coach Rube and pleaded one last time, and he ignored me in front of the rest of the coaching staff. I felt so rejected that at that moment, I decided to make plans to go home.

"Sir, I know I am good enough to play here . . . I have shown over and over that I deserve to play, but there are three local players that the coach took over me, and I know I am a better player. I believe I was left out for political reasons. I can't fight that anymore.

"Sir, I stopped going to classes. I stopped going to practices and games. I am getting married to a local girl and will be going home.

"If I could change things, I would in a minute, but some things will never be the same, let alone be right, if they don't happen naturally, sir, if you follow what I am trying to say."

After a few minutes, the dean sat back and looked at me with sad submission. "I hope nothing but the best for you, Frank. You have a lot of potential to do pretty well anything you set your mind to do. But do one thing for me?" the dean asked with a fatherly smile.

"Okay, I'll try," I answered.

"Do not let anyone tell you that you can't. Get that word right out of your vocabulary and your mind. The biggest test in life, and this goes for everyone, is to never give up. Now, good luck and keep trying."

"Thank you, sir, for everything," I concluded.

A sense of relief eased my stomach as I quickly left that great hall for the last time. I went directly to the arena, knowing the team was on the ice practising. The wedding invitation fit perfectly in the centre of the billboard outside the dressing room. No one noticed as I put it up, for all eyes were on the ice. As I turned to go, I saw the team skating as I looked through the walkway.

I stopped and watched one more time. My eyes were filling up with water as I could still envision and feel that rush while I was flying down the ice and scoring. I could hear the crowd lift the building while they cried out in appreciation for a goal well placed for the love of the great Fighting Sioux. Yet while reliving those vibrant memories, I was feeling so dejected from the coaches' lack of concern for me. I wanted to say goodbye, but I knew they wouldn't have responded, for who was I? Just another short-lived wanna-be who couldn't take the heat . . . or so they may have thought.

Two weeks later . . . my parents landed safely at the airport, and accompanying them were my youngest sister Vickie, Aunt Marg, and Aunt

Dorothy. Their arrival was a surprise and was touching and comforting. My family was not one to show too much emotion, but they did like a good wedding. Monica had done a fine job coordinating the final details and was totally unglued as the wedding day approached. Rehearsal went as planned, and we all went back to the motel, where both sides of the family took refuge before the big event. We were not in my parents' room more than five minutes when a loud knock on the door interrupted my mother, who was telling us we needed to be sure to get a good night's sleep.

"Okay, Hammer, you're ours for the night!" Dean, Bobcat, George, and Yosemite barged through the door and grabbed my father and me, intending to drag us out into the night. They had plans . . . big plans to finish off my bachelorhood in North Dakota style!

"You are going nowhere, Fred," my mother yelled in fear.

"Oh, come on, Rita. This is my son's wedding. He's my boy. I've got to go!"

"No, you won't if you want our marriage to last. I'll take a plane tomorrow if you leave."

"Oh Rita, you always ruin everything," my dad replied sadly.

"Dad, you'd better stay. It's okay. We'll go out some other time."

This was the first time my dad had ever showed his excitement about having some wild fun in front of us kids, especially with me.

Monica came running down the hallway, crying. "Don't go. You won't make the wedding! They'll put you on a train for some unforeseen destination. I heard that's what they do! Don't go!"

"See you tomorrow," I yelled as they carried me out to the car.

"Where are you taking me?" I asked feeling excited.

"You're history, Hammer. You think you were getting away easy? Not a chance," replied everyone in the car, in laughter.

Within minutes, we pulled up to an apartment building not far from the campus dorms.

"This is my brother's place," stated Yosemite. "Remember John said he'd not only take your wedding pictures, but he'd supply a surprise for you?" John was the Green Beret. He'd just got back from another special mission in Vietnam.

The door to the third-floor apartment was open, and overflowing into the hallway were wall-to-wall guys and girls. I knew everyone there, so I thought. As I entered, screams and yelling began with adulations of congratulations and innuendoes of, "Sucker, you're dead now. Congrats, you just graduated with a degree in Marriage 101!"

I couldn't believe my eyes, for standing in the middle of the room was Frenchie, the local college pub owner, who was an NCAA referee in his off time. Beside him, stacked to the ceiling, were at least ten cases of beer. "Hammer! Give me a big old hug," he yelled.

I could tell he was half in the bag already.

"I couldn't think of anything better to get you for a wedding present than a party and a whole lot of beer, ha!"

Everyone joined in as he cracked open my first of many copious quantities of Coors beer. Time seemed to stand still, for I really did not want to be anywhere else. My friends for the past two years were all in one room, saluting in traditional college fashion: loud music, boisterous story-telling, and yes, a lot of bachelor pranks, but none that would cause anyone harm.

"So you're the Hammer!" a drunken voice echoed from behind me. I turned casually, unsuspecting any need for caution.

"Let me introduce myself. I'm the guy Monica was supposed to marry . . . you asshole!"

I reacted instinctively and caught his fist with my left hand as it travelled directly toward my nose. I then pushed him against the wall and put my forearm against his neck in a restraining hold. "Who the hell are you?" I yelled at him.

"You don't know me? I was to marry Monica when I got back from 'Nam, you jerk! I come back, and all I hear about is this guy from Canada has stolen my girl. You won't get away with it. I'm gonna bust you up good!"

Before I knew it, John had him on the ground, and within seconds, this intruder was no longer there. John and Yosemite quickly escorted him out to the cold night and sent him on his way.

"Who the hell was that?" I screeched and as I shook with adrenalin.

"He was telling you the truth, Frank." Dean Hyack, my best man, knew him and had known about the story all along. "I didn't want to be the one to tell you, for I thought Monica would have told you by now. I guess she didn't."

"No shit!" I replied in shock and disgust. "What a thing to find out on your wedding night."

"Ain't that the truth? Have a beer," Frenchie yelled. "Now, you put the can down, and you're gonna chug it back till it's gone. Got that? This goes for the whole night."

"Yeah!" A big, unified bellow filled the room.

"Okay, okay, no problem," I reassured everyone. The guys then picked me up and sat me on the cases of beer, and we all chugged well into the morning hours.

Before I knew it, I found myself face down on the floor and alongside me was everyone else passed out. John had turned the lights out, so sleep could be accomplished.

Movement startled me, and as I looked up, there was John dressed in ninja black with a samurai sword in his hands. He was creeping around the sleeping bodies as if he were in combat, sneaking up on the enemy without a sound. He noticed I was watching. He signalled me to lay still and not move. I began to feel a real sense of fear, for I had heard stories about these Special Forces guys and their obsessions and potential danger, especially at night. He seemed to be reliving an event, for every move was calculated and precise not to stir the sleeping bodies.

I learned very quickly that any ambition I might have had to enlist and go to Vietnam was futile and totally out of my league. Once John circled the room and successfully completed his mission without waking anyone, he went to his bedroom and resigned to silence.

I awoke to the familiar smell of bacon and eggs cooking in a very greasy pan. John again was out in the kitchen. This time I got up and walked in to see what he was doing.

"Smells good, buddy," I said quietly not to disturb him.

"This will get you ready for this afternoon," John responded.

"What time is it?" I asked.

"11 a.m.," John said.

"What?" I shouted in shock.

"Yeah, I let you sleep so you could sober up."

"I got to get going, man. I got a lot to do. Holy shit. Monica will think I'm on a train to Alaska," I joked.

The morning was cold, very cold, as Dean and I walked back to the dorm.

"If anything will sober me up, it's the cold," I shivered out to Dean.

"You want to believe it, buddy. What do we have to do?" Dean asked.

"I'm not sure. When we get back, I'll call Monica and find out. That's if she's still talking to me," I responded in a worried tone.

"Where the hell have you been?" Monica cried out as I tried to tell her I was all right and ready to go.

"You have to pick up the cake and the food and take it to the church. You'll never do it! Your mother is beside herself, and my parents don't know what to think."

"Is that so, Monica? Well, guess who I shared a beer and a fist with last night?" I questioned sarcastically.

"Who?" she queried.

"Yeah . . . your fiancé," I stated.

"Who?" Monica nervously asked.

"Come on, Monica. The guy you were supposed to marry. He showed up to the bachelor party the guys put on, and he wanted to kill me," I answered.

"I told you about him," she said.

"You didn't tell me he still thought he was going to marry you. We need to talk. There seems to be a lot of untold stories I need to hear about," I firmly responded.

"We haven't got time for this, Frank. We'll talk later. Get the stuff!"

She hung up.

"Where's Charlie? It's 1:30. We got to be at the church," I said to Dean.

"No one has seen him since last night."

"Great! My usher is missing."

"Wait! I'll break into his room. He's here," Dean blurted.

"Great!" I yelled.

"But he's out cold," Dean answered in fear.

"Wake him up!" I responded.

"I'm trying, but he won't move."

"Is he breathing?" I quickly retorted.

"Yeah . . . but barely," Dean responded worriedly.

I rushed in, and to my shock, he was out cold. "Pour water on him!"

Dean grabbed a glass and began emptying glass upon glass but with no success.

"Look, Frank, you go ahead to the church, and I'll get him up and ready. I found his tuxedo, and I'll call Bobcat to pick us up," Dean ordered.

"Don't be late," I yelled as I showered, got dressed, and left to complete the last-minute errands.

The church seemed full as I peeked out from behind the curtain near the vestibule. I noticed six hockey team members had arrived, and there were a number of classmates on both Monica's and my sides, but no coaches. My mom and dad, aunts, and sister were sitting appropriately in the front row to the left, and all of Monica's family were positioned traditionally to the right . . . but there was no Bobcat and no Charlie. We were already five minutes late, and I could see Monica pacing at the back of the church. I could tell she knew why the guys were missing. Then, like an explosive interruption Bobcat and Dean entered the back of the church, both on each side of Charlie's arm and virtually carrying him up the aisle. When they reached the front, you could hear a muffled chuckle from everyone in the room, except for a gasp and an, "Oh Fred . . . is he alive?" that came from my mother.

"Rita . . . he's breathing. He'll make it through," uttered my father with a tone of embarrassment.

"Fred! There is going to be a storm tonight . . . I feel it coming!"

"Shut up, Rita . . . my God, woman!"

Then, like a lifeless rag doll, Charlie began to fold neatly to the floor. His head rolled back toward the crowd and revealed the most peaceful, angelic smile for all to see. Quickly, Bobcat reached down, grabbed the back of Charlie's collar and pulled him up like a puppeteer would take control of his puppet . . . but still no sign of consciousness from Charlie. Bobcat took charge of his fellow usher for the remainder of the ceremony.

The rest was very much what you would expect; the vows, the tears from family, the commitments, the jubilant walk back down the aisle. Smiles on faces and joy to all there. Unfortunately, Charlie stayed at the front of the church for many hours after, propped up against the pulpit, neatly and strategically duct-taped to the railing by none other than Yosemite's brother, the Green Beret.

"He ain't goin' nowhere . . . let him sleep it off," he blurted casually while we greeted our party outside the church.

As the day went on, so did the deep sleep of Charlie . . . I never did see him again after that event. However, I did hear he went on to earn his PhD in Psychology and has been lecturing at some Western Canadian university for the past thirty-five years.

The reception went on with little distraction or discord—the friendly handshakes, the introductions, and the fond farewells. There was even a hint from two of the bridesmaids that they wished they had partied with us the night before. From what they had heard, it was a smash hit event even before midnight and was known to all of campus by early the next morning. News travelled fast on campus, no matter what it was . . . great party, fights, anything that related to campus individuals and life there on site. It was part of the culture and part of the close connection one felt while attending UND.

The time was closing in on 10:00 p.m., and Monica was pushing for us to get the car loaded to head back to Ontario. We knew it would be a three-day trip, even though we used to do it in twenty hours. We had decided to enjoy the drive to our new home and make a honeymoon out of it. Dad gave me his Mastercard to charge the cost of the adventure to it, and Dois Dallas, my new father-in-law, gave us his 1967 Plymouth station wagon to carry our personal belongings and wedding gifts with us to our new domain.

Yes, our new domain . . . where would that be? Cunningly enough, my father carefully slipped past that discussion all through the reception. Mind you, this question must have been asked at least 100 times by everyone, even the priest. I was afraid to even touch that question, for I knew it was clearly on the top of Monica's list to get straight by the moment we landed in Chatham, at my parents' home, 45 Chippewa Drive, previously known as Frank's last-known address before university.

Hell . . . I still thought I lived there. Wouldn't you?

Chapter 4

The first forty miles went by copasetic mainly because Monica was asleep. I could barely keep my eyes open due to the many beers I had consumed the night before and the half dozen I chugged with the boys at the reception. The snow was almost to blizzard conditions when I woke Monica up and begged her to switch drivers or stop. She was not happy. We ended up spending our first night in a bunkhouse behind an all-night diner outside of Fargo, North Dakota. Fortunately, this was at the most southerly point we had to go before connecting with I-94 and driving east to Minneapolis, Minnesota.

Our first night went by very quickly and cloud-like, for as soon as I closed my eyes, I was opening them to sunlight and felt well-rested. I glanced over the edge of the bunk bed and saw Monica looking straight back at me with daggers flaring out of her eyes.

"I hope you had a great time at your bachelor party, your morning party, and your wedding party . . . asshole!"

"I had the best time of my life . . . didn't you?" I sarcastically answered.

"You fucking asshole ! How could you think that I had even a fraction of the good time that you did when I was locked up with my parents, your mother—who I am convinced was patrolling the hallways for fear your father would get out—and, of course, my commitment to you that I would be perfect for you on the MOST IMPORTANT FUCKING DAY OF OUR LIVES . . . YA THINK?" She couldn't get much clearer.

Well . . . that gives you kind of an idea of the tone set for the rest of our trip back to Chatham , Ontario, Canada . . . my home?

"Married at twenty . . . Married at twenty," I kept on repeating this to myself. I would periodically look over at Monica and say it again, "Married at twenty . . . hmm."

Her penetrative glare hit me as hard as an incoming grenade . . . like my Vietnam veteran buddies had embellished and verbally painted in living colour for me over many a beer.

"Come on, Monica . . . We've got a long way to go and two more nights to get through. Let's call a truce and enjoy our honeymoon . . . honey?"

"Give me at least four hours," she replied with a great deal of reservation. "That will mean I will consider it by our next sleepover spot."

"All right . . . that's my girl," I said with relief laced throughout my vocal tone.

"Don't get too excited," she quickly responded. "I didn't say for sure."

"Okay . . . okay. I can handle it," I said to myself . . . but, my God, she can hold a grudge. This one's new to me! First flag! I would arrive some years later at a place where this event would come to haunt me . . . permanently.

We arrived on the southeastern side of St. Paul, Minnesota. It was late enough for both of us to quickly—without deliberation, by debate, or through just plain arguing—find a motel for the night. The same went on over the next day and night, which took us to the outskirts of Detroit, Michigan. This was where we were to pass over to Canada and be only 50 miles from Chatham. I pulled up into the lineup to cross through the tunnel and, before the hopefully uneventful three-minute drive under the St. Clair River, a quick but clean passage through US Customs.

"Look! The US and Canadian flag point . . . on the wall . . . over there! Ye-haw!"

And as quick as I said that, Monica yelled, "FUCK!"

"What!" I answered with rapid, impulsive fear.

"The fucking weed jar! We forgot to get rid of the weed jar.'

"What . . . you still have the weed? How could you still have it? What the fuck are we going to do? Where is it," I asked, panicked.

"Oh man . . . it's at the very bottom of the luggage in the back of the car."

"We can't pull over, Monica . . . you'll have to get back there and find it, then get rid of it," I ordered.

So, she crawled on top of the presents and bags, then like a worm, she dug herself to the bottom.

"I got it!" she screamed.

"Get up here and start dumping the weed out."

"Frank... Why are we stopping?"

"Shit! The guards are doing a visual inspection."

"We are fucked!" we both said in coincidental harmony.

"Roll it under the car," I said.

"What?"

"Just do it. They can't pin it on us if no one sees you doing it. It still is dark, and we are stopped. Do it!" I was almost screaming under my breath but loud enough for Monica to hear.

Tap... tap... tap.

I rolled my window down.

"Sir, where do you live?" the border agent asked.

"Canada," I answered.

"You, ma'am?" he asked Monica.

"I was born in North Dakota, and I am a US citizen, but recently married to this man... three days ago."

"You were born where, sir," the guard asked me again.

"Canada," I quickly answered.

"I know, but where?" he asked more firmly.

"Petrolia, Ontario," I responded.

"And you are going where?"

"Chatham, Ontario," I again answered.

It felt like minutes, but within a few seconds, the officer stated, "Go through to the gate."

"Yeah!" both of us said as we approached the gate.

"Wait, sir, I mean you've got to go to the checkpoint to your left... we have to inspect your car and approve your papers," the guard shouted out.

"Is it gone?" I asked Monica with fearful hope.

"What? You don't think I could get us through the border? Frank... you have seen me get through many things before... this was a cinch," Monica confidently replied.

Well... they, the border patrol, went through the car, our luggage, and every bag and package we had in our possession. We were free to go after about two hours of sweating out the search. We laughed all the way through the city of Windsor and almost halfway to Chatham. Then I thought, *Monica not only saved us from total devastation that would have ruined both of our lives for the rest of our adult existence, but she also showed me a sign of a potential ongoing problem that had not retreated or retired benignly to be chalked up to adolescent behaviour.* The little voice quietly went away . . . for a while.

I want to sidetrack for a moment and bring out a very important issue that had been haunting me during my last six months at UND. Work, vocation, career! When I made my decision to leave university and get out into the working world, I still had this relaxed overconfident attitude about my future. For some reason, I thought very optimistically that everything would fall into place.

In the back of my mind, I really thought that Monica and I would hang out at my mom and dad's for a couple of months and get low-end "no-brainer" jobs like restaurant or light construction work. I had even pondered going back to school and completing my BA once I had figured out what I wanted to do. Sounds familiar, doesn't it? I had even applied to the Ontario Provincial Police three months before we got married and had been invited to write their entry tests. So, there was a lot of *c'est la vie* attitude going on.

Monica, on the other hand, kept quite reserved about her plans for work. For the last eight months, she had left school and was working for a construction company in Grand Forks as a secretary. Her father had helped her get the job. Now, you should understand the complications involved in Monica's situation. We haven't talked about that yet.

Monica came from a very solid Lutheran Norwegian ancestral bloodline on her mother's side. Her mother was of a very black-and-white, almost the perfect housewife persona, with a glaze of rigidity that left you wondering what kind of husband-and-wife relationship she and Dois had. Dois, on the other hand, was a fledgling oilman. He had four drilling locations and a couple of pumping stations. Dallalea Petroleum was his company's name. When Monica and I met, Dois was completing a series of courses in order for him to be accredited with a professorship in Petroleum Engineering. I will never forget the first time Monica took me to her home in Tioga, North Dakota and introduced me to her mother and father.

The moment we arrived, Dois corralled us both into his car, and we drove at least 100 miles to some small town where he had a meeting with some local investor. He was very nervous and kept assuring us there would be no trouble. He just wanted our company for the drive.

As Dois left the car, he looked back and instructed us, "If I seem uneasy, it is because this man I am about to see is not happy with me. He lost some money on my last drill project. Actually, he lost a lot of money.

"So have the car running . . . and in about ten minutes, I could be walking out, thrown out, or running out. Monica, you get behind the wheel. Your friend doesn't know the territory. Monica's been here before, and I trust her driving in a case like this."

"In a case like this?" I asked Monica. "What the hell is going on? What is your family—descendants of Bonny and Clyde's, John Derringer's, Al Capone's? Come on . . . fill me in! Are we in potential danger? Is there going to be a shoot-out? What is this?" I was starting to get very nervous and scared. I had read about deals going bad and heard stories about disgruntled oil investors out West and how angry they could get. But here I was in the middle of North Dakota in some small, nowhere town with nothing but open plains and wheat fields for miles around.

By then, the car was running, and I was ready to crap my pants. I was already half on the floor of the car, on the passenger side.

Monica just sat back and chuckled away at me. "You big time, tough guy. Wow, you must really scare the guys on the ice."

Then without any announcement, I heard the back door open and slam shut.

"Go, Monica! Get us the hell out of here!"

As soon as I heard this, I squeezed myself even farther down into the front footwell of the car.

It seemed like ten or fifteen minutes before Dois leaned over the backrest of the front seat and said, "Son, you can sit up now. You won't get hurt. Welcome to the family. Get used to my sense of humour, son. Ha, ha, what a wimp."

Monica blurted out in fun and gleeful satisfaction, "We got ya, you wimp! Ha! Ya can't mess with the West! You may think that North

Dakotans are laid back, meek and mild, and you-can-get-away-with-anything kind of people. Well, welcome to my home, honey."

Dois was busy going through papers as we drove, and I was licking my male pride wounds while Monica bathed in her conqueror's smile, which was as big as the North Dakota sky and as abrasive as the westerly wind carving its way across the open grain fields that lined both sides of the two-lane ribbon of a highway.

Dois and I did get along very well. We seemed close to a point, but he always kept a slight distance between us, psychologically, as if to say, "I accept you, and I'm okay with you and my daughter as a couple, but you can't get into the real inner circle of this family."

I sensed at that time another quiet little voice telling me, *I will never be totally accepted, and no matter how hard I try, I will always be less than the rest.* I could feel it more from Monica's mother every time I looked at her or even when she talked to me. I could sense the lack of trust. Inadequate feelings and mistrust would follow me for years to come, starting in the Dallas relationship, and because of this flag, I turned down my first real opportunity to future wealth and success, offered to me by Dois on the day of our wedding, working for Dallalea Petroleum as a junior clerk at their head office in Tioga.

"Do you want to see Chatham's downtown before we go to my house?" I proudly asked Monica.

"Sure, but it's your mom and dad's house, not yours, okay," Monica responded.

I took the most scenic route I could remember and did the drive and wave routine that all small-town kids performed.

In my time, the objective was to get Dad's car, pick up your friends, then do the drive and wave until you saw that certain girl that you just had to impress while she was coming or going from the library or the socially chosen restaurant that was strategically picked by that very special limited club, the VIP group. The messages that were sent down to everyone else never came directly from the inner circle but by word of mouth and chain of coolness. I was sort of on the fringe of the VIP. I didn't even know who was really in, but I had my suspicions. It was like they had secretive meetings and decided what was cool and what was not. They even decided what kind of clothing was acceptable for every function we as teens attended. The VIP would even advise who was not to be accepted by the "mass of coolness." We all had an adviser; mine was my buddy, Mike Zyburra. He would keep me informed of all that was released by the VIP of Chatham.

He would tell me who to try to date, who to stay away from (for they were dating someone from the inner circle), who to hang out with, and why not to hang out with certain guys. The most important message and trend to follow while in high school was to get a hockey scholarship. If you got a hockey scholarship, you were in the inner circle. My school, John McGregor, seemed to breed the most prospects out of the other four high schools. Anyone who had a chance to get noticed by an NCAA university or Canadian hockey or football university, attended our school. Not because of academics as a rule, but because we were more of a jock school. We had a great Phys Ed department that developed the best basketball, football, and wrestling teams within the region. Of course, you were very close to the inner circle by attending John McGregor. We also had the hottest chicks, and we knew it. What we didn't realize was because of our status in the city, the other schools felt it necessary to work harder scholastically, which made John McGregor students somewhat "less than intelligent" targets socially.

The message was clear and was well known to all as to which girls from the other schools were on the "hot list." I remember my first conflict with the VIP was when I met up one night with Ann Harwood, the so-called hottest, most gorgeous eighteen-year-old in the city of Chatham. The VIP labelled her as untouchable to the mass of coolness because she was so hot that she only dated twenty-year-old's and was allegedly having sex with them. So, we did not have a chance in hell and thus were told, "So forget about it!" Well, I forgot about only one thing: the VIP ruling!

"Do you need a ride home?" I asked. I had no fear or nervousness about talking to her for some reason; yet one hour earlier, I would have been crapping my pants if this event were taking place in front of all my friends. But it wasn't. I had just dropped them off, and I was there with only one friend, Paul, who knew her through his girlfriend, who, just by chance, was best of friends with Ann.

"Sure, I'd like that, Frank. That's your name, isn't it," Ann responded.

"Yeah . . . Ann, right," I coolly retorted.

So, like all Chathamites, the impulsive objective was to casually direct your driving to the cornfields surrounding the city for a little moan and groan, hump and feel, slobber and sweat for 30 to 60 minutes. You see, we were all on a curfew; at least I was, for I was only sixteen. I found myself lying right from the get-go. Oh boy, the stories and lies that were flowing out of my mouth, just to get it on with Ann. The worst was, Ann did not know my age.

Well, the theatrics worked for about a month. She did everything possible to get me to take her clothes off and have sex with her, but I couldn't do it. If the inner circle ever had known this, I would have been shunned, rejected, and spat upon as a result for the very presence of uncoolness performed by me in this matter.

Unbelievable yet was how Ann dumped me.

As usual, we were at Paul's girlfriend's house, for at sixteen, I really couldn't take her anywhere. We were in the basement and making out on the couch. She was so inviting, yet a voice in my head was saying she wouldn't respect me if I went for it. Going for it would have meant taking her clothes off. This message was constantly rewinding and stopping my advances, over and over again, until she got up and, in disgust, sat on the floor and announced, "I'm going home. I have to take my 'pill' and call my twenty-year-old boyfriend and have sex!" She got up and left. That was the last time I was ever with Ann.

I thought I was finished socially, for the conquest of all times had been in my clutches, and I'd let Ann Harwood slip away. But not so. A few days later, Mike Zyburra came rushing up to me at school and demanded a full account of my adventures with Ann. I was befuddled, for I had no idea anyone would have known. Somehow the VIP knew. A news flash was sent to all corners of the city that Frank Trousdell had carnal knowledge of Ann Harwood and that I'd broken her heart. I was the talk of the town and the target for a number of local girls. Very quickly, my reputation began to grow as a "catch" amongst the dogs of the city. Oh, how I thanked Ann Harwood for what or with whom she embellished our short but innocent affair. What a time, what an awakening . . . what a memory!

"So, this is it," Monica sarcastically said as we completed the main drag of Chatham.

"Yup! This is it! Now you know what I did every Saturday night," I replied.

"Right, buddy! I know what you did on those innocent Saturday nights. You went hunting, just like all the guys do. You had to get some unassuming, starry-eyed local girl, probably a grade niner, you pigs . . . and be the first to have her, knowing she was so hungry to be accepted as part of the 'in' crowd. Canadians are no different than US boys, you know," she blurted with disgust.

"Not the 'in crowd.' The inner circle, controlled by the VIP group. It sounds like we were more sophisticated and more hip, socially speaking, ha," I said.

"You jerk." Monica retreated until we got to my folks' driveway. "Nice home, Frank. Very much like my parents' home, don't you think?" Monica suggested as we walked up to the back door. The back door was a basement door accessed through the carport. Dad had trained the whole family and all of the attached members to use the back basement door. This way, Dad could control the dirt. He loved his basement.

Dad spent the very first year after we moved into the house building the basement. He even put a fireplace in the middle of the rec room, as we called it. He had maybe two or three log fires before Mom convinced him to change it to gas. She didn't like the smell of smoke; it reminded her of the farm—the place she had always wanted to forget.

"Straight ahead, Monica. That's our room." My bedroom was off the rec room in the basement. I'd had that room since Dad finished it.

"Well, you finally made it," Dad announced with welcoming pleasure.

"Yeah, we're here," I said.

After the hugs and handshakes, Dad looked at me with concerned eyes and said, "We need to talk before you go upstairs—to both of you."

Monica looked at me like, "What the hell is this?"

I'd sort of expected something like what we were about to hear, for all my life, I had seen or experienced a similar sermon or gospel from the book of Fred and Rita to my sisters and a couple of times to me.

My dad began, "The honeymoon is over, and the fun is now behind you. The two of you have chosen the greatest path of your lives: marriage and adulthood. I know it's early, but you have just walked through reality's door. My responsibility as your father and father-in-law is to guide you while you are setting out into the world.

"Your mother, Frank, has set out some very direct requests. As you may remember, when you announced that Monica and you had decided to leave school, your mother was very clear about the two of you not crashing in her basement. Well, her position still stands. We have decided to give you exactly four days after New Year's to get established on your own. That means a job and an apartment."

Monica looked at me in total terror, and my heart sank to my knees.

"No buts, son," Dad responded to the look in my eyes. "This is the way it is, and your mother has spoken. You got from today, the 22nd of December, the 23rd and 24th, which is Friday, and the 27th, 28th, 29th, 30th, 31st, and the first week in January to get established. You can do it. I recommend that you leave what won't freeze in the car and bring in only what you need for now."

I could tell his speech was not well-taken by Monica, and my responsibility to complete our mission seemed to be two-fold. Get me a job and help Monica find one for her. Practicality was clear that, as an American citizen, Monica would find job-hunting more difficult than me, especially because I thought she would be extremely picky and not settle for just anything. So, we reluctantly decided to head out into the cold world the very next day.

As we got ourselves temporarily set up in my old bedroom that was now past tense in the sense of ownership, I couldn't help but notice Monica's change in demeanour. Every move she made showed a loss of excitement and hope for the future. The bubble had burst, it seemed, for her.

My sisters and their husbands started arriving and again, all the greetings began and well-wishing went around rampant all that day. After dinner, I gave my old friend John Hobbs a call and, by chance, he was at his home, six houses down the street. He invited us to visit his family and introduce my new bride.

Now John and I had a very special friendship. Five years earlier, John's family moved to Chatham from Toronto. Jack Hobbs, John's father, worked for Union Gas, as did my dad, and they befriended each other. Dad felt I, at age fourteen, needed an older brother-like companion, and John, being seventeen, was the perfect candidate. Jack felt I might be able to help John's transition to small-town Ontario with some ease.

Neither John nor I perceived what both of us were to embark upon, respectively. You see, John had been attending St. Michael's College in Toronto, a very prestigious high school and was a budding musician/lead guitarist in a local Toronto band. The family moving to Chatham was not well-taken by John or his older sister, Ann Marie, who was completing grade 13. John had plans of grandeur to take the Toronto music scene by storm, and Ann Marie had plans to find a rich lawyer or doctor and live in the lap of luxury for the rest of her life. On the other hand, I was this snotty-nosed kid that dreamed of playing baseball, football, and hockey for every professional team in existence. I did love music and had taken drum and piano lessons for the past four years. I even had a little band put together, just for the fun of it. Again, the reason for the band was because if you were a jock and a musician, you would definitely get the hottest girls.

So, Dad hooked me up to meet John at a dance at my high school. John's band got a gig there through the local radio station. I watched the show, and saw John and his band, named The Soul Reason, perform cover tunes from Motown to R&B and Blues. I was totally swooned by what I saw and heard. My buddies from my band were also taken aback by the exciting and fresh music the band played. We had never seen or heard this type of music played live before. I then went to the dressing room at the end of the gig and introduced myself to John; he was so cool and aloof. He was like a superstar, and I was meeting him for the first time, and I was giving out all this gratitude to him for allowing me to meet him. I did not even know where this flow of inner emotion was coming from. John then introduced me to the radio announcer, who was the MC of the show live on the air that night.

"Frank, this is Paul Godfrey. Paul, this is Frank Trousdell."

Trousdell? You got a sister named Jackie?"

"Ah yes."

"Well, you and I are going to be best friends . . . you are now my young and 'fresh blood understudy' and the golden key to your sister's heart."

"Understudy... what does that mean, Paul?"

"You're going to learn the radio business, and I'm going to teach you."

"Wow, thanks, Paul."

"I'll pick you up Friday night at 10:00 p.m. I work the graveyard shift on air. You will spin records while I do the talking. So, when can I meet your sister, Frank?"

"I'll line it up, Paul, no problem."

"Worth your while coming out here tonight, Frank?" John bantered out with fun and confidence. "Listen, Frank, I got a lot to do tonight but come to the house tomorrow, and we'll hang out."

"Cool, see you then."

Right from the get-go, that's exactly what we did... we hung out! I would always go down to John's house. I'd start my day by walking down and going into his backyard, and there he would be, sunbathing. We'd listen to music, play our guitars and drums, go downtown and play pool. I introduced him to all my friends wherever I could. John would join in with the gang for afternoon baseball and football games. My closest friends unofficially nominated him "King." There was only one criterion to win this role amongst my friends... he had a car.

Away we all would go to Rondeau Park on Lake Erie. Rondeau was the most righteous and coolest park ever for the entire local community. Michigan State chicks would spend their summers at their family's cottages and campgrounds during the summer weeks. Rondeau was also the home of the legendary Rondeau Pavilion. I always believed that the gods of music and summertime fun had given us the Pavilion as our unadulterated playground blessing us and only us, the class of '67 to '71. Why? The greatest rock and roll and Motown out of Detroit entertained us first before the whole world even knew or heard a song from them.

Bob Seger and the Silver Bullet Band played every month for two years before he released his first album. Bob spent the whole year of 1967–68 writing and recording in the basement of the old Kingsmen Bar and Biker Club in Windsor. He used Rondeau as his sounding board. The Four Tops, Martha and the Vandellas, The Supremes, George Clinton and the Parliaments who later formed the legendary Parliament Funkadelics, and George Oliver and Mandala (Domenic Troiano) all played there, just to name a few. We were definitely spoiled musically. The parties were endless.

My friend Eddie Bush, Jr., whose father was a retired NHL all-star from the fifties, had a houseboat anchored right behind the Pavilion. Remember the VIP and its inner circle? Well, if you got on this houseboat, you were considered as in as you could get. Many a Friday or Saturday night, they allowed me to crash on the deck but never inside the bunkhouse. Only the girls gained access.

The ones Eddie and his crew would corral, and any of the ones we brought aboard who met the okay from Eddie, were the only ones allowed access. It was always okay with us because we looked at it as our sacrifice to the VIP that might grant us privileges someday to be part of the inner circle.

Then John Hobbs arrived. It was like the waves had parted, the gates were opened, and Moses appeared. I introduced John to Eddie, and the next thing I knew, John and I were welcome anytime, not just on the boat but to sleepovers, anytime we wanted. I became so cool. So cool that every morning I would wake up singing a song, doing the slide, a dance move from the Toronto nightclub scene that John had taught me. I was developing such a confident attitude, my friends started to notice and commented about the change in me.

Paul, the DJ, was noticing the change in me as well. At first, he thought I was hilarious, but as time passed, he began to show concern. One night, Paul picked me up to go to the radio station, and as we got onto the street, he said, "We have to go to Wallaceburg for a minute." Wallaceburg was about fifteen minutes west of Chatham.

"Sure, what's up?" I asked.

"I have to meet someone for a minute at the Legion. You wait in the car."

"Okay," I answered.

The drive was quiet, and little was said. Paul got out of the car after parking it in the Legion's parking lot. "Sit tight . . . I'll be back in a minute."

Well, the minute turned into thirty minutes. Then an hour. I was getting really scared for this bar was notorious for its fights and violence. Just the week before, a man had been shot right in the very parking lot where I was sitting. I actually was shivering scared. Then finally, Paul came out.

"Hey . . . you're driving," Paul chirped.

"What? I have no licence," I answered.

"You're cool enough. Get in and drive."

"Okay."

Half scared, a quarter excited, and the last quarter pissed off at Paul for leaving me alone in the parking lot of that bar, the toughest bar in the area, I climbed in and naturally started the car.

"You've done this before!" Paul blurted out in amazement.

"What did you think? I was born and raised on a farm. I was taught how to drive when I was eight."

"Damn! I thought I had one on you," Paul said in disappointment.

"Well, I'll give you the 'gotcha' on leaving me in that parking lot alone for an hour."

"Oh shit, did that scare you?" Paul asked with concern.

"Hell yes, a guy was shot there last week. What do you expect?"

"I didn't plan on that one, but . . . what the hell. I'll take it."

"Gotcha!"

Away we went to the studio, and like all the other times and many more in the future days to come, Paul never ceased to amaze me with his humour, wit, and caring about my well-being as a young teenager. He was my guide into a world of music and star-filled acquaintants that I had only dreamed about ever being able to meet, let alone communicate with to that point in my life. In years to come, Paul would take me to greater heights beyond my wildest imagination, both in my personal life and in the music business. Paul never did get very far with my sister Jackie . . . as far as I know.

For the next three summers, I would experience the most memorable life awakenings and lessons of the heart one could ever expect out of meeting a seventeen-year-old young man when I was fourteen. My friendship with John Hobbs and Paul Godfrey evolved into a closeness that could be considered almost romantic, yet there was no desire or implied homosexual attraction. However, there was a closeness that became spiritual for all of us. In particular, John Hobbs was my big brother, and I was his buddy. He was all that I needed to feel alive and to lean on when the outside world was not so clear or became unreasonable to accept.

I would wait for John to come home, even if it was late at night. I was so obsessed with just being a part of his existence that I would call his family and ask when John was expected to arrive on a Friday night from Toronto. John would drive home on the weekends from school. I would sit in our living room chair for hours into the night, looking aimlessly out the living room window which faced onto the street, waiting for him to drive by in his little red 1968 VW Beetle. I know now I was experiencing a hint of obsessive-compulsive behaviour. I can tell you that I can still feel the pain and anxiety I felt for hours and days on end, waiting for John to come home. Then like a blur, the red Beetle would blaze by, and I would count the minutes before I could call.

"Hey, man, you're home."

"Come on down, you little shithead."

"Cool!" Away I would go. On to another adventure, for every weekend, every day and every hour, John seemed to know how to get the most out of it all. He opened my eyes to life and its amazing gifts . . . and curses. My first drink was with John. Later on, my first toke on a joint and hash knife took place in his bedroom. Interestingly, before we did it, John made me read a pamphlet on grass and hash. He wanted me to know what to expect, I guess. Maybe it was more to justify his actions.

By this time, John had me, lock, stock, and barrel. My parents were beside themselves with me and were beginning to fear my excessive behaviour and attachment to John. The summers were spent out at the lake with John and his sister and her friends. I was fourteen, lying on the beach with seventeen-, eighteen-, and nineteen-year-olds, giving Ann Marie back rubs and massages. I was beginning to find myself fantasizing about Ann Marie. She did catch on later that fall.

John, Ann Marie, and I went to Toronto for a weekend to take in the music scene. Again, here is a fourteen-year-old being exposed to Toronto nightlife. John had an apartment attached to St. Michael's College on Bathurst near Dundas. On the Saturday night, John decided he was going to show me Yorkville. I couldn't wait, for it was the late sixties, and Yorkville was where everything came from, musically, in Canada. If you were in Yorkville clubbing at that time, you would be the coolest guy ever. We were able to get into a couple of small, underground clubs before the doorman ushered us out. But it was still the greatest because I was there and saw it for myself. Hippies could be seen up and down the side streets, smoking dope, wandering aimlessly from one club to the next. All you could smell was incense in the night air, everywhere you went.

John still was not satisfied, so we got in his car, and he said, "You are going to be christened by the most ultimate club ever, and no one will ever be able to outdo you on this one. We're going to the legendary Hawks Nest on Yonge Street."

And we did.

We had absolutely no trouble getting into the main room, up two flights of stairs. I still remember the room. It was dark and long. John ordered two beers, and we stood at the railing, facing the stage. Playing at that moment was the most exciting act I could have ever seen. Rhinoceros! I had their album, and John had introduced me to their music. They were the early version of Domenic Troiano-style of rock and funk, the former lead guitarist of the greatest Canadian R&B blues band, Mandala. Dominic went on to form Bush, then joined The Guess Who, The James Gang, and finally had commercial success on his own. The night was lifetime memorable.

So was the drive home to Chatham the next day. It was cold out, and back in those days, the car was not very warm, so Ann Marie cuddled up in the front passenger seat with me. For two-and-a-half hours, I had this beautiful, full-breasted, warm, outrageously gorgeous nineteen-year-old wrapped up in my fourteen-year-old arms. I was constantly at full erection while we were intertwined in each other, under a car blanket, for the duration of the trip to Chatham. She knew it too. Annie would act like she was sleeping, then she would slowly drop her hand onto my crotch, giving me a subtle, complimentary squeeze, as if she were doing it in her sleep. She would cuddle up to get more comfortable, then slightly kiss my neck while she was seemingly dreaming. I didn't complain about it. I captured every moment with full intent to replay those Kodak moments at a later, more opportune time.

New Year's 1969 brought my sexuality to a new height. John and I were invited to the house of another of my "passion girls," who lived directly across the street from me. Janice Nixon. Janice and Ann Marie were close friends and were about the same age. Janice and I would play golf and tennis together, usually once a week, and joined John and Ann Marie from time to time to watch movies and hang out. I had gotten my sister's boyfriend to sneak a case of beer over to John's house without my sister knowing, for she definitely would have squealed to my dad, who in turn would have beaten me to a pulp. John had arranged that we would go over to Janice's party at about 11:00 p.m.

We were very much ready for a good time and feeling little pain when through John's door came Ann Marie and Janice and Shirley Steel, Chatham's Queen of the City, literally. They had been drinking as well and were in the mood for more. Immediately, John and Shirley disappeared. I had suspected his interest in her for many weeks, but he didn't discuss it much. Ann Marie began to kiss me and hug me, telling me how much she cared for me and hoped for me to have a great life. She also reminded me of our age difference and tried to explain to me what she needed in a man. All the while, she continued to make out with me passionately, and she got more aggressive as the night progressed. Occasionally, Janice would wander over and join in our kissing fest and as well assured me of her fondness and good wishes. As all good things would end up, the girls collected Shirley out of the bedroom and left after midnight off into the Chatham party scene and brought in the New Year until the sun came up.

The next year flowed in and went out as it came. I began to dedicate more time to hockey and football. I rekindled my old friendships that were all a part of the respective sports teams I joined. I found myself wanting to focus on the scholarship hockey programs more than music. I had to devote more time and energy to make the Junior B hockey teams and high school and regional football teams. This was the beginning of the metamorphosis and passing of the close bond between John and I. Change was in the wind.

Paul was sent to the East Coast for a time, where he found himself in the middle of the largest radio empire in Canada, CFTR, located in Toronto. He was in the centre of the world music culture and made friends with Levon Helm, Robbie Robertson, and "The Band." Paul hosted a TV dance show, which earned him recognition as the Canadian Dick Clark.

I waited up in the chair for John with great anxiousness no longer. I would call him maybe once a month. John rarely came home from Toronto that year, only for family functions. The last summer before I left for university was consumed with playing Junior ORFU football for the Sarnia Golden Bears. I found my true love of the sport but had to choose hockey in order to get a scholarship. Funny, John and I didn't even say . . . goodbye.

"Come on in," yelled Jack Hobbs, as if to warn everyone Monica and I had arrived.

I immediately felt an air of coldness and distance from the room and the people in it. Sitting there was John's mom, his two younger brothers, and yes, my dream girl, Ann Marie. She was outstandingly elegant.

I noticed Monica do the womanly once over, as did Ann Marie.

"Monica . . . is it? Welcome. Well, this is a shock. You two married . . . so suddenly . . . a child on the way?"

"No," Monica answered with great quickness and yet with a respective smile.

"Come with me, you two. John's in the kitchen . . . you haven't met Susanne yet, have you, Frank?"

"No," I answered Ann Marie with jubilant curiousness. "John!" I said with a hint of brotherly emotion. As I said it, a feeling of sadness and almost disappointment came over me.

John's hair was long and unruly. He had aged dramatically, and he was totally stoned on weed. The weed didn't bother me as much as his detached, almost arrogant demeanour.

"Hey, man . . . what's happening? Sit down. What's your name? Monica . . . oh nice, uh, ha, this is my, uh, wife, ha, uh, Susanne. She's pregnant. Isn't she pretty? 'Susanne took me down, to the river' . . . remember that one, Frankie? Leonard Cohen. I taught this guy all he once knew."

John tried to express his role in my life to Susanne and Monica through his inebriated, inhibited speech.

I tried to respond by saying, "Yeah, man, those were good times . . . right?"

"Hey! What do you mean 'good times'? They were . . . they were . . . okay . . . Yeah . . . okay, hum, okay. Let's go to the living room where you and your, ah, new wifey ha, Frankie's got a wife, ha. Now . . . watch and listen to the next great Crosby, Stills, Nash & Young replacement group from Canada ever to perform!"

John sat beside his younger brother, whom I hadn't seen for at least three years. Chris was sixteen and looked just like Eric Clapton. We found out very quickly he could play just like him. John was very good as well, even in his state of intoxication. The two of them played for at least one hour. I must say it was memorable and so befitting, for this time would be the last I would see John's brother Chris and his mother. They both passed away within a year of each other. Chris came down with leukemia and died within six months of that Christmas Eve. Mrs. Hobbs lasted out the year but died quickly of terminal cancer. John quickly disappeared into a hidden culture somewhere in Toronto; I have not been able to find him since. Daddy Jack passed on some twenty years later of old age.

As Monica and I walked home, I took some very deep breaths to clear my head. "It's over . . . I've really moved on." I kept saying out loud and to myself, subconsciously knowing Monica could hear me.

"What's over?" Monica asked.

"John is no longer who I thought he was, who I believed he was. My mentor of coolness, my beloved friend, isn't there anymore. I don't know that man whom we just saw named John Hobbs. That's not my friend, my brother. I can't even recognize him. Is this what happens between friends when you grow out of something as magical as what I experienced with John during those four years?"

Then as quickly as I stated my feelings to the cold night sky, tears fell from my eyes as I sat on the curb in Monica's arms until I couldn't cry anymore. My John was gone, leaving only fond memories for me to treasure throughout the rest of my life.

The gift between John and I were those memories; memories that I have shared with friends and acquaintances and have returned to, pulling them out many times to help me entertain so many people in so many places and situations.

"Let's go home, Frank. Oh . . . I mean, your folks' home," suggested Monica.

CHAPTER 5

YEARS LATER 2001

The phone kept ringing as I tried to collect my senses. Soapberry was done. The investors had walked away. Desperate, I began to panic, for the bank accounts were empty and I had no money. Ty was all over me about what the next step was to recapture what she believed to be remnants of the business. I could only do my best to keep from collapsing in shock, but I knew I had to try to regroup. Every call was from investor partners trying to forewarn me about what the main investor group, Coventry Financial Corp, was planning next. It seemed that every call contained more revealing information about my deepest suspicions as to who had done what and why my lawyer and accountant had not been there to help me or support me when the collapse of Soapberry began.

Some months earlier, my chartered accountant and financial adviser, Peter Coleman, and I had started negotiations with Atlantis Bancorp, a venture capital company, to refinance and roll Soapberry into a US public trading company on the NASDAQ Exchange. In return, we would receive two million shares of the company, named Soapberry International, and I would retain my position as CEO, along with a respectable salary.

The president of Atlantis was Mark Appleby, a very wealthy man with great contacts in the international financial world, or so we thought. Mark had been courting me for some time and seemed to be in the same headspace as Peter and me from the beginning of our relationship. He was always presenting solutions through his finance groups to solve the ongoing cashflow problems of Soapberry, especially the $2 million loan with Coventry that was about to be called due to our inability to continue to pay back at the rate they expected. We, as a company, had already repaid $500,000 up to that point. We felt and were reassured by Coventry that they would not call the loan, pending the RTO process that Atlantis was formulating. In fact, Coventry offered a forbearance of the debt in return for shares in the publicly traded company once the RTO was complete. I felt confident in this process, for all parties at the time were seemingly working together. From January 1999 through March 1999, everyone was communicating properly, and we all seemed to be making progress.

Then out of nowhere, one night in early April 1999, Mark called me. He was screaming on the phone at me in a drunken incoherent rage. "The deal is done. I'm out! I'm so disgusted with everyone in this deal I got money in, and I'm so pissed off with Coventry. I'm pulling the plug on the deal right now!"

He hung up.

I had the phone on speaker so Ty, my girlfriend at the time, could hear. "What the hell was that?" she said, in shock and disbelief.

"I had better call Peter and find out if he knows what's going on."

Peter Coleman, my chartered accountant and financial adviser in this deal, was also the president of Coventry Financial Corp. In addition, he was part of the board of directors of Coventry and of Soapberry. We had been introduced some three years prior and had hit it off immediately. At the time, I was involved in a high-tech company called PageActive as the acting CFO, helping them raise money to complete their RTO. The person I was working with as a consultant to raise money was a man named Jim Trainer, another chartered accountant.

Jim and I had spent a lot of time together on a number of finance projects and had built a solid working relationship. I had gained his confidence as a hard-working consultant, and I showed him an honest eagerness to learn the high-finance business. Jim was impressed with my abilities to learn fast, communicate with clients, and find solid opportunities on both sides of the Canadian and US borders. Jim made some respectable returns with the deals I found him. In return, he paid me handsomely for my services.

While I was working on the PageActive project, Jim presented me with an opportunity to partner with him. He was managing a short-term invoice discounting fund and wanted to expand his lending focus to take over a specific oil company's credit card activity. He needed $2 million and wanted me to raise the money. I quickly agreed to partake in the deal.

At the same time, I knew my involvement with PageActive was coming to an end, for the company had successfully signed on with a venture capital group out of Southern California and no longer needed my services. They offered me a commission position. Rather than limiting myself to one company, I felt that I could better benefit as a business consultant, servicing small, fledgling businesses and raising money for that market.

While working on developing my new venture, Jim introduced me to Peter and the group known as Coventry Financial Corp. This group of high financiers was comprised of ex-bankers and venture capitalists dealing with setting up casinos in a number of Ontario cities. They ran a labour fund under the name of Kensington Group that invested in the oil and gas industry out West and had set up a new invoice discounting service under the identity of Coventry Financial Corp. Peter had been employed by Westin Foods for a number of years. The connection between him and I was that we both had come from the London and Chatham area. Peter was a University of Western Ontario graduate and had played football. He was intrigued by my athletic background, which made an immense first impression.

Jim had set up a meeting with Peter and Jim Boxer from Coventry to review my business plan, explaining what business consulting services I would perform, how and when I would do it, and whom I could approach. They bought in immediately, which shocked me initially.

I was a nobody on the streets of Toronto. I had little to no money. I was barely able to pay rent and had gone through twenty-some years of failures and losses in business. I had, however, accumulated many contacts and business experiences in both Canada and the United States. My past was checkered in many different industries, which had opened my eyes and knowledge base to help me fit in the world of finance. I had a business history that started where I left off in front of my friend John

Hobbs' house that Christmas in 1972, wondering how life was about to change for me and my new wife, Monica.

Back to December 1972

The next morning, Monica and I began the move to London. We both had jobs: me working at the Department of Defence as a delivery boy; Monica as a waitress across from our new apartment in London that we were approved instantly for that very day. Mom and Dad had given us their old furniture from the basement. What more could we want?

The first few weeks were what we had expected: getting up for work, living a new life in London, and working out our initial lifestyle. My pay was so small, and Monica, being an American, found things very difficult at first. She could only get restaurant work. She was starting to show signs of depression even though I really did not notice it at first; she hid her feelings well. We visited my parents every weekend, which didn't help much. My mother was quick to criticize Monica on her dress, demeanour, and attitude. It wasn't long before they started butting heads. I again did not take this seriously, for I was used to my mother's personality and hypercritical nature.

As months went on, Monica finally got a job as a secretary in a law firm. She seemed to settle in better and started making friends. I was getting restless to participate in sports to fill in my time. I went back for my final year with the Sarnia Golden Bears ORFU football team. Our life seemed to settle, or so I thought.

The phone rang at about 4:00 p.m. one afternoon in April. A man started by saying in a very friendly manner, "Frank, how the hell are you?"

"I'm good," I replied in wonderment.

"So, you won't guess who this is?"

"Okay, who is it?"

"It's Jim from John McGregor, remember me?"

"Oh yeah, how are you?" I answered.

"Well, I'm great, but I have some bad news for you. See I'm a police officer here in London, and I have your wife Monica here at the station."

My mind was racing, and I felt a cold chill come over me. "Is she okay? Was she hurt or in an accident?"

"No, no, no, nothing like that. Frank, we have a problem. I had to take her in for shoplifting. I arrested her at the Fairweather store about a half hour ago. She was in possession of about $100 worth of clothes. I need you to come down here and vouch for her and take her home. I'm letting her go on a summary charge with a promise to appear under your care. She'll get a fine out of this. I'm really sorry for having to do this, Frank. We're old friends, and I know this is embarrassing."

I hung up the phone and felt so shocked. Then I remembered her problem that I'd experienced when going to her parents' in North Dakota some twelve months prior. *This is a problem*, I thought. *Maybe this will scare her enough to stop.* What I didn't know was that the events to follow would be even more unsettling and bracing.

Monica was waiting for me in the station, sitting on a bench in the main hallway. Jim was with her, and he tried to make light of the situation, but I could tell she was not amused. Jim left us alone, and Monica couldn't look at me. She just stared at the floor.

"Let's go," I said quietly, not to show any anger.

I was as afraid as she was, but I knew she needed me to be calm. We went home, and there was no talk or emotion, just cold air in the car. We got home, and she went directly to the bedroom, shutting the door. I let the day go by without any confrontation or questions. After a few days of distance, we began to talk about her impulse to steal. She had never been confronted about her actions and found it hard to discuss it. Finally, one day while we were sitting watching TV, she broke down and cried, opening up to what was causing these activities.

"I've always felt so secure with myself, even at college. I didn't think I had a problem. I always got anything I wanted as a child and lived a great life at home. Why can't I adjust to our new life?" she asked me.

I replied, "Monica, I'm trying my best to include you in everything, my family, my life that I only know here in Canada. I don't know what to do more. Let's just deal with it and put it behind us."

She just nodded in compliance and quietly let it go.

Two weeks later, while Monica was at work, a loud knock sounded at the door. I opened it to find two large men standing outside the door with suites and badges. To my shock, they were RCMP officers.

"Frank Trousdell?"

"Yes, sir?"

"We are . . ."

They said their names, but it didn't register.

"We need to talk to you."

"Come in, please."

They stood at the door and began to recite an order demanding me to attend a meeting at the RCMP office downtown on a specific date, alone. "You are required to attend the hearing regarding your wife, Monica Dallas Trousdell."

"Why?" I asked.

"All will be explained at the hearing. Thank you, and we'll see you there."

Obviously, I was taken aback but, for some reason, not surprised. *She is an American citizen living in Canada, and she has a charge against her. I am her sponsor. This is not good*, I said to myself.

We discussed it that night, and Monica seemed casual about the whole thing.

I attended the meeting, and as they began, the intensity rose like the temperature would with a fire burning under me.

"Mr. Trousdell, are you aware of the severity of the situation?"

"Yes, sir."

"Are you aware Monica may be deported back to the US?"

"No, sir."

"Well, unless we can come to a clear understanding, you may see your wife transported back to her home and never being allowed back into Canada again. Is that understood?"

"Yes, sir."

"We are going to give you one chance to deal with this problem. Monica must stay clean of any infractions, charges, even a traffic violation, or else she goes."

I responded immediately, "I promise there will never be another incident, sir."

"You may go."

"Thank you, sir."

The feeling of relief was overwhelming as I left their building; I found the closest bar and sat down just to collect my thoughts. Four beers in, I began to feel the anger start to rise. *Why would she put us in this situation? What effect will this have on us?* I kept asking myself over and over.

By the time I got home, I knew our marriage was in jeopardy. A change came over me that would not go away and cemented deep inside my core for a long time.

Our relationship began to slowly come apart, psychologically at first. The next two months were very quiet and started to show small distances. I was starting to work out more, preparing for the football season, and I changed jobs from the Department of Defence to selling life insurance. I disliked the job because I was the youngest member. I found my dad hated me selling insurance as well, and it was difficult for me to understand the benefits at my young age. He kept saying, "Get a job in utilities. Why won't you go to Union Gas? I can get you in there."

Something kept me from getting a factory job, and for some reason, I had to prove him wrong. I was making more money, but I had trouble getting clients. I was too young. No one would give me respect as an adviser. Rightfully so. I had no idea what I was doing.

Then my sister Marie talked to me about a friend of hers who would give me an interview with the Royal Trust Company. They were looking to hire a trainee in the trust department. This was an entry-level position with long-term potential. I was totally excited yet again, but I had no knowledge of what a trust officer did or what it entailed.

I went out and got a new suit, wrote up my resume (not knowing how to write it to form), and set out for the meeting. I arrived at the address in downtown London to find an empty office. No furniture. No people. Just an open door to an empty-looking bank-type room. There was this man leaning up against a railing in a very expensive suit looking anxious.

"Frank Trousdell?" he asked.

"Yes."

He told me his name.

I didn't even remember it after the meeting. I handed my resume to him.

He quickly glanced at it and said, "Fine. You will start at $660 per month, and you will relocate to Hamilton's training office. You will report to the manager (again, I didn't remember his name) on Monday evening at 6:00 p.m. We will pay for all your relocation costs. I just need you to sign here, and you are set."

"So, I got the job?"

"Yes, you have. I know this seems unorthodox, but I know your sister very well and let's say I did her a big favour."

"Okay," I said. "Is there any training or material I could read before I meet?"

"No, not really. They'll train you, and you'll be fine. I've got to go to another meeting. Good luck, Frank."

All I could do as I walked to my car was to shake my head and say to myself, *I guess this is good. I'm working for Royal Trust. I guess I have made it to the big time of business. Okay, I feel great! I did it! Ah, what the hell just happened?*

I couldn't wait to tell Monica. *She'll be really proud of me. Money is going to be a little tight, but she'll get a good job,* I kept telling myself. Monica was settling in at her new job as a secretary at the university Law Department at Osgood Hall. She had just gotten it a month prior. She had just made new friends and was feeling better about herself.

I really wasn't thinking of her when Royal Trust jumped into my world. Mind you, I had no idea they needed me to move immediately. As I drove home, I decided not to tell Monica that I had taken the job just yet, but to tell her I had an appointment on Monday in Hamilton. That might make it easier.

"What the hell are you saying to me?" Monica responded in quick temper. "How could you just take it without you discussing it with me first?"

"I'll make my decision after the meeting on Monday," I nervously responded.

"I just got this job, and I thought you were never going to leave London. What about my new friends? What about my job?"

"Let's take it one step at a time," I said. "Let's see what happens."

"Right," she quipped. She left the apartment in disgust to see "her friends."

Monica didn't get in until 2:00 a.m. She went straight to bed. I felt she had made a decision that she was not prepared to share with me. Time would only tell, but I knew deep inside it was not good.

The Monday meeting went as hoped. The manager was very kind and optimistic. He reviewed what I was to do and the move details. I fell right into the plan. I took the deal. I knew Monica would fight it, but deep inside, this move was right, and my future was at hand. Prior to this, I had applied for many jobs of all kinds and had been rejected, mainly due to the fact I had no degree or completion of any trade. I was desperate. But Monica never seemed to care about my fears of employment or not being employable. As time went on, I found out why.

The agreement was for me to start in thirty days. I had to find us a place to live and help Monica with the transition; at least, so I thought. Monica was beside herself for the first week. She wanted nothing to do with me and spent most of her time with her friends. In a lot of ways, I learned to accept this change in behaviour, mainly because I was training and playing football. I had left my job at the insurance company and had a lot of free time during the day to relax and plan the move.

To add to the stress, I had bought our first new car, a Firebird Rally Sport 1973. Our payments were $200 per month, and I had just enough money to pay the loan for two months and cover our living costs, but boy, was it great driving a new car. I quickly found out how great it was one morning as I was taking Monica to work. When I got to the car in the parking lot, I found a note under the windshield wiper.

My Firebird friend,

I'd like to meet you . . . here is my number . . . my name is Belinda.

After looking at it for a second, I quickly threw it into the bushes as we left. Monica didn't even catch on. I told her it was a prank. When I dropped Monica off, I raced back to get the note. It was still in the bushes. I picked it up and went to the apartment to look at it. Voices inside me said, *Call it. See what this is all about.*

A very sexy voice answered and immediately said, "I was sure you'd call."

"Do you know who this is?" I asked nervously.

"I watched you from my apartment while you picked the note up. Wise move, throwing it away like you did, my Firebird friend."

"Do you want to meet?" I asked.

"Of course . . . your place?" she asked.

"Okay," I responded. "I'm home now."

She finished by saying, "I'll be down in a minute."

What did I just do? I asked myself. *I'm in control,* I kept saying. *I'm not going to cheat. I won't do it.*

A knock came at the door, and as I opened it, I was taken aback by the vision of a beautiful young woman standing there. My fantasies all came to fruition as she entered my apartment.

"I have nothing to drink," I said.

She replied, "Not necessary. We don't need anything, do we?"

"No, I guess not."

She sat on the couch as if she knew where to go and what she wanted. "I noticed you one day about three months ago, just after you moved into your apartment. I thought you were really good looking," she said.

The excitement rose in me like a hot surge of blood rushing throughout my body. I was already perspiring. She then reached over, put her hand on mine, and gradually pulled my hand and, in turn, all of me close to her. All I saw was her face and lips lean into mine, and I felt her warm breath and body as we entwined like two clutching, long-lost lovers holding each other for the first time.

After about an hour of undoing, disrobing, touching, and sexual exploring, with seemingly mindless and wild abandonment, we both exploded into a threshold-breaking, mind-bending climax. Only then did we realize, in shock and embarrassment, what we had just done. As I rolled off her, I clearly saw, for the first time, that we were on the floor. Then, as I had presumed, anxiety and guilt began to set in, to the point of me shedding tears.

"What's wrong?" she asked sheepishly.

"I never thought I would allow myself to give in to someone like you or anyone for that matter. I've only been married for four months."

"Did I cause you to cheat or was this coming?"

"I don't know. I think it was a little of both. Maybe I've been alone too much these past months. You're a very attractive girl. By the way, how old are you?" I asked her.

"Eighteen," she replied quickly.

"I hope you are protected?"

"Oh yeah, don't worry about that. I just broke off with my boyfriend two days ago. We had been doing it for two years, and I went on the pill for that same amount of time. Am I going to see you again?" she asked with a sense that she was hoping for a yes but also to imply that if I didn't want to, it would be okay.

"I don't know. I'll need some time to figure out just what happened here. I hope you won't contact my wife and tell her, will you?" I asked, almost pleading with her not to speak with Monica.

"Oh no, I would never do anything like that. It's more exciting to hold a secret than cause destruction in your life," she convincingly replied.

I could feel my fear and anxiety ease up to the point of feeling comfortable with her near me.

She showed the same body language.

"I'll be gone for the next two weeks," she said. "My girlfriend and I are going to hitchhike to California and back."

"Are you nuts?" I asked. "Do you know how dangerous it is?"

With carefree confidence, she said, "We'll be just fine. Truckers will be our ride there and back. I bet we'll get our ride all the way there just outside of Sarnia and probably get one back from the same guy."

"When are you going?" I asked.

"Tomorrow night," she responded.

"I could take you as far as Sarnia if you could leave about 4:30 p.m." I had football practice that day and thought nothing of it to take them that far.

"Hey, okay," she said. "I gotta go . . . my girlfriend's coming over and is probably at my door now."

She got dressed and gave me a big kiss, and said as she left, "No matter what . . . I want to still see you, okay? Friends?"

"Sure," I replied.

For the next two hours, I was a ball of confusion. I felt excited that I was attractive to other women and was able to experience an affair just like I had recently read in a Harold Robbins novel. I remember how the lead man of the story was at a garage sale and spotted a beautiful, sexy woman gazing at a vase on the corner of a table. He watched her handle the vase so closely and described how she ran her fingers up and down the vase with full sexual suggestion, only for him to see. Then she began to rub herself quietly and so secretively against the corner of the table until she reached climax. Then through a series of events, she led him to her bed. I never could believe that such an event could happen to me in real life, but it did, right there in my apartment.

The only big problem was that I had just broken the most sacred vow between Monica and myself: fidelity. But somehow, and for some distinct reason, I felt deep in my core that this was about to become a justifiable event. For some unexplainable hint of logic, Monica had something she was hiding even after we married. *Only time will tell*, I kept saying to myself. *Only time will tell.*

Chapter 6

At first, Monica was very disappointed with my decision to take the trust officer job in Hamilton. Once she saw the city and looked at houses and apartments, she gave in to the move. It only took us two weeks to find a small home to rent and, luckily, Monica got a temp job with Firestone's Canadian head office as a secretary. The future already looked optimistic. I was still playing football for Sarnia but found I could travel easily to the games myself because most of them were played in the Hamilton and Toronto areas.

My first day with Royal Trust was very unnerving. I had no clue as to what I was to do or what daily tasks I was expected to perform. It was 8:30 a.m., and I was sitting in the waiting room of my new office area when a short, wiry, thin man walked up to me and introduced himself.

"Mr. Trousdell? My name's Jim Aschroft. Now, I don't know why they hired you or what connections you have here, but I can tell you it was not my idea. However, you're a very good hockey player. We need a ringer for our bank league team. That is the only reason I went along with hiring you.

"Follow me, please. Along the left wall are all the agency client filing cabinets, and along the adjacent wall are the management client files. Anything you need regarding the list of clients you will be managing will be found in those cabinets. Behind this door is the vault. All important documents and items held by us on behalf of our clients' estates can be found there. You do not remove anything without proper authorization from me.

"Follow me, please, and stay close to me so you can hear me the first time. I do not like repeating myself.

"This is Evelyn. She is the typing pool. You give her all your dictation and any correspondence that needs to be typed. I must approve all correspondence before it goes out. Do you understand?"

"Yes, sir."

"Jim, not sir. Do you understand?

"Yes, Jim, sir."

"Oh my God, you will be difficult; I can see already," Jim said with a tone of frustration.

All the while, my mind was racing to catch everything he was saying. I had absolutely no clue what anything he was saying meant. All the while, I was looking at the people sitting at their desks that were neatly lined up along the windows, trying to size up who seemed to be open to accepting me enough to tell me what I was to do. Every time I made eye contact, Jim would catch me and take me to another area, which raised the bar of confusion and anxiety another notch.

"Now, here's your desk. The man sitting in your chair is Peter Delianko. He is being transferred to Toronto head office. Peter is our rising star as a trust officer. He will advise you on all you need to know. Peter, take it away, and Frank, God help you. I hope you can last the week." Jim disappeared back to his window office and left me with the guy I was replacing.

"Hi, I'm Peter."

"Frank Trousdell," I quickly responded with an earnest attempt to shake his hand.

One thing my dad always said: "Be forthright with your handshake. People judge you by your handshake. Some will have wet palms and fish-like grasps. Others have no grip, and there are those who shake with a lifeless hand. They all have positive or negative meanings about that person."

Peter's handshake was firm, and his body language was all business. "So, you are taking over the desk?" he asked.

"I guess so," I responded nervously.

"I'll get you on your way, Frank. It won't be too bad of a learning curve."

I asked Peter with caution, "What is it that I am supposed to be doing?"

"You are managing this list of estate accounts, management accounts, and agency accounts." Peter handed me a five-page list of names and numbers.

"Now, what am I really supposed to do?" I asked as if to say, now tell me the real truth and don't bullshit me.

"You keep the files up to date. Correspond with the beneficiaries on a regular basis, keeping them informed of what's happening in their file, things like that. Oh, and every month, keep in touch with the estate lawyer. You'll find each one is in the file."

"Is that it?"

"Pretty much," Peter answered. "Now, I've got a lot to do, and you have a lot to learn, so watch closely. Sit back here." Peter pointed to the window ledge behind him.

I could feel that this process was going to be painful.

The first three hours were dreadfully arduous, watching Peter sit there and read and write little notes. From time to time, he would blurt out, "Keep an eye on this situation in this file. The first beneficiary cannot be revealed to the second beneficiary because the deceased specified so in the will."

"You mean his first beneficiary was his mistress?"

"That's right, Frank. You're going to see a lot of crazy things on this job."

"Doesn't the wife have any clue?"

"She knew of her but isn't aware just yet that the other woman is really the first beneficiary."

"Holy shit!" I said, almost disturbing the other officers.

Then a voice from behind the left kiosk said, "Is that the Eagerson Estate?"

Peter responded, "Yeah, Phil."

Phil Scheiding was a three-year veteran Class 1 Trust Officer. He was an honours grad from MacMaster University with a Bachelor of Commerce. His father was a very successful banker. Phil was the quintessential budding businessman during the week, but on the weekends, he was a wanna-be biker hippie. Monday through Friday, he would wear the three-piece suits with a pipe constantly in his mouth. On the weekends, he was in blue jeans, smoking weed from Friday to Sunday.

"I'll fill you in more over lunch, Frank," Phil spoke with affirmation. "Frances? Are you joining us?" he spouted out to this gorgeous, black-haired, long-legged, short-skirted, twenty-something female sitting in front of my desk.

"Sure, Italian today, guys. Okay?" Frances asked.

I felt quite good and somewhat confident as we all got up from our respective desks and headed for the elevator. I could immediately tell Phil was the ringleader, the hotshot, and good-looking man of the hour. He always was in front of the pack, always talking, joking, and wearing a big smile. You could tell he was going to do something big at any time. The last desk we passed by to collect another person was that of Pat Brown. Tall, slim, and timid in nature, he had a very pale look about him. He smiled with caution and had sort of a snort as he laughed. Yet he walked with a quick step and upright confident stature. Pat was second in command of the trust officers and was the one you would go to before seeing Jim Aschroft, the big little guy. Right from the get-go, I felt that Pat and I could become very good friends.

I quickly learned that lunch was everyone's favourite time of the day. There was a unified sigh of relief as each found their spot at the table. The laughter was loud and cheerful, and the stories would resonate around the meeting place. We were the Royal Trust gang—all for one . . . and so on. Our correspondence girl joined us and sat across from me. Phil noticed me eyeing her up and down.

"Evelyn, you have a new admirer. This is Frank Trousdell. He just started today.

"Yes," Evelyn responded, "Jim introduced me this morning. So, Frank, where are you from and what did you do before you came here?"

I began to recite my history for her but found most were listening.

"Why did you leave UND? What a great opportunity," someone asked.

Phil piped up, "That's not fair, Frank. I apologize. You don't have to answer that.

"Oh, that's okay. I took a crash course in Marriage 101."

Everyone laughed to ease the tension of the moment.

"I may go back to get my degree. I don't know just yet."

"Well, we're glad you are with us. We've got to win this year's bankers league hockey championship, and you're the one who'll take us there," Phil stated with great optimism.

The table began to shout, "Yeah, we've got it in the bag now."

While they were all spouting off, I felt somewhat nervous about their expectations. I shrugged it off and went on to enjoy my lunch. The rest of the day was totally uneventful.

That night, when I went home and sat on the front porch, I started wondering what if I could ever get a shot at a pro camp, even a shot at a rookie open walk-on camp with any NHL team. I sat there and daydreamed.

"What's going on inside of that head of yours?" Monica asked jokingly.

"Nothing, really."

"Come on, let me in.

"Okay, I was just thinking about finding a rookie camp and trying out for an NHL team."

"Where is this coming from?"

"Oh, at lunch today, everyone got me stirred up about hockey. You know that I haven't really got it out of my system yet. Don't worry about it," I said to shake it off and forget about the crazy dream. But that dream would not go away. Instead, that dream would escalate daily for the next year.

Every day seemed to drag on a little more. Peter was pretty much done with my training and was preparing for his move to Toronto. I could tell he really didn't care if I understood what I was doing or not. He just wanted to get out of this office.

Finally, the day came, and we all went out after work to send Peter on to the new chapter in his life. As usual, the rounds of beer were flowing, and food was circling the table. Everyone had great stories of clients and events from years gone by, especially, a story that everyone had a bit to add about a certain Christmas party some two years past, when Peter and a secretary were found by the general manager having sex in the vault while everyone else was in the open office adjacent to the vault door. As the story went, the secretary was apparently a screamer and stopped the party and drew everyone's attention to her outcries, "Give it to me, Petey

Boy, and give it to me hard! Keep slamming me from behind, big boy!" As she climaxed, everyone shouted and applauded her accomplishment.

However, the general manager was not amused. He then opened the door to the vault and caught them half-naked on top of a filing cabinet with papers and files all over the floor. The message was very clear that they were about to be reprimanded. By the next day, the secretary was fired, and Peter was written up. He actually thought that he'd never get any kind of placement or advancement after that. But he worked really hard, kept his nose clean, and got a second chance.

The party lasted for a few hours, and everyone was starting to drift off on their own ways. I was sitting there, talking with Peter and Pat Brown about the job and life in general. I found both of them very interesting and very intelligent. They were accommodating to me and included me in every aspect of the conversation. I really felt like a part of the group for the first time in my life. I felt that I was accepted even though I really did not have a clue what I was doing.

There were many more parties and gatherings as time went on. The unique part was that Monica was never there. She was never invited. Looking back, I do remember that no spouses or girl- or boyfriends were there. We were a very tight-knit group and kept to ourselves most of the time.

The hockey season in the bank league started with a bang. No wonder they wanted me to play. No one could skate, let alone shoot the puck. Our goalie had only played hockey for two years. He was lucky to move in the net from one side to the other. The other teams were chockablock full of decent players. I immediately assessed that there was only one thing I could do: hog the puck the whole game. I'd pass the puck to a player just to catch the rebound off him, then skate past the other players and blast a shot past the opposition's goalie. All my teammates were so happy I was on their roster, for they'd never had won a game in the past.

Jim Aschroft would say after each of the weekly games we won, "Frank, your job is safe for another week."

All the locker room would laugh, but I knew Jim was not kidding. He watched me from his office every minute and read any correspondence I was preparing to send out. He repeatedly red-penned every letter I wrote and made me re-write them four, maybe five times, just to teach me how to write a business letter. I really felt self-conscious and intimidated. Phil was always there to intercept my frustration, and he'd say, "Don't let him get to you, Frank. He's just playing little Napoleon games on you."

"What's that mean?" I'd ask.

Phil laughed and replied, "You know, the small man syndrome. He has to flex his power and position to look bigger than life."

Phil and I spent a lot of time together out of the office. He was almost like an older brother. We went to the YMCA four times a week to train. He was into karate and had a number of belts. His goal was to teach someday, so, he taught me. We also played basketball with a bunch of his buddies. He included me everywhere he could.

The hockey season came and went, and as I anticipated, it was fun but very weak in the challenging department. I knew I wasn't going to get very far playing in this league. I had met Joe D'Amico, who played for one of the other teams. He owned a small sports store at the Ancaster arena. We talked a lot about hockey and my past. One day, he said, "You should come out and play with our Italian team. We play in a higher competitive league." So, I did. I found it more enjoyable, challenging, and demanding. The best part was that they played all year round. That meant I would be on the ice every week. The other best part was that we were all about the same age and, finally, they were all Italian . . . some of whom were connected to the mob. I found out many years later how important it would be to know them.

We played every Wednesday night at the triple rinks in Ancaster, Ontario, always around the 10:00 p.m. mark. The games only lasted one hour, so I was never tired out the next day. Again, I led the pack in the scoring and could outskate most that we played against. The really neat thing about the Italians was that they appreciated good talent, and they would always let you know it.

One night, Joe pulled me aside to forewarn me that we were playing a team that had a guy, Giles, who played in the American Hockey League. Giles was home (in Hamilton) for a few days and wanted some ice time. He knew one of the guys on the opposing team and came out to play for them. Obviously, I was to check this guy and keep him from scoring. What I didn't realize was that he had played a number of seasons for the New York Rangers in the NHL. Well, needless to say, he put me through my paces. We were back and forth, forechecking and backchecking each other as if we were playing for the Stanley Cup. The other teammates were very impressed with the battle ensuing between Giles and myself. The hour went by as if it were fifteen minutes, with both of us quite exhausted.

"We finally broke out in conversation as our time ran out."

"Where are you headed from here?" I questioned Giles.

"Oh, back to Hershey, I think, unless they send me someplace else. What are your plans?" he asked me as if he expected me to reply that I was on my way to some pro camp?

"Oh, I really don't have any plans just yet."

"Oh man, you're telling me you aren't signed yet?"

"Oh no. I left UND a year ago, and I haven't connected anywhere yet."

Giles replied as if he was counselling me. "I would write to every AHL or SHL organization and at least get a walk-on tryout, or if you know someone somewhere in hockey, get them to call you on a tryout."

"You really think I'm that good?" I asked in an adolescent tone.

"You gave me a real run for my money for the past hour. That told me you got all it takes to at least play AHL or SHL. AHL and SHL are leagues a step down from the NHL. They're teams usually owned and run by the mother NHL teams. They're called the minors or feeder teams."

We rambled on for the next half-hour and parted with hopes for good things to all, and then into the night, we went our own ways.

At the next week's game, Joe said to me, "You were so damned good last week I made a call to a friend of mine that works for Citibank in Burlington. He plays with us once in a while. His name's Pat Gregor. His brother's Jim Gregor, Manager of the Toronto Maple Leaf's."

"Holy shit!" I said in amazement.

"Now, don't get your hopes up, Frank, because I can't speak for him, but if he likes what he sees, he promised he'd call his brother on your behalf."

He played against me to really see if I had what it takes. Pat had a shot a couple of years prior with a semi-pro team, so he knew what he was talking about. Pat was impressed, and he couldn't stop raving about my wrist shot and how hard and fast my slap shot was.

"You're a very strong skater, Frank. You can tell you were trained in the NCAA. They really push speed. So, I'll call my brother and see what he says. That's all I can do, but I have a good feeling I can get you a shot with someone. My brother Jim has a very close tie with the Buffalo people. I wouldn't doubt he could get you in there. I'll let you know in a few weeks."

The weeks went by, and no call. The job was getting more difficult, and I was always in trouble with Jim Aschroft. My letter writing was so bad that he refused to let any of my correspondence out. He started questioning my ability to do my job. The others continued to step in to help me without Jim knowing. Pat Brown would watch over me from a distance. Frances Manno, who sat in front of me, continued to look over my work, trying to make sense of what I was supposed to do. She was so kind and helpful. We even played tennis one day. I think she was trying to be a friend, but of course, I screwed it up by hitting on her. She found me to be immature. I was. She saw right through me. Every time I met an attractive woman, I always interpreted the meeting as a possible invite for sex.

"Aren't you married, Frank?" she asked.

"Yes, Frances, but Monica's on holidays back in North Dakota. Do you want to go out or something?"

"Frank, if you were a single man, then I'd say yes. You're not, so forget it. Okay? Now let's get back to work," Francis responded as if she were shaking it off as a joke.

It was no joke to me. She was very attractive, with long, straight black hair, a fit frame, and very long, shapely legs. She always wore miniskirts. Every time she stood up and bent over her desk, all that should be covered became bare for me to see. One day she had no underpants on, exposing me to the view of a lifetime. My jaw was on the floor, and my eyes felt like they were almost protruding up her rear end. I could hear Phil chuckle from the other side of the kiosk.

"Settle down, big boy!" Phil blurted out, causing a unified instant series of jeers and laughter from the rest of the room.

Frances went on doing her work as usual, not responding to the incident at all.

April of 1974 was upon us, and the Royal Trust slo-pitch league was gearing up. We all agreed to meet at a local baseball diamond at the south end of Hamilton Mountain. As the team all straggled in, I noticed Pat was getting out of his car.

"Hey, buddy, what's happening?"

"I've been very busy at work. Citibank is in the process of moving me to Halifax next month."

"Holy shit!" I exclaimed.

"I got some news for you, Frank. I didn't get back to you yet because I had to wait for my brother to do his thing on your behalf."

"Well?" I questioned.

"You've been granted what they call a walk-on tryout with the Buffalo Sabres' farm team, the Charlotte Checkers of the Southern Hockey League."

"Holy shit," I kept saying over and over again.

Pat's vocal led in, "Don't forget you still have to make the team. It won't be easy, and you'll be competing against a lot of really great players from all over Canada and some from the US. Let's not forget that the players from last year's squad are returning and will be miles ahead of you. So, you have until September 6th to train like Rocky Balboa in the movie *Rocky*; that's six months. Think you can do it?" Pat asked in a positive tone.

"I know I can do it. I've been waiting for this shot all my life."

"Chances are you'll only have one, so make it your ultimate best."

As the practice went that night, all I thought about was making the team. I stood in left field all night, catching balls, just so I could daydream about my shot with the Checkers/Buffalo Sabres.

It's funny how your mind takes over at a time like this, knowing that six months in the future anything could happen. I could be dead, for all I knew. But the saying is true that you have to prepare yourself physically and mentally before you even get to the rink. I had six months to give it all I had to do just that—prepare myself to make myself stronger, faster, and tougher than I'd ever been.

When I got home that night, Monica and I sat up on the front porch, speculating what could happen if I made the team.

"Well, we would move to Charlotte, and you would find work to keep yourself occupied while I'm playing somewhere along the East Coast of the US. I would come home each week, and we would have great fun in the sun, living on the Atlantic coast."

Monica replied, "I could start a business, maybe a little retail shop selling clothes or something like that, along the beaches maybe."

"Yeah, that would be really cool," I answered.

That night went on with us filling our minds with dreams of what-ifs until we couldn't keep our eyes open anymore.

Five in the morning came very quickly, as the alarm rang like a fire bell directly implanted in my ear. "Oh, that's painful," I said out loud.

Monica grunted as she rolled over to my spot once I lifted myself upright, preparing to stretch and get moving. *This is my first step to greatness*, I said to myself.

Every day, seven days a week for the next six months, I would start my day at 5:00 a.m. and eat a quick bowl of cereal with some juice and vitamin B complex. Then I would run two miles on the surrounding streets. I had also set up to go at least three (if not four) days a week at 6:00 a.m. to the local rink to practice and skate for one hour. As well, I joined the YMCA, which was located two blocks south of my office. Every lunch hour was my time to weight train, swim, and use the different training equipment that was available to members to improve muscle strength and elasticity.

I worked the plan religiously, every single day. I even quit drinking beer on the weekends, except if we were at a friend's house or gathering at a nightclub, socializing with friends. These events were far and few between. Over the six-month period, we participated in out-of-house events maybe three or four times.

Living next door to us was a really cool family, the Brandinos. Tony, who was my age, had two younger brothers. His father was named Tony as well. Tony senior was a retired boxer, a lightweight Golden Gloves champ. He owned a barbershop in the north end on Barton Street. This was a very old Italian neighbourhood and, of course, Tony knew everyone. Son Tony was a probation officer but was the typical hippie leftover from the sixties who'd graduated from university and had recently got his first professional job. He'd obviously trained to be a probation officer and sociology major but would not jeopardize his morals or lifestyle for the "Man" or anyone else. Yes, he smoked weed. In those times, if you were caught, you would be arrested for an indictable offence and jail time would be eminent. Hypocritically, Tony had clients that were convicted and sentenced on marijuana charges. Tony's justification was, "I do not or will not cultivate to traffic my weed, man. I grow only for myself, and well, some for you, my neighbour. I hope I can trust you, man."

"You can, Tony. I could always use a hit now and then," I replied.

I trained extensively every single day. My skating was getting really strong, coupled with new levels of endurance that I never had before. I rigged up a full-sized hockey net in the basement with a shooting board with corner targets. The basement was long enough to give me a realistic distance to be effective. I also drilled a large hole in a dozen pucks and filled them each with lead to give weight to each puck, and I added lead straps on each side of my hockey stick in order to strengthen my shot. The floor was covered with concrete floor paint, giving it a real smooth surface, almost like ice. You could hear me for hours down the street, hammering away at pucks. The neighbours didn't complain because they were all rooting for me. In fact, everyone at work was too, except for Jim. His evil eyes met me every time I walked in at 8:00 a.m. after completing my morning workout. I would arrive carrying my hockey bag containing wet gear and underclothes. Obviously, the office started to smell like an arena locker room. I really had very little choice but to take a bus from the arena to the office. That meant I had no place to leave my bag for eight hours a day.

"I want to know why you are playing hockey seven days a week," Jim asked. "If I am investing in having to stand the stench you bring to this office, then I have a right to know."

"I'm training," I answered him casually.

"You're training for what?" Jim quickly asked.

"For the fall season," I answered.

He shrugged, then walked away. No one in the office was telling him because they were afraid he would lay me off or, worse yet, fire me.

Mid-August rolled around, and I finally had to have the big talk with Jim about what I was really doing. My plan was to take my first year's vacation, which was two weeks, go to training camp and then, if I made the team, I would quit Royal Trust.

"Well, Jim that's the story and my plan. What do you think?" I asked with nervous optimism.

Pat Brown sat in to give me a mediator in case Jim got over the top.

"Pat, what do you think?" Jim asked.

"I think it's a good plan. Frank isn't abusing any company time."

After a long pause, Jim looked square at me with those steely eyes and began to talk. "This has been the most ridiculous year for me, trying to train you for a career as a trust officer. You can't even write a decent letter without messing it up. Okay, this is my final answer. You may take your vacation only if you take an actual vacation and then come back to work. If you go to camp, then there will be no job here for you if you do not make the team."

"That's not fair," I said.

Pat immediately stepped in. "Frank, Jim is saying you had better make the team."

"Fine," I said to Jim. "I quit."

Jim said, "Good luck."

I then went and packed up my desk and personal belongings. I really didn't get it for some time after the meeting. I did not see what the real message was. Burn your bridge to give yourself no option but to succeed. My issue was I did not want Jim to get the better of me. So, I had the final word. "Boy, wasn't I so smart?" I said totally disgusted with myself.

I had all the time in the world to train now. Every day I was either on the ice, running, or weight training. I started to realize the amount of weight I was losing. When I started training, I weighed in at 205 pounds. That last week I weighed 170 pounds. *That's too light*, I said to myself. *I'm too small.* Even though I was in the best shape of my life, I feared that the big boys would tear me apart. I only had a week left, and even if I ate nothing but pasta and fatty foods, I could not increase my weight enough by the time camp started.

I was left with only one thing to do. Practice taking hits on the ice. I had two friends who were defencemen come to practice for the final few days. They would line up along the boards with enough room for me to get past between them and the boards. When I skated past them, they would body check me as hard as they could to force me to stay as close to the boards without getting myself hurt. I had two options; the first was to take the hit. Eventually, I would get hurt. The second option was to be smart and find a way to avoid the direct impact. That meant falling to my knees as they attempted to hit me or trying to hit them first in an attempt to soften the concussion of the hit. Then it dawned on me. All I had to do was to make sure when they hit me I was right against the boards. That way, the force of the hit would travel right through me into the boards, then travel back out, causing them to absorb the hit. I remembered this tactic from football practice when we hit the tackle bag being held by one of the coaches. Just as we hit the bag, the coach would knee the bag. The concussion was so painful it knocked the air out of you.

    I ran this drill for four days until I felt confident that I could take any hit, big or small. I knew that physically I had done all I could do to be ready. But was I mentally prepared? I would find out in just a few days.

Chapter 7

I arrived in St. Catharine's on the Sunday as scheduled and checked into the dressing room. My nerves were running rampant, and my heart raced as I walked into the room. In front of me were people talking and rummaging through boxes of gear. I walked up to a little, overweight man wearing a sweat suit with "trainer" written on the back and tapped him on his shoulder. "Am I to check in with you, sir?" I nervously asked.

"Who the hell are you? And call me Lefty, would you, for fuck's sake?"

"Yeah, okay," I mumbled. "I'm Frank Trousdell."

"Who? Let me look at the list. Stand over against the wall. I'll get to you shortly."

As I stood there, I gazed around the room and saw the Buffalo Sabres sweaters hanging in each stall. Hundreds of hockey sticks were lined up in a very large rack in the middle of the room, and at the end of that rack was a long table with tape, socks, under gear and all sorts of equipment. This was expected and reminded me of my university days.

"Okay," Lefty yelled out. "Follow me." I had to almost run behind him to keep up.

"Here's your equipment list for you to check off as you take it out of the boxes, off the table, etc. Now, anything special, you have to get it from me. Here's your dressing stall. Label everything, and if someone takes it, remember it's your fault. You will pay for it. Practice is tomorrow morning at 8:00 a.m. Do not be late, or you're immediately cut.

"You're staying at the YMCA behind the arena. Go there after you're done here and see the desk guy. He's expecting you. Sorry for the lousy accommodations, but until you make the team, this is what you get.

Now get busy, and I'll be here at 7:00 a.m. if you like to take an hour to get ready."

"Okay," I replied, feeling a little more relaxed. I sat down on my chair and started to soak up the environment.

"Hi, my name's Chris MacGregor."

"Frank Trousdell," I responded and stuck out my hand automatically.

He began saying, "I'm staying at the YMCA. Are you?"

"Yeah, have you checked in yet?"

He said, "No. Do you want to go together?"

"Great idea. Maybe we can bunk in the same room?"

"Sounds good to me."

"Where are you from?"

"I live in Hamilton, but I come from Chatham. I played my junior there."

"Oh, yeah . . . the Chatham Maroons."

"No," I replied, "the Blenheim Golden Blades Junior B."

"Right . . . okay," Chris answered.

"Then I played for the University of North Dakota, Fighting Sioux."

"Holy shit! he blurted out. "Great school! Man, you must be pretty good."

"Where's home for you? I asked respectfully.

"Toronto. I played my junior with the Dixie Wild Cats Junior B. Then last year, I played in a men's industrial league."

I started to feel more confident, knowing that someone else was in about the same situation as me.

Chris and I checked in at the YMCA and arrived at our room. "Well, they really want us to suffer during training camp," Chris sarcastically rambled as we walked into a very small room with two small single beds. The washroom was dirty, with leaking shower pipes dripping into a tub that must not have been cleaned for years. The walls were all cracked, and the ceiling looked like it was about to collapse at any time.

"Which bed do you want, Frank? Or, should I say, how lucky do you feel?" Chris joked as we began to settle in to that rat trap.

"Don't matter," I replied. I was just happy to be there and a part of the whole thing. "I can't believe the Sabres are staying here," I quipped.

"No, they're at the Holiday Inn," Chris responded. We are not allowed to go there. Lefty told me that they're off-limits, and if we're caught over there, the Sabres will personally kick our asses as target practice."

"I'm not interested to find out," I concluded with a chuckle.

"Are you done? Chris asked. "Do you want to go watch the Sabres skate? I heard they're having their first opening warm-up shinny today."

"Cool! Let's go see what the competition is like," I said with a tone of cockiness.

It was five o'clock in the afternoon, and we had a quick burger, then sat in the top rows of the arena. There on the ice were Gill Perreault, Richard Martin, and Jim Schoenfeld, along with many more of the greats that were playing for the Sabres. They not only looked larger than life, but were amazingly fast, with a great deal of confidence in everything they did.

Chris said, "Do you see that right-winger playing on Martin's line?"

"Yep," I replied.

"That's the new rookie Danny Gare. He comes from out West. They signed him, giving him a $250,000 signing bonus."

As we watched him play in the practice game, we couldn't believe how great he was.

"So, this is what it's going to take to make the Sabres?" I asked.

"And more," Chris replied. "I heard they have maybe two or three spots open. Then it's all about filling the Hershey AHL roster. They've only got a few open holes to fill. It's like this every year, Lefty told me," Chris said with apprehension.

"It's all about what you got," I said quietly.

I started remembering, while watching the Sabres practice, back to when my father moved us from Brantford in 1965 to Chatham.

My first practice with the Bantam travel team had seemed so surreal. There I was on the ice with a bunch of kids who'd grown up together, all looking at me, talking quietly to each other, literally sizing me up. I could still feel the fear and the feeling of inferiority as I waited for the first drill to be called.

The whistle blew and I immediately reacted. I raced down the ice as fast as I could go and completed the drill instinctively and before everyone else. This went on until the coach picked lines and placed people together. I knew this was where I had to shine not only to win a position on the team but to gain acceptance amongst the other players. The first shift I was on, I scored two goals. I felt like a king. The excitement and adrenalin consumed my very soul.

"Trousdell, you made the team," the coach yelled out over everyone there.

Yes! I shouted in my head.

All of a sudden, the goalie, Mike Zyburra came over and said, "You can call me Zyker. That's my nickname. Everyone's called me that for as long as I can remember."

From that day, Mike and I became best of friends. Our practices were every Tuesday, Wednesday, and Thursday mornings at 6:00 a.m. I'd be woken by a tapping at my bedroom window. Mike would be standing there, waiting for me to let him in so we could have a cup of tea before practice. We had this ritual for the next three years. Between one week to the other, we interchanged homes and duties no matter what weather prevailed.

Oh, how I wished Zyker could have been at the Sabres' tryout with me. He'd be so proud. We used to dream about playing in the NHL. All our road hockey games were emulating some big event that had just gone on TV the night before or was about to happen. Usually, we played out the Stanley Cup finals or something of that stature.

Mike had experienced great heights in his own right. He went to Providence College on a full scholarship and played four years as a starting goaltender. He also made the honours list scholastically. He graduated with honours as a math major. Mike wanted to be a dentist, so when he came back to Ontario, he attended the University of Western Ontario, gaining an honours degree in math and science.

This was where things changed for Mike. He applied to dentist school and was rejected. His grade-point average was a B+, but due to the limited acceptance quota the government had set for dentistry school, he needed a straight-A GPA to have a fighting chance. The entrance board told him that they had to accept 75% foreign students before Canadian-born students. Thus, his GPA had to be perfect.

Mike was totally dejected. He felt as if he was being treated like a loser or an outcast. This was his first visit with personal defeat. For a long time after, he could not accept the outcome of that event. His lifestyle started to change. He was not that fun-loving buddy anymore. He only wanted to work in a factory and party. He played with the London Kings of the senior hockey league and was a shining star, but he had lost his drive to run for his dreams.

All the while, he was desperately trying to keep a relationship together with his girlfriend of four years back in Providence. She came from a very wealthy family, and lo and behold, her father was a dentist. She could not accept Mike's failure to follow in her father's footsteps and eventually faded off into the mist of her world. Mike was quite devastated, to say the least, but struggled to hang in until his light would shine.

I always felt Zyker would lock into something great, and he did some two years later. A close friend of his from Providence got him an executive accounts job with a metallurgy company. He was on his way.

"Do you want to stay and watch the St. Catharine's Black Hawks Junior A play? They're up next?" Chris asked.

"Might as well," I agreed. "We aren't going anywhere."

The next morning, 6:45 a.m. came real quickly. Chris and I got ready and headed for the rink. Before I knew it, I was getting dressed in the locker room. As I turned and reached for a sweater, it dawned on me that I was about to put on a sweater that some pro from a previous year had worn while playing in some professional ice stadium, somewhere in Canada or the US, against one of the NHL teams. As I put the sweater on, I realized my dream was about to unfold. I was trying out for the Buffalo Sabres organization.

You have to understand that even though I was attending the rookie camp, I was still at the Buffalo camp. The Sabres owned the Checkers. If you made it, you signed an NHL farm team contract.

We all started slowly exiting the dressing room and made our way to the ice. What a feeling! I could see the same sensation instantly showing on the faces of all the rookies as they touched the ice with their skates. Away we went doing the traditional warm-up manoeuvres as we moved in unison around the parameter of the rink, left to right. Ironically, since

I can remember, even back to peewee hockey, we skated left to right the moment you hit the ice.

Hockey is a world of tradition, systems, and coordinated activity. All is directed by a group of coaches while on the ice. In fact, your off-ice daily plan is somewhat controlled by the intentions and desires of the coach. During your training period, you are told not to drink, smoke, or have sex. Of course, the drinking and smoking are quite obvious, but the sex thing was believed to drain energy and testosterone out of your system, especially the night before a game. Whether it was true or not, we all adhered to the coach's demands.

Without warning, the whistle blew. "Gather round me, men," the coach yelled. "I'm going to make it short and sweet. There are fifty-two of you on the ice. By the end of today, there will be twenty-five. Twenty-seven will be asked to leave the camp. In advance, the club wishes to thank you for coming out and all the best in the future. Now, let's get on with the workout. We are going to warm the goalies up, and then we will have a scrimmage. Remember, everything counts as to whether you are here at the end of the day."

That message resonated loud and clear. I looked at Chris, and he was smiling while he sort of chuckled at me. I skated over to him and asked what was so funny. He said, "See that guy with the white helmet and green and red gloves?"

"Yeah," I answered.

"Well, he arrived here last night from Saskatoon with his wife, dog, and all his belongings packed in a 1968 Volvo. I bet you ten dollars he's gone by tonight."

"You're on," I said.

The coach began shouting out the lines we all were assigned to after we warmed up the goalies. I was playing right wing with Richard Martin and Pat Hobin. These guys were both seasoned pros, each with at least five years' experience. We got to start the scrimmage! Chris looked over at me, and I saw the smile of approval as if to say "impressive for the first day". The puck dropped, and as if a light switch was turned on, I instinctively began to perform my play. There was a lot of manoeuvring on both sides for the first few seconds. Then, like a slingshot, the puck skipped across the ice and landed on my stick in our end. I raced up the ice, and as I crossed our blue line, I saw Richard Martin free on the left side, making his move. I quickly passed him the puck. All I saw was a clear view of the right side of the net, looking from the opposition's blue line. I knew to skate toward the side of the net. As I approached the corner, Richard passed me the puck. In a split second, I cut in front of the net and back-handed the puck over the goalie and into the net.

After cautious congratulations we were ushered off the ice to make way for another lineup of hopefuls. This went on for the next hour or so. I was able to get on the ice a couple more times, and I thought that I performed above the average.

The whistle blew again, this time with a very loud, almost ear-piercing tone. "Gather over by the boards, men," the coach yelled.

"As I told you, half if not more of you are going home right now." He started calling out names that I had never heard of before. One at a time, they were leaving their ice of dreams for the last time. For them, all that they had ever fantasized about as young boys playing road hockey or skating on an open-air rink on a farm or in a schoolyard was about to evaporate into thin air.

It seemed like eternity while the coach kept going through the list. "Okay!" Coach said with a sigh of relief. "I'm glad that's done. Now for the rest of you, it ain't over quite yet. There are five of you that'll have to go by the end of this week. We're taking a long hard look at you and will give you every opportunity to show us what you can do. You're back on the ice this afternoon at two o'clock. Get some rest."

Off we went and got changed and showered. Chris and I decided we were going downtown for some breakfast. As we were leaving the arena, we saw the guy from Saskatoon getting into his Volvo. His dog and his wife were all packed in snuggly.

We walked over and asked, "Hey, man?"

"Hi guys," he responded. "Well, what a reality check this was? Did you guys make the cut?"

Chris and I answered, "Yeah, man. How about you?"

"No. I was the first name called off."

"I'm sorry, man," I responded.

"It's okay. Now I know what I have to do," Volvo-man said. "Right, honey?"

I could see the relief in his wife's eyes as she said, "Yes, baby. It's back to the real world."

"What are you going to do?" Chris asked.

He answered, "Back to my dad's farm. It's all okay. I'll play locally, I guess."

As Volvo-man drove off, Chris and I stood outside the arena and watched the outflow of terminated players leave the complex. We said very little but did comment about each one's play as they left. This was a big reality check for both Chris and I.

Dreams were broken. Plans altered. For most of them, this was their first interaction with rejection and failure. I could see disparity in their body language as they wandered aimlessly out into the morning sun. Even though I knew they had just hit the lowest point in their lives, I couldn't help but feel optimistic as they walked off into the distance to start their new journeys that would take them to all corners of the world.

I lasted three days in training camp until the fateful words were spoken to me by the coach. "Jack Kelly wants to see you in his room after practice."

I knew what that would mean. I was being let go. The hallway was filled with five other guys, and we all just looked at the floor or ceiling while we waited to hear our names called out.

"Trousdell! Have a seat. Well, you had a good camp, but this is not the life you want with a wife, and, well, you know what I mean, don't you? She'd be held up in some apartment in Charlotte while you are on the road for a week at a time. Then if you did well, I could see you going to Hershey. There's even more travel, and what if you get injured? You're on your way back to Canada because you are on a player's visa, which means you've got to leave the US until you're ready to play again." Jack was trying to convince me that I was better off not playing for him than wanting to stay.

"But Jack, this is what I dreamed of doing all my life."

"Am I not good enough, or what is it?"

"Frank, I'll just say it. You don't fit the profile."

"I need a different style of player. Here take this as your final pay."

I opened up the envelope and saw there was US$250 in fifties. I thanked him for the opportunity and the money and went directly to my room.

There waiting was Chris. "So, you got cut?"

"Yeah," I replied.

"Man, out of all of us, I really didn't think you would be cut, let alone so soon. I bet I'll be gone next."

"I don't think so, Chris. You're their kind of player."

"What kind is that? Goons?" he asked.

"Kind of like head-hunters, aggressive hammerheads."

"Thanks, Frank. I like you too."

"No, Chris, I say this in a positive way. That's what they want on their team, a very aggressive, hard-hitting bunch of bullies . . . not that you're a bully, Chris."

He smiled and said, "You're probably right. We'll see if I last."

I called Monica from a payphone and said, "Come and get me. I'm coming home."

"You got cut," she answered.

"Yeah."

"I'll be there in about an hour. I'll pick you up in front of the arena."

"Okay," I said and then hung up.

Chris and I walked over to the restaurant and had dinner and some beer, then waited at the arena until Monica arrived in the parking lot.

The ride home was long and quiet. When I settled in and sat down in the living room, I sensed a real nervous and weary feeling come over me like I was about to lose control of myself. *What am I going to do? I have nothing left*, I kept saying to myself. *I failed to complete university, I quit the hockey team at school, and now I got cut from my lifelong dream to play pro.*

What I was living out, yet I did not know it, was the realism of letting go of my childhood dreams. I really did not want to let them go. I started to feel that it wasn't my fault, that if only I had not married Monica. If only I had not listened to my mother and father. The excuses kept flowing out of me by the second. I was starting to drive myself crazy.

I picked up the phone and called my dad.

"I didn't make it, Dad."

"I'm sorry to hear that, son."

As soon as I heard him say that, the tears began to flow like a watershed. He could hear me crying, and he kept saying, "It's all for a reason, son. Look further than the pain, son. You're destined to do something worthwhile and meaningful. You'll find it. You have to start looking. I say right tomorrow morning, go down to the Manpower centre. Meet with a counsellor and get some sense of direction."

Monica had disappeared into the bedroom when we first got home in Hamilton. I hadn't noticed something was not the same with her at first because I was so wrapped up in my pain. But after hanging the phone up with Dad, I began to come back to reality, and I noticed she hadn't been there all this time. Even in the car, while coming home, she was distant and almost upset that I didn't make the team and not for the same reason that I was disappointed but for some secretive reason . . . it seemed.

Is this paranoia, or am I getting the first signals of another shock to come? I thought while feeling the nervous tingles set in all over my body. *I'd better go to bed so I can get a big jump on the morning.* The trauma of the day, the feelings of despair, and now the suspicions had taken a toll on my mind. I was tired, and I really wanted to sleep. I accomplished that without any problem.

Chapter 8

I awoke the next morning, anxious to get a start on finding a job. I needed to go to Manpower early to beat the lineups. Even though it was October, and all the students were back to school, the steel factories were down and layoffs were running rampant. I was up and out of the house by 8:00 a.m.

Manpower was surprisingly empty, and I was able to get an appointment almost immediately. I came prepared with a resume and background information. I was assigned a counsellor and seated in an interview room. A man appeared, almost faceless in his approach. We talked for five minutes, then he took my information and went back to his office. Fifteen minutes later, he reappeared and sat down quickly.

"Have you ever thought about applying to the police?" he asked inquisitively.

"Yes, as a matter of fact, I had sent away for the OPP's application package before I left university."

"Did you submit the application?"

"No."

"Okay," he started to say as he rustled through some papers. "I have an interview set up for you with the Hamilton-Wentworth Marine Police. Now, this is a federal police force. It is a little different than city. They don't process you as long and the requirements are a little more lenient. I think this is what you are looking for and should work in line with your background. You can go down and report to Chief Bailey right now."

"Alright!" I said with excitement.

I arrived about fifteen minutes after leaving the Manpower office. The building was the harbour office tower, situated right on Hamilton Bay. I had to go to the seventh floor to the harbour master's office. I was ushered right into the chief's office. Sitting behind a very big desk, overlooking the bay with a panoramic view of the city and harbour, was Chief Bailey, a very short man with the steely eyes and weathered face of a seasoned seaman. He was a quiet man, but he looked right through me as we talked. The conversation was a blur, but all I remember was the chief standing up, reaching out, and saying, "You report back here next Monday at 9:00 a.m., with a suit on."

"You've been chosen to be one of the finalists."

"Thank you, sir!" I replied, shaking his hand firmly.

Monica couldn't believe me when she got home that day and we sat on our front steps like we did every night after work.

"You've got horseshoes up your ass, my man," she joked with a sarcastic tone. "I had to beg almost on my knees to get my job at Firestone head office."

"I know how difficult the last six months have been for you. But you kept applying, right?" I stated with a supporting tone. "That's one thing I love about you, Monica. You never give up." She went silent and just smiled at me.

What could that mean? I asked myself. I shook it off and went inside to eat.

I arrived at the harbour office early that Monday morning with full intent of making a lasting impression. Sitting there was a young man about the same age as me. He had a three-piece suit on, and he was toting a black cane with an ivory handle. I was looking at that cane and saying to myself, *This is a little too much, don't you think?*

"Hi, I'm Frank Trousdell." I spoke as I noticed he was watching me size him up.

"Burt Lucosious," he replied in a monotone voice.

I reached out to shake his hand. He just waved like don't touch me.

"You'll probably get the job," Burt stated.

"Don't cut yourself short, man," I answered.

"They're going to find out I was involved with the Red Devils motorcycle gang, and they won't want me."

"Do you have a record?" I asked.

"No . . . no . . . no, but they profile anyone that has any connection to a bike gang in Canada."

"I cannot believe they can discard you because of association as a minor or juvenile with someone you might've known."

"We'll see," he said.

Burt was called in first, and I waited at least fifteen minutes before he came out the door and breezed by me without saying a word.

"Mr. Trousdell, please, come in," the officer requested.

"Well, Mr. Trousdell," the chief opened with a hint of conviction. "You must be really ready for a challenge by chasing after this opportunity. When I was your age, son, I had no idea that I would end up as police chief of the marine division. I started out as a merchant seaman in Halifax. I worked on lakers and sea-going vessels for twenty years." Chief Bailey was spewing off on a tangent reminiscing over his past.

"Oh, it was a great life," he went on. "I was quite a ladies man back then . . ."

"Chief, we're out of time, sir." I could hear a voice from the doorway bring him back from his memory lane ride.

"Right . . . right. Mr. Trousdell, you start today as a cadet. In three months, after your probationary period, you will write the entry exams, then graduate to fourth-class constable. What are your thoughts?"

"I'm in," I replied enthusiastically.

"Follow Sergeant J.J. Johnson, and he'll get you started."

"Wow," J.J. said as we walked down the hallway to the elevator. "That was the fastest hiring I've ever seen!"

"What's the accent?" I inquired respectfully.

"Irish, my son," J.J. responded proudly.

"Were you born there?"

"Oh yes, I came to Canada not five years ago."

"How did you get on the force so quickly?" I asked.

"I was a captain in the Irish Military."

"Why would you leave such a beautiful country?"

"I wanted a better life for my family and, mostly, I was getting a little nervous of the constant unrest in Belfast."

"Oh yeah... the civil wars between the Catholics and the Protestants," I replied.

"We were fighting all the time. The bombings and sniper fire were rampant. Too many were dying. My children were at risk daily. Canada looked really good from where I stood back then, and I have never regretted the move since."

"My granddad came from County Clare in 1905. He lived near the coast."

"I knew it," J.J. responded with a joyful overtone. "Trousdell is a real Irish name. You have relatives back home?"

"I don't think so," I replied.

"You probably do from way back. One day you must go visit and go to your grand-pappy's hometown. You never know what you might find.

"First things first, we're on our way to headquarters, where you'll be fingerprinted, a background check will be performed, and then you'll be issued your uniform and service equipment."

"Do I get a gun already?" I asked with a childish hint.

"Oh no, my son. We do not carry guns here. We are federal police, and we call the city if an occurrence requires firepower."

"What service equipment do we carry?

"A billy club, flashlight, and handcuffs.

"Okay... what's the difference between us and the city?" I inquired.

"Weapons are about the only difference. We actually have a wider geographic jurisdiction than the city. The city has to include us when pursuing a perp or occurrence on federal property, which includes and circumferences the bay area and the lake up to Bronte Harbour to the north and Port Dollhouse to the south shore."

"We patrol all that?"

"Yes, we do and more. We do it by boat."

"Alright," I replied.

"You better like boating because you will be spending as much as eight hours a day on board."

"I can't wait!" I excitedly replied.

J.J. started laughing in his Irish way, which instantly made me feel so comfortable to be a part of this new venture in my life.

Maybe this is the reason I didn't make the pro-hockey team, I quietly and optimistically assured myself.

Headquarters was a very busy place, with people hustling and bustling all about. We walked up to a side door in the front fore, and I heard a buzzer sound and a lock disengage.

"Let's go. We're free to enter."

I was then greeted by a very big and overbearing man in uniform.

"You got his papers, J.J.?" the man asked.

"He's our new meat, lad," J.J. responded.

"Oh . . . I thought he was going to join us for the night," the guard responded.

J.J. began to laugh. "No, no, he's processing as a cadet, Bill."

"Hmmm! I don't know," Bill responded with reservation. "Follow me, meat!"

"Go!" J.J. commanded. "I'll meet you here when you're done."

"Okay," I nervously replied.

The whole processing was like a blur. Fingerprinting, picture-taking, measuring for clothes, shoes, and hat . . . all were completed in seconds, it seemed. Then they gave me two vouchers and a filled-out form for me to sign. This was my acceptance of police property. I was ushered to a back wall with a cage window to hand this voucher to a man who could have been no more than five foot two inches tall. He started yelling orders out "Now, sign here and don't lose any of my property, or you will not like me at all! Do you understand?"

"Yes, sir!" I shouted my compliance. A cart was given to me to load my five shirts, pants, two pairs of boots, two hats, one belt with cuffs, and one Billy club. Finally, the man handed over to me one beautiful, leather police waist jacket; leather gloves; one winter parka; and one winter hat. I was totally equipped.

"We're now off to our station, son," J.J. advised me as we started driving in the police SUV. "Have you ever been to our station before, son?"

"No, I can't say that I have."

"We are at the end of John Street, next to the rowing club and boat storage warehouses."

"Okay . . . I think I've seen the place." There it was—a two-storey building, tucked away from street sight, sitting on its own large, secluded slip. Docked beside the building was this very large tugboat. Four officers were on board, busily scrubbing and cleaning the decks and apparatuses attached to this very interesting vessel. As we walked toward the building, me pushing the dolly with all my gear, I could hear the men start jeering at me.

"New meat!"

"Where did they find this one?'

"He won't last!"

Then from atop the tug, a giant of a man appeared. "Get him dressed and give him to me as soon as possible! I have an introductory task for the new meat that will make him or break him real fast!"

"Give it a rest, lads," J.J. retorted somewhat in defence for me. As we entered the station, J.J. turned and stated as a reminder, "This is the first and last time I save you from Sergeant Jimmy."

"Great," I replied. "What is he, the squad's goon?"

"Be careful! Jimmy can be your best friend or your worst enemy. You ever heard of the wrestler Jimmy Red Sims?"

"Of course, he wrestled professionally all across Canada for years. That's him?"

"No, that's his son. Jimmy Junior."

"Holy shit!" I replied. "He's huge!"

"You should have seen his father. Let's get you a locker, and then you start your shift."

My first day consisted of introductions to the people on staff, locker rooms, equipment rooms, the various boats, vessels, and ships at our disposal. The most fun that J.J. bestowed upon me was the boat tour of our patrolling perimeters. This ride took approximately three hours of travelling along the shoreline of Hamilton Harbour and Lake Ontario. Of course, we went as far as Grimsby on the south shore, then cut across north to Burlington, rather than going all the way to Port Delouse then across to Bronte; that trip would have taken another five or six hours.

By the time I got home, I felt like I had been on a summer vacation or a Boy Scout camping trip all wrapped up in one day. I was even given homework to do that night, with full instructions to be ready before shift the next morning. I was to write the Canadian Power & Sailing Squadron's licence the second day in because I was to be qualified for marine duty by the end of the week. Also, J.J. ordered me to have a police code haircut by the start of the next day's shift, or I would be fined $50. The haircut was no problem, but the prep for the test was unnerving. I was never one for tests or exams, as I've mentioned before. But I knew this test would be one of many over the next year or two, so Monica left me alone all night while I hit the briefs and books that they gave me to study.

Morning exploded on me like a mortar hitting without warning. I jumped up, heart racing and eyes wide open, while I scrambled to focus on the moment. I raced through my morning ritual like an Indy 500 driver, eating my breakfast, getting dressed, and saying goodbye to Monica all within a matter of minutes. The drive to the station was a continuation of the first, and I found myself parking and getting out of the car, and then walking up to the front door of my new place of employment, the Hamilton Marine Police, John Street station.

"You must be Cadet Trousdell . . . Captain Frank Smith." His hand was in front of me before I had absorbed his welcome.

I shook his hand and said, "Yes, sir . . . Frank Trousdell, reporting for duty."

The captain started to chuckle and looked at the older man sitting in front of a microphone and a table of radio gear.

"He is a spark plug, don't you think, Cappy?" Frank Smith joked. "I am pleased to see you show respect first day in . . . but the formalities are not as important in this station. Downtown, however, you'll learn fast enough that protocol and rank and file is very important. Now, this fine man sitting at the radio dispatch and harbour master desk is Cappy, officially known as First Station Harbour Master. He has been a fixture in this office for thirty-five years."

"Yeah, and I'll be a memory in about thirteen months," Cappy responded with a tone of great anticipation. "I'm retiring to a life of wine, women, and song! Ha, Ha."

"In your dreams," Captain Frank kidded back.

"Okay, young man, you have a full day ahead of you. First, you need to book in. Book in is a pre-requisite for everyone and to be properly done before starting your shift. If you don't, you will be reprimanded and written up the first time; the second time, you'll be written up and fined. There won't be a third time, for this is grounds to be immediately terminated. Now, you need to dress in uniform. When you get back, report to me in this side office adjacent to Cappy's, okay?

"Yes, sir!" Off I went, upstairs to the locker room.

I was still early for shift, so I thought, *I must have impressed Captain Frank first day in.* I hoped.

"New meat!" I heard from behind a locker.

"Hi, I'm known as Ruddy the Rudder!"

"I'm Frank Trousdell. Hell of a nickname," I answered.

"Long story, but I'll tell you my short version," Ruddy responded, almost wanting to tell me.

"Well, my first year here, this division was very small and totally unorganized. There was very little training, and our work was predominately rescue-related. Needless to say, there was hardly any supervision.

"Well, one cold winter night, a couple of us boys decided to bring along a little warmer on our lake patrol. We had to cruise in the old Chris-Craft custom skiff because it was the only boat that could handle the cold. Well, my lad, while we completed the first lap in the bay, we had already downed the bottle, or warmer, as we called it. I was feeling the buzz pretty quick, and within a second, I fell backward off the stern. If it hadn't been for my parka catching on to the top of the rudder, I would have been chewed up by the propeller. Once I got back after suspension and recovered from my minor wounds, the boys had found a name for me ... Ruddy the Rudder."

The next three weeks went by pretty quickly. Each day was a new experience with the introduction to more fellow officers. Like me, some were new, but most were seasoned old-timers on their way to retirement. I spent most of my time in the station, polishing brass, cleaning floors, and scrubbing the bowels of the marine vessels. The hardest task was scraping the finish off the inside of the Chris-Craft. I had to lie on my belly as far as I could get up to the nose of the bow, inside the cuddy cab. There was no light or much air to breathe. The dust from the sanding and scrapping was devastating, to the point I had to surface every few minutes to get air.

"You'll get used to it!" I heard from on deck. I looked up, and there was this thin, fair-haired, thirty-something guy in uniform looking down at me through round-rimmed glasses, wearing a grin from one side of his face to the other. "Come on up and take a break." He reached down and gave me his hand, helping me up.

"I'm Tommie Ion. I'll be working a lot with you."

"Hi, I'm Frank."

"That's Trousdell, right?" Tommie started to spell my last name, "T-R-O-U-S-D-A-L-E?"

"Close. E-L-L."

"Oh . . . I got it. J.J. told me you were a good old Irish boy."

"My granddad was," I replied.

"Well, my lad . . . so are you! And so is half this force. You're in luck, as they say!" Tommie responded in an Irish accent. "This morning, you got to finish the sanding because our newest meat is arriving on the afternoon shift, and he has to start applying the varnish. You think you had it bad. Oh, be Jesus! He maybe dead meat after a few minutes painting in the hull."

"Who's the new meat?

"Oh, the guy you beat out the first time, Burt . . . something."

"Burt Lucosious?"

"Yes, that's it!"

"Holy shit!" I exclaimed. "I thought he didn't make it."

"Somebody insisted he get hired; somebody from way up the ladder. We have a special prime cut of meat starting today."

About thirty minutes to go in my shift, I heard a loud rumbling pull up on the dock. I walked out of the station, and lo and behold, there was Burt, dressed in full leathers, riding up on a full-blown chopped-up Harley Davidson. He shut it down, planted the kickstand, and took off his helmet, looking like Peter Fonda in *Easy Rider*.

"Get that piece of shit, two-wheeled pile of metal off my dock!" said a loud, screeching voice from the second-floor front office window of the station and, of course, it was the captain, yelling at Burt. "Get your sorry ass up to my office now, Lucosious. I knew this was a bad idea, letting front office push me around!"

We could hear the captain yelling for the next few minutes while Burt re-located his bike and reappeared in uniform.

"Fuck it!" Burt snorted as he walked up the steps. The noise stopped about two minutes after Burt got up to the captain's office. Twenty minutes later, Burt came running down straight to the boat wells, where he quickly jumped into his coveralls and began scraping the haul.

Days, weeks, and months passed me by with very little but the same routine day in and day out. Patrol after patrol came and went. I was getting more marine time in, and they were finally sending me out on my own with a crew member as my mate. The crewman was a young eighteen-year-old from Grimsby, Ontario. He would tow the lines and tie down the boat when coming to shore. He would also man the life gear if we were on a rescue mission. From time to time, I would be sent out to drag in a small craft that got loose in a storm and landed on the west side of the bay, which was only approachable by boat.

Finally, I was called to search for a floater. That's reference to a body that had been in the water for some time. Unfortunately, it was a four-year-old boy who had gotten through the fences along the docks. The missing boy had been in the paper for the past three days, and both the city police and our detachment were getting a lot of heat from the mayor's office. I spent the next three hours tracing every possible path the boy could have made along the dock area.

At the end of Sherman Street dock, there was a fence with a hole in it large enough for a small boy to climb through. I walked from the hole directly to the edge of the dock, then alongside the deck of the dock. A very large laker freight vessel, about one hundred feet long, was moored there, its anchor directly alongside the dock, out front of the bow. I grabbed hold of it and looked down in the water.

Through the murky shadows, I could see an object floating about three or four feet below the surface. Not knowing what it was, I called it in to dispatch. Within minutes, our Boston Whaler rescue vessel arrived, with Tommy Ion and Jimmy Simms manning the boat. They had a pole out and began prodding the area.

Then without warning, Tommy ordered me to drive the road cruiser back to the station and get Sergeant Frank Smith to return to the site with the b-bag and tags. I quickly found out that the b-bag was for a body and the tags were to identify the remains as to where and what was found. When I got to the station, Sergeant Smith ordered me to stay at the station and man the phones. He also ordered me not to reveal to anyone what was going on or what we might have found.

Within five minutes, Sergeant Smith called on the radio, wanting a city squad leader to get to the dock as soon as possible. I called headquarters and gave the message to the desk sergeant. Within minutes, detectives and city cops from everywhere were swarming the whole area. Tommy, Jimmy, and Frank returned to the police dock house carrying a small, bagged body in the Boston Whaler. I could tell by the grim looks on their faces that it was probably the missing boy.

The coroner's car arrived and backed up to the dock area. The coroner and a city officer lifted the bagged body out of the boat and onto the gurney waiting outside the car. They pushed it into the back hatched area, closed the door, and then drove away. I turned, and Frank Smith was standing waiting for me.

"You did a good job, Frank. Unfortunately, this is just the beginning of many you will have to deal with. I didn't think it was time for you to be in the boat and do the dirty work. There will be lots of time for you to learn that job."

I walked into the locker room only to find Tommy and Jimmy sharing a mickey of whisky.

"You never get the smell off you, Meat. You can't wash it off," Tommy kept repeating.

Jimmy just stood there, leaning against a locker, drinking away at that bottle.

"I remember my first floater," Jimmy started reminiscing but with a very sad tone to his voice. "It was a woman who'd jumped off the Burlington Street Bridge. She'd been in the water for at least two weeks.

"You ever seen a body after being in for that long? First, they drop down almost to the bottom of the bay. Then they start to expand. That's because all the gases and fluids start to ferment. The skin stretches as far as it can, which will cause the body to become buoyant like a balloon. That's when the body begins to rise to the surface.

"In the case of the woman, she'd hit the water so hard from her fall that when we started to crane lift her out onto our boat, she exploded. Guts and body parts were everywhere—on the boat and all over all of us. The stench was so strong that to this day, I can still smell it on me from time to time. That's why we call them floaters. I hate having to do this detail."

Tommy was washing his hands with a special cleanser. "It won't come off. It never fucking comes off. Fuck . . . it's not going away."

"Here, swig this," Jimmy said to Tommy as he handed him the last of the small bottle of whisky. "Let's get out of uniform, Tommy, and get out of here."

I walked out of the locker room and sat in the radio room for the rest of the shift.

They say an incident like this always makes a person feel a need to get closer to their family or kids. I didn't have any kids, yet I was feeling the need to hold my wife. I did have nieces and nephews. They crossed my mind as to their safety. I planned to call them when I got home.

Not much was said after that day, except the local paper ran stories about how the harbour had to reinforce the fenced areas to ensure no more of these incidents and occurrences. The stories started on the front page and eventually migrated to the last page until they stopped publishing the story. The chief was glad to see that one disappear from the media's attention. We all thought he was going to have a heart attack every time a problem happened.

I witnessed two devastating series of events while I was foot patrolling on the Wellington Street slip, the busiest loading dock throughout the whole bay. The activity was so busy that we had four officers on-site the whole day. There were two ships in, unloading from South Africa. These ships always caused a problem because of the crews on board. Most of these men were not allowed off the ship due to their criminal backgrounds or because they were suspected drug runners. The police and RCMP always kept these things quiet, mainly so as not to alarm the city that these hardened criminals were that close to entering the bars and restaurants of Hamilton.

I got a call to run to west door 35 of the Wellington Street dock on the Canada Steamship Lines side of the warehouse. As I got there, a crowd had gathered around a flatbed trailer and truck. A very large piece of machinery that stood ten feet high and about fifteen feet long was sitting crooked on the very back of the truck with a crane attached to it.

As I walked around the front of the truck, I saw a human arm, leg, and a shirt hanging off the side of the truck. As I came into full view, I could see the big object that must have weighed at least a few tons on top of this squashed body and what looked to be the half untouched remains of this man. I don't need to go into the gruesome details of the blood and guts spread all over the back of the truck and flatbed. It was, however, so surreal to me that I felt totally detached from what I was seeing. The other officers were already on the occurrence, and all I had to do was monitor traffic and crowd control.

As the day carried on, the tension on the dock seemed to get stronger, and while the activity was shut down during the investigation and cleanup, you could have cut the air with a knife. The longshoremen were a very unruly group. They were hard-working, and you definitely did not want to piss them off. They would and could cut you into little pieces and have you swim with the fishes without any forethought.

We all agreed to do overtime, and I was asked to double shift. I agreed because it was double time on the weekends, and this was a Saturday. Things seemed to calm down on the docks about dinner-time. The unloading had resumed, and the lights were on. All went well for a few hours, then, "Trousdell!" J.J. blurted over the radio while I was sitting in the warehouse talking to a couple of longshoremen. "The cruiser is on its way to pick you up. We have a 10/14 on the ship *Vestavia*, anchored in the middle of the bay."

"Great . . . what the hell will I see next?" I said to the longshoremen. They both chuckled nervously, for they suspected what had probably gone on. They had a sixth sense about all that went on in the harbour. If there was any kind of criminal or violent activity about to take place or that had taken place, they all knew about it.

"Be ready for something ugly!" Butternuts yelled at me. They all had nicknames on the docks. It doesn't matter what corner of society you come from; one thing is common . . . nicknames. I could never imagine someone calling a longshoreman Muffy or Chas or Skip. They would keep the names rough and scary, like Skull or Bones or Racker. Butternuts got his name because he fell off a rig one day and landed on a pole and fence, instantly castrating him; from that time forward, all the boys called him Butternuts.

Burt picked me up and raced back to the station. We loaded onto the Boston Whaler, and Al White drove out into the night. We approached the vessel and, with caution, ran up beside the ship to the boarding ladder. There seemed to be little to no activity while we boarded until we got to the main deck.

The captain and first mate greeted us. "Follow us, officers." There were three of us officers and one sergeant. I was at the back of the pack while J.J. and Al White were first in line to see the shocking sight that was waiting for us. Lying on a bunk in the sleeping cabin was a man wrapped in bedsheets soaked in blood. As J.J. pulled back the sheets, you could see hunks of meat pulsating in rhythm to his heartbeat. Even though he had lost so much blood, the injured man was still alive. J.J. immediately called in for an ambulance to dock side and ordered the captain to let us use the ship's gurney to move the injured man to shore. Al and Burt took the man down to the Boston Whaler and eventually got him to shore and to the ambulance.

The fun for me was just beginning. The captain gave us the story he was prepared to state at that time. Allegedly, an argument broke out between the chef and a deckhand over dinner. Supposedly, the argument had been brewing since the ship left the African shore. Well, the chef had had it and wasn't going to take it anymore, so he grabbed a machete and started to hack at this sailor. By the time he was done, the man was found somehow in his bed with the bedsheets covering him up. Then we were called in to investigate.

Now, as it goes on the sea, marine law applies even in the Hamilton Harbour while on board. The RCMP were called in and arrived about an hour after we had secured the area. We were not allowed to take the chef into custody because this event happened where it did. The captain was allowed to turn him over to the RCMP. But something strange happened. The RCMP officer pulled the captain aside, and when they reappeared, the chef was released into the custody of the captain, who was to take him back to South Africa, where they would turn over the chef to the South African authorities. When we got back to the station, a report from the hospital came in stating the machete man would live.

"Zyker! Where the hell have you been for the past year?"

Mike called out of the blue and informed me he was coming back to Canada to work in London, Ontario and go back to university to qualify for dentistry school.

"Oh, great, Mike. We've moved to Hamilton, which is two hours down the road, and you go to London."

"Why don't you play for the London Kings Senior A?" Mike asked me.

"Too far to travel, Mike. I tried it last year, but the travel and the shifts at work got to be too much. I even tried playing in Woodstock, but it was still too much."

"Why not try the Preston Jesters? That city's only twenty-five minutes from Hamilton?" Mike suggested.

"I might." I responded.

Mike agreed to visit that weekend. Ironically, Monica's best friend from Minneapolis was going to be here as well. *This could be real fun*, I thought after hanging up with Mike.

I will never forget the time that Mike and my youngest sister went out on a date and didn't get home until six in the morning. My mother met them at the door. "Where have you been all night? Mom screamed.

"Mother!" Vickie retorted back.

"Get in here, Mr. Z. You are not getting away with this so easy, young man."

Mike knew he was in deep shit with my mother.

"Sit down in the living room. You had both best tell me every detail of what you two did last night that took until six this morning."

As Mike told me the details of how Mom had grilled him, he said he'd actually thought he was going to be put in jail or something. My mother had a way about herself; she could intimidate anyone she so chose to confront. This event was when Mike christened my mother "The Queen of the FLQ." FLQ was the name of the iconic sixties-era French liberation movement of Quebec (the Front de liberation du Québec). Mike was always frightened of my mother, even as a child; when he'd come over to play with me, he would find her very much a threat. My mother was very protective of all of us in the family. She also was the same with the neighbourhood kids. That was the teacher in her. Every kid was her responsibility, right to the day she died.

Monica was in her glory being visited by Angela, her university best friend and roommate, who had also been her maid of honour. As soon as our two friends met in our living room, the tension was so thick you could hardly breathe. Mike started firing cheap shots the moment we started the introductions. Angela fired right back. I pulled Monica aside and asked, "What the hell is going on?"

She was as stunned as I was, so we agreed to split up for a while. Monica and Angela went shopping, and Mike and I went to the pub.

"What the hell is eating your shorts?" I asked Mike sarcastically.

"She's a bitch!" Mike spewed out in defence of his actions and his disgust with Angela.

"Have you two met before or what?"

"No, sometimes you can just sense you're not going to get along right from the beginning. She may be a very nice person, but, man, can I feel the hate. You know, like a cat and a dog in the same room for the first time. After a while, the dog gets tired of snarling at the cat, and the cat becomes bored with trying to intimidate the dog. The two of them may settle down and ignore one another, or maybe not."

Mike and I agreed to let things chill out and focus on rekindling our friendship, being that we hadn't seen each other for a good year. I brought him up to date—the affair, the move to Royal Trust, and the hockey tryout disaster, which led me to becoming a police officer.

"I never thought you would ever try being a policeman," Mike said, shaking his head. "I can see you selling insurance or even getting your securities licence and being a stockbroker, but police? Holy shit, Frank! You can get killed," he exclaimed.

"It's not that bad," I said. "There have been moments that shook me up, but the kind of work we do is more limited to guarding property than pursuing criminals."

"Then what are those scum bags that arrive on the ships from all over the world?" Mike asked.

"Yes, but for the most part, they stay on board because they know we'll stop them once they try to go ashore."

"If you know who's not allowed on shore, right?"

"Yeah, you're right," I conceded Mike's point. "What are you going to do, Mike?"

"Well, I had to take one more year at UWO in order to apply to dentistry school."

"I thought you got an honours degree at Providence College in math?"

"Yes, I did, but in order to qualify for dentistry, I need to complete eight credits related to medicine especially credited by a Canadian university."

"You'll ace the courses, right?" I asked.

Mike responded, "Oh, acing is not the problem. Getting past the board of acceptance is the tough one. The Canadian government pushed for immigration increases, and part of the give-back plan the Liberals so nicely implemented was to give immigrants a loophole so if they are entering Canada to complete a profession such as dentistry, they get a "pass Go" card and a leg up on acceptance over and above Canadian applicants. So, I have to have straight A's and will probably have to blow a board member, or I'm crap out of luck."

"You'll do it, Mike," I said reassuringly.

"What, blow a board member? Not a chance, you motherfucker," Mike joked back.

"Hey, heard from Danny Motherfucker?" I asked Mike enthusiastically.

"No, I tried to locate him through his father, but his dad said that he's living in the southern states, is married, and he hasn't seen or heard from Danny for two years. He seemed very deflective about the whole thing. I still can't figure Danny out," Mike said.

I told Mike about the other vets I had met at UND and what I had learned from them and that Danny might never come around to wanting to see us again. He was not the same guy we'd once known.

"Man, let's not ever let life change us like that, Frank," Mike stated with a brotherly tone.

"I'll toast to that," I responded as we raised our drinks and firmly clicked the glasses in agreement.

Mike and I returned to the apartment not much after the girls had arrived back.

"Well, what did you buy?"

"Not much. We couldn't find anything worth stealing, ha," Monica joked in reference to her previous brush with the law.

"Let's not go there, lady," I quickly said. No one else had anything to say on the matter.

Mike left the next day, and Angela stayed on for the rest of the week. When it was time for her to go, I could tell Monica was starting to show disappointment and sadness that her close friend was leaving. As they were saying their goodbyes, I caught a look between them that was very much secretive, which caused me concern. When she had left, I asked Monica what was up, and she flew off the handle, accusing me of meddling in her and her friend's private woman thing. The discussion was quickly dropped.

Events became expected, and days became weeks. The fall was creeping in, and my urge to get back on the ice was nipping at my heels. I was getting pretty relaxed with my job at the marine police force and found the guys had personal systems to work around the mundane life of shift work. Everyone cut a deal with two or three fellow officers to trade off days to suit their needs. I questioned this activity with my sergeant, and I was told that if I needed to do this from time to time, it was acceptable but beware not to abuse this unwritten privilege. So, I set out to build my alliances. I worked Tommy, Burt, and Rick to back me, while discussing my desire to continue my hockey. They saw value in what I wanted to do, and they all agreed to work with me. I then felt confident to go out and find a team that would let me try out.

The most likely organization close to me living in Hamilton was Dundas. The Real McCoys were Senior A OHA. They were considered the last rung before professional level. I went to the owner, who was a very successful owner of a refinery north of Hamilton and Dundas, and asked if I could try out. He just looked at me and said they had already picked their team, and I would not be given a tryout. Before he left the room, he quickly stated, "You should focus on your job and forget 'the dream.' It's over for you, son," he said. He was an older man with steely eyes and a personality as hard as the steel casts his company forged.

I got back in my car and said, "You think it's over, old man? Watch me." I then headed out to Preston, which was only twenty minutes down the road.

"Excuse me," I asked the first person I saw walking in the Preston arena. "Do you know who's coaching the Jesters this year?"

"Yeah, matter of fact, he's in the dressing room, right over there."

I was surprised because it was late in the afternoon on a Friday.

"Hi, my name's Frank Trousdell."

"Bill. I'm the coach. What can I do for you?"

I began to recite my hockey background and then asked if it was possible to get a tryout.

"Be here tomorrow at 7:00 p.m."

"See you then," I answered as I left the room.

I could hardly stop myself from running out of the arena, full of excitement. I couldn't wait to tell Monica that I was getting a shot with the Preston Jesters. I didn't even know any of the players or what my chances were, but just getting the tryout meant everything to me. I had played against them once before while playing the four games with the Woodstock Royals. They had a couple of decent players and a great goaltender.

Monica was not too excited for me when I sang out my achievement of the day. "How are you going to make this work if you make the team?" she asked with a hint of insult.

"I have it all worked out with the guys at work. We just trade days off and re-schedule."

"I don't think this'll work," Monica negatively responded. "What am I going to do while you are at hockey all this time?"

"You can come with me, or you can find something to do on practice nights."

"We'll see, you selfish prick," she said under her breath.

I knew enough to let it alone, for the message was loud and clear that there would be a big price for me to pay. I had better make this all be good for both of us, or I was embarking on the road to destruction.

Since we'd moved from London to Hamilton, Monica had started to show changes in her attitude about almost everything. She had, however, found a great job at Firestone in Hamilton the first week after we'd moved there. She made some good friends as far as I could tell, but again, she kept them at a distance from us as a couple.

We were starting to live separate lives, though I didn't realize it at the time. Over the past two years, we had twice gone back to North Dakota to visit her family. These trips seemed to sprout new vitality in her, almost like a recharge to our marriage. She was starting to spend a lot of time with her closest friends from work, which concerned me a bit. There was one friend, in particular, who was very sexually suggestive and had come on to me once while Monica had gone home for a week. This "friend" had actually called me at work and suggested we go out and have some fun. She also suggested that whatever happened would stay between us. I quickly but with courtesy declined the offer. She was offended. A day after Monica returned, she confronted me about the incident. Her friend told her what she had done and explained it to Monica as a test while she was away. I almost thought it was a setup on Monica's part.

I started to get the feeling we needed to add something to the marriage. I thought something with more commitment or a joint project the two of us could work on together. So, in my infinite wisdom, I suggested we buy a house. Monica liked the idea. For some strange reason, I had no fear of making such a monster of a financial move.

Two years before, I had walked in off the street and bought a brand-new Firebird for $5,000 with only $1,500 in the bank. The dealer had asked, "Where are you getting the rest?"

I said, "I'll have it tomorrow, so get the car ready for delivery by tomorrow." I then went to the bank and walked in unannounced to see the manager. He sat me down and I began saying, "I just bought a new car!"

"Great," he responded.

"I need four thousand dollars, please."

His jaw dropped, and then he proceeded to process the loan. After we signed the loan, he said, "You got this loan just because of your gutsy approach. Who knows where you're going to go in life?" the manager kidded as he handed me the bank draft.

The first thing I did was talk to Al White at the station to get his advice as to where we should look for a house. He turned us onto an agent, and for two weeks, we went house hunting. We learned about bungalows, side splits, raised ranches, new builds, old renovations, and so on. Nothing really appealed to us. We started to think maybe we should look outside the city for an old country-type home. A bit of a fixer-upper would give us something to do. The agent advised us we should get pre-approved for a mortgage. That would help us determine what price range we could afford.

I went back to Royal Trust and went to the mortgage manager, whom I had done some work with while working there. John was a self-made millionaire, and he not only worked for Royal Trust but owned funeral homes. He was not a licensed mortician, but he'd bought three locations and some real estate within the towns and villages surrounding Hamilton. He immediately approved us for a mortgage of up to $40,000. In 1975, that was more than enough to buy a very nice house.

John suggested two homes he owned that he would sell to us. One was a raised ranch only two years old. The problem with it was it was almost one hour away from Hamilton, and I knew I would get grief from my work. The second was a very old house, about 125 years old, to be exact. This house was located in a village called Cayuga. My next day off was a Saturday, so Monica and I set out to visit the house and town.

"Well, John, you really know how to pique our attention."

"I told you this would do it for you," John said quietly.

We were standing outside the front of a 125-year-old heritage house situated on Cayuga's main street. The old courthouse was perched on top of a hill, right across from a large mature lot with maple trees and plants growing in gardens strategically placed on the property. When looking at the front of the house, you could have sworn it was an old southern plantation with its white wood siding and green window and full-length door shutters accentuating the French doors on either side of a grand main entrance. The main door was made of 100-year-old oak with a one-inch bevelled glass window, which took up a good third of the door itself.

The dining room was at least twenty feet by twenty feet, and the living room was exactly the same size. Both rooms focused on the fireplace that dressed the room with its beautiful hearth and mantle. The grand hallway and its gracious wooden stairway led to four bedrooms and a bathroom. Monica was truly excited and constantly remarked on its full potential.

I kept asking, "Is this too much to renovate? Do you think we can do it?"

John kept saying, "Do a little at a time. Don't take on more than you can afford."

By the end of the day, we had bought the house and John, being the owner, gave back a private mortgage for the balance. The purchase price was $42,000, and we put $3,000 down. Our payments were around $450 per month, plus utilities and taxes. Then we had car and travel expenses going back and forth from work. We were pretty confident we could do it and have enough to live and renovate on a very small basis.

I was very excited, but my dad and mom thought we had bitten off too much and were worried about the whole project. My dad refused to help me, which disappointed me. I thought he would have jumped right in, but he was not excited at all. He did advise me as to what to do and how to do it, but Dad certainly did not offer to come down on weekends and help me. I was very confused about this response. I started in anyway, without his help. The outside was first on my list, and I began cleaning up the yard, both front and back. We had bought the house in the early spring of 1975, and we were now embarking on the summer. I got the yard cleaned up, and Monica was busy setting up and space planning the rest of the house.

I got a call from my sister Cheryll Hackborn on a Sunday afternoon.

"Can you come and pick up me and the kids?"

"What happened? Is Bob all right?" I responded.

"He's in jail for the night. I'll tell you when you come and get us, Frank."

"Okay, I'll be there as soon as I can."

"What's wrong?" Monica asked as I hung up the phone.

"Cheryll and the kids need to come here for a bit. Bob's in jail overnight. I know nothing until I pick her up. Are you coming for the ride, Monica?"

"No, I'll stay here and get the rooms ready."

Chapter 9

I pulled up in the driveway and hoped not to be confronted by Bob, my brother-in-law. He had been diagnosed with type 1 diabetes when he was twenty-two years old. He had been insulin-dependent ever since. He was trying hard to manage the disease but would go off on drinking binges from time to time. He had experienced many diabetic delusional reactions that were horrendous for Cheryll to handle. I figured this one might have been too bad for her, and she'd had to call the police.

When I picked her up and got the kids all in, she started to tell me that Bob had had a very bad reaction, and the neighbours had called the police. The police were so used to him having these reactions that they decided to take him into a cell, thinking he would get the message. They had no idea what the real problem was or how to properly deal with diabetics.

Police are still not trained properly to deal with these kinds of situations. Bob had a reaction, a few years ago, in 2012 in a park walking his dog. The police were called to help him. When they arrived, they immediately handcuffed Bob, thinking that he was drunk. Then the officer called EMS when Bob started to go in and out of consciousness. EMS was able to control Bob's reaction, and Bob came around.

I always felt so sorry for him because of these events. I know these situations always embarrassed him. Cheryll was at her wit's end and needed a break away from him and the disease, just to think of anything else. I felt her pain and fear. I was there for her no matter what Monica or anyone else had to say.

The one-hour drive from Ingersoll to Cayuga was comforting enough that all in the car except for me were asleep in no time.

Early evening came quickly for all of us. Cheryll got my nephew and niece tucked away in their rooms, and they both fell fast asleep without any fuss. The previous twenty-four hours had worn heavy on them, and they really needed to feel safe and comfortable. Cheryll and I sat at the dining-room table and talked for a long time. She was able to expose what her family had been going through over the last few years.

"I remember when you and Bob would bring the kids to Mom and Dad's for the weekend. We'd have a great time on Saturdays, playing catch or garage hockey. Then, especially when Jackie and Al would show up, we'd play cards and have a few beers into all hours of the night.

"Then the trouble would start. We'd all go to bed when, without warning, you and Bob would be in a fight. Then Bob would get dressed, and he'd leave you and the kids there, and he'd go home. The next day, Dad and I would drive you back to Woodstock and drop you and the kids off. There was Bob, all apologetic and sorry for his actions. What was the problem? And what is the problem, Cheryll?"

"Every time Bob would drink, all would be fine, like you said, until we went to bed. Then he would jump up out of bed, and all hell would break loose. He always went into a reaction after a night of drinking."

"Aren't you afraid of him hurting you or the kids?"

"He never involves the kids, which is amazing. It's always me," Cheryll pointed out.

"What happened this time?" I asked.

"He went too far and hit me. I couldn't control him. He gets the strength of five men. He is like Dr. Jekyll and Mr. Hyde. He was in bed, and like Superman, he flew out of the bedroom and ran off the stairwell, landing face-first into the wall. He got up and chased me around the house. I started throwing things at him, and he finally grabbed me and hit me in the face.

"My neighbour could hear all the commotion and called the police. By the time they got there, Bob had fallen asleep on the couch. When they woke him up, he remembered nothing of the event. They got him dressed and took him to jail. The officer told me to leave for a few days and figure out what I should do."

"Do you know what you want to do, Cheryll?" I asked with comforting concern.

"No. I really don't know what to do."

"What do you think he's going to do?"

"That's up to him. I told him before they took him away that if he ever wants to see his kids or have any chance of getting us all back, he'll have to get help medically and mentally."

"Well, I think you're right, Cheryll, and I think you need time to really think all of this through. I'm only twenty-three years old, but I've lived through a few occurrences with you guys, and to be totally honest, I don't know how you get through these events. You're a very strong and patient woman, my dear sister. I think you should just take this time and relax, enjoy the house and the town, and just do whatever you need to do. The answers will come to you, and time will take its course. Don't you think?"

"We'll see," Cheryll wearily responded as she headed to bed.

This was my first rude awakening to the real dilemma of diabetes. I had seen Bob go into reactions many times, but it never hit home what damage the disease was doing to everyone around him, let alone to his own well-being. Bob was like my closest brother. We enjoyed the same things and loved to spend a lot of time together. Sports were our common denominator. Since he'd started dating Cheryll, he was very much a part of my life, and this was good because I was nine or ten years old and needed a big brother. He made a point to involve me in his games and take me to his hockey and baseball games. I felt accepted, and I was very proud of him. I also experienced sadness when he had to go through so much pain with this disease. I was glad Cheryll came to me because she needed family and a safe resting place to work this trauma out.

After the third day, I could tell Cheryll was missing Bob and their life and home. She was getting restless around the house and would go for walks around town. The kids were doing fine as they explored the old house and its special places, like the attic and the basement.

"Frank, I talked to Bob this morning," Cheryll said. "He wants to come and get us."

"Are you sure it's time?" I asked.

"I don't know," Cheryll responded with a tone of uncertainty.

"Cheryll, I don't know if I am ready to let you go," I blurted out my immediate reaction as her brother. "I'm going to talk with him before you can go, Cheryll."

"Okay, Frank."

Bob arrived at the front door, and to my surprise, he knocked on the door and stayed out on the front porch.

I walked up to the door and just said, "Hey, Bob, what can I do for you?" without opening the door.

"Can I talk with you, Frank?" he asked in a very calm and respectful voice.

"Sure." I went out on the porch with him.

The first thing he did was reach out to shake my hand.

I responded, and with a firm grip.

"I've come to talk to Cheryll and ask her to forgive me. But I need your approval as her brother first before I talk with her."

I was somewhat taken aback by his intent to follow a mutual protocol from family member to family member. I almost felt like I was the surrogate father in this matter. "Okay, Bob, you can only talk with her if she's ready. I'll go ask her." I didn't have to go far, for Cheryll was sitting on the stairs in front of the door, listening.

She just looked at me, got up, and said as she walked by, "I'm ready, Frank."

Bob and Cheryll spent a good hour outside, talking and walking around the yard. The kids were busy playing in the house somewhere during this interlude. Then, finally, Cheryll came into the house and announced they were going back home.

I had a good feeling this would be the last of their relationship problems but just the beginning of Bob's health issues. I sensed they would only get worse.

As Cheryl and Bob's issues subsided, clouds were gathering on the horizon in my relationship with Monica. One day, she announced she was going to take a two-week vacation and go to see her parents in North Dakota. I was a bit shocked, to say the least, for we were somewhat tight in the money department and needed to start renovations on the house.

We were rounding into fall, and we had to re-insulate the walls in the main house area. I could tell that Monica was losing interest in the house, and the pressing house development cost issues were no longer a priority with her.

I was never one to stop her from doing anything if she really felt it was important. Seeing her parents was an important point of contention, for I had always felt that she sacrificed closeness to her parents to come to Canada with and for me. I couldn't say no. We couldn't afford for her to take a flight, so she decided to drive. She and her friend Vickie would drive together for a while, then Monica would hook up with her close friend Angela in Minneapolis and drive to Fargo. From there, Monica would drive the rest of the way by herself. She never feared long distances, and I had a great deal of confidence in her. I had hockey anyway, and I was busy taking on extra shifts at work.

The next two weeks flew by very quickly, and Monica had only called maybe twice while away. I was starting to feel uneasy about her being so far away and not letting me know when she would be home. I called her parents' house on a Sunday, hoping she would give me an idea of her plans.

"What do you want?" Monica answered when her sister gave her the phone.

"Well, hello to you too! What's the attitude about?" I responded in a bit of a trembling voice.

"I'm not ready to come home," she stated with nervous conviction.

"Why not?" I asked.

"I want to stay for a while longer, then I'll return. You've got your life there. You won't miss me that much, will you?"

"Of course, I'll miss you . . . I miss you now!" I almost yelled through the phone.

Monica, in a short, conclusive, and very expressive tone, advised me that she would be home within the week. She then hung up the phone on me without any "I love you" or anything.

This was the exact moment that I started to experience anxiety pains and flashes. I had to replace my emptiness while waiting for her return with other things. The house was the biggest event, and hockey definitely took a lot of time out of my days. But late at night was the hardest time.

I would lie in bed, looking at the ceiling, and imagine that Monica was seeing her old boyfriend from school or some new guy she might have met. I also began having nightmares that she would get in a car accident or be kidnapped and killed. My sleep deprivation was getting to the point of being uncontrolled. Then I got a call from her.

"I'll be home by Sunday. I'll call you along the way, starting Saturday afternoon. I'll drive through the night like we used to do back in school," Monica announced, her voice weary and tired, with a hint of concession.

Someone in the family must have talked with her about her responsibilities as my wife or something like that. Needless to say, she was coming home. I felt relieved and excited. *Maybe things will be better now, and we will get back on track,* I thought and hoped. I wouldn't know, though, until she arrived and was nestled inside our house, curled up in her blanket like she always did when she got tired and cold. I would tuck myself up behind her and feel the warmth from her body while we talked and cuddled. I couldn't wait to do just that when she arrived in the next seventy-two hours.

I spent the whole of Sunday cleaning up around the house and property so Monica would feel excited and comfortable when she arrived from her long trip. The rest of the day seemed to drag in anticipation of what mood she would be in when she pulled into the driveway. The clock passed 6:00 p.m. when I heard the car come to a stop. I walked out to greet her, and I presented my biggest, warmest smile. "Hi!"

She just looked up and smiled as she started to pull her luggage out of the trunk.

"Don't I get a hug or anything?" I asked with a nervous tone in my voice.

"Yeah, hi," she answered and then continued to unload the car.

I quickly concluded to keep quiet and help her unpack. "How was the drive?" I started with the simplest of questions to keep things light as we sat in the dining room.

"Long, as usual," she replied. "You remember how long it can be, especially when you don't want to make the drive."

I got the message from her tone. She really did not want to be here.

"I think I'm going to take a bath and get some sleep, Frank. We can talk in the morning, okay?"

I agreed with some compassion, respecting the 1,800 miles she had just driven. I was so wired up just to get a whole lot of questions off my mind. I was starting to feel a major distance between us and had felt this gap for some time. I knew it was our time to open the books on what was wrong. I had been feeling the tension build ever since we'd moved to Hamilton. There was a massive change in her mood and attitude about me that kept spreading us apart. Sex was becoming almost mandatory and mundane. There was no spontaneity or excitement. She had gone from ravishing me to lying there, waiting for it to be over. She was going to her doctor on a regular basis, complaining about her cervix. He had put a device in her to correct the positioning of her uterus. This was a very uncomfortable item and got in the way of her freedom during sex.

As I sat listening to music for the rest of the night, I thought of all those issues and, of course, I felt very guilty due to the affair that I'd had in London. My mind was quick at wiping out my ill thoughts to keep me from feeling so bad that I'd decide to tell her. Then panic set in, and I began thinking she might have found out about it. *Why wouldn't she have said anything by now?* Somehow, I countered the paranoia and blanked it all out of my mind. I began thinking, *Maybe she has found someone new? But is he in North Dakota or Hamilton?* The questions kept flashing in my mind until I was about to wake her up and question her. I stopped myself halfway up the stairs to her bedroom. *Don't be a fool*, I said to myself. *You will blow it for sure. Wait until the morning to get your answers and do it diplomatically.*

Monica slept in until noon the next day. When she did get up, she went straight to the bathroom and locked the door. I had woken up some hours before her and prepared her breakfast. She found her way down to the kitchen and poured herself a coffee. I sat down across from her and smiled. She didn't look up.

"Are you ready to talk yet?"

"No," she said. "Give me a chance to wake up."

A few minutes later, Monica started by asking simple business questions about money and the house and demanding to know why I hadn't gotten more done than what I had. She then started in with questions about how much time I had actually been there at the house and insinuated I was out partying most of the time.

I came right back with, "I was here all of the time except for when I was working or playing hockey."

She laughed and said, "You were out."

"How would you know what I was doing? You never called, and when you did, I was here."

The banter went on most of the day. I concluded she was edging toward an argument. By early evening, I laid into her and let her have it with both barrels. I let out all of my frustrations, doubts, and suspicions. She sat back and just stared into space. I did not accuse her, but I tried to egg her into a debate on each issue I brought up. She refused to challenge or defend herself. I could tell I was hitting nerves when I brought up her determination to stay in North Dakota. I brought up the commitment we'd both made to stick it out and to make changes and return to her home if we both agreed Canada wasn't working.

At that moment, Monica stopped me, stood up to me, and asked a question as she stared straight into my eyes. "Would you leave Canada and move back to the States with me?"

"I would if I knew we had work," I replied, staring back just as intensely. Deep inside me, I knew I was lying.

Monica just looked without blinking an eye for minutes, it seemed. Then she backed off, sat down, and said, "We'll see. I don't believe you. You've got it all here. You're with the police; you've got your mom and dad and your sisters, your friends and other family. What do I have besides you and your family?"

"Good question," I replied almost sarcastically. "What have you got going here, Monica?"

She immediately jumped back at me. "I'm not cheating on you, if that's what you're implying."

Then the whole thing broke loose. We fought for hours about everything and nothing. We had to get it all out, whatever it was that was causing our anger for one another. By midnight, we were both tired and had tapped out any energy we might have had. We agreed to call a truce so both of us could get some sleep and go to work the next day. The next day turned into the next week and then the next month. We avoided the fiery hot points completely.

We both got really busy with work and I with hockey. I saw Monica only in passing, except for days off. Hockey was a great relief, so I focused my energies on excelling as a player. I was leading the team in scoring and making a name for myself, not only on the team but in the league. I hung out more with the players and their wives. We were becoming a close family. I was starting to talk to some of the wives about my marriage, and they felt that trouble was brewing, so they made an effort to include Monica whenever I could get her to go to the home games. It seemed to ease the pressure a bit.

Then the team announced that the next weekend we would be flying to St. John's, Newfoundland to play an exhibition series against the St. John's Capitals Senior A champions. It was a chance in a lifetime to be a participant. The bonus was that we were taking Eddie Shack with us as a signed player. Eddie was an NHL all-star, recently retired from the Buffalo Sabres. He had played almost fifteen years with the Toronto Maple Leafs and was on all three Stanley Cup-winning teams. I was so excited about the opportunity. I immediately got to work to re-jig my work schedule, so I could go, and I planned the weekend with Monica so she wouldn't be alone. She didn't seem to mind or care, whatever the case was. She seemed to have it already under control.

The team all met at the airport in Toronto at 7:00 a.m. on the Saturday. We all congregated in the café near the check-in booth. Sitting by himself drinking a coffee was the man, Eddie Shack. I immediately walked over and introduced myself, and he said, "Have a seat." We started small talk about how great of a career he had.

I could immediately tell he really did not want to hear me adulate his achievements, so I changed course and talked about my tryout with the Sabres in 1974.

He seemed to get a chuckle out of it and agreed that it wasn't easy for a walk-on like me to get noticed. "At least you had a shot," he said. "Not many get that far, so don't look back in disappointment. Get on with it."

All the players and coaches were standing around us, listening to our conversation by that time. It was time to board, so on we went to get our seats. Eddie yelled up to me in front of all the guys and said, "Hey, Frank, come sit with me."

I was excited and felt so cool that Eddie wanted me to join him.

Eddie kidded in a loud voice, "Us pros sit together, right, buddy?"

Wow! He really made me feel important. *What a great guy*, I thought. I could tell one of the players was not impressed. Cam Crosby was the other player on the team who'd had a shot with Toronto three years prior, and I know he felt jilted by Eddie's comment. I really didn't care because I'd got the nod from the man!

Later that night, we played, and what a game to remember. I was positioned on right wing, and no other but Eddie Shack was on left wing. Cam was centre most of the game, but the coach interchanged centres off and on. I played like I was on an NHL squad. Eddie was unbelievable. You could tell the difference between our level of play and his. He was toying with the other team all night. He scored twice, and I scored twice. We won the first game. We actually felt like we were pros that night.

After the final buzzer went off, every kid rushed down to ice time to get Eddie's autograph. What a feeling we had, seeing all the fans' affection for the great Eddie Shack. After we showered and got dressed, I went out of the dressing room, and I was immediately hit with kids wanting my signature on their magazines. I knew this was what I'd always wanted, to have these kids look up to me just like when I was a kid watching the greats like Gordie Howe and Bobby Hull.

My dad had taken me to summer baseball games that were played by the NHL all-stars as a promotional series, and I got to stand in line and get their autographs. What impressed me the most was that Gordie and Bobby never left the field until all kids got their autograph. I know because I was the last kid on the field every time. To me, that was a pro. They loved every kid because they knew how important they were to them.

Later in life, I played against Gordie Howe in an exhibition game while I was playing junior hockey for the Blenheim Golden Blades. I was not only scared to bits but proud as hell to be on the same ice as the greatest hockey player ever to play the game. He remembered me and came over in warm-up and commented that he never forgot me because I had played against his sons Mark and Marty throughout minor hockey.

He reminded me of one year when he'd come to watch his sons play against us. He was standing by the dressing rooms when one of our players ran out of the dressing room and demanded Gordie sign his shin pad. Gordie didn't like his tone, and he took the guy's approach as an insult. I stood in and got our player to back off. I was injured that game and was in street clothes.

Gordie said, "You're on this team, aren't you?"

I said, "Yes, but I've got a broken collarbone."

"Why don't you sit with me and watch the game tonight . . . Frank, isn't it?"

"Yes, it is, sir, and I would be proud to sit with you." We talked all through the game about what I was going to do and what I wanted to do with my life and, of course, I was all about playing pro hockey.

Gordie said very clearly to me, "Get your education no matter what. Get a scholarship if you can. I want my boys to do the same, but they are going to be offered a pro contract, and I doubt if they will go on to school. But you really should Frank."

The game ended, and Gordie said his goodbyes. He left me with a message that, to this day, I have never forgotten. "Remember, Frank, that you made an impression on me. That speaks volumes in the real world. Make your dad proud, son." Then he left the building.

The kids were mounting by the fifties outside the dressing room. Without warning, I heard them yell, "There's Eddie!"

They all ran for him, leaving me without one kid to sign their book. Then I realized half the team was watching the whole event and was laughing at me. "Oh well!" I said. I'd got my fifteen seconds of fame. "Let's go for beer, assholes!"

They followed in line with me and left the arena. We were entertained for the rest of the evening by the local brewery, and then we all retired to our rooms for the night.

Sunday's game started at 2:00 p.m. We were so fired up to win, and Eddie couldn't have been in better form. Between whistles, he would skate by the fans and use his stick like it was a fishing pole, luring them in as if to say, "You suckers." He used to do that trick when playing throughout his NHL career. It was his signature move.

The game ended in a tie. I scored the only goal of the game. I felt so complete that I never wanted the feeling to go away. The owner of our team herded us onto the bus to go for dinner at some well-known restaurant in a town outside of St. John's. Only half the team went. The rest went back to the brewery for more free beer. I wanted to be a part of the show with Eddie, my newfound friend.

The restaurant was full, and quickly we found out why. They were forewarned Eddie was coming. We let Eddie in first, and what a scene. Everyone lined up, yelling and clapping for Eddie. He had on his great big ten-gallon cowboy hat and his handlebar moustache. What a sight to see. Then he yelled out to us, "Meet me at the bar, boys. Drink all you want!"

We all looked at each other and said, "Yeah, Eddie's a great guy!" So we did. Countless beers passed our lips, and the stories were running rampant.

Then Eddie reappeared and said, "They're setting up a room just for us, and I'm going to the kitchen. Go get settled, and you'll have a feast bigger than you've ever imagined."

"Eddie's such a great guy," everyone yelled, laughing endlessly. We then found our respective seats. Cam sat right beside the man and talked stories with him during the feast of our lifetime. We ate, and we drank endless glasses of wine until the late evening hours. Eddie looked at Cam while all of us were celebrating our victory and feast and quietly said, "Get the bill, would you?"

Cam responded, "You know, Eddie, I've heard stories about you of how you always stiffed people in situations like this, but I think you're a really great guy!" Cam handed the bill over to the man and watched him take a great big drag off his huge stogie. Then, in shock, Cam watched Eddie sign his name on the bill. "Best wishes, Eddie Shack!"

"No, Cam, you make every mother fucker player pay his fair share and make sure you leave a damn good tip. I've only got a grade three education, and all of you fuckers have university. You owe me, motherfucker!" Eddie got up and went out to sign more autographs.

"We got a problem," Cam announced in an earthshaking voice.

"Yeah, what's up, buddy?" everyone said in scrambling symmetry.

"Eddie just stiffed us for the drinks and the meal." There was dead silence all around the table.

I stepped up and said, "No, there has to be a mistake. Are you sure he didn't have this all arranged?"

"Yeah, he had it all arranged. He had it preplanned to have us pay the shot, including his tab."

"What? Are you sure?" I responded again.

"Wake up, Trousdell. This is for real. Your new buddy just fucked us. Asshole!" everyone cried.

"Divvy up, boys." Cam somehow worked out a round figure for all of us to pay the $700 bill, including tip.

"Where's that fucker?" I said in total disgust.

"He's already on the bus," someone said.

I knew I had only enough room on my Mastercard to get me home when we landed the next day, and I was in shock about having to cover my end. But as a team, we covered the bill.

When we got on the bus, we all sat at the back while Eddie was seated next to the bus driver. He knew he was in shit and probably was in no mood to take on eleven of us. Needless to say, the ride back to the city was very quiet. When we got back to our rooms, we all gathered to discuss the event. The owner said he was shocked, but the event and financial loss were not his responsibility. He would never hire Eddie again.

But the score was not over for us. We were bound and bent to get him back. One of the guys suggested, "Let's go get a beer." Without thinking about whether we could afford a beer or not, we just got up and went. We didn't even know where we were going.

A friend of one of the players was an RCMP officer. He came over to his friend and me and suggested he knew a good place for us to go and drink our sorrows away, being we were fellow police officers. He promised a good time. So off we went to this bar and nightclub. Within minutes, we were pounding down shots and beer and getting extremely drunk. The night went on forever. The brother officer brought over a couple of girls to our table, and away we went into no man's land of playing with the women. He kept saying, "Whatever happens here stays here!"

Of course, the challenge as to who was going to get the girls began. Before I knew it, I was leaving the bar with a lady, and we headed for my room. The rest of the events are quite evident and need not be detailed. After I escorted her out of the hotel and into a cab, I went to bed.

The alarm went off, and I woke as if a shot had been fired. *What time is it?* No one was in the room. I grabbed my clothes, got dressed, and packed up as quickly as I could. Lo and behold, I saw a clock. It was seven o'clock in the morning. The plane was to leave at 8:00 a.m. I checked out and ran to get a ride with our goaltender, who was one of the last to leave. When we got to the airport, we were just in time. The plane was boarding. I reached for my ticket and found I did not have it. I ran to the booth, and they said, without it, I could not board, and because it was a charter flight, I needed to either find the ticket or buy a new one. I had no way of exercising either option.

I thought as best I could through the fog of alcohol and said to myself, *I must have left it on the counter when I was checking out.* The coach had given me cash for transportation when I got to the Toronto airport. I had to use it to get to the hotel. I grabbed a cab and pleaded with him to take the fastest way to the hotel. He got me there in ten minutes. He waited for me while I went in to the desk. The clerk was waiting for me. I grabbed my ticket and ran back to the cab. The cabby pushed the pedal to the metal and got me back to the airport in ten minutes again. I thanked him, and he said, "I could've charged you a lot more, but I think you're gonna need whatever you got to get through this one."

I ran to the front desk, and as I pleaded to have them put me on the plane, they all looked out the window in unison and said, "Only if you can fly as fast as that plane taking off on the runway."

I watched my plane leave in the sky. My heart sunk. "What am I going to do?" I asked in desperation. "I have to be back by three o'clock to go to work."

"The only flight we have is what we call the 'milk run.' I can't be sure what time you will arrive in Toronto."

"I don't care. I have to get back today, please."

The milk run was exactly that—landing at every stop from the East to the West Coast of Newfoundland; then every stop in Nova Scotia; one in Montreal; and then, finally, I landed in Toronto. I looked at a wall clock and realized it was three o'clock in the afternoon. *Okay, how am I going to get to Hamilton and report for work even though I'm late?* I kept asking myself. *Bob Palmer, my buddy from high school!* I called him and begged him to come and get me. He hemmed and hawed, but finally agreed to pick me up.

When I got into the car, I thanked him with a sigh of relief.

He said, "Don't get too comfy just yet, Frank. I'm taking you as far as the GO Train."

"Okay, Bob. I appreciate your help." We laughed all the way to the station, and then I hit Bob with another favour: to lend me train fare. He did, and off I went, arriving at the GO Station in Hamilton at 6:45 p.m. I had already called in to work, advising them of my journey and the calamity of events. The desk sergeant was not amused. I asked if a cruiser could pick me up at the GO Station, and he promised one would be there. My desk sergeant was there, waiting in the car and, again, he was not amused.

Jimmy met me in the locker room while I was getting dressed for my shift. "What the hell is all over your back?" he screamed in shock. "It looks like a cat went nuts on you and scratched and clawed you good!" As he was speaking, he saw my fear set in very quickly.

I instantly realized that in the throes of the illicit sex earlier that morning, my unknown partner must have carved me up pretty bad for him to notice it that quickly. I did my best to cover up the truth by shrugging it off as the result of a fight in the game. "The other guy must have had sharp nails," I said.

Jimmy looked at me with disbelief. "You'd better come up with a better story than that before you get home." As Jimmy began to walk out, he stopped in the doorway, looked back at me, and said, "I think it's time we had a good talk. I think this hockey thing is getting out of whack, and it's starting some grumbling among the other guys here as well. I think you should spend the night in the guardhouse at Wellington Street dock. You need time to think."

He was right. I did need time to think. Too much was starting to get out of hand. My issues began to mount up. Hockey was now starting to interfere with work and my marriage.

I got home at about eleven that evening, and Monica was waiting up for me. We sat in the dining room as we always did when it was time to discuss anything. "Well? How was the trip? I heard you won, and you played great!" Monica started in with all this pre-emptive information.

"How did you know?" I quietly asked.

"I talked to Murray's wife today. She was concerned about you getting home safe."

"So, you heard about me missing the flight?" I asked.

"Oh yeah. Everyone on the team was talking about it. What really happened?" Monica asked with a patient and comforting tone.

I responded quickly, trying to shrug the question off. "I missed my flight." I tried to divert the events by telling the story of Eddie Shack. The more I talked about it, the more I started to feel the guilt build up inside me. Without warning, I began to cry helplessly like a little kid who had just lost his best friend. *I can't take it anymore. I feel so terrible and dirty.*

"I have to tell you something, Monica. I'm so afraid to tell you, but I also can't take it anymore. I do not know what has taken over me, but I'm not myself. I got really drunk last night. Really drunk. A bunch of us went out on the town after the Shack incident and went crazy."

"Did you get in a fight? Did you hurt someone?" Monica quietly asked.

I couldn't even look at her. Then when I did, I lost it. I was crying uncontrollably.

"Just say it, Frank. I'm here," she said over and over again.

Then I knew it was time to let it out. No matter what she might do, I had to tell it all as it happened.

"I cheated on you, Monica. I don't even remember all of it. It just happened. I was drunk, even though that is not a good excuse, but it just happened."

All the while I was fessing up to the events, Monica just sat there listening with a complete demeanour of patience. That's the only way to describe her posture and stature. I was expecting an outburst of rage and anger, but she was the complete opposite. I continued to denounce my actions and pleaded with her to try to understand my stupidity. I insisted that I did not want to lose her over my actions, and I pleaded with her to try to forgive me.

When I was done, she started to respond. "I am really surprised with you. I could have never in a million years believed you would do this, but you did. I know it happens in marriages from time to time, but I was hoping not to us. I believe this is a one-time thing of stupidity, and I will give you this one. Now, go and get some sleep."

What a saint! I thought. *I am so lucky to have her.*

The next day all seemed behind us until we came home that night after our home game. Monica had come along for the ride.

As soon as we got into the car, Monica lit up like a firecracker. "Forgiving you is one thing, but all of the wives joking about you in the stands with no discretion? Having to sit with them while they openly described the events as clearly as if they were there? I can't believe they would be so cold. I will never go there again with you. I want nothing to do with your hockey world again. Is that clearly understood?"

"Yes," was all I could say.

Time rolled by, and Christmas came and went. Monica and I wrapped our lives up into our work schedules, and I finished out the season. We got as far as the finals and lost in the last game. I won the scoring championship. I was extremely proud of my accomplishment but knew if there was to be a future with Monica, this was to be my time to hang the skates up for good. At the end of the final game, the coach asked me if I would be back, and I firmly stated that I would not. He seemed to understand.

The next year was filled with work and an attempt to fill the void of hockey by coaching a new Junior D team in Cayuga. I found great pleasure and joy in coaching teenagers playing their final years of competitive hockey. Work was getting tenuous. Fellow officers were not very friendly anymore, and there seemed to be little cliques developing. This was a cause of staff turnover. A lot of older officers were retiring. There were a few firings due to crazy events that just could not be swept under the table. One officer, who had five years on the force and just so happened to be waiting for a transfer to city placement, got drunk on duty one night. He drove the new $100,000 Boston Whaler onto a berm and wrecked the transom. He was suspended for a month. He never came back.

Then there was Rocky Platt. He was a retired Montreal Alouettes pro football player. His knees were shot, and he was constantly on painkillers. He had been an offensive lineman and was so beaten up that he could barely get through a shift. One day, his wife found him in his living room with a bullet hole in his forehead. His two-year-old son had been playing in front of him while he'd committed suicide. I never got over that one. The old guys on the force would look at me and remind me that was how I could end up if I didn't get my shit together.

The next summer was full of fun and visiting with my family at their homes and cottages. Jimmy invited a crew from the force up to his trailer on Honey Harbour to fish for a weekend. We lasted a day because we only had a van that I had bought to deliver frozen food to daycare centres in Hamilton and Burlington. Bob Palmer, my high-school friend, had gotten me into it to keep me busy. It had started out as a one-day-a-week fun project, but it had grown to be a side business that took five days on my off shifts to manage.

I would set up new clients, and then deliver frozen food to them. I would buy from Bob, who was becoming a going concern in Toronto, and then sell to local businesses. As soon as the word got out to the longshoremen that I was selling frozen food, especially seafood, my business doubled. Every payday, I would park the van at the gates and unload a van full of shrimp, fish, and frozen food of all sorts. I'd bring in $1,000 a day at the gates alone. All the marine officers got in on it and bought from me. Then I got the word. One day, I got a call from Jimmy while I was doing guard duty. "I have been trying to get you on the phone for the past hour. Who have you been talking to?"

"I had a few calls to make. I hope you don't mind?" I asked Jimmy.

"I don't mind? What the hell do you think this is? You do not run your business while on duty. You will get fired for this if the wrong guy catches you."

"It won't happen again," I stated.

It was time for me to take my exams and go in front of the board to be accepted into the CUPE union. I had completed two years, and it was time to be voted in by my peers. I really didn't think much about it, and I certainly did not think I might not be voted in for whatever reason. Outside the hall, I had to wait for the vote.

Jimmy came out after, and he did not have a very good look on his face. "It was really close. You barely got in, but there was a condition to your vote in."

I said, "What is that?"

"You have to quit your food business."

"What? How can they do that? You got a motel business, and most of the guys do something on the side. Why me?"

"You want to know why? Because you're doing it on the job. I had to write you up for that last event. Then there were all the scheduling hassles over hockey. You got some angry guys in there that say you owe them shifts."

I knew there were some very bad vibes starting in the ranks from that moment on.

The next six months came and went. The winter was very cold, especially at night, walking the docks and sitting in those little gatehouses with very little heat and the smell of body odour permeating all my clothes. The guys were not fun anymore, and everyone started showing jealousy toward me in spite of my business.

Then, one midnight shift, I got a call from the desk sergeant to stay away from Wellington Street dock for at least two hours. I was on patrol, and that dock was my main stop to check inside the warehouse. I knew this was a very strange request but respected the order.

After I completed my rounds, curiosity got the better of me, so I quietly drove around the backside of the dock. I then swung up from the water's edge, facing north. I saw one of the big roll-up doors was wide open, and a light was on. I slowly crawled up to the door and got out to take a look inside. There, loading large planks of teak and mahogany lumber into a large van, were Jimmy, Tommy, and two other senior officers. They all stopped and looked at me. They all had an "I just got caught" look on their faces.

All I could say was, "What the hell is this?"

Jimmy walked over to me, took me by the arm, faced me to the bay, and said in my ear, "If you don't want to go swimming with the fishes, then you leave right now and forget immediately what you just saw. Not a word to anyone. Have you got this message clear, son?"

I knew he meant business, so I quickly said, "Yes."

"Now, get lost for the rest of your shift, and remember, not a word."

I took off that dock so fast you would think I had just seen a ghost. I did ... mine.

The next day, I arrived for the afternoon shift and was immediately ushered into my superior's office. "What happened last night?" he asked. "You didn't report any activity on Wellington Street dock."

"No, sir."

"Why not?"

"I saw nothing, sir."

"Do you know what happened?"

"No, sir."

"There was a theft. Over $10,000 worth of valuable lumber was taken on your shift."

"I was doing my rounds, sir."

"Well, you're lucky."

"Why, sir?" All the while, I could see me being set up to take the fall for those guys, and nothing could be done to save me. It would be their word against mine.

"We arrested a perpetrator just after your shift was over. He was found with some teak lumber in his possession that was part of the bundles that were stolen. Now, do up your occurrence and make sure you place yourself as far away from that dock as you can."

I went directly to the reporting room and started typing my sheet. I was so nervous all shift because all I could imagine was that another event like that one was going to happen again and again, and even worse, the real thieves were going to get me when I least expected it.

Every shift got worse. I tried everything to get a desk job or just move shifts, but no one would listen. I was scared shitless every time I was in the locker room, and I feared Jimmy or the others would sneak in and get me. I began having anxiety attacks, so I went to my family doctor for anti-anxiety medication.

I couldn't sleep. It got to the point Monica thought I was going crazy. Every night I would be awakened by some noise outside the house. I would go into combat mode and creep around the perimeter of the property before I could rest. I had heard too many stories about how a policeman had been found drowned or dead in the woods with no explanation. I really did not want to go out that way, nor did I want to live in fear like I was. Monica and I decided to give it till April, which would clock me in for almost four years. Not that it would do me any good, but I thought it would help my resume.

The day came when I was ready to resign. I wrote a very soft and kind letter to my superior, claiming my interest was to pursue a career in business. He agreed with me after he read it. He then shook my hand and gave me my final instructions as to returning police property. Some guys on the force wished me well, but most of them avoided me.

Jimmy came up to me, shook my hand, and just stared into my eyes, letting me know the threat deal was still on. I couldn't wait to get out of there. I was completely clear by the end of that week. When I got home that day, the first thing I did was call Zyker, then I got a case of beer and a five-pound box of shrimp. Mike and I sat up all night, drinking beer and eating shrimp.

The beer numbed my fear, and the shrimp had never tasted as good. It was almost like eating my way to freedom.

My wholesale food business was now my focus, and I put every bit of effort and time into it. When I told my father what had gone on, he just shook his head and said very little, but I knew he did not approve of my decision to leave the force.

He never let go of the pain he'd suffered when he sold off the farm. He always felt that he was defeated and had failed as a businessman farmer. He did not want me to go through what he had experienced. He always said, "I had many chances to go into business with different people, but your mother wouldn't let me. I wanted to partner in on building apartments in Chatham a few years ago with my friend who had worked with me at the Union Gas Company. You know, the ones near the river by the Union Gas head office. I could have been a millionaire by now. But your mother said no." As he would tell the story, his head would drop, and he showed his sadness quite clearly. It was always Mom's fault.

Now my plate was really full. I had to build the business and finish the renovations on the house. The last winter had been so cold, and the pipes had kept freezing up. We'd almost packed in the house idea that season. The insulation was not good, and the leaks around the windows were too predominant to just seal. I knew a very serious decision was about to rear its ugly head and force Monica and I to either ask our parents for money or sell the house. Now that spring was upon us, we didn't want to leave the old house and its unique and beautiful landscape. That was for sure.

One night, Monica and I went out driving in the MGB that we had recently purchased for $500 from a local mechanic. It was in excellent shape and, of course, it was the car that I loved to drive. We needed some fresh air, and driving at night in the country with the top down was our way to relax. Monica started asking me if I thought we needed a break from what we had just gone through.

I said with confidence, "No. Why would we need a break when I have to work extra hard to make a living by selling frozen food?"

She began talking about Alaska. Her parents were moving to Anchorage within the month. Her father had been offered a professorship at the University of Alaska.

"That's great," I responded. "I guess you want to move up there and live like Eskimos. Wasn't last winter cold enough for you here?"

"But what if we worked on a cruise ship between Alaska and British Colombia?" Monica asked. "Wouldn't that be a lot of fun and think about the adventure of it all?"

I just sat and listened to her dreaming out the possibilities.

Then Monica dropped a bomb. Out of nowhere, she asked, "What do you think if we have a separation for a while?"

I swerved and almost put the car in a ditch.

"I thought you would want to be apart from me for a few months, you know? Just to get the business settled and maybe recharge ourselves."

I couldn't believe what she had just said. After all we had been through, she now wanted out. "Why do you want out? After all, we have some heavy commitments going on right here."

"I know," she responded, "but we're young, and there is so much we can do differently. I am tired of the way we're living. The day-to-day struggle, trying to make ends meet. The fighting over who's doing what. This albatross of a house that we'll never get fixed is constantly scaring me."

"Let me think about this for a while," I said. "Monica, please do not do anything that will ruin us . . . please? Let me think about it?" I asked in a very nervous and almost pitiful tone. The truth was starting to unravel. Over the previous three years, I'd seen the fraying of our relationship happen almost year by year. It all seemed so sad to me. How were we going to keep it together now?

I couldn't believe that this was happening, but at the same time, I was feeling the guilt of my indiscretions in the background as the base reason for our failing marriage.

Yet I also had the sense that Monica had contributed to this dilemma through her own selfish actions and, again, who knew what she was doing behind my back, secretly? *Remember her long trips back and forth to Tioga, North Dakota?* I thought. *Who knew if she had a discrete affair going on with someone from work?* She was spending a lot of time with friends. Only time would tell the truth. One thing for sure was that she was not happy, and she wanted change.

I had shut most of my feelings off in order to deal with our emotional roller coaster and the demands of the new business. I was a full-time entrepreneur, and I needed to establish more of a client base in order to replace my lost income from the police force. I knew that every day was going to be very important, and I needed to establish strict work ethics in order to complete each day's tasks. I had no idea what it took to be self-employed. I knew I would need some sound advice along the way. So, I turned to my good friend, Bob Palmer, who'd gotten me into the business in the first place.

Chapter 10

My friendship with Bob went back to the first day my family moved to Chatham. We arrived at a rented cottage located twelve miles from Chatham, overlooking Lake Erie. Our small house was nestled amongst other multi-sized homes, forming a hamlet called Erie Beach. My two sisters, Vickie and Jackie, Mom, and Dad filled up the 500-square-foot summer cottage and forced each day's activities to be experienced anywhere but inside. Before we moved from Brantford, Dad promised me I wouldn't miss a day of baseball and that he would get me enrolled on a team the very first day. He never let me down. The next day, we were at the beach when Dad announced I was to report to my first baseball game in Chatham. That's when I met Bob for the first time. Ironically, that's when I met the people that I would rely on and consider as close friends for many years of my life.

I'll always remember the coach sitting me down on the bench and giving me the pitching position. Everyone on our team complained that I was getting the position as pitcher before anyone else on the team. I had just arrived, and they had been on the team for the last month. The coach told them, "Let the new guy show us what he has before you pass judgment. Give Frank a chance, guys."

I started pitching and felt very good about how I would do. Then the first batter stepped up. It was this little but stocky Black boy, taking a very profound stance in the batter's box. He looked very powerful. I could hear his teammates call his name.

"Come on, Buddy, show the new guy where he belongs. Come on, Buddy, knock it out of the park. He ain't got anything, Buddy. Give him what for, Buddy."

I felt the adrenalin creep up in me while I started my wind up. Then I threw my first pitch with all my might.

"Strike one!" the umpire yelled.

Buddy shook it off and smiled at me.

Again, I wound up and threw another good pitch.

"Strike two!" You could hear the ump throughout the park and the cheers and jeers filling the early evening air.

"Come on, Buddy, you gonna let this wimpy new kid make you look bad?"

"Strike three. You're out!" The umpire's voice resounded like thunder as Buddy left the box in disgust.

The next batter that appeared was Bob. He was a little bigger in stature than the rest of the kids but extremely well built for his age. One could immediately tell he was destined for pro sport no matter what game he chose. The first two pitches were balls. Then I felt a need to throw a curveball. It was like Bob read it before I even threw it. I could see in his eyes as he was squinting at me that he was smiling, as if to say, "I'm going to ram this ball down your throat, new boy." Well, he almost did, but instead I heard a loud crack from the bat, and there went the ball. It landed a good twenty feet on the other side of the centre field fence. I knew right then and there I had to meet this guy or else I'd be beaten up many times by him.

I was always one to make the initial move when meeting people. I still am. So, I walked right up to the opposition's bench and said, "Hey guys, good game. Look, I just moved to town over at Chippewa Drive, and I'd like to meet up sometime. What do you think?"

"We're always at the baseball field right behind where you live, or you'll find us near where we poor Black folk live over at the Prince Street field. You'll find us there." The voice was that of Lorne Foster, a Chatham-born African American, and he was very proud of it. Lornie went on to earn his PhD in psychology some ten years later.

Not four years after we first met, Lornie and I had our very first fight, and we both learned a lesson in the social reality of the sixties. It was all over a girl, a White Anglo Saxon two years older than both Lornie and me. But she was beautiful and so sexy. She reminded me of Marilyn Monroe with her white-blonde, wavy hair and voluptuous body. Her breasts were at least 38Ds, and she was in such great shape. Her smile drew you in just like she'd drawn me in for the kill. I knew Lornie was dating her and that she was a live-in student at the Roman Catholic all-girls school, The Pines. She was in grade thirteen, and I was in grade ten.

One Friday night at the weekly Kinsman Auditorium dance, I spotted her sitting all alone at the back of the hall. I walked up and asked if I could sit down, and she said yes. We talked for a while, and then I got the courage to ask her to dance, and we did . . . for the rest of the night. Dancing with Diane O'Goreman was like having public sex. When we danced for the first time, she made me feel like she and I were meant for each other. I took her back to her dorm, and she kissed me, which made me feel like I had never felt before, not even to this day. She really did capture me.

We called each other and talked on the phone every day of the next week. Then, on Friday night, we went out to a movie. She stayed in on the Saturday night, but we still talked on the phone. I was totally convinced she liked me more than as a friend.

Then Sunday night came. I walked over to the arena and was watching a hockey game when Buddy came in and warned me that Lornie was outside and was going to kill me. He and a bunch of his friends were pacing out in the alleyway.

I asked, "Why? What the hell did I do?"

Buddy responded, "You stole his girlfriend."

"Who, Diane?"

"Yeah," Buddy answered.

"Oh no, I didn't steal her. She told me she had dumped Lornie and didn't want to see him again."

"Well, you better do some explaining and fast because he's ready to do you in."

I had no choice but to confront my friend and tell him the truth. I really was scared because here I was in the middle of the traditional, old school, White man's thinking and teaching and the facts of the times surrounding me at that moment were all coming to meet me face to face. My dad, who spent many years growing up in Chatham, had a predetermined attitude toward African Americans. He always told me, "Don't get in a fight with a Black (or Negro, as he called them) because you can't knock them out, son."

"Why is that, Dad?" I would innocently ask.

Dad would answer, "Because their jaws are made of stone." He would go on about how their skulls were harder than a White man's, just by nature and genetics. Yet my father would do anything for the African Canadians he worked with or had hired. He was not a racist; it was just his way of communicating as a result of growing up during his time, in the early 1900s. So, at that moment—confronting the fact that I might be in my first fight with a person that my dad said I might never be able to knock out or effectively stop by fighting—I was very scared, subconsciously. However, my mind began to go to work.

As soon as we saw each other, Lornie started in on me. "How could you have double-crossed me and stolen my girlfriend?"

I let him go on and on. Then he did something totally unexpected. He backed down. He stopped ranting and just said, "You know what, Frank? You can have her. I don't want to see you again." He just left in the night. I know he was hurt not just because he'd lost a relationship with a girl but because he lost, psychologically, his prized possession of a White girl to a White man. That was so defeating to him, especially at that time of life and racial era. It caused me great pain. I wasn't competing; I just liked the girl, and she liked me, kind of tragic.

Just a year before, in 1967, Lornie, Buddy, and I had gone to Windsor with Dad to watch the fires burning in Detroit. We all were very close that year. You could almost say that in our quiet and innocent way, we were helping each other try to understand what was going on between the White and Black communities. We had a very hard time understanding why Black and White men weren't able to get along. We were only fifty miles away, and we got along without a problem... unless you stole their White girlfriend.

As they always said, time heals all, maybe on the surface, or so it seemed at the time. Lornie and I did not speak until I came home from university. I made the first move, like I always did, and drove over to his house. I knocked on the door, and his mother came and answered it.

"Hi, Mrs.. Foster. I'm Frank Trousdell."

"I know who you are. What can I do for you?"

"I'm looking for Lornie. Is he home?"

"No, he's at the store. Is something wrong?"

"Oh no, Mrs. Foster. I just got back from school and wanted to say hi to Lornie."

"Well, that's really nice, Frank. I'm sure he'll be happy to hear that. I'll tell him."

You see, Lornie and I did have a lot in common. We'd played in the same R&B band, we played baseball and football on the same teams, and we'd spent a lot of social time together. Diane threw a real curveball in the works. She really caused a rumble in the social works of our peer group. But I have to say she was worth every minute of pain and strained friendship with Lornie. She was a dream come true for a fifteen- going on sixteen-year-old testosterone-filled male.

Diane and I got closer and closer every week. Then she invited me to take the train to Woodstock with her. That was where Diane travelled to visit her parents once a month. They lived in a small village called Norwich, some ten miles from town. I had to convince my father that I wanted to visit my sister Cheryll and Bob, who lived there. He finally bought into it and let me go.

What an experience. This beautiful eighteen-year-old, sitting on the train, holding my arm like we were newlyweds. People would say little things like, "You two are so gorgeous together. Did you just get married?" The attention and emotions were like a dream come true. She made it all happen, and she showed me a side of life that felt so right and so good to me. Her beauty haunted me every day. Her smile, her voice, and her intelligence mesmerized my entire being. I would say to her how beautiful I thought she was, and she would slough it off. Then I would ask her if she thought it possible for us to be together after we finished school. She always answered with a big smile and a very reassuring, "Yes!" Our physical sensuality was starting to heat up as well.

One Sunday, Diane came over to my house when my parents were gone for the day. We began making out by the fireplace, and then, after a short time, we ended up in my bed, clothed. She let me do things to her that we had never done before. I felt so secure with her, and she was so good to me. She was teaching me about sex and how to treat the woman you love. I really thought I was in love with her.

Then my sister Jackie came crashing in and yelled at Diane. "What are you doing to my brother?"

"Nothing, Jackie. We're not doing anything wrong."

By the time Jackie was gone, Diane had to go back to her dorm. I knew she was shaken up from this train of events, but she assured me she would get over it.

The next weekend we went to a show together, then took a walk downtown. It was getting a little cold out, but we didn't want to call it a night. Then a car pulled up beside us, and I noticed it was my friend, Dave Birch. He was a great hockey player and was going to the States the next year to play pro.

"Come on in, you guys," he said through the open window. Diane looked at me with approval, so we did. Dave started the conversation as if he knew Diane.

She turned to me and said, "No, I haven't met him before."

Dave then asked her, "Do you like riding bareback?"

She answered, "Yes."

"What kind of horse do you like to ride?" Dave asked.

"Black ones."

Dave answered, "I thought so."

The whole conversation caught me by surprise but also left me with a very suspicious feeling. After that night, I felt very weird and unsettled about that conversation. Was Dave trying to tell me something, or was he luring in Diane to go out with him? Or were they already discreetly involved?

The next weekend was our regular train trip to Woodstock. Diane and I made arrangements to go out on the Saturday afternoon. We went driving around town, then ended up at the small lake outside of Woodstock. We were on the shore in the car making out when we started to get really advanced, to the point that we did everything except penetration. When we were finished our closeness and hot event, she drove me home to my sister's house.

In the driveway, I asked her, "Are you seeing Dave Birch?"

"No."

I could tell she was taken back by the question. I knew she had just lied. Dave had met up with me a few days before that weekend and told me he'd not only taken her out to a movie, but they'd had sex in his car a week earlier.

I knew, for some strange reason, that if I didn't end this relationship at that moment, she would hurt me very badly in the end. So, I told her what Dave Birch had told me. She was shocked. I got out of the car and just walked into the house without looking back. That was the last time I saw her to this date and time. So many times, I have wished it had never happened, and so many times, I'd tried to find her but with no success. Even to this day, I would love to see her once again and just ask her what the truth really was and why things happened the way they did.

From that time on, I changed my attitude about almost everything.

Bob and I were very close friends, playing hockey together. Then in high school, we were two peas in a pod. Bob began weight training and was growing before all of our eyes. He was our Hulkamania man. He got me going in the weight room, and I was getting the bug to be a jock big time. I had just gotten over the John Hobbs era and started focusing on sports. I excelled even over Bob in hockey, but Bob and I took the field in football. Not too many could hold a candle to us. We knew we were the best in town. The coaches and referees all had their opinions on our abilities and our outstanding personas among the Chatham athletic community. We were proud, and we were confident.

I could always count on Bob, and he could on me. Bob and I wrote when we both were in university. He attended Drake U while I was at UND. He missed his family and his girlfriend, Kris. They were high-school sweethearts, and before Bob went to university, they were inseparable. He wanted to play pro football, and I was focused on a hockey career. He left Drake after one year and attended York U in Toronto. He made a name for himself as a fullback and got a tryout with the Toronto Argonauts. Then he got seriously injured and was finished with football.

That's when Bob gave it all to his business. He had a natural ability to organize, systematize, and replicate, which are the fundamental ideologies of a successful operation, especially in the food industry. He dealt daily with inventory coming and going, then having to manage sales, service existing clients, and develop new buyers 24/7. Quality control is an ever-constant task, not to mention the necessity of a foolproof distribution network that works around the clock, without shrinkage or loss. That's where Bob included me in a very small way.

I was to establish a growth market in the Hamilton-Burlington area, focusing on daycare and nursing home businesses. Bob said, "I'll coach you along the way, Frank, just like we helped each other on the field, playing football. You'd call the plays as quarterback, and then I would run out the play. This time, you do what I call. Just run the patterns as I call them. You got it, Frank?"

"Wow, it's that simple?" I asked Bob.

"Yes and no," he answered. "It looks simple on the surface, but to actually walk out the pattern gets a little fuzzy when you're dealing with different kinds of people and situations. That's where experience comes into play."

"That's why I need you to coach me, right?" I responded in question.

"You see, every person you'll come in contact with thinks you know what you're doing. The worst thing is to let them know you're just starting out, and you really haven't a clue of what's really going on in the food business. Just stick to your delivery turn-around, the quality of food, the freshness, and the price. That's all you need to deal with the client."

Bob helped me set up price lists and sales invoices. The rest was up to me. I had to go door-knocking in order to get new clients. I had never done that before.

Monica was somewhat reluctant to see me go out and sell. She thought I could do it, but she really didn't think it would be easy to get these businesses to buy frozen food off the truck. Her worry was that by the end of the day, I would be coming home with melting boxes of peas and corn and fish, and I wouldn't have anywhere to put the leftovers. She thought I was doomed from the beginning.

I'd only worked part-time for Bob over the previous year because I'd been with the police full-time, so I'd only been an order taker. Now I had to find new clients, on a daily basis, in order to make a profit.

The first call was too easy. As soon as I said I had frozen vegetables, the lady running a daycare out of her basement went crazy. "Let me see them. How much? Okay, I'll take two boxes of this and then that and then the fish. I'll take five boxes. Now, I want you to take an order for next week to be delivered on Monday."

After I completed the order, I drove away, thinking, *This is where I belong, running my own business.* I had the knack to sell. Every call I made that day bought something. I sold over $500 of product that day, out of my van. Boy, did I feel great. After I paid Bob, I still had $100. This was what I wanted to do for a living. I didn't have to answer to anyone again, or so I thought.

I had my little setbacks over the next three months, but I still managed to get clients and service them. I was able to add some restaurants to my route, which opened the door to needing meat and poultry suppliers. I had met a man who had a little furniture store on King Street in downtown Hamilton. He allowed me to use the basement of his store in order to operate out of Hamilton, which saved me the drive back and forth from Cayuga.

Jim the furniture guy, was always watching me and stepping in when he thought I needed help. I think he had a thing for Monica. They spent a lot of time together when Monica got laid off from Firestone in 1976. I had her work in the basement of the store, taking orders, calling, getting orders, and finding meat suppliers. Jim suggested Monica call a company that was out in Grimsby, way on the mountain east of Hamilton. They were Hamilton boys, and Jim knew them well. I had run into Joe D'Amico just around the same time as Jim told me to go see these guys, who had a meat-packing plant, and I might get a deal.

I drove out to the plant that next day and had to go way out into the sticks on a dirt road to find the packing plant. There it was, nestled back amongst trees and long weeds. I could hardly see the building from the road. The banging I had to do seemed to go on for minutes before anyone came to the door.

"You Frank?" A short, hairy Italian in a white apron, covered in blood, appeared in the sunshine from a dark, cold-looking room.

"Yes, I am, and are you Peter?" I asked.

"No, I'm Joe. Peter's my brother. He's inside butchering right now. Come on in, and I'll show you around."

I had always been interested in butcher shops since my dad had taken me with him to witness the slaughtering of our last cow left on the farm before we moved. I remembered the event as Joe walked me through the many rooms, all tiled in white. Every room was cold, very cold.

Meat and butchers were working everywhere. Boxes of wrapped meat were constantly being moved on a conveyor to the cold storage freezers and refrigerators.

"Where do you slaughter the animals?" I asked.

Joe answered, "We don't do that here. We have that building elsewhere. Most of our meat comes already slaughtered and graded from large national operations. It's easier to deal with the process and government requirements."

"Doesn't that influence the price?"

"Not really. We buy in volume enough to give us a really competitive price point."

Sounds good! I thought as we ended our tour back to his office. Then I realized where I'd met them before. We'd played hockey together on Joe D'Amico's Italian hockey team. "You bugger!" I shouted. They began to laugh, and we shook hands and patted each other on the back.

"Now, let's figure out what we're gonna do," Joe began.

"We'll take real good care of you, Frank," Peter added with assurance.

"Guys, I really am quite new to the food game, and I'll need a lot of help here."

"Oh, don't worry, Frank. We'll show you the ropes. You gonna be a big help to us too. We got product that needs to get out of the ice, and you gonna find homes for da food, *capisce?*" Joe stated in his Italian-Canadian accent. "We'll show you the way, Frank. Always remember, don't think about it."

"Hey? You still play hockey, Frank?"

"Not this year," I responded. I joked about the Shack incident, and they got a real good laugh out of it. The real joke was on me, which I found out later in the newspaper headlines. "Local meat-packers found trafficking pot; where's the beef?" Needless to say, Peter and Jon went away for a while.

Most people got a laugh when I told them the Shack story and finished with, "Where's the beef?" I found that telling that story always softened the room when I was trying to get to know someone or get accepted by a group of people. Even in the sales process, I would look at the pictures on the walls of offices and see if they were hockey fans or involved in team sponsoring. Then I'd ask questions about the picture, expanding to my career events and, of course, the Shack story. What an ice breaker.

Months went on, and I was selling a promising amount of food and meat. Bob and the Italians were happy, and so was I. I was supplying a nursing home in Burlington and got to know the owner comfortably when he exposed one day that all the nursing homes were forming a buying co-operative. He felt I should meet with the other homes and offer to be the central supplier of frozen and meat products exclusively for the co-op. I was beside myself. He had also told me the potential volumes that I'd be dealing with, and I almost lost it. We were talking in the millions of dollars.

For more than a week, I spent most of my days putting together a proposal. I got Bob and the meat boys on-side for the presentation. I then went out to all the nursing homes I had contracted and got them to sign a petition agreeing to centralize, using my services. Then I submitted it all to the head of the board of nursing homes. They thanked me and advised me that they would include my proposal in their overall co-operative planning presentation to the new investors group. I was so excited and so sure we had the deal wrapped up. For weeks, we believed it was all in the bag. Business was growing on the smaller side of things, but new doors kept opening for those few weeks of blind anticipation.

Then I got the call. A decision had been made. The group insisted that we take my idea of central supplying and give it to a national company. Hickson and Lang were awarded the contract. Not only did they get the contract, but they also started immediately taking away my existing contracts, one at a time, by undercutting my prices and services. Within a week, I had lost all my clients. Every single one was gone. They all had to sign exclusive service contracts in order to secure their prices. Not one client was left. I had never seen it coming. This event coined my very first business loss.

It didn't take long before Monica was very angry with me. I had taken a hit in business, and I was not going to recover from it. I was starting to feel very much on my own by then. By her actions, Monica was making it very clear that she had taken enough failure for one lifetime. I really didn't blame her for the way she was feeling. It seemed even to me, the quintessential optimist, a little bit disturbing. But one thing I lived by that stemmed from a very early age was never to give up, no matter what was happening.

Chapter 11

Not long after the business collapse, I ran into a man whom I had met through one of the players on the Preston Jesters team. His name was Gord Lee. I was at a hockey event at the Preston arena one night, and Stewie introduced me to Gord. Sitting across the table was this sharp-dressed man with red hair and neatly trimmed beard, with wire-rimmed glasses protecting his two beady eyes. I could immediately sense he possessed a level of intelligence that crossed business and social coolness. His stylish dress and haircut gave his materialistic presence away.

"Hi, my name's Gord Lee. Frank Trousdell?"

"Yes, that's me," I responded lightly.

"I watched you all last year play for the Jesters. You had quite a year."

"Thanks, Gord. I wish my business had as good a year," I sarcastically responded to Gord's compliments.

"What business are you in?" Gord asked.

I told him the story and, like a broken record, added my Shack and "where's the beef?" stories for good measure. Everyone at the table laughed, and the co-players from the previous year added their anecdotes.

"Frank, I have some ideas that could work for you. Can we talk?"

"Of course, I answered. When and where?" I asked.

"Come to my office in Hamilton on Monday morning, and I'll introduce you to my manager. We can share some thoughts."

I saw very quickly where this was going, and I felt excited and good about the possibilities. Selling life insurance seemed to be an honourable challenge to me.

Gord suggested to me that he had made well over $100,000 the previous year. That was a lot of money for anyone to make in the late 1970s.

I walked into Imperial Life's office, situated on the eleventh floor in the CIBC building on the corner of John and King streets, overlooking the centre square of downtown Hamilton. The clock on the wall clicked to 9:00 a.m. just as I reached the reception counter. I introduced myself, and immediately the pleasantly mannered girl directed me to the board room. Sitting around a very large board room table were at least twelve well-dressed men and one woman. Beside Gord was this somewhat plain-looking woman who smiled and introduced herself as Jane. I quickly surmised the majority's reason for being there was the greedy vision of anticipated easy money.

Not long after the grand poohbah, the illustrious leader and branch manager, Wes Lilley, arrived in all his glory, I realized I was about to be drawn into the fold like a lost lamb and become well on my way to great things only accessible to the life underwriters of this world as we knew it. Wes was profound with his words, which were carefully chosen to answer any question that could even be conceptualized, answering our unasked questions with succinct precession.

Then, like a light bulb turning on, I remembered where I had seen this man Wes before. He was a referee in the Senior A league. *Okay, I am putting the pieces together. I am not just randomly picked.* The dots were quickly connecting. *Amazing!* I thought as I listened to Wes preach on and on about his great adventures as a life underwriter. As I listened, I could feel a slow warmth grow inside me. *I think I belong here*, I commented mentally. An acceptant smile appeared on my face for our leader and all to see what I was feeling.

That's when Gord leaned over and said, with his convincing, conquering look, similar to a cobra's just before it struck, a look he probably used in every closing part of his sales process, "Welcome aboard, Rainbow."

"Rainbow?" I queried with an amused but puzzled look.

"Yeah, Trout as in your name, and you're always looking for the shooting star, right, Rainbow?" Gord laughed out loud. He had a bellowing and real distinctive laugh that I would hear and remember for many years to come.

Becoming a life underwriter was not an easy challenge. The in-office courses of study were arduous and seemingly endless. I did, however, plow through the paperwork and testing, finally reaching the best part—obtaining my licence. I was a registered and licensed life underwriter. I was on my way to earning a great income and community recognition, so I thought and hoped. I found myself preaching to my family and friends about the potential great success that was about to unfold for me, and I encouraged them to buy a policy or even look at the business, for their benefit.

This is where I first was hit with the hidden flaw to all that was taught about client building and acceptance to the world of life insurance by society at large. I was immediately hit with every objection my family and friends could come up with to ward me off from their pocketbooks. How was I going to make a living? I was only making a guaranteed base salary of $600 a month, and I knew that if I did not sell enough to cover my base, I would not last more than two or three months before losing my job. What was I to do?

Wes called me into his office one morning, and he began to talk with me. "I'm going to give you a kick start, Frank. I want you to come over to the window behind my desk and stand there and look out over the city."

I got up and stood looking aimlessly out over the skyline of Hamilton.

Wes stood behind me, and as I looked, he started talking quietly, "What do you see, son? Take a good look and tell me?"

"Well, I see Ivor Wynne Stadium; I see Stelco buildings near the bay—"

"No!" Wes interrupted me. "Look down on the street. Now, what do you see?"

"Oh," I said, "people. Lots of people."

"Right!" Wes exclaimed. "That's your market. Every one of those people is your potential client. Now you have to figure out how you are going to meet them. There are many ways for you to accomplish that goal, and you have to figure that challenge out.

"I recommend that you do the most obvious. Go stand down there on the street corner and start handing your business card out and shaking the hand of anyone who will let you. Now, remember, take your project 100 sheet and fill in the name, address, etc., of anyone who will give you their information."

My immediate thoughts were, *This won't be too hard.* But as I passed every floor going down on the elevator to greet the thousands of people waiting for my arrival, my enthusiasm slowly diminished to absolutely none by the time the elevator door opened at ground zero. I feared Wes was standing at his window, vigilantly watching for me. I felt the pressure rise and embarrassment creep into my psyche. *How can I escape this moment? I do not want to do this. Why can't I get out of this exercise? There has to be a different way to get prospects.* Then it came to me. *I will go into every store and meet the people working and hand them a card. I'll get their cards, too. This way, I can get their information and try to sell them.*

That's exactly what I began to do. I thought, *This will fuck up old Wes. He won't be able to see me. He'll think I've taken off and failed the test. I got one on him!* Mentally patting myself on the back, now I felt confident and a little more relaxed. *I will take my time and go into the stores I so choose.*

The first target was the Real McCoy Sports store. I knew Mr. McCoy from hockey. He owned the Dundas Real McCoy's Senior A team. They were the team that rejected my request to try out before Preston. "Can't help you, Frank. We're all taken care of by one of ours on the team. Keep kickin' at the can, boy," old man McCoy had said to me.

That afternoon was filled with rejection. Every store I went into had already been serviced by someone special in their lives. A brother, sister, cousin, father-in-law, or some unique and personal relation seemed to dominate their repletion. I was mentally tired but not beaten. I knew in my very inner being that eventually someone would say okay and let me sell them insurance, but when? That was the ultimate question, and would I make some money? Every time, before I entered a store, I would stand in front and wonder what kind of connection I could make with them. I wondered if there was something I could do for them to get them to listen to me. Finally, I walked into a bridal shop and asked this beautiful lady if I could talk to her about her business. She replied, "I just work here, but I would be interested in talking. Not often does a good-looking young man come into this shop." She was soft-spoken and had a smile that would stop you right in your tracks. Well, she stopped me.

"Hi, I'm Liz, short for Elizabeth uh Hamilton."

"As in Hamilton . . . Ontario?"

"Ha, ha," she laughingly replied. "Your name?" Liz asked while she stuck her hand out to shake mine.

"Frank Trousdell," I answered, shaking her hand. I felt an electric sensitivity while shaking her hand, and I sensed warmth in her grip of acceptance that caused me to not want to let go. Her eyes were drawing me in to search her soul, it seemed.

"How about lunch tomorrow?" I asked quickly.

"Sure, meet me here about twelve noon, okay?"

"See you then."

The rest of the day went by quickly. It seemed almost a blur. Liz consumed every moment of reflection that day. I daydreamed a lot about her and what might be in store. I saw desire in her eyes. I felt warmth and a need for her to expand her emotional needs, so I thought, *What will be in store for us?*

We met across the street from her store at a cozy restaurant. We both showed ourselves to be uncomfortable, yet one could surmise there was something more in the air than small talk. But small talk was all that occurred. As we parted, she made sure she let me know with a look that she was expecting me to ask her to meet me in a hotel room and have wild passionate sex all afternoon. If I could have found the nerve to ask, I would have done it with her in a heartbeat, but for some reason, that daydream would stay saved only for the memoirs. I did, however, sell her an insurance policy.

My manager Wes was encouraged by my results in that first week. He kept motivating me to keep door-knocking and cold-calling. I hated every minute of it, but all I could imagine was earning my first big paycheque. On and on I went, talking to people, eventually selling two, maybe three policies a week. I was barely making more than what I had been making when I'd worked for Royal Trust, but this time, I had control of what I could potentially make, based on my effort. I found that the more I sold, the more I became hooked on the business. Wes was a great motivator. He had a way with all the young recruits fresh out of the gate. He made us feel that there was no other business, and if we failed in this one, we would never achieve much anywhere else.

As time went on, Wes directed us and suggested that we get involved in community events to network. Networking back then was the same as it is today. Get involved with groups of businesses and advertise your existence. You feed off each other. Well, I was a little too young to join a service group, so I set out to get to know some local Cayuga people.

That's when I met Danny Horvatis. Dan owned the local garage, and as well, he operated the local sports shop in the garage. His two sons, Peter and Paul, ran the business. I started hanging out there and became a regular. The next thing I knew, I'd agreed to coach the brand-new Cayuga Junior D Red Wings hockey team. Dan had just purchased the franchise rights and organized the team. I finally began to realize I was out of the playing part of the game.

We put the first team together, drawing players from the local minor teams, and finding a couple of key players who were about to quit hockey because their chances of going further were improbable, and their eligibility was running out. I remember one practice, a somewhat frail young boy came up to me, wearing a big smile. He had that farm boy look about him. "Hi, my name's Chris McSorley, and I want to play for your team, sir."

I looked at him and smiled back. "How old are you, son?"

"I'm fourteen, but I'm tough, and I am a good player, and I don't quit. You see, sir, I have four older brothers, and we all play hockey. My oldest brother is Mark, and he just signed a pro contract with the Edmonton Oilers. I got another brother, named Paul, and this is his last year for junior, and I can get him to play for you, sir."

I turned and looked on the ice and responded to this kid, who'd had my heart from the get-go, "Get dressed. You're going to play junior hockey, and you'll be great!"

"Thank you!! I won't let you down, sir."

"Don't let yourself down, and never forget what I just said." When I said it, I looked into his young impressionable eyes, and the sparkle was so bright that I knew he would go a long way. He truly loved the game. Not long after, his brother Paul was our number one defenceman and eventually earned my confidence as captain of the team. He was, as well, my on-ice coach, which really upset Danny, the owner, because he wanted his sons to be the leaders on the team. Peter and Paul were very supportive of my decisions and understood my choices. But their father never got the message.

I really upset Danny by bringing on a local guy to help me in practices and assist me on the bench. Jim Wilson was a very personal and fun person that every player liked. He was the type of young man who attracted most women, and he played the part very well. The main quality he possessed was a commitment to the project. He was willing to learn, and he always was there, willing to do whatever was asked of him, and he was always on time.

Jim and I became very good friends, both on and off the ice. He was single, and he drove a brand-new Corvette. His history with the local girls was well-known to most, and he enjoyed his popularity. Jim worked hard, and he played hard. That was the way we were all taught back in those days, especially those of us working in sales. Jim was a salesman for Ultramar and sold water softeners. Jim and I would meet for lunch most Fridays in Hamilton and share notes. He always had a wild and wacky story to tell, usually on a farm where he found himself cornered by a lonesome farm wife. He quickly became Ultramar's number one salesman.

The team I was coaching worked hard and was vigilant. They trusted me and hung on to every word I had to say. I was really enjoying my new venture, and things seemed to help my relationship with Monica for a while. Then, close to Christmas, Monica dropped a bomb. She was getting laid off at Firestone. That was not good news at all. In fact, this was devastating. The loss of her income meant financial trouble for us. She kept assuring me we would find a way to bring in extra money. I immediately went to Wes and asked if he could increase my draw. He responded too quickly with a firm no. I was set back on my heels. I felt he'd abandoned me in my time of need. I was not too happy with Wes, and I lost faith in him from that moment on.

One of my players was an eighteen-year-old goaltender named Billy, whose family owned and operated Cayuga Dragway Park. Not only was the park the only one of its category in the region, but it was the busiest in the NASCAR Drag Racing association. Billy and I hit it off right from the start. His younger brother was on the team as well. The family was very supportive of their sons and the team as a whole. I became very close with the family, so close that Billy and I developed the first Drag Way Park magazine. The two of us spent most of our spare time writing articles and selling advertising, trying to set up the magazine. We thought this would be our ticket. It certainly filled our time. I, of course, sold small policies to the family. I was quickly taught by Daddy Melenbalker, Bill's dad, that insurance was not a priority on the farm; his cattle were number one. Bill senior raised cattle, and so had his forefathers and their fathers before them. The farm had been in the family for three generations. The problem was that the boys did not want to farm. They were addicted to drag racing and the business of it. Bill senior never showed that he disapproved at all. He was as much involved in the park as were his sons. As well, Bill was very much in approval of whatever Bill Jr. wanted to do. He was right because Bill Jr. was a great lad and very committed to his family and the business.

The Cayuga Junior D Red Wings finished out the season, winning their division and entering the playoffs. This accomplishment was recognized throughout the league. Never before had a team reached the playoffs in their first year of operation. Cayuga was even more proud because we did it with players who were throwaways or had no experience or were finished as potential future stars. We did it all on the strength of will and motivation. We trained hard, and we utilized unorthodox training methods as well. For example, at one practice, in order to help keep our goalies from moving too far out of the net, Paul McSorley suggested we rope them to the net during practice. I thought that was a great idea. It worked within the first week. We tried unique hitting drills. I was afraid that little Chris would eventually get hurt because he had no fear. There was no player too big for him. He came off the ice bloodied from fighting or just plain never giving up until he'd won the puck and put down the man.

Ironically, not once did Chris come off the ice without that smile on his face. I remember one time as if it were yesterday. He had a gash on the side of his face, and I thought he was going to need a lot of stitches. He looked at me, smiled, and said, "Get me some bandages. I'm alright. I'll be ready for next shift." And he was ready enough to set up a goal. That was my boys. I was so proud of them and all that they accomplished that year. The team eventually lost out in the league finals, but to all of us, they won big time in our hearts and our minds and will always be my greatest achievement as a coach for the rest of my life.

Every week the team and I would either get together at my house, or a bunch of us would jump into a car on a Saturday afternoon with a case of beer and go crop dusting. Back in the day, crop dusting was just that: we would load up the car with beer and drive up and down the dirt roads between fields, out of the way of anyone and everyone. We'd talk, tell stories, and drink beer. The boys would share their problems, and I would give my point of view. When you think about it, I was only three years older than most of my players. They were very much my friends rather than children to me. Their girlfriends looked at me as cool and very much a target from time to time. I was finding myself in questionable positions with one or two of them. I was very much flattered but knew there would be trouble if I carried out any such knee-jerk activity.

On the other hand, Jim Gibson had no conscience when it involved women. He was addicted to sex, without a doubt. He was like a dog in constant heat. Many times, I had to back him off of Monica and her friend Vickie View. Vickie didn't like him and would make it known to him every chance she had. That only fuelled the fire. Jim loved primal challenges. A girl says, "No," but he hears, "Yes . . . just try a different line." Away he'd go like a hound dog on a rabbit trail.

The month was April, and spring was starting to roll in like the breezes through the trees. Monica and I were getting along better, and we started setting plans to maybe sell the house and get something more finished and easier to maintain. We had it up for sale for two months, and there was absolutely no interest. In fact, the real estate people all said we should tear it down and build new. We were shocked by this advice and began to feel stressed out about all that we had done. Then, the final nail in the coffin came unexpectedly. Monica announced that she was going back to North Dakota for a few weeks to help her parents move to Alaska. Her father had been offered a professorship in Petroleum Engineering. The whole family was moving up to the northern state. I was devastated by Monica's announcement and immediately felt this would be it. "When do you plan on going"? I asked her.

"I think in two weeks. I'll drive to Bismarck, leave the car with my sister, and then fly back when I'm done."

"Okay," was all I could say.

The two weeks went by quickly. The night before Monica was to leave for her journey, Vickie arrived. I went out with some of my hockey buddies. We pretty much partied all night. I had given up and lost any kind of respect for Monica by that time. I strolled into the house early enough to catch them both before they headed out down the road. They were much disgusted with me, and looking back, maybe they were right, but I was hurt. *I am hurt for the last time,* I thought. Not long after Monica left, I started feeling the slow creeping pangs of anxiety and loneliness take over. *I should have done this and maybe said that*, was going through my head. *It really doesn't matter anymore,* I thought, *for she is gone. For how long? Who knows? But one thing is for sure: I'm going to be on my own for a very long time. It's all up to me to survive. The bills, the mortgage, the food, the car, and anything else are all my responsibility to pay for going forward. Thank God we don't have kids*, rang through my head. *Well, let's get on with it. I've got some work ahead of me*, I thought.

You always hear from time to time that answers are all around you that will either change your life forever for the good, or move you in a direction that will cause an equal and opposite reaction, but you never see them coming. I was riding down the elevator in the office building a few days after Monica had left and beside me was a familiar face. It was Phil's girlfriend, and her name slips my mind.

"Well, hello there. How're you doing?"

"Great," she replied.

"Are you still at the law firm?"

"Oh yeah."

"How's Phil?"

"He's doing great. He left Royal Trust and is now Vice President of Trust Services at Equitable."

"Wow, I always knew he'd make it big."

"You should call him, Frank; he'd love to hear from you. How's Monica?" she asked.

"Oh, I guess okay," I answered somewhat sheepishly.

"I detect problems. Want to talk?"

"Yeah, I would," I replied. She had a way about her that always built comfort in the other person while talking to her.

We chatted for about fifteen minutes, and by the end of the discussion, she suggested I get a lawyer. "Monica isn't happy, Frank, and she has given you the final word by leaving for an indefinite time. My boss will see you. Let me set up a meeting."

"Okay," I replied, not really knowing what I was getting myself into.

"Hello, have a seat. Frank, is it?" asked the lawyer, Mr. Collins.

"Yes, sir," I replied nervously.

"This process of separation is very unnerving for the weak-hearted. How old are you?"

"I am twenty-three, sir."

"Drop the 'sir'. I'm not your dad. I am your lawyer, your new friend. You will learn how much or little of a friend I will be very shortly," the man of law retorted. "I need to know how old the children are and how many you have."

"Oh, we do not have any children," I quickly answered his question.

He cringed as he pondered my response, and then he asked, "Why are you separating?"

I laid out all the differences I thought we had and the psychological struggle we were both experiencing and that I thought it best to set Monica free, and maybe I could get on with a new start. I found myself talking to him as if he were my priest taking confession.

"I get the message," he said, trying to get me off the true confession bit. "I'm not a psychologist. I'm a lawyer, so this is what I think. The two of you should see a marriage counsellor first. Then you should get some guidance second. Then, if the two of you are still at odds, come and see me again.

"The final antidote is you got one of two choices to get a quick divorce in Canada. Either you admit adultery, or she admits it. Either one must have a willing participant to go to court and make such an admission. Call me if you need me, Frank."

"Thank you," I said and went out to the street, gasping for fresh air.

I walked toward my car and asked myself, *What do I really want to do. Do I continue the way things are, or do I stop everything and divorce Monica?* I decided that day to try living as if we were separated while Monica was away and take each day at a time. *How do I know whether Monica had made the same decision? Maybe she's living a single life right now?* When I got back to the house, I pondered my steps as a temporary single man. *Whatever happens will happen.*

For the next few days, that's exactly what went on. I found going out of my routine was very difficult. I had to plan my activities and try to include other people to coincide their schedules with mine. Then the activity always included two things: nightclubs and booze. The whole single thing was becoming very costly and weary on the body. Finally, the repetitive explanations to my friends seemed endless.

One night, I decided to call Monica's home. It had been a week, and I hadn't heard a word since she had left. Her father answered the phone and seemed very surprised to hear she hadn't arrived after being on the road for five days. He said he would call once he heard anything. I worried about her safety and where she was, so I began calling her friends, starting with Vickie View.

She explained Monica's agenda as she knew it, which was a bit of a surprise to me. First, she was going to drive to Madison, Wisconsin, and stay at a friend's for a few days.

"A friend in Madison? Who's that?" I asked with a bit of a heated temper. "What friend?"

So, then I called Angela in Minneapolis and asked what she knew. Angela only knew Monica was staying at a friend's, then coming to her house for a few days. I asked her to have Monica call as soon as she could to keep me aware of her safety. Mentally, I was steaming with the suspicion she was cheating on me. Every moment of the day, I imagined her with some other guy, driving back to North Dakota like we used to do. I envisioned the two of them stopping alongside the highway and having sex in the field, like we did from time to time, and the trucks honking their horns at us as we made love. I was beginning to drive myself crazy.

I called my friend Jim Wilson, and we met up for a beer. I told him what was happening, and he listened with great intensity and compassion. "I've got an idea for you, Frank. I think this'll straighten you out once and for all. If you can't get her out of your mind after what I'll do for you, then you belong in a loony bin."

I asked, "What is it you're going to do?"

"I'm going to give my friend the best surprise he has ever gotten from anyone. Meet me tomorrow at Hanrahan's strip club for lunch."

"Jim, I really don't need a lap dance, but lunch there is good. See you then."

I arrived at the club the next day and found Jim on the phone. After a few moments, he sat down, and we began drinking our beers. I looked at him and said, "Okay, what's the big deal?"

He had this funny look on his face and began to tell me how he met women through work. He had been promoted to sales manager, and was responsible for interviewing and hiring sales staff. "You won't believe this, Frank, but I've never had so much sex since I got this new job. For every five women I interview, I sleep with at least one. I think that most women will do anything to get a job."

"I don't believe you, Jim."

"Well, you're going to meet someone that I hired just a week ago, and we've been meeting every day for a quickie."

"No," I replied in shock.

"I'm telling you the truth. She's unbelievable. I think she's a nymphomaniac. She never gets enough. I was just lining up for us to meet her in about an hour in Waterdown. You know what the best part is?"

"What?" I replied.

"She's engaged to be married in about a month."

"That's the best part?" I asked.

"Yeah, she's totally discrete. My girlfriend will never know," Jim stated with excitable conviction.

"Wow." Deep inside. I started to feel anxious thoughts of Monica doing the same thing that Jim was talking about. "Maybe Monica's been doing the same thing?"

"That's the point, Frank. I've come to believe that a lot of women compensate their fear of their spouse cheating by cheating first or at least balancing the scale."

"This sounds pretty screwed up if you ask me," I retorted.

"You think so, Frank? Just look at yourself. You can't tell me you haven't cheated on Monica or at least thought about it."

"You're right. I've done both."

"There you go, Buddy. What makes you think you're so righteous to think you can do it and she won't?"

"Oh my God! I'm really fucked up. I've messed this marriage up from day one," I sadly responded to Jim.

"Yes, you are, but you've got to get a grip on yourself. Do you realize that at least forty-six percent of all women cheat on their spouse at least once in their marriage and/or relationship? This has been proven by many studies done on marriage. Why do you think I'm not married? I already know that my girlfriend has had a relationship with her boss. The prettier the women, the more they have to prove their sexuality.

"Let's get out of here and enter into the world of wild sexual encounters. Drink up, my friend," Jim requested with a sense of urgency.

So, on we went to meet this mystery woman. While we were driving, I thought of what Jim had said, and I felt so jaded and confused. All that I had suspected of Monica was probably true. The trips back to North Dakota were probably preplanned to meet with old boyfriends or maybe even with new mates. This was getting really ugly for me. I guess my sexual hunger and desire for other women were a tempting demon, controlling my mind, as it is with most people. The only difference was that I allowed myself to act out the opportunity and fulfill the fantasy as I was about to do that afternoon. Jim was very convincing on top of it all.

We arrived at the Waterdown pub and entered the back door. Sitting in a booth was this gorgeous, stunningly beautiful, young woman about twenty-two years old. At first glance, you noticed her perfect, long black hair accented by her symmetrical eyes that caught your attention and almost melted you once you made contact. Her smile was sultry and inviting.

"Hey Melinda, this is Frank, who I told you about."

She reached forward to shake my hand. As we touched fingers, I could feel the almost electrifyingly warmth instantaneously. Jim sat beside her, and I was across the table from her. We chatted for about five minutes, then she looked at Jim, gave him a nod of approval, and suggested we leave. The three of us went in Jim's car and drove to a small motel down the road. Jim went to the office and signed in. He came back and opened the door to a room almost in front of where we'd parked. Once we were in, I sat in a chair across from the bed. I began to watch their movement as if it were a choreographed dance. The two seemed in perfect harmony as they disrobed each other and began reciprocal touching and stroking.

All the while, she was looking at me, smiling and gazing with great pleasure as if to say, "Come with us and join in." Then, without notice, she said in a deep pleasurable tone, "Come here. I want you too."

Those first few seconds seemed like minutes of reservation and hesitation. I felt uncomfortable and childlike but emotionally aroused by the occasion. Within minutes I was fully participating in an afternoon of shared sexuality between three friends yearning for an escape into a fantasy known to me only through the written works of Harold Robbins.

She got out of the bed and looked at her watch. "I really have to go. I am to meet my mother for dinner. We are making the final plans for the wedding." The way she said it was as if what had just happened was insignificant and just part of her day.

"We should get together soon, do you think?" I asked her.

"I don't think that will be possible, Frank, but you gave me the greatest afternoon, and I will remember this for the rest of my life. I have a friend that you should meet. I'll let Jim know when you can meet her."

"Cool," I answered as we drove away to drop her off.

"So, what did you think of that?" Jim asked.

"I'm in total shock but feel so free for some reason. I don't feel guilty at all. There's almost a peaceful feeling going on."

Jim chuckled as we drove to my car. "Maybe you and Monica should split, Frank. I think you guys weren't meant for each other. You need some time to yourself and explore a bit, don't you think?"

"I don't know, but I'm ready to think about it more seriously. Monica really feels like she's in North Dakota. I'm feeling the distance more and more."

"I think it's time to move on, Frank. Don't dwell on this anymore. You might drive yourself to do something crazy, like jump off a bridge or something."

"No, I'll never do that," I replied with a tone of self-confidence.

The next few weeks were filled with some work and a lot of drinking and chasing women with Jim. I even tried to get together with Vickie View. That never materialized, only because I stopped myself from following through with the dates we had set. Vickie was ready; I was apprehensive. I was originally smitten by her when Monica first brought her into our lives, but there was something about her manners that turned me away. Monica had made a statement the day before she had left that behooved me. We were sitting in the dining room, and Monica suggested that while she was gone that it would be okay if Vickie and I dated. She suggested we go to Toronto for a weekend. Vickie was nervously in agreement. I questioned Monica as to why she would suggest this, and she replied, "You guys are friends, and I feel okay about it." I never followed through with it because of this questionable setup.

I actually thought Monica was trying to pair me with Vickie and, in some strange way, was handing me off to Vickie. I could never get over that event. In fact, I began to feel that Monica was preparing me for her to leave me permanently.

A letter arrived for Monica from Firestone, and they were offering her a new position for her to come back. I immediately called her father again, and he said that she was due to arrive that day. He would pass on the message and have her call me.

Later that day, I got the call. I was shaking when I heard her voice. Anxious feelings of missing her reappeared. She was happy and carefree, as if we were long-lost friends.

"What are you going to do, Monica?" I asked.

"I'm going to help Mom and Dad move to Anchorage, then I'll come back and look into the job."

"When will that be?"

"Next month," she responded.

"Next month?" I questioned with a bit of anger. Then the fight began. The argument went on for over an hour. The call ended with her hanging up. I was so disappointed and hurt. My first instinct was to call my father. I told him all I could, and he responded with one very firm and strict demand. "Call her back and tell her you will meet her in Bismarck, North Dakota, and drive her back now, or else the two of you are finished."

There was a lot of calling back and forth between Monica and me until she gave in and agreed to meet me as suggested by my father. Dad lent me the airfare, and I flew out two days later.

My plane arrived minutes before Monica's landed. I got off, and no sooner did I get into the airport waiting room than Monica landed. She walked through the arrival gate, and I ran up to greet her. She stopped me inches from hugging her.

"How dare you?" she screamed. "How dare you take me away from my family? Grab my bags," she demanded, then walked off to the exit door. We had to travel to her sister's to get the car, which was a very long and uncomfortable small commuter plane ride. Then her sister picked us up and drove us to her home. The next day we started the long drive back. We did absolutely no talking for over six hundred miles.

Then, like a thunderclap, Monica started to yell and scream.

I pulled the car over off the interstate, and both of us got out of the car. We began to rip each other apart verbally for seemingly hours. There was not an event that we didn't cover. Then without any notice to each other, we both broke down and cried and fell to the ground. We were holding each other, shaking and sobbing.

"Let's end this insanity," she said.

"Okay, okay, I agree," I answered.

"Can't you see we're killing each other, not to mention our families."

"I know," I said in full submission.

"Let's put an end to it, okay?" Monica placed her hands on my face and kissed me. We had ended our painful journey, so we thought.

The rest of the ride back to Cayuga went like a blur, ending late the next night. Both of us dropped on the couch and slept for a full night and almost the next day. I planned to get rid of the house somehow, so I called the original owner back from Royal Trust and told John what had happened. He suggested that we do a legal resolve with him called a quick claim deed. What this meant was we signed full title back to him, forgoing any asset value that could be in the house. This transaction would be consummated in writing and with the passing of a dollar between both parties. The very next day, John was at the doorstep with the papers. He gave us a month to vacate and unload our belongings.

Chapter 12

I remember the next few days as if they were today, driving in Brantford to see my friend Robbie Lockington. His brother was opening a pizza shop, and Robbie had networked a meeting between us so I could sell them a director's insurance policy. After the meeting, I asked Robbie if he knew a good place for me to get a haircut. He sent me to a place on the main street and said to ask for Patty. She was really good, and I might enjoy her company. So, I did do just that. I went to have some small talk with a hairdresser.

The shop was in the basement of an old building, and I had to walk down the stairs to the entrance. A window was adjacent to the door, and I noticed this young girl with long auburn hair, a tight-fitting striped sweater, and a pair of tight black slacks, standing by the barber's chair, looking right at me. She had this big smile and looked very pleasant.

Without hesitation, I walked through the door. "Hi."

"Hi, are you here for a cut?" she asked.

"Yes, I was actually referred by my friend, Robbie Lockington."

"Oh, yeah, what's he up to?" she asked without breaking her smile.

I told her of his business venture as I sat in the chair. As usual, I started giving her the once over with my eyes, trying not to be obvious.

"You like what you see?" she sheepishly asked.

"You are very attractive," I responded, trying to be polite.

"What do you want for a style?" she asked. I began to direct her as to what I wanted, and as I went on about my wants, she stopped me and revealed that maybe I should come back when the regular girl was in because she had just started that day. I could immediately tell she was very unsure about her ability to cut my hair.

"You got to get started someday, so it might as well be me," I said with great encouragement.

"Okay, but don't blame me if I total your hair."

"I don't think that will happen," I assured her.

The small talk went on as she went through the motions, and when it was over, she stood back and said, "I think I did a pretty good job."

I looked in the mirror and replied, "You did a great job. You got yourself a new client." I could tell she was very pleased, and she showed her appreciation for my encouragement. I then began to sell her on insurance and how she should get some to cover her in case of disability. She thought it was a good idea and asked for my card. I gave her one and asked her to call me. We shook hands, and I left her a very nice tip.

A few days went by, and I got a call from Patty, asking me to visit her at her mother's house to discuss the insurance. I agreed, and later that day, I met up with her as she had requested. The house was a small wartime home with a very large backyard. I knocked on the door, and within seconds, an older man came coughing and sputtering to the door. "What do you want? Don't be selling me anything 'cause you won't get far here."

"Dad, fuck off," I heard from behind him.

"What . . . it's just another fucking salesman," he said in defence of his gruffness.

"I asked him to come today, for fuck's sake. Go sit in the kitchen," Patty demanded as she came to let me in the door. "Don't mind him. That's my dad, Don. He hates salesman, can't you tell?"

"Oh yeah," I responded in laughter. "I get that a lot in my business."

"I bet you do," Patty replied.

"Hello," said a robust-sized lady in the kitchen. "I'm Patty's mom, Pat."

"Hi, I'm Frank."

"I know. You're all that's been talked about for the last few days around here," Pat replied.

I sat in the kitchen across from Don, who had to have gone through a pack of smokes in at least a half-hour. The clock hit five, and he jumped up and said, "It's Miller time. Want a beer?"

"Sure," I responded.

As soon as he drank the first beer, he began dominating the conversation. "I know what you're saying, but I am telling you up front, my daughter does not need any fucking insurance. She can't afford it. She can't even hold down a job for more than a day, for fuck's sake."

"Shut the fuck up, old man," Pat interjected. "You keep it up, and I'll kick your ass out the fucking door!"

"Yeah, yeah, always threats, bitch."

I was really getting nervous, and I was definitely not used to this abusive bantering between spouses and children. Patty kept trying to lighten the conversation by implying this event was all in fun. It was their way of jibber-jabbering back and forth. The beer kept coming, and I was getting drunker, and so were Don and Pat. I was seriously waiting for an all-out brawl to break loose any minute when I stood up and suggested I'd better go before I couldn't drive.

"Oh, you can stay over. There's a couch in the basement."

"That's okay, I have to go, but thanks for everything," I quickly and politely answered. I then made my way to the car.

Patty followed me out and apologized for their behaviour. I responded that I was okay and that it was quite an event but still fun. She said, "We should get together under better circumstances."

"Sure, I'll call." While I drove home that night, a whole series of events passed before my eyes as if I could see the future. I envisioned myself in that house months and years later, doing the same thing as they were doing. It was very disturbing, yet there was a sense of down-home acceptance. I could see through the rough and gruff façade a family closeness that was comforting in a very primal way.

The next few days were more of the same between Monica and me. There was a constant distance and non-emotional gap. She went her way, and I went mine. Oddly enough, Monica was not showing any activity toward packing or moving. She made no reference to her getting her own place or wanting to get things legally cleaned up between us. I thought that this was better left alone so as to not force any undue arguments.

The next morning, as I was in the office, Wes called me and asked me to shut the door. I thought he wanted to have another one of his father-son talks, but I was wrong. "Frank, I'm going to show you a little trick that saves you and the client a lot of time and money. Come over to the window for a moment."

"Okay," I said.

He had an application in his hand, and it was filled out completely, except there were no signatures on it. "Now, you see that app on my desk?" he asked. "Pick it up and look at it."

"Okay," I responded.

"That's the app you submitted yesterday, right?" he asked.

"Yes," I answered.

"Okay, look at line twenty-five. Do you see the mistake you made?"

"Oh, I did," I responded in surprise.

"Now, I'm going to show you how to do something that, in some eyes, is illegal, but you don't have time to go and get the client to sign a new app. So, you're going to trace their signature to speed up the process."

"That's fraud, isn't it?"

"Oh no," Wes responded in a tone of confidence and assurance. "The client should always do it, but in business, these are the grey areas we have to live with to get the job done."

"You're the boss . . . boss," I answered in apprehensive acceptance. Even though I knew this was forgery and fraud, I had no idea that I was about to commit my first white-collar crime. I did whatever Wes told me to do, and so did everyone else who worked for him. I would find this out over the next few years.

The phone rang just as I sat down at my desk, and it was our receptionist. "There's a call from a Patty, wanting to talk to you about insurance," the receptionist said with a hint of excitement as if to say, "You've got a sale, brother!" You see, life insurance salesmen rarely get calls from people wanting to buy insurance. Only car and house insurance agents get those calls. That's what makes the job so difficult. You have to find someone who is interested, and then you have to sell them to buy.

"Hello, this is Frank Trousdell. How can I help you?"

"Hi, Frank, it's Patty MacGrandles . . . the hairdresser. You remember, the one with the wacko parents?"

"Oh yeah, how are you?"

"I'm fine."

"Listen, what are you doing Saturday night?"

"I don't have any plans as of yet," I answered.

"Would you come to a wedding with me? A friend of mine's getting married. You should meet them, and you might get a sale." It didn't even dawn on me that she was actually asking me out on a date, let alone the fact that it would be impossible to sell them anything at that time. But I did think that it would be a great way to meet more people as insurance prospects. We set the time and place and signed off the call pleasantly.

"I'm going to my sister's on Saturday until Sunday. Is that okay with you?" I tried to be accommodating to Monica by giving her enough information without telling her the whole truth to avoid confrontation. I had no intention of going to the wedding as if it were a date, even though Monica and I were virtually finished as a couple. I still felt compelled to be respectful, at least on the surface. I also didn't see this as a date because I was going with business intentions. Monica did, however, show a sign of interest in coming along. I carefully said that I needed this time alone. She let it go, and so did I as I packed and went out the door.

I got to Patty's to pick her up and found that she was a bridesmaid in the wedding. I was very confused because I'd thought I was going as a guest. She then apologized for not telling me the whole truth and gave me a beer. I calmed down and away we went to the wedding. The whole event was a little uncomfortable, but by the time we entered the reception hall, we were all good friends as if we had known each other for years. The night went on, and we had a real good time. I guess I needed the release from all the tension I had gone through and was experiencing every day while living with Monica.

Patty then suggested that she change clothes and we go out to a bar after the wedding. We had more drinks, and I thought I should go home. It was about two in the morning. We sat in the driveway of her home and got hot and heavy. Before we knew it, we were having sex in her parents' front yard. We said our goodbyes and I thought that would be the end of it from there on.

My parents called me a few days after and suggested Monica and I come to Chatham for a family reunion. All my sisters and extended family were to be there, and I should show a good face by making sure Monica accompanied me. We agreed, and off we went to the weekend reunion. Everyone from the family was there, and we partied, as usual, all day long. Pictures were taken of us in groups and as individuals, which made Monica and me very uncomfortable. We dealt with it as best we could, especially at night when we had to sleep together. We made a big mistake that night by temporarily falling in love again. We would try again, we decided.

The next week went by with little confrontation, but by the end of the week, Monica and I started arguing again. On Friday, I got a call from Patty at the office. She wanted to see me again. I agreed. So, I orchestrated another excuse and off I went to Brantford and partied away the weekend while Monica had Vickie visit her in Cayuga.

On Sunday, there was a river party in Cayuga, so I arrived and went looking for Monica and Vickie. They were in their bikinis, lying by the river in the midst of a large crowd, obviously trying to attract the hungry boys. They were doing just fine at getting the attention they wanted. I got jealous and caused a scene. Jim came over and walked me away from them. He calmed me down, and I went to the bar and got drunk, then went home and slept it all off.

The drive to the office was at least forty-five minutes from Cayuga, which always gave me enough time to think. *I'm going to make the move*, I kept saying mentally. *I'll get an apartment and move to Brantford. Monica can deal with herself, and maybe she'll get her own place in Hamilton.* We only had two weeks to vacate the house, so maybe Monica would get the message to move. That night, I drove to Brantford and started apartment hunting. I signed the first one I saw and made plans to move in that week. I called Dad and told him, and he said he would bring a pickup and help me move. He thought it was the best thing to do.

Dad and I arranged to meet early morning, just after Monica went to work. We took only what I needed and moved quickly so Dad could get back to Chatham before dark. I was set up and ready to stay in my new apartment by the end of that night. I had also left a note for Monica as we left the house, telling her I had gotten an apartment and would be back by the weekend to help her move, so she should find a place to go.

I called her, and we agreed to meet on the Friday night to do the final packing. That night was pretty exhausting for both of us, and we cleared all we could and cleaned the house. Monica and I went to the bedroom to pack it up when she looked at me and asked me to stay with her one more night so she wouldn't be alone in the empty house. I reluctantly agreed.

As we got comfortable in bed, Monica came over close to me and looked me in the eyes. I saw a look like I had never seen in her before. It was a weary look and one that told me she was scared. Monica began to talk to me in a way she never had before. She was apologizing for all that she thought she had done wrong in the relationship. She knew I wanted a life with kids and to grow together. I had always talked about it, but she wanted nothing to do with kids until then. Before I knew it, she mounted me, and we cuddled with so much affection I fell for her all over again. She was so different and warm. She really wanted me like it was the first time we ever had sex, and she was so giving and wanted to be loved. There was no reservation between us. Why couldn't she have shown me this side of her before? Why couldn't we have talked things through? I really wanted us to be back together and make this work.

We talked and made love all night. We didn't even sleep.

The morning came, and we began taking the old junk furniture out to the local used furniture store and threw what we didn't want out. By noon, we had finished the job. I had lined up our friend that had a pickup truck to cart what Monica had wanted to her new, small flat in Hamilton later that day. We had an hour to go, and so we sat in the dining room on boxes while we waited. Then the phone rang. Monica looked at me as if she didn't want me to pick it up.

"Who'd be calling here?" I asked.

"I don't know," Monica replied.

I picked it up.

A voice came on. "Frank?"

"Yes."

It was Patty's sister Sherry. "I don't want to disturb you, but Patty asked me to call and find out what you are going to do."

"About what?" I asked in a confused tone.

"Are you going to stay in your marriage, or are you going to split for good?"

I looked at Monica, and she looked at me as if to say she knew who it was and why they were calling. "We're busy packing right now. I'll have to call you back, okay?" I hung up the phone.

I turned and looked at Monica as if to ask, "What's going on here?"

She said, "Well, are you staying or are you going? Don't argue with me, Frank. I know who was on the phone, and I know why they called. Make a decision."

Let's get you moved, and then we will talk about it, okay?"

"Whatever you want, Frank. I'm getting tired of all this back and forth," Monica stated with weary overtones.

"What I experienced last night was the woman I want. I'm afraid you'll go back to the old Monica," I blurted out, almost in tears.

"Do you love her, Frank?"

"No, I don't. I like her, have fun with her, and even care for her. I love you and always have. Can you say the same, Monica, or is it too late?"

"Let's get the move done," she said and left the room.

By late that night, we got Monica moved into her new flat and sat and ate pizza and had a couple of beers. Our friend decided to leave, and as he was walking down the stairs, he turned and asked Monica if she wanted him to stay. I got the message that he might have a thing for her. As I got up to leave, Monica got up, held me tight, and almost begged me to stay. "If you go out that door, Frank, I don't think you will ever come back again."

"I want to stay, Monica, like you would never believe. I have to think about it. What about my apartment? What about this place?"

"We can make the adjustment. It's only money, Frank. Don't go, please, Frank."

"I have to go for now. I'll call you in a day or two. Let's just take the time and think this through, okay?"

Monica didn't answer. She just smiled and slowly closed the door.

As I left into the night, I looked back one more time, hoping to see her looking out the window. She wasn't there.

I drove back and forth from Brantford to Hamilton daily for a number of months before I realized that most of my clients were being developed in the Brantford area. I was also a bit concerned that I was not making the commissions that I'd heard others were getting. This in itself was becoming a new awareness for me. I started questioning Wes as to my opportunities with Imperial Life, and the answers were always the same. "You have to get your sales up, and then we'll talk."

I was getting frustrated by the day and couldn't find any avenue that would open up for me. I finally decided to call the guy who'd gotten me into this business, Gord Lee. He was breaking loose from Wes and Imperial Life to represent Maritime Life as an independent agent. When I heard about his move, a light flashed in my head, and the realism of his actions started to make total sense. I could see that the life insurance business was opening up and becoming a new opportunity for those who wanted to expand the paradigm of the old traditional image of a life insurance agent. I always felt a sense of reservation going into a house, as if the client really did not want to deal with me . . . me being the product. The old image was this person arriving at your door and bringing up the topics of death and destruction. The real reason was that I was there to take money out of their paycheques and strap them even more for something they would not realize until they were dead.

I'll never forget the day that Wes went out on a call with me to a friend's house. Wes always wore the three-piece suit and a wide-brimmed fedora hat. He was the quintessential life insurance agent, if there ever was one, representing the uniform dress of the traditional door-to-door salesman. As soon as we entered the house, Wes took over.

"Let's sit down at the dining room table, please," he said to the couple.

We started some small talk when, out of nowhere, Wes jumped out of his chair, ran over to the refrigerator, and pulled open the door.

"Who is going to fill the fridge with food when you're dead and six feet under?"

"Who is going to clothe your wife and your kids?"

"Who's going to pay your mortgage when you're not here to provide for your family, sir?"

Then he ran to the curtained window in the dining room. All the while, he still had that hat on that made him look like an old forties detective.

"I'll tell you who will, if you let me? Are you interested to know, sir?"

I immediately looked over to my friend, and he was as shocked and befuddled as I.

"Uh, yes, I would like to know, ah, honey, do you know who is going to take my place?"

"The next guy, I guess," she jokingly responded.

We started to laugh, except for Wes. He stood straight and looked square in my friend's eyes, putting his face no more than a few inches from his eyes.

"There won't be anyone to take care of your wife and children." Wes paused for the longest time without moving. Then he slowly backed off and quietly began to talk.

"If you'll let me, I'll show you who will be there for your family. My company will be there to support them. Yes, that's right, my company."

"How's that?" my friend asked Wes.

Wes then went into a whole series of question answers and almost comically used the curtain as his flow chart. My friend was mesmerized by the show and production Wes put on in front of us. In the end, my friend bought a policy for $25 a month. That was a lot of money for him at the time, but he saw value, I think. I wasn't sure whether he bought just to get rid of Wes, help me, or because he really wanted the insurance, but Wes got the job done.

I never forgot that event, and from that moment on, I swore I would never do that to anyone or become that controlling in front of anyone as long as I was in this business.

"Rainbow," grunted Gord, "have you made your millions yet?" he asked sarcastically but friendly.

"Not yet, buddy. That's why I'm calling you," I stated with great enthusiasm.

"What's up, Rainbow?"

"I'd like to meet with you and talk about my future. I want to look at what you're doing and maybe work with you," I said.

"I don't know, Rainbow. I'm really busy, and I don't have the time to train you. I also have to tell you upfront, Frank, that I recently had to make a very big decision in order to be successful in what I'm doing. You see, Frank, I can only associate myself with successful people and those who will make me money. I cannot be associated with people like you anymore."

"People like me?" I asked in shock.

"Yes, people who can't think for themselves, who flounder around, kicking at the business when they feel like it. Most importantly, people who haven't made it successfully. You see, I have to think in big numbers like hundreds of thousands of dollars, not five hundred dollars. I have to stay in the circle of multi-millionaires and think like them so I can become them.

"Listen, Rainbow, let me know how you're doing from time to time, and maybe one day you'll be ready. Got to go now and see you later."

When I hung up the phone, I was totally destroyed. I had never been talked to like that before, and I'd thought Gord was my friend. Then the light switch came on. He'd told me what I had to do. *Think like a millionaire.* How was I going to do that?

A few days later, I called Gord again, and we talked over his point of view as buddies rather than business associates. He came up with an idea.

"Why don't you put together $100 and join me at a seminar I'm involved with in St. Catharine's next week? I think you might get something out of it."

"Alright, I'll be there. Who's speaking?" I asked.

"A man who's been through the business wars like no one has. He built four janitorial companies and has been bankrupt nine times. His name's Bob Proctor. He owns and operates Xeoxes Seminars. Imperial Life funded him to lecture every branch operation in Canada."

Gord met me at the hotel at 8:00 a.m. on the morning of the seminar. We sat in the front row, and Gord pre-empted me by saying, "This is your chance to be a part of my future, if you get the message today."

A slim man with reddish-blond hair came walking out to the front of the stage and stood beside a table. On the table was a funny-looking contraption, somewhat familiar to me from my high-school physics class. It had six silver balls, each attached by string hanging from a wooden frame. Without saying a thing, the man swung the end ball closest to him and let go, hitting the next and causing an ongoing pendulum reaction.

The whole crowd sat and watched for minutes before Bob Proctor began to talk.

"What do you see?" he asked.

"You're watching an illusion. This illusion is the fundamental element to all that goes on in our mind, action, and the very being of oneself. We're going to study today the human factors that make or break your aspirations, dreams, goals, and the very thing that creates the results to take you farther than you've ever have been before. You will learn today that, like this apparatus, for every action, there is an equal and opposite reaction. For every word you say, there will be a reaction, good or bad, right or wrong, motivating or indecisive."

I sat on the edge of my chair for the rest of the day, taking in every word Bob Proctor had to say. He brought on to the stage assistants who had gone through many adverse times in their lives. He presented concepts to help motivate the mind and exercises to train the mind to think and practise being successful.

By the time we left the room, I was so pumped up and wanted to get going that I felt like I was running out the door before reaching the hallway.

Gord laughed and said to me, "Use what you learned today wisely, Rainbow. What do you remember from the lecture and why?" Gord asked like the old man in David Carradine's TV show that ended each series by saying, "Snatch the pebble from my hand, grasshopper."

"Yes, for every action, there is an equal and opposite reaction. You got it, Rainbow. Now let me know how you do."

The first thing I did was go to a car dealership and stand in front of the car I really liked. I had the salesman take a picture of me and the car. It was a 1978 Porsche Cabrera 911. The price tag that year was $50,000. The salesman kept saying, "You're nuts to think you'll sell enough to buy this car."

I told him the story of the lecture and Bob Proctor, and he was very interested to see if I would accomplish this goal. Bob's theory was to imagine your goals and immediately bring them as close to reality as possible. The best way to accomplish this was to touch, feel, and see the goal. So, he recommended going and standing by the item and taking a picture. Then you would be motivated to earn the money to obtain the goal. He also talked about how each of us has a bank account with one million dollars in it. Our mission in life is to find the key to open up the account. The key is hidden in sales and the planning of the process. His theories were so fresh and new to me that I believed every word he spoke.

That day changed me in thought and actions for the rest of my life... both for the good and for the bad. As he stated, for every action, there is an equal and opposite reaction.

Chapter 13

Another hockey season was upon us, and I felt the need to go back. This time I had other motives. I needed to network and develop new clients. My intensity in my game was surely affected by my change in focus. I was not the player that I had been a few years back. The year coaching took a toll on my conditioning, but I was still able to keep up with the rest of the league. There were very few players from the 75/76 team, and there were a couple of new ones that came aboard. Still, we had fun.

I was taking Patty to the games, and we were getting closer as a couple. We were a bit of an odd couple, but we had fun most of the time. Doug Scheonfeld and his new wife hung out with us most of the time. We did have a lot in common. Doug and I went similar paths hockey-wise and ended up pretty much the same. Doug worked for a manufacturing company in Cambridge, and his wife was a secretary. I thought Patty might come out of her shell by associating with new people who were hard-working and fun-loving.

For the first while, Patty was getting more into the lifestyle our friends lived. Yet she struggled with her self-confidence, which caused concern for me. She was somewhat out of most people's level and found herself saying and doing things that made people take a second look at her.

We moved into an apartment in Cambridge, Ontario, and I found a job with Prudential Life. We were beginning to settle into a common form of life while I again struggled to get ahead with the company. Prudential was not a progressive, innovative marketing company but was entrenched in traditional systems of selling insurance. We had to maintain the old manual journal credit/debit book of clients, visiting old retirees, collecting the weekly premiums, ranging from twenty to thirty dollars a week to fifty cents. Selling new insurance was almost impossible because our day was spent accounting and bookkeeping and then prospecting for new clients. The products available at the time were redundant and out of touch with the times. I was ever increasingly becoming bored and restless.

I met a fellow salesman named Norm Caseren, and we became good friends. Norm was in a band called Copperfield, and I was very interested in Norm's ventures with them. Copperfield had a successful run in the early 70s with a hit song that reached regional levels of radio airplay. I spent many nights practising with them and then eventually became a member as the keyboard player and backup vocalist.

The Christmas party for Prudential that year was a crossroads for Patty and I. Norm and I played as a duo at the party and caught a lot of attention from the crowd. Patty was especially annoyed by one of the secretaries, who made it known that she was quite attracted to me and was obviously flirtatious. While I was talking to my manager and in deep discussion, my manager stopped and looked at me in shock. I immediately felt a wet and cold sensation overflowing on my head. Without warning, Patty was pouring a beer over my head. I then slowly turned to face her, and she began to scream, "You fucking asshole."

I slowly walked toward the coat check, got my coat, and walked out to my car. I was in total shock as I started my car and began to leave the parking lot. Patty came out of the building and stood in front of the car. I stopped, and she got in. I cannot remember all that she said, but she didn't stop yelling until we reached home. As we entered the apartment, I began to load up her belongings in garbage bags and then sat her down on the couch.

"I refuse to be embarrassed like this, and I will not live with someone who cannot control themselves in public. I do not know who you are, and right now, I do not want to be with you. I will take you back to your mother's in the morning." That night we slept in separate rooms.

In the morning, I got up to find Patty sitting on the stairs, waiting for me. She began to apologize and begged me to let her stay. I did after a lengthy discussion.

Two weeks later, she announced that she was pregnant.

Mentally, I was always thinking about being a father. I really wanted to have children. I had wanted children with Monica, but she wasn't prepared to even discuss the possibilities of children and family. Patty was always prepared. She was born to be a mother. Even though she was experiencing some psychological malfunctions, she showed her maternal instincts right from the get-go.

The next nine months were textbook. Patty took good care of her health and totally enjoyed the attention everyone was giving her. I was in a very good space because the attention was on her, and I could do no wrong. My time was spent playing music in the band and assisting Patty. I took a new job with a communications company selling two-way radios, and as well I worked part-time on a loading dock, trying to raise extra money to buy a house.

In Patty's seventh month of pregnancy, we finally were able to get married legally. Due to the circumstances at hand, we went to the justice of the peace in Brantford and officially commenced the paperwork at 12:00 p.m. on June 27th, 1979. After the ceremony, our witnesses—Patty's cousins, Ted Carriere, a Brantford police officer, and his wife—met us at MacDonald's restaurant in the drive-thru for a "Big Mac Meal Deal" to celebrate the marriage. Out of the police cruiser, Ted uncorked a bottle of Baby Duck, and we drank it in the parking lot in MacDonald's sippy cups.

Then on October 11, 1979, at approximately 11:30 a.m., while we were eating breakfast at a restaurant located across from the Cambridge Memorial Hospital, Patty went into labour. All she kept saying, while I was trying to finish my bacon and eggs was, "This damn kid is kicking the hell out of me. He's either a hell of an eater, or he's going to be a great field goal kicker. Oh . . . I think my water is breaking." I then carried her out of the restaurant and got her across the street to the emergency room. Within minutes she was ushered into the delivery area.

The pain seemed to be steady, but Patty held her own through a long and painful labour period of, I think, three or four hours. The doctor decided to induce her. The actual birth was quick and straightforward, but the doctor had to cut Patty to give more room to allow a less stressful birth. As the head appeared, I was overwhelmed with joy and excitement as I witnessed the birth of my boy, Daren. He was a healthy and very much awake seven-pound eleven-ounce bundle of happiness.

I'm a father with a son! God has blessed me, I kept thinking as I held my little man. How beautiful he was and alert. His hands and fingers were so tiny, and they moved with mine as I gently rubbed his palm with my finger. I will never forget that moment for the rest of my life.

There were a lot of tears and fears that took up our emotions as we fumbled through the first few months of baby care. But we learned and got really good at it. I finally made enough money to make a down payment on a semi-detached house in Kitchener, Ontario. We were very proud and enjoyed our life as parents.

Money was an issue, and I just couldn't seem to make enough to cover the bills. I did have a decent job, but after taxes, there just wasn't enough to cover everything, so Patty agreed to get a part-time job at Zellers. I would work until 5:00 p.m. and then go to my second job Monday through Thursday. On Friday, Saturday, and Sunday, Patty worked. That was my time to be with my little man. Saturday afternoons were our special time. I would put the record player on and listen to Supertramp while Daren bopped up and down in his stand-up jumper and played with his toys in his playpen. Sometimes my long-time friend Paul Godfrey, the radio broadcaster, would drop by, and we'd drink beer while caring for Daren. It was good times, and memories were really made for me during those months.

Except for one night while Patty was working, when I had just put three-month-old Daren to bed in his room on the second level. I had just begun cooking some French fries in a shallow pan when the phone rang. We only had one phone, and stupidly, it was located in the basement rec room. So, without a thought, I ran down to answer the phone. I wasn't on it more than twenty seconds when coming back upstairs, I could see a flickering reflection on the hallway wall, and I could smell something more than French fries burning.

When I arrived in the kitchen, I was shocked to find the pan of fries on fire and the cupboards burning. My first reaction was to grab the burning pan and get it outside. It was winter, and snowbanks lined the driveway. I rushed to the door, threw the pan in the snowbank, re-entered the kitchen, grabbed some baking soda, and tried to put the fire out. I was able to douse the flames, but the smoke was so bad I had to open all the windows and doors.

Then I realized Daren was upstairs, and the smoke would all be in his room. I ran up and grabbed him out of his bed and ran to the next-door neighbours. While running, I cleared his nostrils from any black soot and checked his breathing. He was fine. My neighbours were our babysitters, and they were right there for Daren. As my next-door friend and I started back to my house to check the damage, pain set in my hands like I was on fire. I looked at my hands, and all I could see was red flesh and skin hanging off the back of my hands. I almost passed out. My friend drove me to the clinic to get attention. I had third-degree burns on both hands and a burnt sweater. I was very lucky to have gotten Daren out in time. My injuries were not an issue for me. Daren's safety was everything.

When I could find the time, I was still a playing member with Copperfield, but my time was limited. I eventually had to leave the band. My friendship was ongoing with Norm, and we would get together from time to time.

However, Patty joined a baseball team run by her brother-in-law. His coach was an old coach of Patty's. One night, Patty was out until two in the morning, and I was quite concerned and upset that she would stay out that late. I noticed headlights pull into our driveway, and by the time I went outside, I caught her and her old coach making out in the car's front seat. I lost it so bad that the coach sped out of the driveway so fast he almost hit a sign on the other side of the road. Patty and I got into a verbal fight. I was never able to get over that incident. I could never trust her again.

There were to be many similar events that occurred as time went on. We separated for a month but got back together after I had a long conversation with my dad. He made it very clear to me that I had made choices to raise my child, and I must not walk away from Daren. I swore to my dad that I would never leave my son. My dad made it very clear that Daren was more important than my life. He said, "No matter how tough it gets, you're living for your child. Now get on with it."

So . . . I did. Two months later, Patty was pregnant again.

Selling two-way radios just wasn't doing it for me. I wanted more, needed to make more money, and needed to be in a more lucrative environment. I went back to selling life insurance for Imperial Life in Hamilton. The management was new, and I felt I could do more and learn how to get into better sales markets.

Patty agreed to move to Hamilton, and we rented an old, very large house in Ancaster just outside of Hamilton. Our Kitchener house was rented out until I sold it for its original value. My father was not happy with me. I was very depressed by this time. Nothing seemed to be working for us. Money was very tight, and sales were not going well at all. I had to rent rooms out of the rented house just to cover the heating bill. We were getting further and further behind financially.

Patty was acting up again, and this time, she was not taking care of herself like she had during the first pregnancy. She was drinking a little, and she was smoking. I had to drag her out of a bar one night, which caused us to get into an argument. She ended up breaking my guitar over my head. After that incident settled down, I knew things had to change, so rather than leave, I decided to sink myself into making money. I had to do something drastic, or we would perish and have to go bankrupt.

The second baby was about to arrive. It was January 30, 1981. The weather was cold, and the time was closing in on 10:00 p.m. "It's time," Patty announced while she screamed in excruciating pain. Off we went to MacMaster University Hospital in Hamilton. Michael arrived with a bit of trouble. He needed to be turned around inside the womb, and if that wasn't enough of a challenge, when he popped his head out, the umbilical cord was wrapped around his neck. So, back in the womb he went while the doctors scrambled to save him. They did a great job, and Michael came into the world screaming—seven pounds eight ounces, lungs like a screech owl, and an appetite like a bobcat constantly on the hunt. He was definitely attached to his mother right from the get-go and was never too far from her clutches. He was a handful, but I saw great physical potential in him the moment he was born.

Now with two boys, a wife, and a looming bankruptcy, I had to do something quickly. We were sinking fast, and I saw no way out. *What can I do?*

So, I called Gord Lee again.

"Rainbow! What's shaking?" Gord asked in his half-baked tone.

"Gord, I really need to talk with you. I want to work with you. I'll do whatever it takes to work for you."

The phone went silent. Then Gord started in, "Okay, you got me at the right time. I need an understudy because I'm in a very lucrative stock deal that requires all my time, which means someone's got to take care of the insurance side of my business. I'll teach you, and you'll make more money than you ever imagined. Be in my office in Cambridge tomorrow at about 11:00 a.m."

When I arrived, he was sitting in his office on the phone and motioned me in to sit down. When he got off the phone, he walked over to a tripod and started to explain the new methods of selling a revolutionary product line offered by Maritime Life. The plan, in a caption, was to replace existing policies, held by competitive companies, with new, higher-interest-bearing products. You must understand that the insurance industry was traditionally against and/or very cautious about the replacement of existing policies between companies. It was legal only if the necessary forms were signed and properly submitted to the appropriate departments. The plan and system actually made sense to me for the first time, and I could see myself doing what he was telling me to do. By the end of the day, I had it down and was ready to go. Gord then said, "Be in the office the next day by nine in the morning because we're going on a road trip to Toronto."

I was excited. He was really taking me under his wing. I was about to be exposed to the big-money world I'd always wanted to experience. I couldn't sleep that night just thinking about the changes I was to make and how my world would open up to meet my dreams.

Gord and I talked all the way to Toronto about everything from business to personal goals. As we parked, Gord instructed me to stay in the car while he met with some people. He assured me he wouldn't be long.

Well, he was almost two hours. I was getting nervous by the time he arrived but forgot all about the agitation as we drove away.

"I've got to go see a house on the Bridal Path. I might be buying it."

"Holy shit," I replied. "That's about one million or so dollars, right?"

"Yeah, probably more like five million, Rainbow," Gord replied with a smile on his face. As we pulled up onto the circular drive, I was amazed at the size of the mansion and the large lot. It was like in the movies.

A strawberry-blond-haired guy about our age came out of the front door and motioned Gord very nervously to go inside. "Who's this guy, Gordo?" the guy asked, abruptly motioning to me. "He's my driver," Gord answered. Many years later, I would find out this was the son of George Mara Sr., one of the Silver Seven that literally ran the Toronto Maple Leafs with Harold Ballard during the 1960s Stanley Cup era.

To date, George Mara Jr. has become one of my best friends, as you will learn later.

Gord wasn't more than fifteen minutes with George. We left and headed back to Cambridge. When we got to the office, Gord said, "You're to be in the office every day by nine o'clock. You're running the show. Make me proud."

"Okay, but Gord, do I get a paycheque or am I on commission?"

"Rainbow, a thousand a week until you make enough commission that you don't need my thou ... got it?"

"Right on!" I replied with excitement. I was only making $600 a month with Imperial Life at the time. I immediately went to my office in Hamilton, emptied it out, and quit Imperial Life. The manager looked at me and said, "You've made a very bad mistake."

I said, "How can going from $600 a month to $4,000 a month be a big mistake?

"Gord's in deep with the wrong people, and he'll take you down with him. I know what I'm talking about, and you need to trust what I'm saying, Frank."

"How do you know this?"

"I just know. Remember, I'm a retired captain in the Canadian Armed Forces. I have friends, very special friends."

"I'll take my chances," I replied.

And so I did. The first month was amazing. I sold almost $6,000 in commission. Gord was pleased. Soon I was getting calls from ex-employees of Imperial Life's Hamilton office, looking for work. Bob Ward, a fifty-six-year-old guy who I thought was the right choice to work for us was more than welcome to join our little group. Bob used to own a very successful clothing shop in downtown Hamilton during my time at Royal Trust. I used to window shop almost every day at lunchtime and dream about wearing his suits. Unfortunately, he suffered some bad times and went bankrupt. A friend introduced him to the life insurance business, and Bob joined Imperial Life. We trained and worked together. He was so much fun and very funny. His enthusiasm was infectious and addictive, which made him a great door opener.

So, off we went to make our fortunes with the master, Gord Lee.

"Rainbow, come into my office for a minute," Gord asked in a quiet tone. "I need you to do something for me, and there is a great reward for you personally by doing what I need you to do."

"Okay, what do you need, Gord?" I asked enthusiastically.

I need you to go to London and meet a stockbroker—his name doesn't matter—and sign a DAP account in your name. I'll be depositing stock and transacting stock in your name through this account. You're fully safe from any liability. The upside is you will be establishing about $250,000 worth of credit under your name. You'll be able to create lines of credit at any bank for yourself." Gord sat back with a big smile on his face like he had just handed me a brass ring.

I was overwhelmed with excitement, thinking I had just hit the jackpot. I didn't realize that Gord had just set me up to help him box stock. Boxing stock is how promoters stimulate an increase in day trading and inflate stock prices, mainly to excite and entice new investor groups and attract more investment activity. The downside to this manoeuvre is that if stock prices drop and are below the account's margin, the brokerage house will call the owner of the account to pay the difference in cash within seven working days.

I was completely ignorant of these facts and had no clue what Gord was up to. I didn't even know what stock I was trading. Needless to say, off I went to London, Ontario to sign my life away; at the time, I thought I was signing my way to becoming a millionaire. When I got back, Gord announced he had lined up a meeting for me with the local CIBC bank manager to set up my personal accounts and new credit lines. *Wow*, I said to myself. *This is for real!*

The meeting went well with my new friend, CIBC Guy. The first thing he did was establish a checking account with a $2,000 overdraft. He then set up a Visa card with a $2,000 limit. Finally, he set up a personal signature loan for $10,000 in order for me to buy stock. All of the above was done on Gord's word. I had no assets, and my credit, by that time, was questionable. There were no questions asked or answers required. I filled out the paperwork, and away I went.

The next day, Gord sat me down again and began explaining the stock play that he was so entrenched in with another man named Rob Kelly from Kitchener, Ontario. Rob was a well-known stockbroker and real estate and business owner. His prize holding was the Doon Racquet Club, situated between Kitchener and Cambridge, located on land in the country nestled alongside the 401 highway. You could barely see it from the highway because it was built in the middle of the forest that lined the countryside. To get to it, you had to drive through a thick section of evergreens that almost covered the paved one lane. Only the who's who of K/W and Cambridge were members at the time. The wealthy who played their games there—and I mean games both on the court and off—would have made most private clubs jealous, to say the least.

This was 1980, and the stock and real estate markets were strong and healthy. We felt that the opportunities and flow of money were endless and readily available to that specific group. I was only invited to the open receptions because I was not accepted as a qualified member, and I had not paid $10,000 as an annual member's fee. Also, there was an inner circle that followed Rob and Gord. This group was old friends that had grown up with both of them and were together through high school and university. Their parents were either doctors, lawyers, or owners of prominent businesses located within the area. The "Rat Pack" of K/W and Cambridge had made it big, especially with this stock play that Gord and Rob controlled.

Gord began to unravel the deal to me as we sat in his office. "We're running two stocks, both listed on the Alberta exchange. Both stocks are oil and gas holdings. The assets are lease holdings in the provinces of Alberta and BC. We're negotiating two properties in Utah and Montana. The actual drilling company is Surf Oil, and the holding company is Redial. Both separately listed. Now, you will buy on my direction, and all your stock must be held in the DAP account you just opened in London. You have signed a power of attorney document, which was amongst the papers you signed the other day, which gives me the right to direct any activity in that account. This is done to control the account due to potential market fluctuations. This is to protect you, Frank. The stocks have just completed a stock split, giving three to one. The price is $8 and will drop to around the $3.50 mark. This was done to open up more stock to offer the open market. Oh, I've just bought in your account the full $250,000 available under your name."

I did not understand a single word he said except that my mind led me to believe I'd just got $250,000 of stock. I had never bought a stock in my life to that point, and I definitely did not comprehend what had just happened.

"Now get on with your business and go and make money. I'll fill you in as we go." Gord got up from his desk and left the office.

I walked out in a daze and went into Bob's office. "Let's go get a drink." Bob was always up for a drink. "In fact, let's shut the office down and take the two girls out. The two girls were our secretary and Barb, who was a salesperson brought in by Gord."

We partied all afternoon, eating and drinking until five, when the girls had to go home. Bob and I stayed and had one last beer.

"You wouldn't believe what happened this week, Bob."

"No, you won't believe what happened this week, Frank," Bob responded in a joking tone.

"You first, Bob."

"Well, Gord had me do something that totally changed my life." Bob then began to detail the exact same trail of events that I had just gone through.

When he finished, I sat in shock and wonderment. *What has just happened to us?* I asked myself as Bob rambled on about how he was going to be able to put his daughter through university now, and this would change his status with his wife. Gord had just saved him from another bankruptcy. Before I said a thing to Bob, I couldn't believe Gord would have done what he did out of goodwill. *What was his motive? What's going on here?*

"Doesn't this all seem kind of strange to you, Bob? Like, why us? Who in their right mind just turns over half a million dollars to two employees?"

"Yeah, Gord is a weird one and lives in a different world, and maybe this is the way things are done in the big game world but, man, why us?"

Bob sat and was a little bent over the table, fidgeting with a coin as I was talking, then he looked up and said, "It's not only you and me. Barb's in as well."

"Holy shit!" I blurted out in surprise. "You know they just did a stock split—"

"Three for one," Bob quickly interjected. "It really doesn't mean anything significant to our position. For that matter, we're just holders of the stock, Frank. We get the benefit at the bank, not the money."

"Bob, what do you mean?" I asked.

"You can leverage the holdings from the DAP account. The CIBC guy won't check it out. He's on the take with Gord. He'll call on Gord's holdings if there are problems. That's how Gord's got it set up."

I started fidgeting with a straw and then I responded to Bob, "So Gord won't be out a dime on the wages he's paying us? The bank is on the hook?"

"You got it, Pontiac!"

"What a fucking con," I answered in disgust. "What do we do now, Bob?"

"Ha, go for the ride, my son. Now, this is not confirmed, what we have just been talking about, and we must never let anyone know what we are thinking for two reasons. First is that Gord would fuck us up so bad financially that all of us would be bearing down over a million dollars of debt to repay. Secondly, this smells of fraud right from the get-go. You were a cop, Frank. Don't you see this?"

I hadn't gotten that far in training yet. The criminal code was the sergeants and the chief if we needed interpretation. Nowadays, the marine police are trained in Aylmer at the police college. They know what they're doing.

Bob started laughing and finished his beer. "You are so naïve, Frank, for a guy who has been a cop, worked for Royal Trust, and been in the insurance business for the past four years. I have to admit, Gord saw you coming. You were perfect for his plan."

"What about you, Bob?" I responded. "What the fuck is different between me and you?"

Bob looked up with a smile and answered after looking me in the eye. "This is my last chance to make a hit that will get my family back. I told you, my daughter is counting on me and my wife? Hell, she has had enough. I'm fifty-six years old and in bad health. What chance of landing a big-paying job have I got? I'm finished on all counts. I need this more than I need air!

"You're twenty-seven. You have time for second and third chances to turn things around, and you're healthy and good-looking. Anyone would hire you—"

I cut Bob short. "Time to go, Bob. I got a lot of thinking to do."

Bob responded, "Don't think too much, or you'll fuck it all up! Go home and take the wife and kids out for dinner."

That is what I did, and then I drank at least ten more beers until I passed out.

The next two weeks were spent selling and learning the new methods of selling replacement techniques from the Gordo. He would come in at 11:00 a.m. and leave at 1:00 p.m. He was off somewhere, busy promoting the stock.

As that month went by, Gord was harder to find. Days and, eventually, the whole week passed without even a telephone call from him. We were getting worried.

Bob arrived on a Monday morning at about 10:00 a.m., almost running into the office. "Have you seen the news on TV?" he asked in a very loud and nervous voice.

"No," I answered as I emerged from my office.

They just announced trading is halted on Surf and Radial. The stock had split three for one two weeks earlier, dropping the price from $13 a share to $4.50. The stock had dropped within the first two hours of trading to $1.13!" Bob cried out in despair. "We're so fucked!"

"What the hell?" I responded as my heart started to race and panic crept into my body.

"Get on the phone, Frank. Find that motherfucker now!" Bob demanded.

The phone rang and rang at Gord's house, but no one answered. We tried to contact him for the rest of the day, to no avail. At about 7:00 p.m. that night, we all decided to go home and keep trying to contact Gord.

"Let's be here tomorrow morning at 8:00 a.m., everyone, and we'll investigate what's going on and see if there is any change in the status of the stocks," I commanded.

The next morning, we all arrived at the office, and the team was very tired from a lack of sleep. Anyone get a hold of Gord?" I asked.

"No."

"Let's call the brokerage house and talk to James." I picked up the phone and first ring he picked it up.

"Frank Trousdell, here, so I think you know why I'm calling, James."

"Yes, Frank . . . not good, not good," he answered in a shaken tone. We're trying to find out what took place on Friday and who's involved that caused the collapse. You see, Frank, usually when this happens—and it does happen sometimes, not often, mind you, but it happens from time to time—"

"What actually happened?" I asked James.

"You don't know?"

"We haven't seen or heard from Gord for the past five days. No one has said anything at all to us here in Cambridge."

"You've got to be kidding! Well, I'll fill you in. Last week, Gord and Rob were negotiating a very big transaction with a group in Alberta. They were to buy a very large amount of stock that would bring the value of the stock up to $10. Midnight Thursday, they backed out, causing the stock to drop Friday morning. But on top of that, an unsuspecting group began shorting the market at the same time.

"Normally, a well-financed company would be able to offset the short from the treasury, buy off the short calls, and stabilize the activity. Unfortunately, this short-call activity is part of the game, and most big deals billed contingencies for the possibilities. Obviously, there is something wrong in this whole deal, and there will be serious questions by the Securities Commission on this one. That's why the exchange halted trading so fast.

"Frank, you and the crew there had better make arrangements to cover your accounts by next week. I can only hold off the 'house' from taking action on your accounts for so long. I'm really sorry, Frank. Good luck!"

"Fuck!" I responded as I hung up the phone.

Bob looked at me and knew the results were going to be devastating. "What are we going to do now, Frank?"

We're going to wait and find Gord. We're not reacting to this just yet. First thing we need to do is contact Rob Kelly or Gord's brokerage house here in Kitchener. He deals with a broker there that's on the inside. I've heard his name spoken by Gord many times, referring to him as a partner. I think it's Jim Garland."

"Okay, then what?" Bob and Barb asked.

"We keep selling insurance; one fuck of a lot of insurance. I think we're going to need a lot of money in a very short time frame."

"You don't think we are going to get stuck with the DAP accounts do you, Frank?" Barb asked.

I looked out the window and pondered the answer for a few seconds. "I'm afraid we are going to be sued, at least, if we do not negotiate something first."

"Well, I bet you guys are ready to hang me out to dry about now, aren't you?" The familiar gravelly voice of Gord came from the doorway to the board room.

"Where the hell have you been?" we all responded almost in unison.

"Sit down, everyone. There's a lot to discuss."

"What happened?" was our first question to the elusive Gordo. We told him what we had learned and what our fears were.

"I'm busy for the next while, trying to straighten out this event, so I need all of you to continue to work as usual and sell insurance. Frank, I'll need to talk to you alone, so . . . get back to work, everyone."

"Not so fast, Gord," Bob interrupted. "What about the DAP accounts? We're gonna get a margin call, and you said not to concern ourselves about the accounts. What do we do?"

Gord looked at Bob with cold and vicious eyes like I'd never before seen Gord use on anyone. "I will cover everyone's accounts. I promised you no one would get hurt, and I will stick to my word."

"How do we answer the calls we're going to get, Gord?" Barb asked calmly.

"Advise the caller to call me and tell them I will be resolving the accounts." Then he turned to me. "Now, Frank. My office, please," Gord commanded.

As we left the board room, I looked at Bob and Barb, and the looks on their faces told it all. They were scared shitless.

"So, Rainbow, this is your time to rise up and take control. You now own my brokerage firm as of this moment on. I will advise Maritime Life to direct all residual payments to you so you can keep the office open, and you are now the agent of record on the existing clients."

"Why are you doing this, Gord?" I asked in complete bewilderment.

"I'll lose everything I've built if I do nothing, Frank. You'll need to contact Maritime Life within the week and arrange banking etc. In the meantime, you'll have to deal with the landlord and the utilities. I haven't paid them for at least two or three months . . . I can't remember." Gord trailed off as he looked out the window like he was trying to think of what to say next.

Gord and I spent the next hour going through his desk and files, so I knew where to get everything I needed to figure out what we were left. I could see Gord's weariness and shaken confidence start to show while he exposed to me more and more business problems that he had ignored for the past two or three months.

Then, like nothing was out of the ordinary, he stood up and said, "You're on your own now, Rainbow! You won't hear from me again for some time. Please don't try to contact me or try and find me. I have to go away for a while to work on the stock mess. Maybe we'll be back in business again soon. Either way, Frank, you have the opportunity of a lifetime. Make the best of it, Rainbow!"

Gord left like he'd arrived that morning—quiet, quick, and without notice. I knew he was really gone, and he wouldn't be found by anyone. I suspected the worst for him from that moment on. Yet deep inside, I sensed he would surface bigger and stronger than ever. We had no idea who he owed or who would be chasing him down. I was starting to worry about how we would be implicated if there were people looking for him. *What if the police started an investigation?* I began thinking as I sat in Gord's chair. *Will we be instigated as associates? Should we get legal advice?*

The rest of the week was spent organizing all the bills that had not been paid. Bob and Barb stepped in to help. "What a mess," Barb said on the Friday morning. "In order to keep the office open, we need to raise at least $30,000 by next week just to pay up the outstanding accounts. Then we have to raise enough to carry on the operation."

"That number is at least $15,000!" I responded.

"I ain't got it," Bob snorted out in disgust.

"None of us have it," I responded. "Let's put our heads together and find a way out of this without losing the book of business Gord's left us. Don't forget, Gord has made over $150,000 a year for the past four years. He has one of the best books in town. Ninety percent of the clients are doctors and professional specialists in the medical field. The book is a gold mine, and we own it."

Just as I made the statement, a voice rang in my head. It was Gord telling me he had given the book of business to *me*, not to the group. I felt it best not to argue this point at this time in order to avoid a mutiny when I needed them the most.

I explained, "We cannot disturb the accounts in order to perpetuate the residual income, and to the best of my accounting, it would be far in excess of $100,000 per annum."

Bob sat back and said, "Why not close the actual office and sell the book to someone who will pay at least that and take us on as agents?"

"I think that's a very good possibility and is what we should do after I go through the transference procedure of the ownership of the book," I responded.

"Bob, you contact the most successful broker in Hamilton-Wentworth and set up an appointment. Don't reveal anything to them. Just tell them we're interested in discussing a merger or a sale. Don't tell them anything about what happened."

"They're gonna want to know what happened to Gord to give us the business, aren't they?" Bob asked.

"More than likely, Bob, and your answer will be that we acquired the business from Gord some time ago. That's all you say."

"Okay, I've got it."

"Barb, any ideas?"

"Not yet, but I'll make some calls over the weekend. By the way," Barb continued, "how and when are we going to get paid now?"

"Good question. I will see if the bank is still on, or if we are screwed there as well. If I can activate my overdraft account, I'll advance enough for all of us to get through the next couple of weeks, okay?"

"Thank you, Frank," both Barb and Bob responded.

"Let's get the fuck out of here and get drunk!" Bob commanded with pleasure.

"I think we all deserve it," I stated with finality.

"Unbelievable," was all Barb could say.

Monday morning, Bob stated with enthusiasm, "We got an appointment with Colling and Baird in Waterdown tomorrow. I'd talked to them before I joined Gord, and they were going to hire me. They weren't too happy when I'd turned them down."

"What did you tell them?" I asked.

"Just that Gord had rolled his business over to pursue other business ventures. We got the book and feel that selling and merging with another company such as theirs would be a more practical solution than running it ourselves."

"Would they consider setting up in Cambridge?" I asked.

"Possibly," Bob responded. "They're expanding their outlets and are going more into the life and benefits business. Their core focus has been general insurance for the past twenty years. They are one of the leading companies in Ontario."

"My only concern is that we're somewhat of a group of renegades in the business. We're on the cutting edge of transitional sales approaches to the life business. A lot of traditional companies don't like us because we're attacking their clients," I interjected.

Bob answered, "We can only determine whether they are our kind of people and think as we do."

That same Monday early afternoon, I got a call from a fellow Kinsmen member, Cam Yule. He was a representative of McClellan General Insurance Agency in Kitchener. His company was the largest and most successful agency in the area. I was very impressed with the company, especially their innovative approach to their niche market. They only dealt with successful multimillion-dollar businesses and professionals earning incomes in excess of $100,000 annually. I was fortunate because he took me on simply out of fellowship as Kinsmen.

He'd heard the hints of what was going on and was interested in getting the skinny on what was happening to the book of business. It's real funny how the word gets around, especially in Kitchener/Waterloo. The sister cities were modest in physical size, but had a population of about 250,000. The uniqueness of the area was its fundamental wealth. The rest of the country could be suffering terribly, but K/W never missed a beat. No one was in financial trouble, it seemed.

There was a reason for this stability. The old money is very old and well protected. The city was founded by German immigrants some 200 years ago. The farms and businesses were entrenched and financed by old German heritage money brought in from the fatherland, some say secretly, in gold bullion and artifacts. Some even go as far to suggest quietly that during the Second World War and early after, K/W was a drop point for stolen Jewish wealth. Anything was possible back then, and those early families were very intelligent and well connected, both governmental and otherwise.

"So, Frank, what the hell is going on?" Cam asked in his humorous fashion.

"It's a very interesting time, Cam," I responded.

"Fill me in, my friend; I might be able to help you."

"Well, Cam, I think we may sell the book," I revealed with caution.

"I thought so, and so do my partners over here," Cam answered. "I can set up a meeting for you, Frank. Is tomorrow okay?"

"No, Cam, we're meeting with another party tomorrow. Let me get back to you after the meeting, and we'll set up with you. I promise you that we won't make any decision until after we meet with your people," I answered with confidence oozing over the phone. I could feel the smile on Cam's face as we concluded the call.

"We're in the most powerful position anyone could ever be at this point," I spewed out to Bob, who was standing in the doorway. "Okay, Bobby, my man, let's get our paperwork together for tomorrow. We're about to make a shit load of money by the end of the week, which I can taste as if we were eating a juicy steak right off this desk," I joked as we started to prepare our presentation.

I've got to tell you, at this point, none of us had any idea what we were doing. I had no clue about the proper form the paperwork needed to be in or the system of presentation. I had never sold a business or completed proper books. All we had were the previous statements from Gord's accountant and current statements from the existing insurance companies carrying the clients. Barb brought in a book to show examples of forms and statements that we could copy. So, for the next twenty-four hours, we began to build a prospectus and business plan.

Chapter 14

Three of us arrived simultaneously in Waterdown for the 11:00 a.m. meeting with Donald Baird, the founding principal. Don was a thirty-four-year-old self-made millionaire who started as a chartered accountant after university and then bought his first general insurance business five years into practising accounting. Over the past six years, he had grown his business to be a very successful agency within the Burlington and Hamilton area.

I always find it amazing how you can tell that a person is a CA just by their appearance and physical stature. Stone-faced, pale-skinned, and somewhat frail. They always wear less than expensive suits but usually three-piece and mostly polyester. Sitting at the head of the board room table was this short, white-skinned man with a blue polyester three-piece suit, hair parted perfectly on the side with no indication that he was in any sort interested in partying whatsoever or going for a drink at a local strip club after work. He didn't even smile as we entered the room.

"Have a seat, please. Let me see your presentation before you start, thank you. I need to read what you have before I am prepared to hear what you have to say."

Totally taken back, I gave him his copy. He leafed through it very quickly a couple of times and then began to speak in a quick and monotone voice.

"You have a very interesting opportunity. I am interested in expanding into Cambridge and establishing a new market niche. Your book is very interesting in that you control a sound fundamental client base. The income looks to be adequate to cash flow the first year of operation. Now it comes down to your ability to sustain sales growth and meet the kind of targets required to meet the business model we have here at Baird. I do not see that here in your proposal," Don said as he vigorously leafed again through our pages, mumbling to himself about how he would have to install accounting systems and train us to function as a Baird operation.

Then finally, he looked up and said, "I am fine with your suggested offer but must review it to counter your price for the book. I will respond within the next twenty-four hours. Thank you and have a nice day." He showed us to the door, and that was it.

"Well, we got a deal!" Bob said as we went to the cars.

"What the deal really is has yet to be determined," Barb added.

"Let's go to the office and make some changes to the presentation for tomorrow's meeting with Cam's people," I responded to them both.

Bob asked, "Who we are meeting with tomorrow?"

"We are meeting the firm of Lackner, McPhail, St. Hill Life Insurance Agency . . . the most prestigious and wealthiest operation in K/W," I answered with a great deal of pride and confidence.

The next day we drove together and arrived outside of a large, converted heritage house situated two blocks from downtown Kitchener. We were immediately asked to sit and wait in a very posh, comfortable room furnished with wing-back leather chairs. We could tell the building had been renovated to perfection. A well-dressed lady ushered us to a very large second-level office that projected the image of a very successful, wealthy director or lawyer. Sitting at a large hand-carved wooden desk was a man who one would think had stepped out of an international magazine advertisement selling very expensive suits, ties, and shirts. Everything on him looked brand new and fit to perfection. I noticed he must exercise daily and was military fit.

"Hello, I'm Jim Lackner, the principal director of Lackner, McPhail, St. Hill." I stretched my hand out and introduced my colleagues and myself. He smiled and directed us to a round table for us to sit. The same lady arrived again, and this time, Jim introduced her as Lynn, his personal administrator.

"Coffee or juice, anyone?"

"No, thank you, I responded, but Barb and Bob both obliged. I had learned this move from Gord, not to take a drink if you are leading the discussion. The rest must have a drink to divert the attention of the two that are to be in the conversation.

"I heard that you are now in control of the Lee book. Frank, you have a very valuable commodity in your possession."

"We think so," I answered.

"What has happened to Gord?" Jim asked in an innocent non-suspecting tone.

"He's now focusing on the stock market and his oil and gas companies."

Jim chuckled and said, with a bit of sarcasm, "You think he'll survive this mess he's in? I know some people in the area that have lost their life savings in that deal. They're selling almost everything in order to bail out. Let me tell you, they are not very happy."

"I'm not one to say, Jim. I have no knowledge of what, who, or how much is involved. We're only involved in selling life insurance and have a book of business that we feel needs attention."

"Well, I am all ears, Frank. What's your plan?" Jim asked in a casual but suspicious voice.

I walked through our presentation and numbers with some stumbling but satisfactorily completed the first part of the task.

"So, what do you propose we do for you?" Jim asked.

"Number one, you buy the book at a fair market value. We believe the book is worth three times its annual revenue."

"That would be at least $300,000," Jim responded without twitching a muscle.

I looked directly into his eyes and continued. "Number two, you must house the three of us as employees, paying annual salaries plus bonuses of $60,000 per annum and a 70/30 split on the commission."

"Interesting," Jim responded. He then continued, "Would you mind waiting here while I have a quick meeting with my partners?"

"No, go right ahead," I respectfully responded.

As Jim left the room, Bob looked over at me with that big smile and said, "Where did those numbers come from?"

I smiled back and answered, "If we're going to do a deal with these guys, we've got to go big or get completely ripped off. They're going to try and take us to the cleaners; that's what they do in this league."

"You don't think they'll pay us the money upfront, Frank?" Barb asked.

"Hell no," I responded. "We'll be lucky to get a salary."

"Well, there's no deal," Bob grunted in his normal quick reaction. "Baird will pay us something. Baird will do the same as these guys."

"What we want is stability and guarantees for once, don't you think?" I answered.

"You're right, Frank. That's what I want," Barb quietly stated.

"Well, whatever you think is right, Frank. It's in your hands now," Bob concluded.

Jim re-entered and sat down almost seconds after we finished our confidential discussion. "My partners are reluctant to pay the upfront fee. They feel there isn't enough security to ensure that the book stays on the books once the word gets out that Gord's gone. No offence to you folks, but every seasoned agent will be gunning to replace carriers the moment they can. But we feel very supportive of you and your dilemma that Gord has left you to handle. So, our offer is this; we will hire the three of you to manage the book and sell new insurance. We will train you to sell our way. You will all be on three months' probation and must meet an agreed target for completed business. If you fail, you are released from any involvement with the firm. There will be no buy-out of the book. Your wages will be $42,000 the first year with the 70/30 split."

Bob piped up and asked, "But we haven't been paid for the past month. Can you not see your way to invest something in us upfront?"

"What do you need?" Jim asked

"I think at least $5,000 each should get us through."

Jim thought for a few seconds and came back with his offer of $3,000 each . . . only if we took the deal right then and committed to start Monday.

I looked at Barb and Bob, and they acknowledged yes. "We'll sign and receive the cheques today, and you have a deal, Jim."

"We can do that," he answered me with a smile. He knew he'd got us good, but he showed respect to me personally just by the way he looked at me and with the firmness of his handshake. I felt that I could work with him. I wanted to work for the firm. I was really excited. The image of the building and the people were like my fantasies of the perfect successful environment. *I've made it*, I was thinking as we walked through the building to the door.

Jim pulled me aside. "Can I have a quick word with you, Frank?"

"Sure," I said as we ducked into the small waiting room.

"I want you to know, in full confidence, it's you we want, not the other two. We're convinced that they'll fail long before the end of the probation period. At that time, you'll have complete control of the book. We'll renegotiate at that time. Okay, Frank?"

"Thank you, Jim," I responded with a committed look and gave him a very firm handshake.

Jim had just solved a very big problem I'd had hovering over my head from the get-go of this case. Control of the book was everything and more. The real value of that book of clients and business was in the future potential of the projected new business with those clients and the upsalability. That value was worth four, maybe five times its present value. I knew what I had in terms of present opportunity. I had absolutely no clue of the journey that this book of business was about to launch for me.

My office was on the third floor. At first, I accepted the three flights of stairs as a new form of exercise. I didn't realize that I would be up and down those stairs four to five times a day. But just having that great office and all these beautiful, successful people around me was worth every minute and bead of perspiration.

Gary sat across the room from me and was the first to introduce himself. He ran the benefits department. His claim to fame was managing some of the largest corporate group plans in K/W. Then there were Carl and Hubert, who managed the Ontario Teachers' Pension Plan, among other large pension group plans.

Al, whose last name I will not mention, was new but came with a very successful book of business, combined with corporate life and benefit clients earning twice what my book generated. From the get-go, he unnerved me. He seemed nice enough of a guy, but something just didn't seem right. He was always looking at me very curiously, as if he wanted something from me. He and his secretary would disappear for an hour or two during the day. No one ever commented, so I didn't ask any questions. I assumed they worked very closely with clients, and he needed her there in the on-site meetings.

The secretary pool consisted of two girls on the second floor, Mary and Brenda. They handled all correspondence for the entire operation, except for Jim. He had his own personal administrator, Lynn. On the basement level was McClellan's General Insurance operation, and that's where Cam was situated. I would go down and chat with Cam from time to time, mainly to dig up new leads from him and vice versa. There was one other man that would turn out to be a very important player in my life, John R.; I will not expose his name to avoid any allegations or inferences.

Jim's partners were situated on the second floor of the building. Louie St. Hill was next to Jim, and Doug McPhail was across the hall in the sunroom. Doug's office was the most unique with surrounding windows. His desk was a well-milled and finished hardwood slab about four inches thick. Doug was a short, very fit man who dressed well. He was a sailor and ran his business as if it were a military operation. I think he had what many would call "small man syndrome." His Napoleonic personality was very prevalent around fellow staffers. Everyone else in the business was inferior. But I strongly admit that Doug was my best teacher, and I learned many new techniques from him. He was the one that introduced me to the formulated presentation called *needs analysis*. No one in the life business was using such a tool or approach at that time, except for him and a few well-schooled brokers across Canada. It was clear that if you intended on selling the big and complicated policies to professionals, you had better learn how to prepare a complete *estate analysis*. Doug immediately took me under his wing. He did so reluctantly, as he would remind me every day, but deep inside, he was revelling in self-indulgence and power-mongering as he trained me.

Bob and Barb were seriously left out in the cold, and only a fool could not tell they weren't wanted. Bob and I would meet and discuss what was going on from time to time. I had to play dumb in order to let the Lackner plan unfold. Barb caught on after the first month, and she resigned without notice or even saying goodbye.

I was starting to sell reasonably larger-valued policies, and I found myself getting more attention in the firm. They were starting to involve me in their activities, such as after-work gatherings and partner discussions. I was asked to join in on new product seminars that only partners were privy to, and I felt a real sense of belonging. I was very much entrenched in the Lackner fold by the third month.

I became a member of the Doon Racquet Club and began playing tennis almost every day of the week. I was taking lessons and had been asked to join the club's travel team, competing against other regional clubs. Louie St. Hill took an interest in me because he was a professional tennis pro many years ago in Bermuda, where he was born and raised. Louie would invite me to his house to play on his court from time to time. He was in his late fifties and took a real liking to me. He offered me a mentoring role, and I felt comfortable around him. He was a real family man, and I liked that in him. He was not as flamboyant as the other partners. He was more down to earth. His house was very large and eloquent, situated about five miles outside the city on about one acre in a gated community. He was living the life, as they say. As we drove to his house, I would tell Patty how much I wanted this to be our lifestyle. She would hem and haw and say I was a dreamer. I would respond, saying it was to happen very soon.

My two sons were growing fast and required a lot of attention. Patty was a stay-at-home mom, which was very important for the boys and my new career. We didn't do a lot as a couple, but we did visit her family or mine from time to time. Patty spent most weekends at her mother's with the boys. It was a tradition in her family. I didn't complain because it freed me up to do my work and live in my work environment. However, we did go to the racquet club together a lot. We began making friends that were members, and we began socializing with their group. Patty became close to a couple of girls, and they started to go out every week. Patty needed to establish friends, I thought, and all was okay.

The only problem that was developing, it seemed, at the time, was her drinking. I was always a drinker, and the two of us were starting to do too much partying. We had moved again to Kitchener and bought a townhouse not far from the house we'd had two years earlier. The house cost $25,000 and we had a $20,000 mortgage. In retrospect, we were living on the cheap. I was starting to make more money, and we were able to make ends meet and have some savings. We even took a vacation to the

Bahamas. When the New Year arrived, being 1982, I decided to make that year my most successful earning year ever.

Jim called me in and advised me it was time to change my compensation plan. By this time, I was very much aware of what the firm was being paid for new business, and I realized now that my sales were becoming consistent every month. I would earn more than the salary I was being paid. The insurance companies were paying the firm 160% of the first year's annualized premium. This commission was one of the highest-paid in the country.

So, if you do the math, you'll realize how much money we were making on the sale of a life insurance policy. If the premium was $1,000 a year, the firm would receive a one-time cheque for $1,600. In the general insurance business, it is totally different. A car policy would pay the firm 60% on the first-year premium. You had to sell a lot of insurance to make a business out of it. The only difference was that the general business would pay 60% every year, not just the first year.

"So, Frank, you've successfully completed your probationary period, and you've shown great promise here. We are going to change your pay to commission and give you a new challenge. We'll offer you a partnership in the firm within one year if you reach a sales target of $250,000 of premium paid over the next twelve months. We'll retain 20% of the gross commission and set it aside in a trust account as your down payment for the partnership. You'll receive a net of 100% of the premium annualized. We retain the remaining 40% for office and administration costs."

"I'm more than happy with that, Jim," I responded, trying to hold back my excitement. "Oh, by the way, what's going to happen to Bob?" I asked in a more sensitive tone.

"We're giving him his walking papers today. I think you should take the rest of the day off and stay out of sight just to let him take it on his own."

"If you don't mind, Jim, I think I should be here. He would think unkindly of me if he thought I knew before he did, and I think I should have a word with him to clear the air. He does think he holds a right to the book even to this day," I responded.

"Whatever you think, Frank. That's honourable of you."

"Meet me at the Edelweiss Room in twenty minutes," Bob spurted out at me as he grabbed his coat and bags from his office and ran down the stairs. "Unbelievable." The Edelweiss was an Oktoberfest pub, located on the south side of Kitchener, where we used to meet from time to time.

"I didn't see it coming," Bob kept saying over and over as we drank our beers. "You knew, and don't tell me you didn't, Frank."

"Yes, I had a suspicion you would be next but only because you weren't producing. If you would have sold to cover what you were making, you'd still be here," I stated in a direct manner, trying to pacify him and justify the end results at the same time.

"If we had only done the deal with Baird," Bob said.

"You think there would have been a difference? Baird would have chewed us up and spit us out without thinking within the first month."

"We would have got a sizable cheque upfront, Frank!" Bob yelled.

"Absolutely not," I responded firmly. "We had nothing but a pipe dream. We were trying to make the best out of a very bad situation that Gord had left us in. By the way, we aren't out of the woods yet on the Gord thing."

"What do you mean, Frank?" Bob asked nervously.

"Haven't you been following the news? Rob Kelly was front-page news in *Maclean's* magazine this past month. He's under investigation for fraud. They're suggesting that they bilked over $52 million from local and area investors. Businesses and doctors are going bankrupt. People are selling their houses to cover their losses. It's the biggest scam this area has seen in over eighty years. Even the *Globe* is doing a story on Surf and Radial."

"Fuck," Bob snorted. "What a mess. Have you heard anything yet on the DAP accounts?"

"No, but I have a friend who's a litigation and securities lawyer, and a Kinsmen member, who's looking into my situation for me. He thinks we're safe because of Gord's manipulation and misrepresentation. The broker is in deep shit because he knowingly set the accounts up without verifying our ability to pay and without verifying our net worth, qualifying us as sophisticated investors. We were duped," I stated as finality to the issue. What now for you, Bob?"

He looked out over the pub and then dropped his head and said, "I have no clue. I don't know what to tell my wife and daughter. This is the worst day of my life. It's not your fault, Frank," Bob tried to assure me and held out his hand to shake as he got up from his chair.

"Keep in touch, Bob," I responded with a smile that took all I had to give.

"Sure, buddy," Bob responded as he always did, with that grin and laugh that I will never forget. I never heard from him again. Not long after that day, I learned he died a very lonely man.

I sat at the table that day for at least two hours and thought about the previous six months and what had gone on in all of our lives. There was a message for me and a direction to take that I had feared and didn't dare to go. My mind kept referring back to the book of business. I hadn't yet touched one client. I was afraid to unravel the imaginary bow that tied the book up so carefully. I knew it was time to take what I could without remorse or fear. I had to meet some very large numbers to get partnership, and that alone was all that mattered to me, it seemed. As I thought about my next move, I felt a sense of guilt, like I was about to do something wrong, like cross an illegal line that was underhanded and evil. It was like making a deal with the devil. I took my last drink from the glass in front of me, looked around the room, and said only to myself, *May God forgive me for what I am about to do . . . get on with it!*

The very next morning, I began to read through all of the files and data cards of each client in the book. As I studied each case, I discovered that most of the key clients were doctors and about a half-dozen were owner-operators of long-standing, successful local businesses. I also found a common denominator with every client. They were all stockholders in Surf and Radial Oil and Gas. I'd found my door opener. They'd all talk to me in order to get a review done on their file. I would offer them an updated estate analysis and policy review.

The first thing I needed to do was find the right product that would allow me to roll their existing policies into one, consolidating their coverage with a bonus like a single-premium plan or a higher coverage for the same money or some benefit that made sense to the client in their present situation. More importantly, I needed to figure out how to protect their losses from the stock deal. I knew I'd have to implicate Gord as the evildoer in all of this and portray myself as the white knight, proposing a practical solution to offset their financial imbalance. The insecure part? I was unsure how Lackner would view my approach. Mostly, I didn't know what the carrying insurance company would think or allow. So, I decided to contact the president of Maritime Life, who held the bulk of the clients.

My initial call was to set up a meeting with him to discuss the present situation and how to deal with the book management. He invited me to Halifax to meet and direct the future plan. My youngest sister was about to get married the following weekend, so I thought if I flew out on the Thursday night and met with the president on the Friday morning, I wouldn't interfere with my sister's wedding. I met with Jim that day and outlined my agenda. He gave me his okay. There was one caveat he requested, and that was for me not to upset the book. In fact, he wanted me to discuss Lackner becoming a broker for Maritime. They hadn't approached Maritime as of that date, and because of the book being mostly Maritime Life policies, they needed to finish the arrangement and contract. I gladly took on the assignment.

I was very nervous about meeting the president and feared he wouldn't take kindly to my approach because I was about to roll hundreds of thousands of premiums into new policies that would cost the company new first-year commission. I was anticipating a session of heavy negotiating. I was prepared to go for broke, to threaten to move the clients to a different carrier if he disallowed my intent.

The flight from Toronto to Halifax went by very fast, and all the while, the meeting was on my mind. I was very anxious to get it over with, but at the same time, I felt like I was living in a dream. I'd only read about these types of meetings in books before this day. Only six months before, my biggest challenge was paying my bills, and I'd had no clue where the next paycheque was coming from. All the books I'd read talked about this moment as a defining crossroads. This was where a real man was made in the business world, when you were confronted with the opportunity to either win large or lose everything. In my case, if I made the wrong choices and failed to come out a winner, I would remain a mediocre salesman and continue to dream rather than live the dream.

What I also realized was if I did not succeed and get the approval to go forward, I knew in my heart and gut that someone, especially in the firm, would snatch up the opportunity and replace every client they could. I could feel it almost daily.

Al was my biggest fear. He continued to ask questions about the clients and who they were. I just knew he was a snake waiting to coil and strike the moment I wasn't looking. I had to strike first. This was no business tactic. This was survival. I was learning very fast that business was warfare in a completely different venue and theatre. The battlefield was the market, and that could be right in your own office. You'd have saboteurs and double agents all around you. Your fellow colleague could very much be your nemesis. The firm could very well be the biggest thief ever and use fraudulent tactics and manipulation to gain control of your assets. These events are never discussed or investigated by police or the legal system unless you are fingered by the firm itself. Then the tables will be turned against you as a corporate governance preservation move.

These traumatic stories unfold almost every year, somewhere in Canada and the United States. The little guy always takes the fall on behalf of the board of directors or executives. A very successful criminal lawyer once told me that if there was anything at all that was valuable out of earning a master's degree in business, it was learning the protocol of corporate preservation and the art of the down-line set-up of lower staff to always take the fall. He said the banking system lives by this rule. Most mega-corporations, like the auto giants and drug companies, are the masters. Someone will always take the hit on behalf of the board. A board member will never go down for the company. That's why most CEOs are paid those astronomical wages and bonuses. They are on the legal and public front line and will always be slaughtered in the good name of corporate brand integrity and prudent governance, the so-called watchful eye.

The building was very modern and looked very much like the Maritime's image as an innovator in the insurance business. I was ushered up to the top floor and directly into the president's office. I cannot recall his name, but his face I will never forget. He was tall, well-dressed, and had a full-face beard enhancing his broad smile.

"Well, we finally meet," he opened, creating an air of comfort and assurance. I immediately could tell why he was the president.

Before we begin, can I get you anything?

"No, I am fine, sir," I answered.

"Don's my name, and we don't have to be formal here," he stated as he sat down in his chair. "You're on the map now, Frank. Let's cut to the chase. You've moved Gord's book over to the Lackner people along with yourself. I think that's a very good move for all concerned. We at Maritime Life would very much like to do business with Lackner. Are you in a position to discuss such an event?" Don asked.

"Yes, Don, that's one of my main tasks today—to set up our relationship as a firm and as well to discuss the management of the book." I knew right then and there we were on our way. This wasn't going to be difficult at all.

I then laid out my dilemma concerning the security of the clients staying with Maritime and feared industry raping and pillaging by every hotshot agent in my area.

Don totally agreed with my concerns. Before I had a chance to even pull out my proposal, he said, "I want you to re-write every policy and use the single-premium plans as much as you can. They're our most innovative and newest to the market plans. I've been thinking long and hard about this since you called, and I know if you don't do this, the clients will be gone."

Don then outlined our commission structure and I almost fell to the floor. We were going to earn almost 180% of first-year commission. I had just landed the biggest deal any brokerage firm had heard of in the K/W area at that time.

"I expect you to make at least a quarter of a million dollars this year, Frank. Good hunting!" Don said.

I could not get out of there fast enough. "The beer and seafood are in deep trouble now!" I yelled as I ran into my family at the hotel.

"Fred, he's going to ruin the wedding! Stop him now before it gets out of hand," my mother barked out his marching orders.

"Rita, damn it, woman. I need to talk to my son! He has good news for us!"

"One drink, Fred. Do you hear me?"

"Yes, Mother," my dad responded as we darted to the bar as fast as we could.

"My God, son! This is truly amazing. Well, it will be something if it all comes to pass," Dad answered in a conservative tone.

"You can count on it, Dad," I assured him as we drank down some scotch.

"What's your next move?" he asked me.

"Have a good time in Halifax this weekend and see my sister married. By the way, why didn't she invite me?"

"Well, son, that's another story. She feared you'd make a spectacle of the event and embarrass her."

"Come on, Dad. I wouldn't do that," I answered in a reassuring voice.

"She'll never forget what you did in front of the whole family last year when she introduced Mark."

"That was a joke, and I'm sure he took it as one." While Mark had been showing us slides of him and Vickie, my sister, I got drunk and made rude comments throughout the showing. Vickie was beside herself. I felt bad after I sobered up, but what the hell—Mark needed to know what he was getting into. Or better yet, what Vickie was getting into. Unfortunately, she found out two years later.

Mom, Dad, Patty, and I took a short tour of the Nova Scotia shoreline and visited Peggy's Cove to see a bas-relief memorial carved into the stone by renowned local artist William de Garthe. To my mother's joy, the artist was standing outside of his house when we arrived. My mother possessed an ability to captivate most people she met firsthand and she did just that with this man. De Garthe stood by his work with Mom as Dad took pictures for about fifteen minutes and got into long conversations with Mom. While they were talking, I noticed a great deal of smoke billowing out of the man's back door, so I yelled to the man, "Do you have a wood-burning stove going in your house?"

He replied almost casually, "Oh, I was cooking some bacon on the stove. Oh, I'd better go and see what's burning." He walked over to his back door.

As he entered, my dad went inside with him. The next thing we heard was my dad yelling as he was running out of the house, "Where's the garden hose? His house is on fire!"

As quickly as the fire had started, the man and my dad put it out. But what a mess the man had to clean up. In my mother's style, she shrugged it off as the man came out to get some air and asked him to take one more picture with her. "Sure, why not," he replied with a grin.

I couldn't believe what I had just witnessed. If it were me, I would have lost it, but I guess this was the way East Coasters dealt with life in general. If it didn't kill you, then who cares? It's just another thing to deal with at that moment. Life goes on. We parted that next morning as Mom and Dad headed out to tour the rest of the Maritime province. Vickie and Mark were not planning a honeymoon, so they drove us to the airport. On the way, I remembered I'd promised the Lackner crew I would bring back some live lobster. So, Mark stopped on the highway at a lobster stand, and I bought two boxes full of beautiful crustacean creatures, joyous to the palate once boiled and doused in butter.

I arrived at the office, lobster in hand, and with great news to present to Jim Lackner.

Jim took the news as if it were expected, and I had done what I was sent to do. Jim had the ability to make you feel less than important at any time. I think this was a defence mechanism he used to keep everyone at a manageable distance. I did not fully explain my next move with the clients just yet. I thought that I should keep that to myself until I got my first deal in the bag.

There were three doctors who agreed to see me right away. I had set up appointments at their office and met with them. To my surprise, they immediately agreed to do what I had proposed, and by the end of the first week, I re-wrote $20,000 worth of premium.

That Friday morning, as I handed the applications and paperwork in to Mary in the administration pool, she looked up at me and smiled. "You have hit a home run, my friend. Keep this up, and you'll be getting a lot of attention around here."

I replied, "I hope from the right people."

She looked at me and gave me a long, staring smile as if to say, "You got my attention."

The rest of that month went by with similar events and successes. I was knocking them off one at a time. My cheques were growing as fast as I was writing the new business. My earnings for the first eight months of 1982 broke $170,000. I could smell the partnership getting closer. Jim was getting more friendly and observant. Doug was beside himself and somewhat jealous. Louie was proud of me, and so were the administration staff.

I was going through the book quite quickly, and I was starting to tackle the business clients. The one client that stood out to me was a sixty-two-year-old mega-millionaire that owned and operated a hydraulic manufacturing company. His situation was very tenuous for two reasons. His existing policy was huge. His premiums were very large, but I saw I could re-write it into a single-premium plan that would eliminate his monthly premiums for life. The initial hurdle was for him to pass the medical. Then there was another big problem. His son-in-law was Rob Kelly, Gord's partner in the stock failure. I had no idea if he would find out I was dealing with his father-in-law or if he would blackball me. The other question was whether he would tell his father-in-law not to deal with me. All I could do was present my case as best as I could.

I will never forget that morning as I was driving to my first appointment with the man. I won't mention his name out of courtesy to his family. My mind was racing over how I was going to present the case to him. A common problem I had—and one I have even to this day—was second-guessing myself before the event. I was trying to talk myself out of doing the deal. I was so stressed about the whole thing that I had to pull over on the side of the street and calm myself down. *If what I am about to do was wrong, then so be it*, I convinced myself. *I want the deal. I will do anything for this deal.* Mentally, I'd actually thought I'd sold my soul to the devil at that moment.

I was brought into the owner's office, and sitting there with him was his accountant. I knew I either had to do the best presentation I had ever done, or I should turn and leave right then and there. Something took over my mind and body the moment I began. I started asking questions instead of telling them what I was proposing. They kept leading me to the solution , so I went for broke and laid out the plan I had prepared for him.

When I was finished, I went right for the jugular. "Shall I start the paperwork?"

The owner looked at his accountant, and he nodded yes.

When I completed everything I could think of, he shook my hand and said, "Good job." The accountant added that he thought this was a wise move for his boss. I left in a professional manner and walked out the front door of his plant.

I couldn't get the car door open fast enough. Have you ever had to pee so bad you can taste it? I had to yell and scream so loud I couldn't contain it. All the way back to the office, I was yelling and screaming and singing at the top of my lungs. I had just written the largest premium and first-year commission that 90% of all life insurance agents in Canada have ever dreamed of writing: $34,000!

When I got back to the office, I said nothing to anyone except Mary. I asked if she could come to my office.

When she sat down, I handed over the application. Her eyes almost bugged out of her head. "I've never seen a life policy this big! The death benefit is over $10 million. The single premium is $34,000. My God, you have just earned . . ."

"$34,000," I said as she voiced the same thing.

"What are you going to do with the money, Frank?" Mary asked in fun.

"Build a new house. That's what I want to do," I answered.

"Smart thinking. Where?" Mary asked?"

"Beachwood," I replied.

"Where the rich live in Waterloo," she replied with some attitude.

"Yeah, why not?" I said.

"By the way," Mary started to say in confidence, "you're going to be a target in here. Do you know that?"

"I figured there might be some backlash from some in the firm."

"The newer guys don't want you in here. They're very protective of their turf, Frank."

"Mary, who do you think they are?"

"Al, Hubert, and, I think, Collin. They've been lobbying to get Jim to dump you. They're planning something to set you up."

"Great," I responded. "Just when I am about there to become a partner, I have another hurdle."

"Are you invited to the Christmas party yet at Jim's house?"

"No," I answered.

"Oh, I think you will be after he sees this deal."

It took no more than a half-hour before Jim called me into his office after Mary had taken the paperwork down to him.

"Well, I guess congratulations are in order, Frank," Jim stated as I walked into his office. "What deal! I reviewed your paperwork, and it is impeccable. I would like to discuss your commission on this deal. You know, with this size of a deal, we would like to pay you out monthly rather than in one lump sum."

"Why?" I responded in a nervous tone.

"To protect the firm from any repercussions if the deal falls apart, and there's a sizable payback."

"Jim, it's a single premium. There is no likelihood of the client changing his mind. The accountant was there and approved the deal."

"My partners won't like this, Frank."

"I wrote the deal, and I've operated under our commission deal for the past year. I expect you to stand by your word," I stated with passion and firmness as if to say, "Don't even think about fucking me now."

"Look, Jim, you had the chance to keep me on salary a year ago, and you insisted on taking me off and sold me on living on commission. Now you want to change the deal? I'm sorry, but that isn't fair or ethical. I demand you stand by your word. Also, I have been contributing 20% to the partnership fund all year, and I'm very close to meeting the numbers you laid out for me. Why are you trying to change the deal?"

Jim sat for a moment, then looked up at me and smiled. "You're right, Frank. I stand by my word. You'll get the whole commission."

"Thank you, Jim!"

"Oh, by the way, don't forget the Christmas party next week at my house." By then, the whole office knew about the deal, and all were there to shake my hand.

I got home late that night; I was very much inebriated, tired, and unbelievably happy. As I sat in my chair, I looked in the eyes of both my boys as I held them and said to them, "We're now on our way. You're going to live a great and fulfilled life. That I promise you." They just looked up at me like they always did, smiled, and played with my face until they fell fast asleep in my arms.

CHAPTER 15

My friend Mark was a real estate agent and a Kinsmen member. He was always on me about investing in more real estate. I called him the week after I sold the big one and told him I was ready to build the house of my dreams.

"Where do you think I should look, Mark?"

"I'll show you some properties around both cities of K/W," he responded enthusiastically. "You'll get a good idea what's out there before you make a decision. Let's spend tomorrow and go hunting."

All that next day, we looked at properties in the country, on the outskirts of both cities, and lots in the cities. Finally, Mark drove me to the subdivision of Beachwood, located in the northwest end of Waterloo. I was immediately impressed with the size and styles of the homes in the semi-gated community. All the homeowners were doctors, lawyers, and business owners.

"You fit in here, Frank. This is where you belong. I have an exceptional one-time deal to offer you here. There's a lot open right in the first section of the area. It's about sixty by one-forty in lot size. The builder is my guy, and he only builds his own design. The homes are all of the highest quality. The walls are plaster, not drywall. I'll show you the lot, then I'll show you the house plans you can choose from."

"Wow," was all I could say. Right off the bat, I knew that was where I wanted to build.

I called Patty to meet me at Mark's office. When she arrived, Mark had already shown me three layouts. All the floor plans were at least 3,000 square feet. Within thirty minutes, Patty and I picked a back split and layout. I put a $5,000 deposit down, and away we went. We were building a beautiful house.

"What are you going to do with the condo?" Mark asked.

"I want to rent it out or maybe sell it. I don't know at this time."

"Let me know, and I'll handle the sale for you."

"Sure, Mark," I responded.

"Oh, do you know a good lawyer for this deal, Mark?" I asked candidly.

"Yes, as a matter of fact. His name's Tim Jansen. We went to law school together in Ottawa."

"I didn't know you studied law," I asked inquisitively.

"I'll tell you all about it over a drink sometime."

"Go see Tim. He needs the business."

"Great, I'll do that."

It always amazed me how critical encounters transpired in my life especially influential friendships. Tim would become my closest confidant for many years to come.

I had retired from hockey and had no outlet except for work. The new year of 1983 was upon us, and I decided this year would be filled with tennis at the club and golf throughout the better weather. What snuck up on me were the old strip club runs that I had made a rare activity up until this year.

The Kinsmen club had elected a new president, Paul, and he was one wild, crazy guy. He was twenty-nine and held a very important executive position with London Life: director of bond trading. They claimed he was a financial genius and was the company's guru. But he had a big problem, and that was booze and sex. When he was not at work, he could be found at the local strip clubs between London and Toronto. He stood six feet two, weighed in at 260 pounds; he was bald and sported a full beard. His choice of transportation was a Harley. When he left work, he would put his leathers on, and no one would see him until the next morning, showered and dressed in a suit, sharp as a knife. He ran his life like he was living as if he were dying the next day.

For the first few months, everyone at the Kinsmen club found him to be a marvel, so we all got on the bandwagon. One night at the clubhouse, we were to entertain one of the Kinsmen governors. So, Paul announced we would set up a special event to take place that he would personally orchestrate. We were all standing around the room when Paul showed up with a boom box going and two strippers in tow. He commanded we all stand around the room in a circle to let the girls dance. As they got going, two of the lawyers and another corporate executive began to undress the girls. Within minutes, the three men and two women were having sex in the middle of the room in front of fifty Kinsmen. Before we knew it, the governor was completely undressed and was getting a blow job from one of the strippers. At the end of it all, Paul announced that the girls were raffled off to two business partners who owned an electronics shop in town. They were given keys to a motel room and ushered off, never to be seen for the rest of the night. We heard the next week that their wives found out and were threatening divorce.

Paul showed up one meeting in a school bus wearing a tux. We all got on the bus, and he announced that we were going on a pub crawl. There was not a nightclub or bar in both K/W that we didn't hit. We were all totally wasted by the end of the night, full of piss and vinegar, and some of us headed over to the strip club to finish the night off.

Almost every Monday night, I would patronize the same place and meet up with old and new friends. One night I ran into my friend from Cayuga, Jim Wilson. He was with Ultramar and had moved up the ladder to sales manager. "What the hell are you doing in K/W, Jim?" I asked.

"Hey, Frank, what's up?"

"Just having a drink as usual after Kinsmen night," I replied. "What about you? Long way from Cayuga, buddy," I added.

"You see this dancer that's on the floor right now?" He pointed her out to me with a sneaky grin.

"Yeah," I responded.

"I've been doing her for the past month. We just did it in her room before she came out to dance."

"Yuck!" I said. "I wouldn't want to be near her, like a lap dance or something," I blurted out.

"I've got a bunch of them going," Jim said.

"You gonna get yourself in a lot of trouble if you keep this up," I said.

"I'm careful," Jim answered.

"Aren't you married now to Lauren?"

"Yup, but I can't help myself. I have this crazy need to get laid every day. I can't stop chasing women. It's like a sport, a release from the pressures of work. I only pick women who understand my position, and that's why I like strippers. They all want a man who'll spend attention and money when they can without any commitment," Jim added.

"You should get into the game, Frank. You getting enough at home to keep you going?"

"You got a point. But man, I don't know."

"I'll introduce you to one of them." Jim introduced me to one of the girls, and I found myself spending the rest of the evening being entertained by this dancer.

For days and weeks, I spent a lot of my free time visiting dancers in the clubs. I found a sense of distraction from the stresses of the day, and I also discovered that the male population in K/W was very much accepting of this behaviour. It was okay to be found in these places. The wives and girlfriends of the era accepted that their man would have a beer from time to time at the local strip club. They hoped it would stimulate and enhance their sex life at home in the bedroom. For some, I'm sure it did, but for others, it was worse than gambling. Some men would spend a whole paycheque on lap dances, drinks, and dinners, and some would eventually support a dancer by paying their rent for weekly sexual favours.

I did not get in that deep, but I was quite the voyeur. I was very much into watching the dancing, but more so in observing the activities of the dancers and how they manipulated the patrons. A few dancers caught on to my game and found it acceptable that I thought like them, in a sense. I understood what they were up to and that they were only trying to make a living, for the most part. The odd one or two had the extra career on the side as a hooker. My girls, as I used to call them, would point those ones out to me to avoid at all costs. They were usually hooked on heroin or some drug that required injections. They were strung out all the time and lured unsuspecting drunks up to their rooms at the bar.

I got to be very comfortable spending time there and became quite a regular. I was, however, only there twice a week. I did have a conscience and loved my children to death. I had to find a way to balance my habit without hurting my kids. Patty was another story.

While all of this business growth and extra activity was going on, Patty was spending more time at the tennis club and with her new friends. Her younger sister, Kim MacGrandles, was almost living with us, and I found that I was supporting her as our live-in babysitter. I really did not mind because she was really good with the boys, and she was a joy to be around. Kim had a boyfriend who was working overtime to get into Kim's pants but was totally unsuccessful. Kim was quietly struggling with her sexual identity. It became a joke in the family because he was so unsuspectingly comedic in his attempt. Kim would almost beat the living hell out of him when he got frisky. I have to tell you that he was the most persistent guy I had ever met. His loyalty to Kim was relentless and vigilant. You could always count on him being there, no matter what.

Well, the house was getting built, and we were all very excited. The move would be happening in April. The house was beautiful, and my mom and dad had visited us a couple of times to see the house. Dad was very proud of his son. He wasn't too sure about my career. He had reservations about the life insurance business and listened to me with caution. "Always put money away, Frank," he would say. "Plan for a rainy day. This ride you're on might not last, son."

Today, I wish I'd listened because he was right. Ironically, I was coaching people to put money aside and invest in GICs, term deposits, mutual funds, and savings plans. I did have an RRSP, but I had no contingency funds. I had this internal voice that always kept me in desperation. I took it as motivation to continually strive to make money. I believe this came from the seminars with Bob Proctor, teaching me to stand beside the car I wanted and sell until I could buy it. Buy the house with nothing down and work to pay it off. He would preach, "Live the life now that you always envisioned in order to self-motivate and set your standard." I certainly bought into that concept by building the house and spending on furniture and things. I went from driving a Volkswagen to a 325 BMW. Patty drove a Monte Carlo with a T-top roof. We were the yuppies of our time and space. The who's who were accepting us and inviting us to join in at their parties and events.

But a problem surfaced. Patty found it extremely difficult to fit in with the professional crowd. I was one of them and felt very much at home amongst their kind. On many occasions, Patty would get ridiculously drunk and cause a big scene. She would slur out embarrassing innuendoes while someone was trying to talk. Or she would insult someone for no reason. I was frightfully frustrated with her drinking and uncontrolled actions. I had to stop bringing her to parties on the advice of my associates and friends, which caused many fights and problems between Patty and me.

But in the world I was in, I had to protect my image and place to continue to attract the right clients. Patty just didn't get it. We were spending more time apart. There was no common ground between us except the kids, and I felt I was living a completely separate life most of the time. The fights were getting constant and louder. They would last for days, not minutes. I was becoming more worried by the day. Again, I kept my instincts intact and forced myself to make things work as best we could. This meant staying away from each other on the weekends. Patty was off to Brantford as usual with the kids, or towing one with her to her parents. I was playing tennis or, later in the spring, golf.

All my activities were starting to get to me, and I needed a break. The type of change to make was unclear to me at that time. I could sense a rustling going on at Lackner. Some were saying there was a corporate move in the wind. McClellan and Lackner might merge. Lackner might sell. Who knew what was happening? I just felt I needed to get my partnership in place before anything took place. I started to turn the heat up on Jim and was questioning timelines for my partnership. He was avoiding the question as if it weren't the right time. I was getting very concerned, and I started feeling a wall grow between the partners and me.

Then it happened. A meeting was called for all the partners off-site. I was invited for the lunch, but not the meeting. You could cut the air with a knife, which made things quite clear to me that I was overlooked.

At the end of the day, Collin came out and told me I was to meet Jim inside. All the rest of the partners were out of the room.

"I'm going to make it quick, Frank. We're not making you a partner. You're not ready in the eyes of the partners, and I have to go along with the majority. That's all I can say except that we'll try again next year." He got up and left.

I stayed seated in the room, stunned. My life ran before my eyes, and the most prevalent vision and memory that hit me was Mr. Mariontette, my high-school counsellor who'd screwed me out of Boston University, looking at me, laughing and jokingly insulting me. "I told you so. You'll never make anything of yourself. You'll never be accepted by the professional world. You're not smart enough! Who do you think you are, thinking you could make partner here?"

"Frank, want to join us at my house?" Collin spoke from the doorway.

I turned, and it took everything I had not to break out in tears. "Yeah, let's go!" I put the happy face on, grabbed a glass of wine, and gulped it down.

"Take it easy, Frank. We've got lots of beer at my place," Collin assured me.

"One for the drive, that's all," I responded.

Only Collin, Gary, Hubert, and Al were there. We all went to the basement and, of course, I was very complimentary to Collin and his house. We hit the beers pretty hard for about an hour and talked about various business things. I found myself somewhat of an outsider in the conversations.

Then, Collin suggested that we do the man thing and enjoy the sauna. I found it strange, but what the hell? I was never one to shy away from most things out of the ordinary. I was quite at one with my body and had been nude amongst many guys in the locker rooms.

In the sauna, the conversation changed to be serious. I was being ganged up on by all of the partners.

"What makes you think you deserve to be a partner, Frank?"

"I was promised a partnership, and I earned it," I responded in a defensive tone.

"You'll never be a partner here," Al added with an attitude of righteousness. They kept hammering me and hitting me from all angles until I broke down in tears. I couldn't take it anymore. I got out of the sauna, got dressed, and as I put my coat on, I turned, looked at them all, and warned them, "You're all going to pay for this. You have just fucked with the bull, and I am going to fuck you all up big time, you spineless fuckers."

"Frank, don't be like that," Al spoke out.

"You, of all the fuckers. The one who tried to steal one of my clients behind my back, and I said nothing to Jim. Oh, guys, I wouldn't be too free to take sauna baths with this faggot. He grabbed my dick last year while we were driving to Oktoberfest. You're lucky, Al, that I haven't busted you up good by now." I turned and ran up the stairs before they had a chance to defend themselves.

I knew I had to do something drastic and quick, so I drove back to the office. The only partner that was there was Louie St. Hill. I burst into his office and told him the whole story. I also told him that I was violated emotionally and would probably go to my lawyer over the weekend. I was so angry that I could have burnt the building down and kicked the living shit out of everyone who was part of Lackner at that time. I was livid to the point I could barely see straight.

"Frank, you must calm down now! Go home and let me sort this out. Jim's gone on holidays and won't be back for two weeks. Please do nothing rash and let this work itself out. I will deal with everyone. Go home, Frank."

How many times in the past had I heard this buffer? "Go home and let it work itself out." I had no intention of letting it work itself out for their benefit. They—meaning Lackner—had planned this manoeuvre for one and a half years, just like they got rid of Bob and Barb. They knew it was going to take longer for me because I had the ability to make the book of business work. *How stupid could I be?* I kept saying over and over to myself.

We were about to close our house deal in a month, and I had a real big problem called a down payment. I had most of what I needed to close, but I was short by at least $2,000. I then got an idea. I went to another Kinsmen brother, Tom Brock. He was a criminal lawyer, working in his older brother's firm. Mark's brother was a lawyer there as well. I told Tom and his brother the whole story, and they felt compassion for me.

"Why don't you set up your own firm, Frank? You made over $200,000 over the last year and a half. You can do it again. This time, you retain it all for yourself," Tom's brother assured me.

"You can rent an office here and work out of here. We can feed you some business. I'll get a small mortgage for you to close your deal, but I will have to do the legals. Is that a problem?"

"No, I don't think so. Tim has not started yet."

"Perfect. Now there's nothing to worry about, is there?"

"You're right," I replied with newfound confidence.

He was right. I would open my own firm. I could get a new insurance company sponsorship and start over.

Monday morning was the beginning of a new life for me, but I had some unfinished business at Lackner. I had to hand in my resignation and clear my desk out. I also had to get my copy of the book of business. Gord was about to be moved again. This time, I knew there would be a war on my hands. I was ready for anything, especially a fight from Lackner.

I walked in and went straight to Louie's office. "Louie, I thought long and hard over this whole matter, and I met with my lawyer. I officially resign from the firm immediately. I hold no animosity toward you or Jim, and I thank you from the bottom of my heart for all that you have done for me. I'm at a crossroads. I can't see anywhere to go but on my own. That's what I have chosen."

Louie looked up at me and said quietly, "Please don't do anything that will hurt this firm."

I responded, "I cannot promise you anything, Louie, but I can say this. I will not take any legal action against your partners as long as there is no action on the firm's part."

"That is fair," Louie said.

"I'll be gone in an hour, and here are my keys," I responded.

Louie looked up and stated, "Thank you, Frank, and good luck."

I said my goodbyes to the administrative staff and specifically to Mary. She looked up with a grin and said, "We'll be talking very soon, Frank."

"Great," I responded, not really understanding her intentions. I couldn't wait to leave the building. I stopped in to say goodbye to Cam Yule downstairs, and as I was leaving, Robson stopped me in the hallway.

"I'm leaving McClellan," he started. "We had a partner dispute. Maybe we should talk," he suggested.

"We can but give me six months to get settled," I answered.

"Fair enough," he responded.

"I'm free!" The drive to my new office was refreshing. "I am now my own man! I have my new business." I kept shouting out these statements as I drove four blocks south of the Lackner building. I was even on the same street. My new office was in direct line to Lackner. *How ironic*, I thought. *This has got to be the right thing to do.*

Now the job to get set up took a lot of favours from a lot of people. That had to be done before a dollar could be earned. There were start-up costs like any new setup, and I had very little money free to start a new business. Tom forwent rent for two months. My Kinsmen buddy, who was an executive with Bell Canada, got my phone hooked up for free. Now, I had to get a sponsor company. My biggest hurdle.

The next day, I started calling every successful broker I'd met over the past six years in the life business. Everyone wanted to deal with me. Everyone tried to take advantage of my situation as well. I found one man in Toronto who was somewhat of a flamboyant type. He wore only the best handmade silk suits and gold chains. He looked a lot like Elvis. He also made over $500,000 per year personally. His firm was grossing well in the millions per year of first-year premium. He had over fifty agents selling through his agency. Some said he never sold a policy himself. He ran a wholesale firm. I didn't care. I needed a source to run my business through. So, I began.

The first two weeks went with a bit of a struggle. I wasn't getting much interest at first. Then a few policies started to come together. My old clients were rallying back into the fold. However, I wasn't going to touch them just yet.

At the end of the first month, I was getting nervous because the house deal was closing in, and I was worried about closing and carrying costs. I still had the townhouse to deal with and had no one to rent or buy it. One night at the strip club, I ran into Rob, who manufactured stereo speakers and was looking for an investor. He was a bit of a rounder, and I could tell he sold more than speakers to the strippers.

There was one dancer who had caught my eye, but I hadn't met her yet. Her name was Cathy. My new friend was buddies with her and introduced me to her one night. She seemed somewhat on the ball and had a very businesslike attitude about her career. Her plan was to buy a house from her earnings, and she needed financial advice. I offered my services, and she accepted. We planned to meet the next week in my office.

In the meantime, my friend Rob, the speaker guy, was interested in my townhouse. I thought I could maybe set up a rent-to-own deal with him. He bit. Now I had to figure out how to make the deal financially work. So, I took the first three months' rent of $1,000 as a down payment and then took the postdated cheques to the bank and convinced them to give him a mortgage for the balance. They did it with my guarantee. Within that week, I set up my own life insurance firm, sold my townhouse, and settled my sponsorship issues . . . all without dipping into Gord's book of business. But time was running out. I had to make a craploud of money fast.

Cathy showed up at my office the next week, right on time. She stood five foot eleven with perfectly styled curly brown hair, and she was the most attractive woman I had ever seen. She was in outstanding shape and wore a very tight-fitting wool sweater and form-fitted blue jeans. The stilettos made her height well over six feet. Her breasts were her marquee attributes, flaunted without reservation. "I hope I am not late, Frank."

"Oh no, you're right on time." The whole meeting was one of trying desperately not to be obvious as to where my eyes kept going, but she seemed not to mind. We got through the sales part, and she picked up on two main areas of concern for her, saving money and disability.

"There's no doubt that I need the coverage because what if I get in an accident and get my tits cut off? Then where will I be? No one will hire me to dance without my tits, don't you think, Frank?"

I just about fell on the floor when she made that statement, and I was sure she'd said it in jest . . . but she really meant it.

We finished the policy application, and when we were done, she invited me to dinner the following week. I accepted the invitation with great anticipation. I had a gut feeling we were about to become very close friends.

As I opened the door, Tom was rustling around outside my office door and was embarrassed as if we caught him peeking in on us. When Cathy left the building, Tom came into my office and said, "That's the most beautiful chick I have ever seen!"

"I agree," I responded with a big smile.

"Bring more of that in when you can, Frank!"

The phone rang. It was the receptionist. "There is a George White to see you."

"Send him up," I quickly responded. *Who is this guy?* I asked myself.

As I opened the door, a well-dressed middle-aged man was waiting to enter. "Hello, Frank, sorry to arrive unannounced, but I didn't want to take the chance of missing you. I've heard nothing but exciting things about you from a fellow colleague of yours, Mary Baron."

"Oh yes, Mary from Lackner."

"*Was* at Lackner," George corrected me.

"When did she leave?" I asked in surprise.

"Last week. I guess there was quite a shake-up after you left. Jim came back from holidays, went ballistic on the partners, and cleaned house. Mary got out as soon as she could.

"I checked into your background. I think I can offer you a great environment to succeed and a compensation plan that no one in the industry can ever touch."

I sat back and listened to George's pitch. He was the branch manager of Monarch Life, a very old insurance company. He wanted to attack the K/W market with new aggressive products and sales methods. The company image was to be current and show innovation. As George talked, I was hearing a lot of what every other brokerage house or insurance company was offering, but then the bell ringer came, the ultimate deal.

"We will pay you the full 160% of new first-year premium ... upfront." George stopped and just looked at me.

I was frozen by the upfront thing. "Upfront?" I questioned.

"Yes, Frank, upfront ... as soon as you submit the policy, we will pay you the full commission. That means we are prepared to process your applications immediately and not hold the commission for thirty days. You will receive full payment on your very next statement."

That was incredible news because on the size of policies I was writing, I could wait up to ninety days before I would get paid and sometimes not in full. This meant getting the cheque as early as fourteen days from issuance; this offer was unheard of in the industry.

"That's incredible," I responded. George then ran through the rest of the terms and conditions. I would have to move to the branch. I really didn't like that idea but agreed to take a look at the facilities. George had advised me that I would be getting my own floor of offices, and I would be able to grow a staff of salespeople and earn override commissions. I finished the meeting by setting up another one for the following day. I went home that night and advised Patty of the opportunity; even she understood the value of the move. I was only concerned about leaving the Brock office and upsetting the brothers. They had been very helpful, and I felt I owed them something.

The office was atypical of a life insurance branch but attractive to me because George gave me the largest space in the building, the board room.

The first enticement was Mary walking up with a pen and an order book from Krug furniture. "What style of furniture would you like, Frank?"

"You can outfit your complete office," George stated like Bob Barker on *The Price is Right*.

"You know, George, I've been through so much the past two years with broken promises and rip-offs, this move has to be the final one and the best one."

"I'll tell you what, Frank. You give me one piece of business, and I'll fly you to Winnipeg, to head office. You can follow the underwriting right up to you receiving the commission and be there as the vice president signs the cheque."

I thought for a moment and remembered I'd already set a meeting with Dr. Achiume, a Zambian middle-aged family practitioner and surgeon at Cambridge Memorial Hospital. I already knew how large his plan was to be, and I also knew he was prepared to sign. "Let's do it, George. If everything goes as planned, I walk away with a cheque, and you have a new agent broker on staff under all of the terms you set forth."

Mary stepped in and asked, "Now, about the furniture, Frank?"

The next two days were meetings with the doctor and a couple of other clients. I walked into George's office on the Friday with three applications in hand totalling $9,000 in first-year premiums that grossed out $14,400 in first-year commission.

George looked up.

"From the beginning of underwriting to the receipt of the cheque, all the same day, right, George?" I asked in a suspicious tone.

George stared at me with a smile and answered, "Right!"

The plane to Winnipeg was set to leave from Toronto on the following Monday evening at about 6:00 p.m. I arrived at the Winnipeg airport around 8:00 p.m., and awaiting my arrival was the superintendent of agencies for Ontario: "Tom." I will not use his real name. Tom drove me to the hotel downtown, and I think it was a Holiday Inn but one of their better locations. It had a nightclub with a live show. Tom had filled me in on the next day's events, agenda, and what to expect. All that was on my mind was receiving that cheque.

The next day was filled with meet and greets, from the janitors to actuaries. The underwriting department took up the first hour and a half of the early afternoon. Then Tom had me wait in a small sitting room outside a grand, hand-carved wooden door. On a brass nameplate situated in the middle of the right-hand door was "The Office of the Vice President."

I must have sat there for almost a half-hour before Tom walked in and said, with quiet excitement, "Your applications were all approved. Everything has been processed. Now we'll meet the vice president of the company, and he'll sign your first cheque."

"How much?" I asked with very little emotion.

Tom opened the envelope and stated, "$14,400."

A sigh of relief went through my body, and I did everything I could not to voice my joy in front of Tom.

The grand doors were then opened from the inside, as if I were to be introduced to the king of some foreign land.

"The vice president will see you now, Mr. Trousdell," the personal assistant stated in a royal tone as she ushered me through a long, richly carpeted pathway leading me up to a humungous hand-carved wooden desk.

"Have a seat, Frank," a directive of introduction and courtesy was voiced from behind a menagerie of hand carpentry and woodworking art. In an extremely large, leather-upholstered, high-backed office chair, a very little man with half-moon glasses sat peering over a file set in front of him with a gold pen in hand.

"This must be quite a day for you, Mr. Trousdell?" asked the little powerhouse. You could tell he had all the confidence of an international poker player and was not afraid to take any calculated risk if it meant money for his company or, even better, for himself. "I see all went well through our underwriting and prep program."

"Tom, have you got the cheque and the agreement?" he asked Tom as he kept looking down at the file.

I noticed that I was sitting about as low as he was; in fact, my eyes were at the same level as his. *Brilliant*, I thought. *Everyone plays at his eye level, no chance of anyone psyching him out.*

"Frank, you need to sign the final contract with Monarch Life as set out in your previous meetings with George. As you do that, I will sign your cheque."

I couldn't sign the paperwork fast enough. As soon as he received the finished documents and Tom witnessed them, he handed me the cheque. It wasn't the size of the cheque that was important to me; it was the deal. I needed to complete this process from beginning to end. I wanted to prove to all who were watching, including my father, that I had really succeeded without any questions of who's who or who did what. I could have run all the way to the airport; I was so happy.

The flight seemed to be fast and most enjoyable. As the plane approached the GTA, I looked out over the landscape of Toronto and whispered to myself, "One day, I'll be here and living amongst those bright lights and office towers. This will be my domain, soon." *I am ready*, I thought, *to be the most successful businessman in town!*

"Where's Patty?" I asked as I set my bags down in the hallway of the townhouse.

"She's at a party with the Ramonos."

"Where's that?" I questioned the babysitter. "I guess I'll be going there. Kids in bed?"

"Yes, they've been asleep for the past hour."

"Okay, thanks. I'll see you later." Off I went to the party. I was always into a good house party, especially if the Ramonos were there. Cathy was a very attractive twenty-eight-year-old of Italian descent with a hunger to flirt. Her husband was supposedly having an affair, which she had learned about some weeks ago. She was bound and determined to make him jealous by flirting with me. He couldn't have cared less. She would grab me and make out with me right in front of him, and I would apologize for the rest of the night. He'd just say, "Forget about it, would you, Frank?"

"There you are," someone yelled as I entered the party. Cathy was the first to greet me, and as usual, she was all over me. One might think she was my wife if they were new to the crew.

"Where's Patty?" I asked her

"Do you care, my luscious man?" Cathy answered with extreme pleasure.

Then, from the darkness of the living room, Patty appeared quite drunk. "What the hell do you want, asshole?" she blurted out like a drunken bar fly. I'm surprised you're not at the strip club, getting a lap dance from the other Cathy, you fucker!"

"Oh great, she's pissed," I said. Everyone started to laugh and took it as a joke because they had heard and seen this all before, too many times. They used to call it the Frank and Patty show. As soon as Patty had too much to drink, she had a habit of going into Godzilla mode and wanting to kill me in front of anyone who just might be there. I tolerated the abuse and insults followed by embarrassment only for one reason: the boys. Most would have departed that relationship long ago. I had committed to my boys, in my mind at least, to stay until they were either in or out of school, depending on how long I could last.

This whole charade was extremely taxing on both of us. We knew we were together for the boys only, but we were resigned not to talk about it anymore because it only created a terrible fight. Two years prior, we had agreed to see a shrink/marriage counsellor/minister. My Kinsmen buddy, Jamie Martin, had arranged the meeting. He had gone to this guy when his marriage broke up, and he highly recommended him. Five minutes into the session, the minister asked me to sit outside while he talked to Patty. I feared this because Patty was a master manipulator. He then called me in and did not give me a chance to talk alone with him. "So, you are having and had numerous affairs on Patty?"

"What?" I shockingly responded

"I have not had any affairs, sir."

"Well, that's not what Patty tells me, Frank. In fact, you have no regard for your family whatsoever, and you stay out all night partying with your friends and many other women."

I just sat there and took all these accusations in like someone was beating me up with their fists while I was tied to the chair.

"What have you got to say for yourself, young man?"

I looked at him in disgust, then turned to Patty, and said, "Either you can leave with me, or you can stay. Either way, I'm out of here." She left with me.

As we drove back to the house, I couldn't believe what had just happened and, more importantly, what a lying and manipulating two-faced bitch Patty was that night. "You sold me out!" I kept saying.

"What are you talking about, Frank? You wanted this meeting. It's your entire fault. You had it coming, you prick."

"You know, Patty . . . if it weren't for the kids, you would be long gone. I made a deal with my father to stay no matter what, and this meets the 'no matter what' time in our relationship. We are through as a couple. You can live your life, and I mine as singles, but we will not divorce, and we will live in the same house."

"Fine with me, you motherfucking asshole," yelled Patty. "It's not over yet, fucker. I will get you so bad one day that you will never get out from under the wrath I will bring down on you."

I decided not to ever bring the issue up again, at least for quite some time. I was only interested in raising the boys and being a very successful businessman.

The move took absolutely no time or energy. The new office furniture had arrived that same day, and no sooner did I sit down behind my brand-new Krug wooden desk than Mary walked in and stood in the doorway. "I'd like to introduce you to your new secretary, Mandy."

Without further notice, this five-foot-five, 110-pound, auburn-haired beauty strolled past Mary and into my office. She immediately sat down, and Mary said, "I'll leave the two of you to get to know one another."

"You will have to bear with me for a while, Mandy. I just got here today, and I won't have much for you to do just yet. However, here are a couple of client lists that I will need you to set appointments with over the next two weeks. Do you need me to write a telephone script?" I asked.

"Oh no, Frank, I am well trained for telephone work."

"Thank you, away you go," I jokingly responded.

"Well," I said to myself, "George and Monarch Life have outdone them all this time. I really have hit the top just like I've dreamed for so many years." I sat there for a while, just soaking the whole environment in, and thinking about the last three years and how far I'd come. I really thought I'd made the big time. All I had to do was keep bringing in the big policies and rake in the money. I knew I would have to turn my back on Maritime Life and re-write all of the policies in order to sustain my position.

I decided, at that moment, that I would not worry about the potential industry fight, if any, because I felt confident that Monarch would back me along the way. Furthermore, Maritime had been ripping off all the other companies over the last five years. I saw the issue as a firefight and warfare, leaving no policy sacred, and no client was to be left alone. All business was open for the taking. Any business held by the Lackner firm was definitely in my cross hairs.

If they could see me now, I was thinking as I shuffled through the day setting up my office and files. The Lackner boys had set me off, and one thing my dad had always taught me about revenge was to let the rope out as long as you can. Then, when the rope runs out, you hit and hit as hard as you can, ten times harder than they hit. They'll never forget you. Vengeance is always served best on a cold plate, some say. "I'll serve it up in due time," I responded to myself while wearing a very wide grin.

"Are you settling in there okay, Frank?" George asked as he stepped into the office.

"George, this is great! I am so happy."

"I'm glad to hear that. Anything to make my rising star comfortable enough to produce millions of dollars of insurance this year," George responded with great expectations.

"Consider it done, my friend," I retorted back with a smile.

"Great applications you submitted today. Keep them coming," George stated as he left.

The rest of that week was filled with meetings, networking, and dinners with the new staff. George and I were hitting it off quite well, and I felt that I could trust him. He, on the other hand, kept just a little distance from me out of self-preservation and maybe respect. I was somewhat of a rounder personality and character, whereas George was all business and family-oriented. I started to feel like I would demand recognition from the younger trainees in the office. I wasn't loud and boisterous, but I definitely let them know when I hit a big sale. I was always trying to outdo Gordo and what he'd presented as his persona back when he was on top of his game.

I had heard just that week that Gord and Rob were being charged with fraud of some kind. I had no clue as to who got charged with what, but they were both indicted as being involved in the biggest stock scam in the region. *I wonder where Gord is?* I asked myself. *I wonder how he's dealing with the mess he's in?*

I have found, over the years, how powerful the mind really is. Memories of situations keyed on the same people re-surface as predominant thought patterns, time and time again . . . until it becomes a reality.

Chapter 16

"Rainbow, how the fuck are you?" that old familiar voice grumbled over the phone line.

"Gordo, you're alive!" I quickly responded in shock and excitement.

"Yes, I am. Still standing, better than ever."

"Okay, I've heard some nasty things about you. And recently, about you and Rob."

"Don't mention his name, Rainbow. We aren't friends anymore. Don't even discuss it," Gord retorted but finished his sentence abruptly. "I called you, Rainbow, to invite you to come to Toronto. I am in a new stock play, and now you are filthy rich on my account, no pun intended," Gord chuckled.

"None taken, Gord, because I've earned every penny."

"Oh, settle down, Rainbow. I was only kidding," Gord interjected. "I've been watching you from afar, and I've heard nothing but good things from some close friends of mine. I'm very proud of you. You've learned well since we were together as the falcon and the falconer."

"Very funny, Gord," I joked back. "Okay, when are we meeting?"

"On Thursday, I need you to meet me at the Brass Rail on Bloor and Young, at about three o'clock."

"I'll be there," I closed off.

I sat in shock and began to tremble. *What am I getting into?* I asked myself. *Was Gord going to try and get revenge on me?* I had bad-mouthed Gord pretty severely to the clients in order to get confidence and trust built over the past two years. *Maybe Gord does trust me and feels I am the one to help him now?* I thought, as if to pacify my emotions laced with a crap load of fear. Nevertheless, the feeling of inquisitiveness overpowered my best judgment.

The drive to Toronto was spent thinking about how I could get the most out of the potential meeting. I decided I was going to get Gord to network me into the stock players and sell insurance to them. I wanted clients to buy into using a prepay or limited pay life policy to protect cash from creditors and tax deferment issues.

I had heard of the giant agents out West using this method with the oil and gas guys mining in northern Alberta. They were making a fortune. *Why not me?* I asked as I drove down the 401.

The streets were as busy as usual on Bloor Street, and parking the car seemed impossible. I walked into the bar, noticing the décor and ambience befitting its name. Brass railings were everywhere, and the seating was all at the bar in a long narrow room. There was only one man in the bar, sitting at the end of the front corner, sipping on what looked like a martini. He kept smiling at me, which kind of unnerved me a bit. As usual, Gord arrived fifteen minutes after me. He sauntered in, dressed in his normal way, sporting a $2,000 suit.

"You certainly look like you aren't suffering, Gordo," I stated in fun as he sat down beside me.

"Long time, Rainbow," Gord responded.

"Want a drink?" I offered.

"No, I got lots to do today, so let's move on. Oh, by the way, Rainbow, what do you think about this place?" Gord asked with his sneaky grin plastered across his face.

"I think I've been here before," I said.

"Are you sure, Rainbow?" Gord answered.

"Why?" I responded.

Gord stood up, looked at the guy in the corner, smiled, then turned to me and announced, "This is a gay bar. Do you come here often, Rainbow?"

"You fucking jerk," I answered, embarrassed as we almost ran out the door.

"Assholes!" the man at the bar yelled after us.

Gord broke into laughter as we walked to his car.

"Things never change with you, Gordo," I said while we walked up to a brand-new Porsche 944 white turbo.

"Nice wheels, but you're as crazy as ever, man! Slow down," I yelled as we sped through the streets.

"Where are we?" I asked.

"Rose and Rose, Rainbow. You're gonna see what I'm doing for cash."

What are Rose and Rose? I thought as we entered the building by the back door and into a room filled with work cubicles.

"I bet you're wondering what the hell this is all about, Rainbow," Gord said as he sat at his desk.

"Yes, exactly," I answered.

"I raise money for the movie industry. I find investors for new movie projects."

"Wow," I said. "Are you working on anything good?"

"Oh yeah," Gord answered confidently.

"Are these all Canadian movies, Gord?"

"No, Rainbow. Most are Hollywood-based, but there are tax advantages for Canadian investors to get in on through the Canadian Film Board. There's a loophole that big money guys like. I've been raising money for a new project that's called *Wall Street*. It's all about the stock market. They're trying to get Michael Douglas to star in it."

"No shit!" I responded.

Gord carried on talking about the movie deals for a bit, but the whole thing didn't really make a lot of sense to me.

"We have to go and meet my partner downtown. He runs the stock deal I'm in right now. This deal, I want you to get in early and make some real money, Rainbow."

"I'll consider it, Gord, but I'll have to be able to offer insurance to your partner."

"Yeah, great idea, Frank," Gord responded with a smile.

I knew he had figured out within a second that I would invest if I got a new client. "I'll make sure it's worth your while, Rainbow. He'll do what I tell him to do, Frank."

The office of the mining company was on the corner of Adelaide and Young, in a vintage building. The elevator was at least eighty years of age, still manned by an elevator attendant. The glass-partitioned offices had wood walls. I felt I was going back in time.

"Rainbow, wait outside the door for a few minutes while I set everything up," Gord asked.

I sat in a chair against the wall for at least twenty minutes before Gord ushered me into the office.

A bald man was sitting behind the desk in a very nice suit. "Hello, Frank. My name's Don Jones. Gord and I have been discussing your proposal, and I'm in agreement, so whatever paperwork you need me to fill out, Gord has all my details. I'll sign, and you do the rest. Call me when you have it all figured out. I need at least $10 million in coverage, okay?"

"Yes, Don," I quickly responded.

He gave me a blank cheque as a void for the monthly premium and then handed me a binder full of policies.

"I understand you'll roll over any cash values to the new one?" Don asked.

"Yes, I'll do an accounting and send you a letter outlining the full transaction. There'll be a full medical first, Don. Any problem with that?" I asked in a businesslike tone.

"No, shouldn't be. Just have the nurse call me. You'll hear from MDS services."

"Thank you, Don."

"No. Thank *you*, Frank," he responded as if I was doing him the favour.

I already knew the premium was going to be large. So did Gord.

"We're not done yet, Frank," Gord stated as we left the building.

"Do you remember Dr. Tom Love?" Gord asked.

"From the racquet club?" I responded.

"Yeah, that's him. You're going to write him up now. He's going to deal with you on the stock play. He'll be your point man for the stock play," Gord instructed me.

"Do I buy through him?" I asked.

"No, you tell him when and how much you buy and what broker you deal with when you place your order. It'll be really simple and clean. He gets credit for everyone he brings into the play."

"What's the name of the stock?" I asked.

"Thor Resources. It's trading on the TSC at twelve cents."

Dr. Love was living near Yorkville in a restored walk-up. I couldn't figure out why he was living there when he practised in New Hamburg, outside of Waterloo. I waited in his living room for at least a half-hour while Gord and the doctor were upstairs talking. I could hear mumbling going on and a lot of sneezing and coughing between the two of them. Then, without notice, the doctor came down to the living room.

"Hi Frank, it's been a while since we met," the doctor said.

I could tell something was wrong. His eyes were all over the place, and he couldn't stop moving from room to room.

"Where are the papers?" he asked in a nervous but demanding tone. "Where do I sign?"

"Right here, doctor."

"Call my secretary in the New Hamburg office and get the details and set it all up."

"Okay, consider it done, doctor," I responded.

"Now, Gord filled you in on our new relationship. Right, Frank?"

"Yes, doctor. I call you when I start buying Thor, right?" I asked.

"Correct, now you do not sell until I tell you, okay? the doctor stated.

"Okay," I responded.

"We're done here," the doctor said as he headed up the stairs again.

"Where's Gord?" I asked.

"He's gone. You take a cab to your car."

"Oh . . . okay," I answered, a bit shocked. As I flagged a cab on the street, I couldn't help but think, *This doctor is snorting coke. He's fucked up! These guys are all playing in a fucked-up world right now. Let 'em get fucked up as long as I reap the rewards*, I said to myself.

"Frank, can I talk to you for a moment," Mary asked as she entered my office the next morning.

"What's up, Mary?" I looked up at her as she swayed toward my desk.

"Do you realize how much premium you wrote yesterday in Toronto?" she asked as she stood against my desk.

"What's the final number?" I leaned back in my chair.

"$74,000 in first-year premium," she responded with a very wide grin on her face as if she was the budding recipient of a commission from my work.

I just smiled at her.

"So, can you drive me to Manulife building at lunch? I have to take a course this afternoon. I really don't want to drive there myself."

I quickly responded, "Sure, I'd be delighted."

Mary acted as if she belonged in the passenger seat of my brand-new Mercedes Benz 300 turbo diesel. The sun was shining through the sunroof, and her short blonde hair glistened, making her skin look tanned, even more so than it always did as a result of her weekly tanning regimen.

"You know, we haven't had a one-on-one talk since you started here, Frank."

"I know, Mary. I've been meaning to ask you how George got the incentive to contact me in the beginning."

"Haven't you figured it all out yet?" Mary responded in a very seductive tone, looking at me like she wanted a close and personal encounter.

"I thought you and I had made a connection back at Lackner, but I wasn't sure."

"Oh, come on, Frank. I tried to let you know I liked you from the start," Mary stated surreptitiously.

I could feel the excitement arouse my body and, of course, my manhood was taking over as she talked. "I'm so proud of you and how you're running strong after all you've gone through and what you are dealing with at home, Frank."

"Thank you, Mary," I retorted in my appreciative way and looked straight into her eyes.

"I want us to be very close friends, Frank. Closer than anyone I know. My husband is a fireman. He is at risk every day of his life. We have an understanding that if anything should happen to him, I should be ready, and that means having a close friend there for me."

When she finished her speech, I knew she wanted us to begin an affair. I just wasn't sure of her real intentions, but it seemed to me to be very clear.

I could remember Gord telling me about the effect success and money had on people. First, you get the money, then you get the power, then you get the women . . . whether you want them in your life or not. But for now, I thought the flattery was fun, and the whole thing made me feel desirable and wanted. The inner need for recognition from all that were hovering around me was very fulfilling, but could I sustain this world I was building or was it going to crumble like a house of cards? Who would be the one to pull on that pinnacle card to bring it all down around me?

No one is immune to failure or collapse. You never know where, when, or how it happens. It could be your family, your best friend, maybe your co-worker, or your spouse, maybe even your trusted accountant. *This*, I thought, *was the enemy that I had to look out for, the one person who was hiding in the wings, waiting for their opportunity to do their deed and end this incredible run.*

Could I be the enemy? I asked in shock as I drove back to the office.

Every day was filled with more parties, luncheons, and doctor sales meetings. The summer of 1983 was upon us, and I wanted to take the family for a week's vacation, away from business. I called my sister Cheryll and asked if we could use their cottage in Turkey Point on Lake Erie, and she agreed. I liked the idea of the cottage because there was no phone, and I didn't want any interruptions, for the kids' sakes.

We settled in at the cottage on Friday night, and the boys were really excited and full of energy. Patty's family showed up, and we had a regular gathering of eating and drinking until all hours of the night. The first weekend went as fast as it came. I have always experienced the speed of time as fast as the speed of sound when you want it to last. When you want time to go by like lightning, it never does. Monday morning was quiet; the boys were busy on the beach, and I started to get restless.

"I'm going down to the store and calling the office to see if all is okay."

"Don't be an ass, Frank," Patty responded. "You'll end up going in for some stupid reason that could wait."

"I'm sure everything's okay; I won't be long." I got in the car and drove down to the store, where there was a pay phone.

"I'm glad you called," Mary responded. "Your stockbroker called and said it was really important you call him immediately. Oh, and by the way, your cheque from head office hasn't arrived yet, and your bank called as well."

"Okay, I'll call everyone," I replied and hung up. *What the hell?* I said mentally. No cheque, and I needed to cover the account because cheques were due. There was one sizable cheque in particular from the brokerage house that needed to be covered, and I figured the bank manager would hold it until my deposit arrived the following Monday. *No problem*, I thought as I called the bank first.

"Al, Frank here."

"Where's the money, Frank?" a gruff voice sounded in quick reply. "I told you no more large cheques until you covered the account."

"There will be a deposit, Al," I responded with assurance.

"I don't doubt it, but this is one that I cannot override without head office approval. I had to send it back."

My gut fell to the sand under my feet. The sun's heat rose about ten degrees in seconds while I digested Al's statement. "What?"

"Sorry, Frank. You'll have to call the brokerage house, give them a story, and promise to replace it once your account here is straightened up."

"Okay, Al. What about any other cheques or withdrawals?"

"You're okay up to $2,000."

I called the broker. He wasn't very kind at all and suggested liquidating the stock purchased the week before to cover the account. If I did that, I suspected I'd have a hell of a problem with Gord and company.

"I need at least to the end of the week to straighten this out, Jim," I asked firmly after explaining the circumstances.

"I won't be able to go any further than tomorrow, Frank," the broker responded.

"Shit," was all I could say as I hung up the phone. I thought for a moment and saw no option but to go into the office and get the cheque due from the insurance company into my hands. I went back to the beach, told Patty of the situation, and headed into town.

"Why is the cheque not here?" I asked Mary the moment I arrived.

"There's a hold-up in head office underwriting on one of the big cases," Mary replied.

"Where's George?" I asked.

"He's not available for you right now, Frank."

"Get Don on the phone, please," I directed Mary.

"Don, I got an issue that needs your attention."

"I have it straightened out, Frank, but you had better be clearer to underwriting with a case this size. We won't be able to process quickly like this much longer if this continues. Now, you'll have to come to Toronto to pick up the cheque if you need it that badly, Frank," Don instructed.

"There goes my holiday," I said to everyone listening in my office. Off I went to my house for the night. I saw no reason to return to the cottage in order to get an early start for Toronto in the morning. As I rested that night by myself, I wondered if my kids would someday understand the demands of business and its effects on your life.

I knew one thing had to change, and that was I didn't have the temperament to invest in the stock market, at least as an investor off the street. The whole game was not as easy as Gord had made it sound. The hidden rules and demands of the brokerage house felt like a loan shark hovering over your head twenty-four hours a day. The domino effect that would take place if I allowed the stock to be liquidated without anyone knowing would affect the price of the stock and could cause a shake-up for the boys in Toronto that I had just insured for an astronomical amount. They would have had to cover the sale of my stock, as required by the treasury rules under the TSC. That wouldn't have been a pretty sight. All I could think was, *Gord has got me in a bind again with this stock deal, just like before. This time, it could wipe me out. The bank is edgy, and my main source of cash through the insurance company is getting testy.*

I got back from Toronto in time to straighten everyone out. I was sitting in the bank when Al, the manager, sat across from me and said, "We have to make some changes, Frank. You can't do this anymore. You'll run into trouble with the bank. That alone could shut you down and force you to sell everything."

"Okay, Al. I won't make any more large purchases."

"I'm watching the stock for you, and if I tell you to sell, you do it. I'd like to see you out of it as soon as possible. You aren't ready for it yet. You built the house, and even with all the money you made, you're already margined to the limit, leaving you with limited equity. You should be paying down the operating account. How long are you going to keep selling these large policies? I'm worried you'll burn out. Then where will you be?"

Al kept going on and on, and I felt he was making good points, but deep inside, my little voices were battling it out as well. One side of me was yelling, "Don't listen! You're going to keep selling the big ones. Not to worry." The other voice was trying to reason with me, telling me, "Listen to your bank manager."

The next day I got a call from one of my doctor clients from Guelph, Ontario.

"Dr. Gelb here."

"Well, hello, doctor. What can I do for you today?"

"I need to liquidate my policy, the one we did last year."

"Why's that?" I asked calmly, panic surging up the back of my neck."

"I'm looking to invest in a new business. I need to generate new income from my practice. I plan on retiring soon and want something to work for me."

My mind raced for a minute, then I said, "Why don't we meet tomorrow and discuss it, doctor? I may have an idea for you."

"Sure, tomorrow it is," he responded positively.

As I hung the phone up, I shrugged the fear from my mind and suddenly realized two things. The first was I had warded off a big problem of losing a large commission that I would have had to pay back if I allowed him to cancel the policy. The second realization was that I had a golden opportunity to offer him an investment opportunity in my business. It could bring in more cash to pay down the operating line at the bank.

"How are you?" I asked the doctor as he entered my office.

"Fine, Frank. Before we get started, I need to confess something. What I really want to do is buy a timeshare in Hilton Head, South Carolina. I play golf, and that would make my life very comfortable. So, if I use my cash in the policy, I wouldn't have to finance the time share."

"How much is this investment?" I asked.

"For two weeks a year, it will require $8,000 US currency," the doctor responded.

I thought for a moment, then suggested that if we got three weeks, I would be willing to share and pay the total for fifty percent. I would let the doctor have as many weeks a year he wanted as long as I got one week guaranteed. The asset would be shared equally if he left the policy in force. When we decided to liquidate or part company, then we would cash in the policy. However, the doctor would have to pay the ongoing fees, such as monthly maintenance costs. He agreed, and we both decided to travel down to Hilton Head and spend a week in October to check out the unit.

The doctor left very happy, and I was relieved as if I had just dodged a fatal bullet. *Oh well, I'll own half a timeshare. I wonder what Hilton Head is like? I guess I'll find out soon enough.* I headed to the bar to drown my nerves in scotch, my drink of choice at the time.

"Frank Trousdell here," I responded as I picked up the phone.

"Dan Robson of South Waterloo Edgar Insurance Brokers in Cambridge here. How are you doing, young man?"

"I'm doing great, Dan. How can I help you?" I asked.

"Well, I thought you and I should get together and chat. I have some information concerning Lackner that you might want to know. Also, we're expanding over here, and I thought of offering you an opportunity to grow your business under the South Waterloo shingle."

"Interesting," I responded. "Let's meet next week."

"Give me a call, young man," Dan replied. Dan was with Lackner's partner, McClellan Insurance, where my friend Cam Yule worked. He'd left to buy into South Waterloo about the same time I'd left Lackner. His sores were still as raw as mine, so I was quite interested in what he had to say. His potential offer was singing in my ear as well because I was getting very tired of the daily chase for cash and new sales. Maybe the South Waterloo Edgar bunch might see the value in my book and buy me out.

Here we go again, I repeated over and over again in my head. *I think I'll discuss this one with George and see if we can make it happen without losing anything we're trying to build.*

"I don't believe this, Frank!" George responded after I told him of the upcoming meeting. "How did this take place?"

I told him of the call out of the blue and then what Don had had to say.

"Look, Frank. We, being Monarch, invested a lot in you, and it'll take at least three years for us to recoup our investment."

"I'm not going anywhere, George. I thought we could build a win/win here by bringing the S/W clients on board."

"Frank, I've been negotiating for the past month with Peter Kennedy, the senior partner. What makes you think your book would have a very large value?"

"I don't know what value it has. How would one go about getting an evaluation done?" I asked.

"Hire an accountant," George snorted.

"I have to anyway. I haven't filed my taxes for the past two years."

"Yes, you'd better, or you'll be in big trouble with Revenue Canada. Don't keep me out of the loop on this, Frank. Both our futures are at stake over this situation."

I couldn't believe I had started a potential problem with George and Monarch. *Something doesn't seem right to me*, I thought as I sat in my office. I invited Mary out for a drink and told her that it must be on the quiet from everyone.

We sat down across the street at our neighbourhood watering hole because it was set up for privacy. I also knew George didn't go there.

"So, what's going on, Frank?" Mary asked with a stinging tone.

I told her and suggested George was upset about the opportunity that had been offered.

"Well, wouldn't you be concerned if you put everything on the line for you and then, in six months, you're looking to jump ship?" Mary asked.

"I'm not jumping ship," I replied.

"It sure looks that way to me," she said.

"No, I see it as a way to get S/W to buy my book of business for a fair market value, then continue servicing the clients and writing new business from their book of general insurance clients. This would be a very large win/win for all parties, including Monarch Life."

Mary sat and looked out the window for a few moments. "I must tell you some very heavy news that must be kept secret for now."

I just looked at her as she spoke. I could tell there was something very disturbing riding on this whole thing.

"Monarch has been bought by North American Life!"

I felt like I'd been hit right between the eyes with a sledgehammer. "When?" I asked in shock.

"It was in the works even before you started with us. You put George on the map, and that insured him a head office job. The real plan was to merge the branch office with North American's office in Kitchener under their present branch manager. You would be working out of here but would answer to that manager." Mary filled in the blanks, and I just sat there listening. As she unveiled the inevitable, the move to Cambridge and S/W looked more inviting by the moment.

"You were the piece George needed to build his branch to the level necessary to capture the superintendent's position and move to Toronto. You got him the position, and in return, you got what you wanted. I was to keep you happy at all costs," Mary stated with a tired voice.

I sat back, finished my drink, then took Mary's hand, squeezing it as I said to her, "I appreciate your honesty and candidness under the present circumstances."

We both left exhausted.

"Hi, Dave Rolofson."
"Frank Trousdell here."
"Well, young man, what have you to say for yourself?"
"I say let's discuss our futures and fortunes."
"Ha," Dan responded. "That's what I want to hear!"

The meeting was set for the next week, so I could get my accounting done before the meeting. I needed to hire a CA and had no idea who to ask. A mutual friend from the Kinsman Club, Ron Madzia, suggested I meet with his CA. Ron owned a printing business and had been introduced to me by another Kinsman prior to joining the club. I'd actually sponsored Ron into the club.

"Why should I think your guy is what I need?" I asked Ron over beers one night that week.

"Craig's our age and has been my CA for the past four years. He's known as a really sharp, knowledgeable, and innovative pro. He was one of the founding members of Molly Maid in Canada."

"You've got to be kidding!" I responded.

"No, he just sold his share this year and made a fortune. You don't want to be on the wrong side of him, or he'll chew you up and spit you out. I'm selling my business, and he's doing the negotiating," Ron stated. "Here's his number. I'll go with you to introduce you."

The CA's name was on the wall of the building in north Waterloo. *W. Craig Keller and Associates, Chartered Accountants*. I was somewhat suspicious because I'd never dealt with an accountant before and had no idea what to expect except that they charged huge fees.

Sitting behind an extremely generic desk with no pictures on the walls was this thin, five-foot-ten, salt-and-pepper-haired man. He was on the phone talking to a client, shrilling out, "I told you not to do that!" He finished quickly, hung up the phone, and jumped up to greet me with his hand stuck out.

"Hi, I'm Craig Keller. Ron's told me a bit about your successes. You have quite a reputation on the streets," he stated with confidence and flattery.

"I hope it's all good," I responded.

"Very much so. Now, what can we do for you?" he asked with a smile.

I learned in due time that Craig smiled most of the time. In fact, he smiled more as he got angrier or more excited. I almost wasn't sure if he was kidding or serious most of the time.

The meeting ended with the usual "let's go for a beer." The beer went on for the rest of the day, and by the time we finished, Craig was my best new business friend. Ron and I became very close as well. He was looking for a career change, and I spent a lot of time nurturing him into the life insurance business as my junior confidant.

Craig and I spent a lot of time preparing my taxes and financial statements for the proposed acquisition. Craig advised me to hire him to present the proposed acquisition to keep me emotionally out of the loop. Also, he was positive he could get me more for my book of business. Yes, the haunting book of business that everyone was so attracted to, even Robson of South Waterloo Insurance had his eye on getting it. I focused on having access to S/W's clients to sustain my future earnings without giving up my residuals. I was very concerned about how Craig would handle this dilemma. More importantly, how much was my business worth?

"Your business is worth one million two hundred thousand dollars as it stands today," Craig announced to me in his office the day before we had to meet with Robson.

"What?" I replied in shock.

"I used a technical accounting method called accrual projected valuation," Craig began to explain in a very professional tone. "Your last two years of earnings minus cost of goods projected over the next five years gives you this value. I can back this up due to your earnings being commission, and you also earn residual income from the book, which will average twenty-five percent for the next five years."

This is too good to be true, kept looping around in my head as I drove home. I knew I had a gold mine but hadn't realized the full value. I was very hopeful that this value was real, but for some reason, I had this little voice in my head, saying, "This could all be a bad dream."

Robson, Keller, and I agreed to meet at five o'clock in the afternoon in my office.

The niceties lasted no more than five minutes, then Robson took the first shot across Craig's bow.

"No disrespect to Frank and his work, but how the hell can you come up with these kinds of figures?" Robson asked.

"I've been a chartered accountant for the past ten years and have done many valuations like this for bigger and worldlier operations than yours. My methods are tried and true, with full precedence recognized by the CCA. I stand behind these numbers," Craig responded in a very forceful voice.

Keller and Robson battled back and forth for over two hours. I was getting very frustrated with the fighting and could not understand why they were so focused on the fight and not the deal.

We paused for five minutes, and Craig ushered me outside for a smoke. He was very anxious and fired up. "I have him in a corner, Frank."

"You do?" I asked in a sarcastic tone. "All I see is the two of you fighting to see who wins the fight. I don't hear anyone agreeing with anything. Why can't we settle on a real good fair deal?" I pleaded with Craig.

"You'll regret this, Frank," Craig answered with grave concern. "Robson's only positioning not having to pay fifty percent up front. He hasn't disagreed with the valuation."

"Frank, I think you should walk from this deal. I don't like what I'm seeing and hearing. I think these guys—Robson, and I'm afraid to tell you, but George White is involved here with Robson—I think they'll agree to anything just to get the deal in their hands then fuck you afterwards, once they have control."

"Craig, I am worried if we don't do this deal. I need to tell you something, I fear."

"What's that, Frank?" Craig asked as he stared me straight in my eyes.

"I need to do this deal because I'm running out of key clients, Craig. I need access to their clients right now," I said in desperation. "They're going to pay me out of the existing value of the book. Let them pay me monthly. Take fifty or one hundred thousand up front, then a fair monthly value over the five years. I also want a guaranteed wage of $10,000 per month to manage and build the business."

Craig took a long drag from his cigarette, then threw it away. He turned to me and said, "You're the client, and I'll do what you asked, but let me remind you 'I told you so'."

Robson agreed to the final proposition, numbers, and payout. I was relieved and somewhat happy, yet Craig's warning haunted me.

The next step was to get the lawyers teed up to draft the final agreement. This was where I became totally lost in the mix. My lawyer was from the largest and oldest Kitchener firm, Martin and Martin. He was also a Kinsman. His proposed method was not a common share purchase, but a preferred share transaction with a conversion factor monthly to be common shares. This was a method the legals called a butterfly flip.

And so it all began with the utmost pomp and pageantry. Robson treated me like he was courting me for marriage. His partners in S/W stood by the wayside with caution in their persona. The one partner's mother was a shareholder of S/W and did not like the deal at all. She was very wary of me. She wouldn't even look at me or talk to me. The worst of the whole event was that George White immediately distanced me, like I had betrayed him. He only talked to me when he had to, and only then did he make any kind of an effort. I started to move my young staff back and forth between S/W and George's office. He was not happy about that, but the staff was part of my organization, and I needed to show S/W what they had bought besides my book of business.

Dr. Gelb and I decided to go on a golfing trip to Hilton Head, South Carolina for seven days to celebrate the business deal. We also decided to look into finishing our mutual timeshare deal. The week went by golfing and looking at the different timeshare offers. Finally, I did what I swore I wouldn't—I bought a timeshare and put it in both Gelb's and my name. I did make the doctor very happy and excited.

We returned exhausted from the week and the long twenty-hour drive home. Life and business were like I had never left. The kids were happy to see me, and Patty said her hello, then packed the kids up and off they went for their weekend in Brantford, as they had been doing regularly. As I sat on my back deck, I realized I had created the rumblings of a potential avalanche. The beginnings of anxiety made me worry about how I was going to maintain this lifestyle even though I had the guarantee, on paper, of a substantial monthly income. I started to doubt the deal and knew I was losing my confidence. The book of business was draining out, and I had to find a new way to market. I didn't have the security of the branch office and George White anymore. I'd really put myself on an island.

Every day there seemed to be a new cost to doing business. The new partners would demand I add more hardware to the operation. I reluctantly added a new computer that cost $15,000. The worst part? No one knew how to use it. We spent a lot of time looking at it. We would turn it on and off, over and over again. I felt like an idiot having it there. My administrator Brenda White took it upon herself to learn how to use it. She finally began word processing with it and learning how to file documents. We had a very expensive typewriter.

I had seven people selling insurance, and one walking in for the first time would be impressed with the bodies and commotion going on, but in reality, I was the only one selling anything. It didn't take long for Robson to get wise to the dysfunction and lack of progress.

Cash was good for the first six months, and I got the urge to sell the house in Waterloo and move to Cambridge, where S/W's office was located. It was also only fifteen minutes from Brantford, making Patty's trips closer. My reasons made sense at the time. Our house sold in thirty days for a modest profit, and we found a beautiful executive property in the elite part of Cambridge, not far from my new client and close friend, Dr. Kirk Achiume. The house was on three-quarters of an acre with a circular drive and a picture-perfect backyard, featuring a very large cement pool. The mature foliage and pool were framed with flagstone. It could have been featured in *Home & Gardens* magazine. My parents were beside themselves with it.

My dad sat poolside with me one day and said, "This is fantastic, Frank. I'm getting close to believing you've done well. Now, somehow you have to keep it and not lose it." When he finished, he turned and looked into my eyes like he always did to see if I understood what he meant. I knew right then and there he saw my fear and uncertainty. The uncertainty was about everything—the business, the marriage, the future, the future of my children, and how I was going to pull it all together.

Dad could always read through me no matter how much of a façade I put on. We were always attached as one. He was my rock and source of reality and, most of all, honesty. My sisters, except Cheryll and her husband Bob, kept their distance. They had their own opinions about me. I was always their little brother and would eventually screw up. Al, my sister Jackie's husband, had a love-hate thing with me. He and I would always have some kind of a bur in the saddle. That had started when he was dating Jackie. My dad didn't really care too much for him because he was a rebel and rode a motorcycle, a James Dean type. Al would park his bike in the back of our house, and while we were all in bed, he would honk his horn, trying to get Jackie's attention. Jackie would come into my bedroom, wake me up, and get me to go out and tell him to go away. Then my dad and mom would wake up.

"Fred," my mom would yell, "he's back again. Go and knock his block off once and for all!"

"Damn it, woman," my dad would reply in agony. "Give me my bat," he would yell, loud enough for Al to hear him. Al would instantly start his bike and peel out into the night.

One day, I'd had enough of Al's bullshit, so I challenged him to an arm wrestle in the backyard. I was fifteen, and he was eighteen. I had been working out quite a bit for football and was full of testosterone. While we arm-wrestled, I got aggressive, and so did he. I ended up putting him in a headlock, and he began to cry like a baby and left. Jackie never forgave me. To this day, he does not like me too well.

The spring turned to summer, and life in the Cambridge house was good. We had lots of parties and get-together events. I was spending a lot of time with Dr. Kirk, playing tennis and partying away from Patty.

We began to plan different business projects, trying to come up with the perfect opportunity.

Dr. Kirk was very focused on developing an import-export activity with his home country, Zambia. I became very interested and intrigued. We finally decided to fly to England to meet up with Kirk's high-school friend, who represented a British fertilizer distributor. My input was to pay the way there and back and do the negotiations. Kirk had connected with a very large conglomerate that owned businesses in Zambia. They were willing to sell off a basket-manufacturing plant in the middle of an aloe vera farming community. The idea was to convert the basket plant into manufacturing the aloe vera to crude, barreling the crude, and then exporting it to Canada. The aloe vera business was just beginning to open up, and we made connections with a man who brokered the crude to all of the national manufacturers that used aloe vera.

We saw phenomenal potential, but there was one fly in the pie. The Zambian government did not allow any direct exportation of local goods out of the country without heavy tariffs. So, with the help of a couple of Kirk's influential friends, such as the Zambian ambassador stationed in Ottawa, we were able to propose a barter plan involving Kirk's friend in London, England—Fertilizer Man. Zambia needed fertilizer, so we would swap in equal value for the crude. We would pay a substantially lower price FOB to Canada for the crude to the fertilizer company. Also, we needed to have a commitment from an international bank to handle the financing and transactions. This is where my accountant, Craig Keller, came into play. Craig set up the relationship with Barclays Bank. We had everything set and needed to complete the deal on the plant and consummate the fertilizer relationship. When we produced commitments from all sides, we would then get the financial commitment from Barclays.

We decided to fly out of Buffalo because there was a very inexpensive direct flight to London from Newark, New Jersey. Kirk and I got to the American border. No sooner had we stopped at the toll gate than the officer took one look at my new Mercedes and Kirk, a very black Zambian, sitting in the passenger's side, and he pulled us over for inspection. We had nothing to declare, but they were very insistent something was amiss, and we needed to co-operate. After about fifteen minutes, the inspector came over and announced to us that there was a rash of stolen

Mercedes crossing the border, and they needed to double-check. The inspector pulled me aside and quietly added that they needed to check on the doctor to make sure he was legal due to his colour and former nationality. I could not believe what he said to me, and for the first time, I was so angry and ashamed that this White officer was so shallow and blind. I told Kirk as we were driving, and he assured me not to worry, for he'd had to deal with that all his life. I tried to apologize for my race.

He stopped me and said, "Don't you go there, my friend. You have no right to do that. I know you mean well, but you are still too naïve. Time may give you the right to communicate your feelings, and you may never know. Someday the White man may be a minority just like me. Then you will learn the true meaning of pain. For now, let us enjoy life and be brothers. We are on a journey, my friend."

A journey was exactly right, and what a time was about to unfold. Here we were, a forty-eight-year-old, Black, Zambian doctor who stood five feet tall and a twenty-eight-year-old, White, blond, five-foot-ten, ex-football and hockey player, ready to tackle international business for the very first time. Naïve? Yes, I was. Did I know what I was doing? Absolutely not.

Was I worried or afraid? The only fear I had was whether my Visa cards would clear in England. I'd brought very little cash. We were scheduled to be in London for only three days, but three days in England could get very expensive, especially if my cards failed to work.

We landed at Heathrow and railed into Trafalgar Square. We arrived at the Gloucester Hotel at 11:00 a.m. London time. The plan was to rest for a few hours, then meet with Howard, the CFO of the international company, to discuss the sale/purchase of the plant. We agreed this process was the most difficult out of the three meetings planned that weekend.

Kirk insisted I call Howard before we slept in order to set the meeting up. I hung up the phone with bad news. Howard was in Scotland at the British Open, where one of the companies he directed was hosting the event. I was assured that Howard would be contacted, and we would be rung by him as soon as possible.

No sooner than we dosed off than the phone rang.

"Frank Trousdell, please?"

"This is Frank..."

"Howard here. I'm sorry. We got our times crossed. I thought you weren't coming until next weekend. I'm up in Scotland until tomorrow. We could meet at my flat in Piccadilly Square. Is that convenient for you?

"Yes, Howard, I'll meet you there."

Kirk and I decided that only I would go to keep the focus on a one-on-one meeting. I found that a bit unusual because Kirk was the money and a professional doctor. What I didn't know was that Kirk felt intimidated by the man and the fact there were two Whites and one Black man. That fear would surface later.

We slept the rest of that day and got up early and had breakfast. My meeting with Howard was at 10:00 a.m.

I arrived in good time and was ushered to a private elevator, which sped me to a penthouse flat. As the elevator door opened, a middle-aged man was waiting in the foyer of what looked to be a very nice, spacious apartment. We sat in the living room, and Howard quickly began the meeting by verbalizing an overview of the property in question. Then he reviewed the financials of the operating business. He pointed out their price, which we had already been aware of prior to our arrival and, again, I was prepared to tell him we were in agreement on the price. He felt good, and I spent the next few minutes outlining our plan. He was impressed to hear how we were planning to move the crud and bypass the tariffs.

I purposely held back that Kirk's family—or tribe, as Kirk described it—was the farming community on that land. He was planning on fulfilling a lifelong dream of giving the land back to his tribe and providing the tribe work, profit, and heritage. All of this I did not even know at the time.

Howard outlined their expected process and chartered diligence to process the deal. I, too, assured him of our due diligence and processes as well. We shook hands, and I left. My first real big international negotiations had just been successfully completed. We were on our way, doing world business. Here I was, a twenty-eight-year-old life insurance salesman doing deals in England and about to be involved in an African export company. I felt I could do no wrong, and I saw myself as a big shot, wheeler-dealer. I hoped this was not just a flash in the pan or a figment of my imagination.

"Come on, Kirk. Let's go see the city today and celebrate."

"When do we meet your friend, Fertilizer Man?" I asked in a confident tone.

"We'll take him out for dinner tonight at seven," Kirk responded. "He'll meet us in Piccadilly Square at the bar that he and I go to when I'm in town. You will love it. It's more of a men's club, where you go to have private conversation and dinner. The rest will be a surprise. Let me show you a real British pub, my brother."

"I'm always into that, Kirk," I replied.

We stood in a corner bar across the street, and, yes, it was the real thing because the place looked as if it had not been decorated since medieval times. The ceilings were low and of old wood. The beer was served in pints, at room temperature. I had a hard time with that because I was so used to Canadian beer, cold and from the bottle. However, I found a way to bypass the bitterness of the heavy, barley body and warm temperature.

We got in a cab, and the driver asked in a heavy British accent where we were going. I answered, "To the Dexter Lodge Inn."

The driver replied, laughing, "Are you Canadian?"

"Yes," I responded.

"I thought so. I have a brother that lives in Scarborough."

"Okay," I responded.

"Have you ever been to the Dexter Boys?" the cabby asked in a suggestive manner.

"No," I answered.

"Hold onto your wallets, boys. You're in for a ride," he said with a comical tone.

He drove down a very narrow side street off Piccadilly Square and stopped in front of this unsuspecting door. "There ya be, my lads. That'll be ten pee, please."

As we entered, we found ourselves in a very small room with only a coat check half-door. A little lady appeared and asked what our pleasure would be, and I answered we were to meet someone inside. She quickly answered, "Everyone that comes here meets someone inside. Follow me."

We found ourselves in another room, a little larger, but there was a bar and about three men standing having a drink. One was Kirk's old school friend, Fertilizer Man. He was a well-dressed, Black Zambian with a big smile.

"My friend, how are you?" Kirk rushed up to greet and hug his old friend. "This is Frank, the man I told you about."

"Oh, yes, what do you think of our London?" he asked, as if England was his home.

"I love it so far. I don't feel out of place here."

"Well, here we are at the Famous Dexter Lodge Inn very discreet and cozy! let us go downstairs and get started," Fertilizer Man stated.

As we headed for the door, a very attractive lady, dressed in an evening gown, appeared and asked us to wait a minute for our escorts for the night to arrive.

"What?" I said in a very surprised tone.

"Yes, you must include an escort for each of you. It is our policy and as well, isn't this the reason for your visit?"

"I'm in!" Kirk and Fertilizer Man began to laugh, and so did the other two men. Then three beautiful women arrived in negligees took us by the arms, and led us to the bottom floor. We entered a room in a larger area, but it had curtains dividing each table area and led up to a circular dance floor in front of a small stage. They ushered us to a table, then shut the curtains on each side, only open toward the stage. The illusion was for us to have our own private showing of whatever was going on. My instinctive protocol was strip joint rules. You can't touch the women, but that was quickly changed because they were touching us. Yet we were reluctant to force any sexual advancement.

There was a lot of drinking and talking, especially Kirk and Fertilizer Man, as they carried on about the deal. I did listen and give input, but I was mostly focused on the escort. The meals were very fine dining, and the wine flowed all night. We danced and partied with our paid friends until the wee hours of the morning.

I noticed a man dancing very slowly and quietly with an escort. He looked very familiar, so I asked my friend, did she recognize him? She replied yes, but she was not allowed to reveal his identity. He looked in his sixties, well-dressed, and for some reason he looked a lot like Prince Phillip. I asked the escort, and she just looked into my eyes and smiled as if to say, "You're very close."

I replied, "I will say no more." I had heard stories about the prince's antics, and some have said that he was a well-known philanderer right under the nose of the queen. I just chuckled and went on with the night.

As we sat down, a waiter came to the table and asked if there was anything more, and we said, "No, except the bill."

He was ready and dropped it in front of me. I opened it, and to my shock, it came to £250! At the time, Canadian value was almost $400.

Oh well, I thought, so I pulled out my RBC Visa and handed it to the waiter. We carried on for a few moments until the waiter returned, and with a smile he said there was a small problem with my card.

"Oh crap," I answered and gave him my other card from RBC. In a few seconds, he returned this time a bit nervous, stating, "Still a problem."

I began to sober up quickly. I pulled out my CIBC Visa and gave it to him. Back again he came, and this time he asked me to come with him to the office. I followed him to a very small closet he called "the office." A very small Korean lady was sitting on a stool in front of a Visa merchant machine. She said, "Your cards are good, but you're over your limit on all of them."

"Shit," I said. "What am I going to do?"

"No problem, Johnny. I fix quickly. You have good time for long time in my place. You come back anytime, okay?"

"Great but what are we going to do?"

"We go under limit on each card," she said. "I break up amount under $100 on each card. Then we real good, Johnny."

"Excellent," I replied in relief. I signed the chits, and as I was about to leave, she said, "I hope you got cash for girls. You pay girls before you go, Johnny. They nice girls. Big tits. They touch peewee. They get paid, no?"

I quickly thought and replied, "No problem."

"Okay, Johnny, you have big time tonight here?"

"Yes, I did," I responded.

She finished by saying, "Love you long time, Johnny. Come back, I give you special girl. She do more than touch peewee, okay?"

"Sure."

When I arrived at the table, I relieved everyone by announcing the bill was paid. Then I pulled Kirk over and quietly announced the final problem.

He said, "Oh no, Frank. You were to pay all the expenses."

"I know, Kirk, but I have a problem, and still, I did not come with much cash."

"Frank, I do not have more than $50. I cannot ask my friend for cash. That would be very improper."

"Then what are we going to do?"

Kirk thought for a second, then grabbed me by the arm and said, "Take my friend out of the building by telling the girls you and he will be right back, and that you are going to the washroom upstairs."

"Okay, I got it. We get out of the building right away and leave without paying the girls."

"That's right," Kirk answered. "I will divert them, and you wait for me down the street. Get a cab and have it waiting."

"Okay," I answered. "Listen, girls, I need to talk to Fertilizer Man for a minute alone, so we will be right back, okay?" I asked, trying not to be too suspicious.

Our friend had no idea what was going on, and he followed through, very unsuspecting as we went up the stairs and directly out of the building. He then asked, "Where's Kirk?"

"He'll be with us shortly," I answered as I nervously kept an eye out for Kirk.

Within seconds the door of The Dexter Lodge Inn flew open, and Kirk started running down the street toward us, yelling, "Get a cab, quick! Hurry, they're coming for us! Get a cab!"

Right behind him were two of the girls and a bouncer, chasing him.

"Holy shit!" I yelled.

Fertilizer Man stood in disbelief and said, "What this is? This is unacceptable. How dare you do this to these people?"

I yelled, "Get a cab, or your ass is grass, buddy!" He looked at me in shock, then turned and, within a second, flagged a cab and got in.

I waited for Kirk, then the two of us jumped in the back seat. "Go . . . go . . . go!" we yelled as the cabby sped away just in time. We looked back, and all we could see was the two girls, jumping up and down in the middle of the street, shaking their fists, and flashing their tits while the bouncer crouched over, catching his breath.

"You men are very bad," Fertilizer Man stated in disgust. "I will not go out with you again! You are corrupting my dear friend! How can I do business with you?"

I was pissed off at him by then. "You won't be complaining if we earn you a few million bucks, asshole, now, will you?" I shouted out at him.

The plane ride back to Buffalo was unmemorable, to say the least. I kind of wanted to be home anyway. I could tell Kirk was not too anxious to talk much business for the time being. In fact, I could tell he was drifting away from the enthusiasm he had before the trip.

A few weeks later, Kirk called me and announced he needed me to go to Montreal with him to pick up his Ferrari Daytona. It was in for repairs, and he needed to drive it back to Cambridge. I obliged, and away we went for a weekend in Montreal. On the way to the airport, he announced we were stopping in Ottawa to meet with the ambassador to Zambia, and we would stay the night at the Zambian consulate's mansion.

We pulled into the mansion driveway through large iron gates, and I was very excited. The door opened, and there stood a very tall, thin, Black Zambian with a big smile.

"Welcome, my friends!" It was the ambassador, and he was already half in the bag, and it was only two o'clock in the afternoon. "Come in, and I will get you a drink!"

I just followed. We talked about the deal and, the ambassador was very much committed to the plan as he poured us our sixth vodka. "We will celebrate the success of our new venture by going dancing tonight in Hull, my friends," the ambassador announced. "I will drive," he stated.

Oh my God, I said to myself. *We'll die for sure.*

All of us piled into the Lincoln, which had diplomatic plates, and away we went to a bar at least five kilometres down the road.

Kirk and the ambassador slipped away into the woodwork as I drifted aimlessly by myself, enjoying the solitude amongst a very energetic, wall-to-wall crowd. It seemed like hours when I finally began talking to a very good-looking young lady sitting at the bar. I immediately discovered she only spoke French. She could understand a little English. Enough to say, "Come to my place."

I sparked to those words and I tried to find Kirk but to no avail. I assumed they'd left to go back to the embassy. My new friend urged me to get a cab, and we headed toward her place, so she said. Fortunately, we were on the same road as the embassy, and I had a very good sense of how to get back when the time came.

The girl was very quiet, and I could tell she was very uneasy with what she was doing. Finally, she got the taxi driver to pull over at a local pub, and she said good night and then slipped away. I looked at my watch, and it was almost five in the morning, so I directed the cabby to drive me to the embassy. I got out at the gates and paid the cab. I assumed there would be a guard or electric communications at the gate to let me in, but to my surprise, there was nothing and no one.

I was getting a bit nervous because I feared that if the group was not back, someone might think I was trying to break in. My initial instinct was to climb the fence, which was what I did, completing the task successfully. The second plan was to check the garage to see if the car was parked, and it was there. I felt more at ease, seeing the car's presence. Last was to try the front door and see if they'd left it open for me. No, it wasn't. "Shit!" I said to myself. "Now what?" I actually said out loud. *Back door, windows, any entrance*, I started deducting mentally. To my dismay, nothing was open. *Well, it's 5:30 in the morning. Someone will be getting up within the hour, and I'll ring the doorbell then. I shouldn't wake anyone up just yet.*

I was starting to feel the morning chill even though it was late August 1984. All I was wearing was a golf shirt, sandals, and shorts. The dew had formed on the grass. The frost-like coating was on everything. I'd forgotten we were in Ottawa. That's on the cusp of north-central Ontario. The chill hit sooner than southern Ontario, where I had been raised to be used to warmer temperatures this time of the year.

So, there I sat on the front steps to the Zambian consulate, waiting for the ambassador to wake up and let me in to at least warm up. Every five minutes, I rang the doorbell, but no one came. It seemed like hours went by. I finally lay down on the front door mat to try to get some sleep. I could barely keep my eyes open.

"Wake up, Mr. Frank. Mr. Frank? Mr. Frank, wake up!"

I could hear someone calling me from a distance in my sleep. I opened my eyes. There was the ambassador, in his pyjamas, standing over me, trying to wake me up.

"What time is it?" I asked as I became awake and sat up.

"It is nine o'clock, Mr. Frank. What happened to you last night? We looked for hours for you!" The ambassador walked me to the kitchen, and there, to my comfort, was everyone waiting for me to sit and join in for breakfast and hear my tale of the night and laugh with me about my attempt to break into the Zambian embassy.

Kirk and I laughed for days over the event and shared the story with everyone at the tennis club. We were getting to be known as the odd couple around town, but definitely the heterosexual odd couple. Kirk always had an eighteen-year-old, six-foot blonde at his side. She was from Austria and attended the University of Western Ontario in London, Ontario. Kirk was paying her tuition to help her and her mother out. I suspected there was a payback in the form of personal favours, but I never broached the question at any time. In fact, when the club members we hung out with kidded him about his tall blonde protégée, I looked the other way and disengaged to avoid confrontation of any kind. Both Kirk and the young lady seemed to appreciate my approach to the situation. But there they would go, a five-foot-nothing, forty-eight-year-old, Black Zambian doctor and a gorgeous, six-foot, blonde, long-haired, long-legged, eighteen-year-old Austrian beauty, off to play tennis or spend a weekend in Toronto, charioted in a 1972 Ferrari Daytona.

Harold Robbins could never have written it better. Robbins was my favourite author of the seventies. His books edged me into a whole new world of sexual awareness and wonderment. I blame him for all that went wrong in my relationships and, in fairness, what went right in the bedroom.

The next few months were of the same type of activity with Kirk, my staff, and my Kinsmen friends. We partied, I attended numerous business meetings, and I embarked on many affairs—short-lived, mind you, but I still ran with new female acquaintances. I was getting to the point I really didn't care whether Patty found out about them or not because she was spending all her time away from the house and me. I was mentally divorced anyway. My focus was on the well-being of Daren and Michael.

Daren had started kindergarten, and Mike needed to have a babysitter. We hired a local girl who was about seventeen and came from a good family to watch Mike during the day and both boys after Daren's school.

One day I came home early, and before I got out of the car, I saw Mike walking on the roof of the house near his bedroom window. Without shutting the car off, I panicked and ran into the house.

When I got to Mike and Daren's bedroom, the door had been locked. The babysitter was nowhere in sight. I immediately opened the bedroom door and found Daren sitting on his bed, playing with some toys. I asked what was going on as I was halfway out of the window to try to get Mike back in safely. I couldn't see Mike, and I was really freaked by this time.

I ran out the side door only to see my new Mercedes roll down the driveway, cross the street, roll onto my neighbour's front lawn, and come to rest, without damage, against their front bay window. Then, like a shot from a gun, Mike ran out of the car's driver's side and down the street. I ran and grabbed him, hugging him, relieved he wasn't even scratched.

"How did you get off of the roof, Mike?" I asked in amazement.

He said, "I can slide down the eavestrough on the garage side, Daddy," as if to impress me with his four-year-old gymnastic ability and strength.

"I'm so happy you're safe, Mike, but don't you do that again, please!"

"The rooster showed me how to walk the roof, Daddy!"

"The rooster, who is he?" I asked in shock.

"Carey's boyfriend. He's a man dancer with hair that looks like a rooster," he answered innocently. "He plays games on us when Daren comes home from school."

"What's that, son?"

"He locks us in our room, and we are to stay there until they are finished."

"Finished what, son?"

"Bedtime," Mike answered as a four-year-old only could.

"Bedtime, I questioned?" Then I immediately put Mike down, quietly went into my bedroom, and found the two of them naked, still humping like animals. I kicked them both out of the house and demanded that they never come back again.

It only took once for me to realize both Patty's and my lives were spinning out of control. Sooner or later, something terrible would happen. We had to stop the insanity right then and there.

The Mike on the roof event was the first signal of bad times to come.

I was called into a meeting with the partners of S/W on a Saturday. They were all there, awaiting my arrival. Peter Kennedy began by almost yelling at me about running the company into serious debt by my overspending and cost of operations, let alone the cost of my buy-out. The others joined in except for Robson. He just sat in a corner and listened. When they stopped, I knew what they had intended the meeting to accomplish. They wanted me to fold and walk.

I got up and looked around the room, straight into each partner's eyes, and then stopped at Robson.

"You know, Robson, I actually thought you were an honest guy. I thought you were a man of your word. I expected nothing from your buddies, and I even had the idea this meeting might happen sooner than later. But I really didn't think you would be such a spineless weasel and hide while I'm being beaten up.

"Tell you what I'm going to do, gentlemen . . . and I use the word 'gentlemen' loosely. I'm going to forewarn you up front. You are on notice from this moment forward. I'm going to file a civil lawsuit action against S/W and you all individually, as directors, for wrongful dismissal, breach of contract, and whatever else my very expensive lawyers can conjure up. I am going to teach you a lesson in humility and honesty. See you all in court." I got up and walked out.

The first call I made was to Craig Keller, my accountant. After a long discussion, Craig guaranteed he would have the best Toronto-based law firm on our side and tear these rip-off artists apart. We set a meeting to go to Toronto and meet with Tory and Tory, located on Bay Street.

"You have a very solid case, Frank," Mr. Tory stated, "and I would like to suggest you could have a settlement in the first three months."

"Okay," I answered, relieved and feeling more confident.

"So, I'll need a retainer, Frank," Mr. Tory stated without looking up at me.

"How much we talking, sir?" I asked in a bit of shock. "Can't you work on a percentage?"

"Contingency," Tory snorted out. "This is Canada, my son. Not the US. We need to cover our cost up front, my boy. How about $10,000 to get started?"

"I'll get back to you, sir."

"Fine, let me know."

Then we left.

"Shit!" I chuffed as we got on the elevator. "How am I going to raise the money for this?"

"Get back to selling, Frank. That's what you do best," Craig coached as we walked onto Bay Street.

I had gotten a call from Gord Lee about a month or so before this happened, and he had asked for a loan of $3,000. He was stuck in Los Angeles, broke. I couldn't let him starve, so I wired him the money. I didn't realize I'd be cash strapped so soon after. I was able to get hold of Gord through his brother and told him the story of what happened. Gord then said, "If you ever need anything, you let me know." He was set up in Cold Water Canyon up on the hill in Hollywood near Bellaire. His house was situated on Cabrillo Drive. As always, he was living high, like a movie star. He had his way, and he was always able to con people into believing he would pay for something like a car, a house . . . anything that was worth more than $10,000, Gord had a way to get it.

I had to call in the loan on Gord because I had no cash left, and time had run out for me. Gord sent me the money. Only half was there in the Purolator envelope.

I got a call from John Hamilton, the branch manager of Standard Life. The office, ironically, was in Waterloo. "Come work with us, Frank. I know all about what has happened to you. The news is everywhere, unfortunately, and you are a sitting duck, as they say. But you still have friends. We'll help you out."

"Thank you, John," I said in response.

My ethics were completely out the window by then, and I busily re-wrote as many policies as I could within about a two-month period.

Christmas came and went, only to deliver two unwanted presents for Patty and I. Patty agreed to a divorce, and we both filed for bankruptcy on December 28, 1984.

February first arrived, and I was sure the next for me would be a nervous breakdown. Patty left the house for Brantford, and I had an apartment in Kitchener. Instead of putting the house up for sale, Patty let it go into foreclosure. I was so beside myself and disillusioned by the lack of help from the insurance business and the helplessness I felt because even my own accountant refused to help after all the money that he had earned from me.

The worst part was the people who had worked for me who still had jobs. They survived without a scratch, like Ron Madzia, for example. I went to lunch with him not long after everything collapsed, and he refused to lend me money or help me in this rough spot.

He simply stated, "You'll be fine. You always find your way through things, Frank."

I began to realize who my friends really were. Ron, obviously, was not one of them.

Then there was Dale Rutky. I not only gave him a job selling insurance, but took him off the streets when he'd lost his previous job. I not only housed him, but lent him my car, which he drove on my insurance without giving me a dime for six months. I even lent him $1,200 to fly to Texas on some TV cable deal. He never repaid me. What he did do was give me his coat from Calgary. It might have been worth $100. "At least you won't get cold, Frank," Dale pacified me as I left his house.

I couldn't raise the money to sue, so I had to walk away from the deal. Tory said I was a fool not to go to my family, but I knew better. My dad would have said no, and no one else would have come to my rescue. I had to do it on my own.

Chapter 17

So, I called Gord and ate crow.

"Rainbow, good timing. I may send you to Vancouver or bring you to LA until you get to know the ropes. Then you'll be my representative in Vancouver. Okay?"

"Awesome," I said. "When do I leave?"

"Well, you need to raise at least the cost of a flight, which is $99 USD out of Buffalo, and some spending and living money. I'll have you earning your own way within a couple of weeks."

"Okay. I'll call you when I have it together," I told Gord.

The first thing I did was contact Cathy Stach, my exotic dancer friend, and have her take over my apartment, which she did in a heartbeat. The second was to make amends with Patty so I could make sure she was prepared to stay away from legals while I was away and, most importantly, to take care of my boys. My dad agreed to help out financially as a necessary stop-gap, on the condition that Patty stayed away from the lawyers while I was in LA. Finally, I had to find money. I went to my friend Les Misner and borrowed $100. I then creatively scooped $200 from the bank machine by depositing a cheque from the S/W account. This was legal, but I was not sure there was any money in the account.

Two days later, I called Gord, let him know the flight arrangements, and then got Les Misner to drive me to Buffalo to catch my flight.

The next morning at 6:00 a.m., I packed up Les' car with one suitcase, a small carry-on, and my guitar. I turned to Patty's sister's house, and standing on the sidewalk was Daren. To this day, I will never forget the image I saw of him. This five-year-old, watching his father go away.

He knew I was going somewhere, but I don't think he understood I was going to come back, but not for some time. I walked up to him, took him in my arms, and hugged him so tight. I whispered in his ear, "I have to go for a while, son, in order to try and make money for us. I may not be here, but I am always there in your heart for you, my son. I will never leave you. You call me on the phone whenever you want to talk to me, son."

"Okay, Dad," he answered. Then he said, as he always did when things got teary-eyed, "Don't you never mind care, Dad. See you!"

As I got into the car, he just stood there with that beautiful smile, and he raised his little hand and waved goodbye to me. I cried almost all the way to the border. Les understood and promised he would look out for the boys while I was away. I thanked him because I knew he would never let me down, nor would he ever let anything happen to my boys.

The plane was on time arriving and loading in Buffalo. Next stop was Newark, New Jersey, which was and is to this day the international hub to go anywhere. When I arrived in Newark, I learned I had a three-hour layover, so I took the opportunity to write John Hamilton of Standard Life and let him know what was going on. John was the last thing to do on my list, and wouldn't you know it, I forgot. Once I had completed the goodbye letter, I mailed it from Newark.

Ironically, I felt free from the last ten years, from the struggle, from the fight to keep myself and whomever I was with happy. Free of the fight to try to prove myself every single day as a husband, father, son, son-in-law, businessman, business owner, and community person—all the things I had been taught to become. Where did it get me? Where had it gotten the people that I'd given a life to and fed for so long? Where were those that lived off me and worked for me? Where were they now?

Looking out the window of a plane was so surreal to me, especially while flying over the Grand Canyon and the Nevada desert. It was like looking at a picture of the same thing. You really can't get a fair judgment of the true size of things unless you are standing amongst them. You know it's there, but you just can't put your finger on it.

From Newark, it took nine hours to fly and land in LA airport. I told Gord that my arrival was expected to be about 10:00 p.m. LA time, and we hit it dead on. The gate customs was very quick because the flight was national, so the real check had been done in Newark. But don't forget this was 1985, not 2010. A lot has gone on since then.

There were his cowboy boots, just like he said, sticking out from the bar. A well-dressed man with red hair and wire-rimmed glasses was sipping on a whisky in a shot glass. "Rainbow, you made it," I heard Gord remark in his gravelly tone just as I walked into the bar. "No time for a drink. We need to get to my house." I'm awaiting a very important call by 11:00 p.m.

He led me out of LAX to a parked Porsche 911 T Cabriolet. The car was new, and it was so fine. I loved this car. Typically, the car was illegally parked right in front of the entrance door to the airport. He was lucky it hadn't been towed away.

So away we went, down the expressway to Sunset Boulevard. Then we turned off of Sunset to Coldwater Canyon, which started us up the Hollywood hill, passing great movie and music mogul estates such as Lionel Ritchie and James Garner's, just to name a couple. Then, just before we reached the top, we turned onto Cabrillo Drive, and then halfway up that stretch, we turned into a gated compound nestled on the very top side of the Hollywood hills. Gord then stated with pride, "We're home, Rainbow. What do you think about this place?"

"Outstanding," I said. It was a beautiful flat-roofed bungalow overlooking the city of Los Angeles. I recognized so many views from TV series and movies as we walked around to the back of the house.

"The house is owned by Paramount Studios. I lease it for $5,000 a month."

I was in total amazement. My room for the first week was a small guest house, tucked against the wall of the hill.

Gord said, "Oh, by the way, the house was originally built by Lawrence Harvey, a very famous British actor of the thirties and forties. He died about five years ago. Then the studio picked it up from the estate. That's what these studios do." Gord lectured on, "They wait like piranhas, and when a star runs into financial difficulties or dies, they weasel their way into buying out the star's assets for a major discount.

"How do you know all this stuff, Gord?" I asked.

"I work in this industry, Rainbow. I find all this stuff out so I know what I'm dealing with at all times. But we'll get into that tomorrow. Tonight, let's get some sleep."

All that night I couldn't sleep because I felt so unsettled. I sensed that I was about to live out a movie of my own, but would I survive the outcome? I would have to wait to see. For some reason, I was sure it wouldn't be long before I learned the truth of Gord's Hollywood world. I really felt I'd had my eyes opened for the first time, and I was ready for anything. There was an empowering feeling of being on the edge this time.

The next morning came early. Gord rapped on my sliding glass door, which took up the whole front of the guest house. "Get up, Rainbow. We got a lot to do today."

"What time is it?" I asked in an early-morning stupor.

"It's 6:00 a.m., Rainbow. I let you sleep in. We get up at 5:00 a.m. in this town. They call it curtain call. Most actors get up at 4:00 a.m. to get to the studio for makeup, etc."

"The businesses too?" I asked.

"Oh, ha, everything operates around the movie business," Gord added.

We got into the Porsche and headed to downtown Bellaire, where Gord left me in the car again like he used to in Toronto. I said to myself, *Here we go again. I'll be his driver, always waiting and not being included.* Gord was back in seconds, then we headed toward Hollywood and Vine, the famous street that everything happened on, like the walk of fame and the Chinese Theatre where the Oscars took place.

"I'm going to introduce to you my partner in the telemarketing business we recently set up."

"What's telemarketing, Gord?"

"Telephone sales, Rainbow. You are about to learn the wave of the future. People are making millions every month from telemarketing. Selling over the phone is the new door-to-door salesperson. It is also the most profitable. I met some guys that drive Rolls Royces, live in bigger houses than I do, and have cash to burn. I am going to show you this world, Frank, because I think you could make your fortune in it. I'm already starting to turn cash, and I have only been doing it for two months.

"We also have a stock play called Thor Resources. This one's a brilliant play. We mine what is called aggregate from the Nevada desert, then ship it off to a refinery that separates the precious metals from the dirt, and then sell the precious metals, like gold, silver, platinum, etc."

"So, you sell the precious metals at a discount?"

"No, we sell the metals for a profit," Gord answered with a smile.

"How do you do that?" I asked, dumbfounded.

"I'll show you. I've told you enough for one day. For the rest of the week, you're going to enjoy Hollywood and get to know your surroundings. Go have lunch in Bellaire, meet movie stars, become a star, whatever you want to do, Rainbow. This is your time to learn and enjoy. You've been through enough over the past four years. Time for you to rebuild, don't you think, Rainbow?"

Yes, I said to myself. *Rebuild is what I have to do. I have to be smarter and not so naive.* "What's next on your list, Gord?"

"I have to meet with someone in the toughest, most dangerous part of LA. Want to come along, Rainbow?"

"Sure, I'm game," I responded like I wasn't concerned at all.

"I have to meet my leader of the telemarketing group. His name's Mike Dungy."

The day was sunny, just like one would picture in greater Los Angeles, and I could recognize the streets not by name but by image because of all the TV shows that have been filmed throughout the City of Angels. We passed by Centre City and the three towers that could be seen from anywhere for miles, especially from Gord's backyard pool. That's where all the movie and TV business happened. The streets and buildings began to show their age and neglect as we went west. The people congregated on all the street corners, and streetwalkers were everywhere. Gang colours dominated the uniform of the street people as we got deeper into the poorer neighbourhoods.

I mentioned to Gord, "Aren't you afraid of getting mugged down here?"

He just looked and smiled at me. Gord rarely showed fear, and I often thought that was one of the characteristics that attracted me to him. He somehow made me feel like he was a big brother in some sense of the title.

"Okay, Rainbow. We get out now and go directly into that hair salon across the street. Do not look at anyone in the eyes and do not stop for nothing, do you understand?"

"Yes," I responded firmly, as if we were about to enter a war zone.

The shop was full of African American women, and the hairstylists were mostly Latina. Standing at the counter was a very large, overweight, Black man wearing a white T-shirt and shorts with sandals. "Gord, hey man, what's shaking?"

"Mike, how's things?" Gord responded.

"This is Frank Trousdell, your new recruit for the team."

"Another Canadian . . . my! You guys are coming out of the woodwork," Mike jokingly responded.

A Latina stylist quirked back, "And he's a cute one at that, baby. Let me cut your hair and get to know you, my man."

Mike and Gord started to laugh at her reaction. "It never takes long for Rainbow," Gord jokes.

"We need to talk," Gord directed Mike.

"Okay, come to the back room."

I chatted for about fifteen minutes with Carina, the stylist, while Gord and Mike did whatever business they were doing. I instinctively sensed they were doing a dope deal. When they came out, Gord was quite red-faced, and Mike was all smiles. Coke, I deducted, but carefully kept my mouth shut and eyes off them. I had learned early to mind my own business, especially when dope might be involved.

"Mike, come with us. We're going to Bellaire for the rest of the day."

"Are you out of your mind?" Mike shrieked. "You want to get me locked up?"

"What's the matter, Mike? You've been with me at Rodeo Tavern a number of times. Let's go," Gord ordered.

"Alright," Mike answered and gave in.

Rodeo Tavern was situated on the corner of Rodeo Drive and Hollywood Boulevard. The place was more of a roadhouse upscaled to a restaurant than a tavern. The floors were terracotta tile, and the walls were stucco. Everyone was in summer suits or tracksuits, the official uniform of the Hollywood community at the time. Sitting at the bar was a very nervous Middle Eastern man, speaking very loud and fast. In fact, he was very animated, waving his arms and gesturing all around him.

"Gord!" he yelled as we came up to the bar. "Where have you been? He yelled almost loud enough to break the windows. He grabbed Gord and hugged him as if he were his long-lost brother. "I have been waiting here for at least two hours. You got my package? Please say yes," he spoke a lot quieter, thinking no one could hear this time, but to his mistake, everyone couldn't help but hear.

"We'll take a walk. Okay, Mick?" Gord quietly responded and led him to the door. "Stay here, Frank. Talk to Mike. Get yourself a beer and put it on my tab."

"Okay, was all I could say except to the bartender. "Two beers, please."

"On Gord's tab?" the barkeep responded.

"Yes, please. So, Mike, do you feel like telling me about yourself?" I asked mainly to change the topic.

"That's easy, Rainbow. Rainbow, how did you get that name?" Mike asked to redirect the question.

"Who else but Gord named me about eight years ago when I was playing hockey in Canada. It's a long story."

"I got you—Gord and his nicknames," Mike laughed. We spent the rest of an hour discussing each other's backgrounds and found a lot of similarities. Mike was from Philadelphia, and he'd attended Penn State for a time. His brother was in football, but Mike had never played. Mike liked basketball. We got along right from the get-go.

We were at least three beers each when Gord returned without the loudmouth.

"Is everything okay, Gord?" I asked.

"I'm back, aren't I?" he responded.

"That's always a sign in LA that all is good," Mike responded.

"Man, you guys are really scaring me now."

"Cool it, Rainbow. There's nothing for you to get your shit in a knot," Gord joked.

Gord and Mike spent the rest of the day outlining the telemarketing program to me, and by the end, I felt ready to give it a shot. Mike said to me, "Not quite yet, my man. You need training, and you have to learn to do it my way. You cannot wing this. There are very important teamwork elements you need to learn," Mike rigidified. "You will participate in a training class tomorrow at the office we have across the street from here. We start at 10:00 a.m."

"I'll be there," I assured both Mike and Gord.

"Good, let's get out of here," Gord stated.

That night I sat in my bedroom and reflected on the events of the day. I was amazed at what I had experienced; meeting Mike, the mysterious backroom meeting, then the suspicious man at the restaurant. You could have thought the whole event was played out on a movie set. Who knew, maybe we were playing out the beginnings of a Hollywood script? In LA, I learned you never knew what was real or what was just part of something bigger. One thing for sure was you'd never know the truth, no matter what. Everyone definitely played a part, even though they might not have had a clue what part they were acting. Only in the final cut, if they haven't been spliced out and dropped on the cutting room floor, would anyone involved directly or indirectly ever have a chance to understand what they had just done or assisted in as an accomplice. Eventually, you might find yourself as the main character for just a few moments. While in LA, you were lucky even to come out knowing what the hell you had just experienced. How well I found out not too long after this day.

Mike was a great communicator. I quickly realized why Gord had picked him to lead the pack. I sat amongst six other guys who obviously needed jobs. They certainly were not executive types or dressed like they could run a bank or insurance company. Pumping gas was more like their style.

Soon after my mental overview and assumptions, I gradually changed my attitude to respect their communicative skills. Their minds were sharp, and they spoke exceptional English. In fact, I felt intimidated. "You can't judge a book by its cover," I said over and over again to myself. As the session unravelled the true mission we were about to embark upon, I slowly started to get the full picture.

Thor Resources was the play. We were selling a product of Thor over the phone to homeowners, sophisticated and non-sophisticated investors, retirees, and anyone who answered an advertisement in an investment magazine requesting more information on commodity investments. Now I got the big picture and most of the little pieces. The package we were selling over the phone was a "dory bar," which weighed about ten pounds. This bar was raw aggregate. Everything you could think of was compounded in this bar. The contents included impurities, along with whatever precious metals existed to make up the whole matter. The truth was that Thor had an old man living in the desert north of Los Vegas. Every morning, he got up and with shovel in hand, filled hemp bags with desert dirt, then stacked them up for pickup. He was our mining operation.

The law stated that we could not sell the precious metals in their purest form, which was why we sold the dory bar. We automatically offered the service of shipping their bar to a refinery to produce the precious metals on behalf of the owner of this bar. Then the precious metals were shipped off to the purchaser with authenticity papers. Sounds interesting, doesn't it? Oh the price was $4,900 US for a precious metal value at today's estimated value of $7,500 US. So, the unsuspecting buyer thought they'd just profited $2,600, tax-free until they sold their holdings. Why wouldn't you do it? You couldn't lose, or could you? That was the illusion of the deal—the hidden pitfalls, the people mistakes, the redirected cash trails and finally, who was in control of the manufacturing of the dory bars? How were they being made? How were they being shipped off to the refinery, and by whom? How were the production systems being reported to the shareholders of Thor Resources? Finally, who was ensuring that Thor was complying with the SEC? We never even dreamed about all of the above while we set out to telemarket our way into the bank accounts of America.

Weeks flew by as we readied to telephone our way to financial success. I had no money by this time, and I had kept in contact with Patty and the kids, missing them more and more each day. Patty had taken a job with a nursing home, and my mom and dad were keeping a distant eye on the well-being of the boys, as were my sisters. I talked to Les on a regular basis and encouraged him to invest in Thor stock, which was ironically climbing the market on the Vancouver exchange. Gord was getting me to promote the stock more and more, giving me the opportunity that I had come down there to learn. I was contacting brokers right across every brokerage house in Canada and the Southern United States.

One day Gord asked me to stay at the house for a meeting with a couple of partners in the Thor deal. He didn't prep me much but did say he needed me to make a telephone call to a bank in Chicago for him in front of the two men. I really didn't think too much of the challenge.

I was standing outside the front door when a white Rolls Royce pulled into the driveway. Two men, looking like movie people, got out of the car and greeted Gord. We went inside and sat by the pool. Gord introduced me to them as the businessman from Toronto that he had told them about. They immediately took an interest in me and asked me very strange questions about my past. "Did I ever do any acting in school or study drama?"

Of course, I replied, "No."

The shorter man asked me to make a call to a number that he handed me and told me to ad lib the conversation with the name I was to ask for on the other end. The other end was a bank executive, and I was to inform him that a transfer of funds was on its way to cover a certain account and that we would require confirmation immediately upon its arrival. That was all they wanted me to do.

Gord sat very anxiously while the two men watched me as if they were studying my every move and listening to every word I spoke. When I finished, and the man on the other end had thanked me for my call, I said, "Goodbye."

At that moment, the two men got up, shook my hand, and left, saying nothing. When Gord came back in, I looked at Gord and said, "What the hell was that?"

Gord looked back with a twinkle in his eye and said, "You just auditioned for a part in a movie called "Wall Street". I told you about that movie some time ago in Toronto, remember, Rainbow?"

"Holy shit," I answered. "Are you kidding me?"

"No, I work with those two, and they're agents looking for actors to fill typecast parts. I suggested you.

"Who knows if anything comes of it, Rainbow? You can't prepare for these things. You just do it. If you got what they want, they will tell you. I've been through a number of these things. Hell, that's where I've met most of my investors over the past few months. Let's go down to the office."

So away we went. I was riding high over the little test I experienced. Needless to say, I was impressed ... until we got to the office. Gord and Mike sat me in a board room with two phones. One was for Mike, and another was for me. Gord placed a list of names and numbers in front of me, and all he said before he left was, "I have meetings all day, and you'll have to find your own way home, okay?" I did not have any time to realize I only had twenty dollars in my pocket as Gord left the room.

"Okay, Frank, let's go to work," Mike commanded. "Call your first number. Oh, and here is the script you must follow to the word."

"Okay," I replied somewhat apprehensively.

To this day, I cannot remember a word I spoke, but I did exactly what Mike told me to do. The person on the other end was following my questions and statements as if they were hypnotized by the script and fell into the telemarketing trap instantly. When I got to the part about why they should not invest today, Mike took over as the supervisor only qualified to discuss the bank/credit card information, and within five minutes, we had a deal and a credit card number authorized for $4,900. My commission was $600. The rest of the day was not as easy, but we landed two more deals. I was excited by my success, but deep inside, I didn't feel right about what I had just done. I could have sold dope, and I would have felt the same way. Even though I had $1,200 in one sitting, I couldn't shake the dirty feeling, and all I wanted to do was go get drunk. Mike asked me if I wanted to go to his place, and I replied that I just wanted to go home. He could tell I was not really happy and saw I was putting on an act.

"I think I'll walk home," I stated.

"Suit yourself. That's a long walk from here, Sunset Boulevard past Bellaire to Coldwater Canyon, then to Cabrillo Drive. You're going to walk five miles."

"I can do it," I replied in confidence. "I need the air."

"Watch out for the pimps and hookers. They can be dangerous, Frank."

"They don't scare me, and I can take care of myself."

"Call me if you need me, Frank," Mike yelled as I left the office.

I didn't get a mile down Sunset before every dreg of the earth began to follow me and gear about how much of a fool I was walking alone. They could tell I was not from the area. By the time I reached the infamous

Sunset Café, a pimp tried to stop me. "Hey, man, get a cab. We all been watching you. You gonna get yourself hurt walking alone, man."

"I'm okay," I answered,

He smiled and said, "Where are you from?"

"Canada."

"Shit, you will be fine. No one gonna mess with a Canuck!"

I smiled and said, "Take care, man." He just laughed and returned to his ladies while they all kind of cheered me on.

The sun was setting as it did about 6:30 every day, and I took a big, long breath as I looked up at the Hollywood sign on the top side of the hill. "This town is really not for me. I want to go home and start over," I said to myself. "When I get paid, I think I'll take a plane and go home." I smiled as I stated my plan to myself. "It's time to get back to my boys."

I remembered when talking to a fellow phone guy that he bartended at Glitters in Bellaire, so when I came up to it on the street, I decided to spend my last $20 on some beers. I had just made $1,200, so I thought I could spend the twenty. The guy's name was Doug or Bob—that I can't remember—but his last name I will never forget: Lynch. He claimed his brother was a famous New York actor and his cousin was a director, David Lynch. He was an aspiring actor but hadn't gotten any good roles yet. I really didn't believe him because in LA, everyone is an actor waiting for the big break.

I sat down at the end of the bar, and within a few seconds, buddy arrived from the back room. "Hey you made it! A cold beer, and you mentioned you like Miller Lite, right?"

"You got it," I replied. "How much are the beers?" I questioned as I reached for my twenty.

"Oh, for you . . . you're good for five beers at . . . no charge. Tonight is on me!"

"Holy shit," I said in a very happy tone.

"It's a slow night, and I'll do my patriotic duty and treat my Canadian cousin to some good old American beer."

"Thank you, my cousin," I said with a big smile on my face. The beer was cold and tasted very good, and was just what I needed to finish the day.

We talked for at least three hours, and then the owner came in and shut the place down. "No business tonight, so go on home," he said to buddy.

"Hey, Frank, I got my car, and I'm going to a comedy club tonight. Would you like to go for a bit?"

"Sure," I said, "but shit, man, I got no money until Friday."

"I'll spot you. Don't worry. I do have to go home for a second, okay?"

"Sure," I replied.

He lived in a modest house about five minutes away, near Brentwood. As we entered, buddy said, "Take a look at my brother's pictures on the wall. You might recognize some of the people." I certainly did, such as Al Pacino on the *Serpico* set, Al and his brother in different bar and group pictures, and countless other famous actors. I recognized his brother right away. I had seen him in TV movies, and he had many bad guy roles in *The Streets of San Francisco*, *Starsky & Hutch*, and *Where Eagles Dare* with Clint Eastwood. They were all there for me to see. I was convinced because of the family photos on the piano and the Tony awards his brother had won.

Off we went to the comedy club—I cannot remember the name, but it was the big one that ended up on TV for a long run. The acts were familiar but not the big ones like Chevy Chase or Dan Aykroyd or John Baluchi. I do believe, if my memory serves me, that Jay Leno headlined that night. I could be wrong, but the event was fantastic. Ironically, it did not cost very much. Entrance was $5, and the drinks were $5 each, I think. Maybe buddy wasn't telling me the real cost. However, fun was had that night. He drove me home, and I went to bed.

"Rainbow, where the hell were you last night?" I was startled by the tone of Gord's voice. I told him, and he just said, "Well, you had me a nervous wreck all night. I thought you were mugged and dead somewhere off Sunset."

"No, I was watched by the pimps, and they took good care of me."

"Unbelievable, Rainbow. You've got horseshoes up your butt."

"You'd think so, Gordo."

"Well, I got some changes for you. Move to the servants' quarters in the back of the kitchen. We have friends staying the weekend. My wife wants you to find your own apartment by next week. You've outstayed your welcome. Three months is enough living off me. I've repaid the debt we've had, so start getting yourself together and get out, buddy."

Just as he finished his statement, his father-in-law came running in and yelled, "There's a tow truck in your driveway, taking both your cars, Gord. What's going on?"

"Fuck!" Gord ran out to see for himself.

I stood in the middle of the driveway, watching the event. Gord came up to me and said, "They confiscated my cars. I owe six months on the leases." No sooner did he finish telling me that than a sheriff's car arrived and served Gord with an eviction notice. He had seven days to get out.

"Fuck! Gord, haven't you been paying your bills?"

He just shrugged it off and walked into the house. I knew this was bad, and he did not seem himself at all. Gord then came to me and said he was busy with his guests for the next two days and asked if I could do a couple of meetings for him. I said I would.

The one that day was with Mike, and Mike was unnerved as well. Mike said some things weren't right, and some people were looking for Gord. They were very nasty people, and Mike thought I might be better off going home soon.

"I got to get paid first, Mike," I said.

"Tomorrow's pay day, so let's see what happens."

I did not sleep all night. Gord and his wife entertained their guests as if nothing was out of line, and I could hear them joke about me. The friends were from Cambridge, Ontario, and I knew them well, for the husband was Dr. Murray Fisk's son. Dr. Fisk was one of my insurance clients. The wife owned and operated the famous retail franchises Cotton Ginny. They had been high school friends, so Gord couldn't let his guard down. When they went to bed, Gord came into my room. He had a joint and shared it with me. He apologized for what happened and the abuse they gave me.

I said, "Don't worry. I'll do your meeting tomorrow with the guy, and all will be good as long as you pay me."

"Pay you?" Gord retorted.

"Yes, Gord, you owe me $1,200."

"Rainbow, you owe me for all the food you ate here and the accommodations!

"So, I worked for free?" I questioned him.

He could tell I was angry. "Okay, okay, you're right. I'll give you cash tomorrow."

"Fair enough, Gord. By the way, who am I seeing for you tomorrow?"

"Remember the crazy guy at the Rodeo Drive bar?"

"Fuck," I said. "What do you want me to do with him?" I asked in disgust.

"Calm him down for me, would you?"

"He thinks you're my bodyguard. He won't fuck with you."

"Where's he from?" I asked.

"Lebanon. He's a real estate broker. He's very wealthy and has invested over $2 million into Thor. He also buys coke from me. Forget I even told you."

"Great," I said as Gord left my bedroom. "I am going to get the fuck out of this crazy town if it is the last thing I do," I kept saying to myself, trying to calm down so I could sleep. *This is it for me and Gord. I've finally learned my lesson. Everything that Gord has done, he has suckered me in and taken advantage every time. I'd thought he was there to help, not to set me up. Am I that gullible to fall for the trap every time with Gord or is he trying to teach me something about myself at my own expense? Either way, this is it. The falcon is leaving the nest. I will now hunt for myself.*

I had to stop by the office to meet Gord to get paid before I went to the meeting. Mike and I waited an hour before Gord showed up. He paid Mike and then tried to leave through the doorway. I stood in the doorway with my arms up, clutching the upper door frame.

"You forget something, Gordo?"

He looked into my eyes and saw my anger rising. "Oh yeah . . . here!" He dropped the money on the floor and ran out the door.

Mike started laughing as I picked up the cash and counted at the same time. "The fucker!" I yelled. "He's short $600. He only paid me half."

"What are you going to do, Frank?"

"Go home, Mike. I'll gather my things and catch a flight out tomorrow. I'll stay one night more without letting him know and leave in the morning."

"Good idea," Mike suggested.

By the time I got to Rodeo Drive, the Lebanese man was there waiting. "Hi, I'm Frank."

"Where is Gord?" he asked.

"He isn't coming," I responded.

"Well, what the fuck do you think you are going to do for me Mr. Man?" he asked sarcastically.

"You and I are going to have a little talk," I stated with quiet confidence.

"We are . . . okay," he answered as if he had a hit of logic. He could instantly tell I was in no mood for him to try to intimidate me. To tell you the truth, I'd had about enough of these idiots, and all caution was out the window by then for me.

" I do not know who you are, what your deal is with Gord, nor do I really care. But I have been sent here to talk to you, so in your best interest I think you should tell me everything. Then I will tell you what I know. Then we can decide what to do. What do you think?"

He sat there for a moment, then sat back in his chair and just looked at me. "For some crazy reason, I feel I can trust you. You're from Canada, right?"

"Yes," I answered.

"You are an insurance specialist according to Gord, am I right?"

"That's CLU, right?

"Yes, I agreed.

"Okay, here it is, Gord approached me some months ago with the Thor deal, and I was referred by a lot of my associates to talk to Gord. They were all in the deal. I had some . . . let's say . . . extra discretionary cash on hand from an undisclosed transaction offshore. Let's say . . . illegal maybe."

"Let me help . . . drug money," I stated.

"Yes . . . but I had to clean it, so Gord took it off my hands and somehow bought me into the stock deal. Now I need it, and he is giving me the run around. I heard he's broke?" he asked.

"Yes, he is at this moment"

"Am I going to get my money?" he asked, getting sweatier and more anxious.

"I personally think you might not, but Gord always finds a way to come through."

He sat back again and just looked at me. "You're his hit man, aren't you?" he asked flatly.

"Absolutely not," I answered.

"Just checking," he stated. "I like you. I think you could help me get out of this problem."

"How?" I asked.

"You set up a short account in Canada, and when the time is right, I tell you when to pull the trigger. We win large by shorting Thor."

I could not believe what I was hearing. It was the same play not two years earlier with Surf and Radial, and Gord was about to get it again, this time by a very dangerous Lebanese. The worst part of it was that I was in the middle again, but this time on the drug dealer's side. I felt like an assassin cleaning up a very dirty mess.

"I want you to call me when the account is set up. Then I will transfer $250,000 into the account. Then you have the ability to call the short when I tell you. Okay?"

"Okay," I responded with a handshake. While I rode in the cab, I realized if Gord were to find out about this meeting's discussion, I would be in serious trouble. Gord, being a coke user, I never knew what he would do. So, I decided not to discuss it with him and see what happened.

I thought that would be the end of it. I was going to forget the whole thing by the time I got back to Gord's house. All I wanted to do was go back to Canada and be with my kids.

I looked at my watch as I entered Gord's house. On the door was an eviction notice. The lights were out. A small light could be seen as I passed through the kitchen coming from the far part of the open space living room. There was Gord, sitting all alone behind his desk with only the small desk light on. In front of him was a mixing bowl full of white substance. He was scooping small piles out, lining it up, then snorting the line into his nose, one line after another.

I stood in the shadows for a few seconds, watching him. The rest of the family was not in the house because they would have been in the kitchen or wandering about. This situation did not look good to me at all. *I had better announce myself, or else he'll get suspicious.*

I slowly and quietly walked up and stood in front of his desk. "Gord, what are you doing?"

"What does it look like, Rainbow? I'm drowning my sorrows in coke. So, Rainbow, you had quite the meeting with my man tonight," Gord suggested as he continued snorting the coke, looking at only the coke lines.

"Your man is a very strange one, to say the least, Gord."

"Strange as a fox, Rainbow. What did he have to say?"

My mind started racing to think of what to tell him. Then I noticed the silver-plated, pearl-handled nine-millimetre pistol sitting on the edge of the desk in full view. "Fuck," I said to myself.

"Your friend is trying to set you up, Gord. He wants to short Thor to get back at you. He wants his money, and I believe he will do anything to get it."

In a flash, Gord jumped up, grabbed the gun, and pointed it right at my forehead. I could feel the sweat run down my face and start to soak my golf shirt. I looked straight into Gord's eyes; I could tell he was crazed, and I believed he would do anything by then. I could feel my nerves start to spring on end and my blood pressure rise rapidly.

"Gord, I tried to get as much out of him as I could for you. You need to know what he's up to. I think you need to talk with him and straighten this thing out before he loses it." It took every ounce of strength to not flinch or go for the gun, which I know would have caused an even worse chain of events.

Gord just looked at me, shaking. His hands were shaking, and then he lowered the gun and put it down on the desk. Gord then slumped down in his chair and stared at the floor. "What am I going to do, Rainbow? These guys are very dangerous. This situation is not negotiable."

I could tell Gord was now distraught, and I needed to get the gun away from him. I slowly walked around the desk, gently picked the gun up, then slid it into the holster that was sitting on the bookshelf behind Gord. I put it at the very top of the bookshelf, pushing it to the back against the wall so it could not be easily reached. I turned and grabbed Gord by the shirt collar, pulled him out of his seat, and looked him straight in the eyes.

In a very low tone, shaking as I spoke, I said, "How could you, Gord? What have I ever done to you for you to put a gun to my head?" That was all I could find the words to say. But he knew I was pissed and scared. I let him go then.

Gord changed his demeanour instantly like nothing ever happened and seemed to straighten up in seconds as he grabbed his car keys. "Let's go get some booze, Rainbow. You need a beer. What a day, Rainbow. You did good, buddy. I'm real proud of you, standing up to that asshole.

"He called me seconds after you left and told me that you were going to sabotage me. He also said he wanted to set you up and have you whacked if I didn't settle the outstanding account I had with him." When Gord said this, I knew he was likely telling the truth. I knew right then I had to get out of LA as soon as possible. This was not a barroom deal gone bad in Cambridge, Ontario, where two guys would sort things out in a fistfight. These whackos meant deadly business. I had to disappear . . . like right that moment.

Gord literally flew down Cold Water Canyon, then across Brentwood to a drug store, and walked in to buy booze. He was staggering, and I was scared out of my mind that a cop, or even worse, the Lebanese guy, would show up. Within minutes Gord appeared and got into the car. "Let's go, Rainbow. Ha ha, open me a beer," he commanded as if we had just arranged a big deal or something. I handed him one, and he gulped a whole beer down in seconds. When we got back to his desk, Gord seemed to get really tired and announced he was going to bed.

I couldn't wait to get to my room. The first thing I did was call Mike Dungy, the guy I was working with in the call centre, and ask him to come and get me immediately. I told him, in short, what happened, and he agreed I needed to get out as soon as possible. By then, the time was close to 12:00 a.m. Doug would be at the gates any time now, so I figured I had better get on the other side of the gates and wait for my ride.

I didn't have to wait too long before I saw a set of headlights slowly climb Cabrillo Drive. As the old, black Lincoln got closer, I could see only the two beady eyes of the driver over the top of the steering wheel, shining like mini headlights . . . it was Mike.

"Get in the fucking car, Frank!" Mike was almost yelling as he pulled up.

"What are you bent out of shape for, Mike?"

"This is Bellaire/Hollywood! Blacks do not drive up the hill after midnight. They'd shoot us if they found me up here," Mike screamed.

"Holy shit," I responded.

He turned the car around and travelled down the hill below the speed limit.

I told Mike the details of what had gone on earlier that night, and he couldn't believe it.

"Well, that's what drugs and money do in this town. You're lucky he didn't snap and shoot you," Mike spoke with assurance. "I think you're right. You had better get on a plane first thing in the morning."

"Where am I going to stay, Mike?"

"I'll take you to a place that is safe and totally out of the way. No one will look for you there. I will come back at nine in the morning and pick you up and take you to Centre City to get you a one-way ticket home. Hopefully, there is a flight out tomorrow."

Well, Mike took me to an out-of-the-way place, alright: 53rd and La Brea Avenue. The Watts district! Yes, the same place where all the riots took place. It looked like a war zone. Boarded-up windows and broken-down buildings lined the streets. Everyone looked like they were ready to do me in if I looked the wrong way. Mike pulled into a motel that looked like it should have been condemned years ago. I walked up to a window, and a small Vietnamese man was sitting on a chair behind a bulletproof window. "Twenty-five dollars, please," the man stated before I said anything.

"Okay," I said and then paid him.

He then gave me a key and directed me behind the back of the building. "You want service tonight?" he asked as we walked to the room.

"No, I really just want to sleep. Where can I get cigarettes and some beer?" I asked.

"Across the street. It's open all night."

"Thanks," I answered. He opened the door and then left very fast. I walked in, and to my horror, the room looked like someone had just used it and left towels and blankets thrown all over the bed. I then looked into the bathroom and shouted to Mike, "Shit!"

"What?" he answered with a bit of a nervous chuckle.

"The shower is a pipe sticking out of the wall! There is no shower curtain. I won't even pee in this thing that is the toilet. I'm afraid something will jump out and bite me." I turned around.

"I could have taken you to the Hilton, but that's a thousand a night. Have a rest for five hours. I'll be back by nine. You'll be alright," he said as he left.

I then went across the street and got my supplies for the night.

I had opened a beer and smoked about three cigarettes when a knock on the door happened. I looked out the window, and there stood a very scary Black man with a thin scraggly-looking Black woman. I opened the door just a little with the door chain on. "Yes?" I asked.

"You want to party, my man?"

"No . . . no, I am trying to sleep, thank you."

"Come on, man. Just a little party, man."

"No, thank you." I then shut the door. I chugged my beer to try and knock myself out. I was starting to get really scared, thinking this was the way I was going to die, here in this rat-infested hole in the middle of Watts. I began to doze off when a bang on the door happened again. I looked out again, and the same Black man was at the door, alone this time. I didn't open the door. "What do you want?"

"You got my girl in there, don't you, Whitey?"

"No, man, I am very much alone and trying to sleep now. Leave me alone, please."

"If she's in there, I'll fuck you up, man!"

I reacted without any fear—just anger this time—and opened the door wide. I stood face to face with this pimp-looking guy. "Now you listen to me, buddy. Look inside and find your old lady!"

He looked inside and backed off. He actually looked and acted a little frightened. "I'm sorry, man. I won't be back."

"Okay," I responded and shut the door. I drank six more beers and smoked a pack of Marlboro Lights, then fell asleep.

I opened my eyes to the sun shining in my room. It was a good feeling but only for a moment. Reality set in, and I jumped up as the fear of the night and the panic to get ready took over. I looked at the clock, and it was nine o'clock in the morning. I was packed and ready to go. Instead of waiting in the room, I walked to the front of the motel and waited for Mike. There he was, not five minutes after I got to the street.

"Ready to go home, Frank?" Mike asked.

"Oh yeah," I responded.

"Well, let's get you a ticket home."

The next flight to Toronto was scheduled for 2:30 that afternoon. Fortunately, it was a direct flight with an ETA of 9:30 in the evening. I bought the ticket, leaving me with only $100 in my pocket. Mike and I said our goodbyes and promised to keep in touch. I then went to the quietest place I could find in the airport, the cafeteria. I sat in a booth in the far corner that looked out over the runways. After about three coffees and a late breakfast, I read myself to sleep.

Before long, I felt someone shaking my shoulder. "Get up, sir. You have to get up."

"What time is it?" I asked.

"It's one o'clock, sir.

"Where are you going?" the attendant kept asking me my destination.

"Toronto. What time is it again?" I asked repeatedly. "Okay, I should go to my check-in area." I started walking toward my gate when a very strange feeling came over me. I felt like the odd person was looking at me from afar. Like they were spying on me or watching every move I was making. Paranoia seemed to set in over this acute awareness thing happening. I felt extremely anxious and couldn't get to the check-in gate fast enough.

As I waited for the plane, I couldn't help but think that Gord, or even the Lebanese guy, had set up a hit just before I left on the plane. I realized how serious exposing Gord to the Lebanese drug dealer was, and in their world that meant death for somebody. Gord had stolen or misappropriated a lot of drug money, and I knew he would pay, one way or the other. My fear was that he might have set me up to take the fall. How many times had he done that to me over the past six years? The ironic thing was I did not do drugs except the odd joint. To that date, I had never done cocaine or any other drug. More importantly, I had never purchased drugs, not even a joint. I always got it free. I was concerned about getting the hell out of LA, and I couldn't wait to be 30,000 feet in a jet, going northeast at a speed of at least 700 miles an hour.

I heard on the loudspeaker that my flight was to board. I was so happy to hear the announcement that I jumped out of my seat and almost ran to the counter to check onto the plane. Once cleared at the counter to board, I began to walk-run to the entrance of the plane. A flight attendant stopped me just as I came to the door of the plane. "Are you Frank Trousdell?"

"Yes," I answered nervously. I could feel the sweat roll down my face and the back of my neck.

The attendant looked at a piece of paper she was holding, then looked up into my eyes. "You have a message, sir. 'Have a peaceful flight, my friend.'"

"Who is this from?" I asked with nervous trepidation in my voice.

"There is no name, sir," the flight attendant answered. "Please board, sir." She directed me to my seat. I was totally shocked and bewildered. Who had left this haunting departure note? Whoever did this knew that I was totally freaked out.

I did not stop sweating and shaking until the plane reached 30,000 feet. The stewardess gave me a scotch on ice, and I asked for two more. She obliged, and not long after the pilot announced we were crossing over the Hoover Dam, I slipped into a deep sleep.

I awoke to the pilot announcing our pending arrival at Pearson International Airport. I awoke feeling like I had slept for eight full hours. I actually had, by the looks of the time I awoke. I had a sense of safety as we taxied down the runway. How good it felt to be home in Canada and close to seeing my boys again. I had called Patty and pre-arranged to stay with her and the kids. Her brother Kirk agreed to come and pick me up. I thought that was a very kind gesture on his part. One thing about the MacGrandles family: they were always there to help no matter what they might have thought of you. I have to say, especially in my case, after leaving the boys and Patty on their own, to chase a dream—or should I say, after the fact, a nightmare.

Chapter 18

Looking down at the boys fast asleep was so comforting and exciting at the same time. I was back safe and sound with my boys. That was all I had really wanted throughout the entire time I was in LA. I had wanted to make money and find my way out of the mess that I had left behind for LA. There was still the looming bankruptcy, possible repercussions from the life insurance industry, and who knows who else that felt I had wronged them or felt I owed them something.

The funny thing about falling from grace is that not only do your so-called friends turn their backs on you and run the other way, but the bottom feeders appear. The ones who think they can peck away at your bones for some leftover meat.

In my case, there was nothing left. My house was sold off for the mortgage, the cars were gone, and my bank accounts were dried up. Patty's family got the furniture that we didn't need and couldn't store. We were down to nothing of any value. We did, however, have our health, and we had the kids.

I was tired of being overweight and not eating properly. I knew I needed to rebuild from the inside out. The excess drinking, eating, and partying of the last six years had taken their toll on me. I was at least thirty pounds over my normal weight, and my waistline was growing. So, I decided to join a local fitness club in Brantford and start over again. In every rebuilding program, there are two very important commitments one must make—a commitment to a series of daily activities to be performed at the same time every day, no matter what and without interruption; and a personal physical fitness program that is to be completed every single day without fail. In my case, I went to the gym seven days a week, then I would walk over to a running trail alongside the Grand River. The trail was about two kilometres long and took me about ten minutes to complete. The thing I liked about it was that it had a number of workout stations positioned along the trail, like military obstacle mini segues, to add to the strength and endurance elements. I got good at this over time.

Every day was routine but enjoyable. The summer of 1985 was a month away, and I had just received my absolute discharge from filing bankruptcy. Now I was free to rebuild my financial life. I started to test the waters and applied for a number of jobs that were advertised by agencies and in the paper. Over the course of a month, I think I sent out two hundred resumes. Not one replied favourably. Every reply that I did receive said the same thing—not at this time, or I was not suited for the job, or they had chosen someone else. Most of the companies just refused to reply.

I even went out in person and tried to convince some of them to hire me. Again, I experienced a major letdown. Only this time, I was usually of interest after they met me. But as soon as their human resources people got involved, I was immediately eliminated. I always asked why and only once did the CEO of the respective company tell me why he could not hire me.

Frank, if it were just me, I wouldn't think twice about hiring you. I know of the collapse of your insurance company, and that really is the problem. The references from the companies you were involved with would not reply or, if they did, they responded unfavourably and negatively regarding your history. You have some enemies from your past, Frank. I believe in second chances, but my HR people do not. I can't help you but keep me informed, would you, and let me know how you make out."

I had at least ten of those interviews. I finally had no choice but to go on welfare. I could not get unemployment benefits for some technical reason even though I had paid in for the past twelve years. The government we have in Canada is an amazing bureaucracy for those who need social services such as welfare and health benefits. But when there is a need to collect benefits that you have paid into, like unemployment, and you had been worth a few hundred thousand at one time and then had to declare bankruptcy, they become very distant and non-empathetic to your case. In the end, you lose for some ambiguous reason. The bureaucrats are very good at lying... or let us say, interpreting the facts. They can verbally dance better than a British pickpocket who just stole your watch.

I qualified for the maximum welfare benefit available for a male. I think it was $800 a month. My father and mother had no problem with me collecting welfare at this particular time because they could justify the government owing it to me for a number of reasons. Firstly, I had been paying my taxes for years and with me not qualifying for UI benefits I was owed the money. Secondly, both my parents and Patty's were WWII vets and felt they and their children were owed any benefit that was made available to the Canadian taxpayer and war vet. They had served their time for the country.

Patty's father had been a foot soldier that partook in the liberation of Europe. He landed at Normandy and fought right to the doorstep of Berlin. His name was Don MacGrandles, and he was a factory man who worked hard and played hard. You never saw him without a cigarette in his mouth, a beer in hand, and a smile on his face. He and Momma Pat had eight children and built a three-bedroom wartime house in Brantford, Ontario. Don and Momma Pat did a great job in raising the kids, and somehow were able to feed and clothe them, living on the intermittent pay of factory life, riddled with layoffs and shutdowns. They survived, and they lived life as if there were be no tomorrow.

Every weekend there was a backyard party, and all the neighbours would be there. Then like clockwork, at about eleven at night, someone got too drunk, and a fight began. The whole backyard was filled with fights and yelling matches between all those who were there until they got tired or gave up and then went their way into the night. Most of the fights were between and started by the siblings. Then someone would try to stop the fight by stepping in between the initial fighters. Then the other siblings would step in to help the ones that had started the whole thing, and before too long, the ones that had started the fight were no longer in the fight but took the position of innocent bystanders, watching these people duke it out.

Don died of lung cancer or some terminal cancer in 1986. The day he was buried, I think, was in November. I remember it was very cold and rainy. Everyone was uncharacteristically quiet and very sombre, reflecting their individual sadness and realization of loss. Momma Pat was flanked by her children and grandchildren. Don was at rest and, most importantly, in peace. He was, I believe, only fifty-nine years old.

You watch the sitcoms of today, and they don't even come close to the events that took place in the MacGrandles' household and backyard. Everyone was involved one way or the other, but they always watched each other's backs to the end. Momma MacGrandles would always say, as she sat in her kitchen, "Don't ever get on the wrong side of the MacGrandles. You will either get a whooping or have to face an army, and we just keep coming." Then she would take a big drag off her cigarette, exhale, and take a sip of her beer. "Smell that turkey. We got a real deal on that bird. We got it from a friend working in that new store across town. I don't even know who paid for it!" I can still hear her laughing and giving out orders from the kitchen, as the grandkids ran through the house as if it were the playground that was located across the street. I can still hear her yell at her own kids, all grown up, but to her they were still children. "Hey, asshole, baste the turkey, pick up their clothes, or watch your own fucking bastard kids. This is no hotel, you shit head," Momma Pat would grunt as one of the sisters strolled through the kitchen on their way to the bathroom while a commercial was on during *The Young and the Restless*, the family afternoon ritual.

Patty had agreed for me to reunite with them when I got back from LA, to try to rebuild my career and possibly our lives together, but firstly for me to be with my boys. Getting welfare was a very big help to the four of us. *Somehow this would all work*, I thought.

The plan began with early morning bike rides to and from the gym some three kilometres away. I had stretched out the workout time, including my run at the trail, to be three hours every day. Then I rode my bike to the local riverside park, lay out on a blanket, and read a number of business/financial magazines. My intent was to get some clear-cut direction as to what I could do for a career and accumulate as much knowledge as I could. I found myself reading at least four magazines and at least a book a week to study. Out of a used bookstore, I found a series of *How to Succeed in Business* books written by a man, who I would meet later in life, by the name of Gordon Hume of Hume Publishing. I discovered the books were easy to read and simple in nature. The lessons were profound and motivational in a sense. So, I set out to read them all. The series included how to be successful in starting your own business, how to own your own real estate business, how to invest, and how to learn to be a business consultant.

Business consultant! Bingo! I jumped up from the ground and started fast-walking nervously back and forth, reading out loud the chapter on what a consultant did and what credentials it took to become a consultant so I could hang my shingle out. All you needed was knowledge of business or how to do certain tasks that someone did not have the time to do and would consider hiring you as an independent contractor to perform those services he required. Also, you could offer fundraising services, and the book spelled out enough for me to get the message that I could broker investors between the companies needing investment and those with money. All services for a fee, of course. The fees could be charged by the hour, a flat rate, and/or by aggregate consideration. I became very familiar with this phrase. These two words mean raising the funds contracted for in its full gross amount to the point of contractual completion; meaning, in the trust of the lawyer, the consultant would receive an agreed commission or percentage of that said gross amount. So, if I raised one million dollars under contract for a client and had an agreement to be paid an aggregate consideration in the amount of five percent, I would earn $50,000. "Yes! I can do this," I yelled out so loud I was sure it could have been heard across the park.

There was another fee that I found very doable. The work fee was earned by doing contracted duties and/or services for a period of time, per job, and/or to completion. This was the variable that could be charged out per month by invoice, for these services rendered. This fee was like a lawyer or an accountant, but I wouldn't have to go to school to earn a degree in order to offer the service. I could not offer legal or chartered accounting services but could refer the client to a lawyer or a CA as part of my billable services.

Now I needed to figure out just what services I could offer and how I was going to market myself. Remember, I had no money; I was bankrupt and living on welfare. Who would believe in me and how was I going to advertise, and who was I going to approach to promote my services? I had just seen the mountain in front of me and realized I had to find some people to help me climb this mountain. The first lesson I learned was that you cannot do it alone! No, unfortunately, no matter who you talk to, everybody always had someone or a group of people such as angel investors, first clients, advisory boards consisting of high-profile public leaders, family, professional confidants, their church, or a business consultant that guided one through the start-up phase. All of the above was needed to get off the ground successfully.

I had none of the above. My dad refused to get involved, my family rejected me, and Patty's family did the same, only because they too had no money. Then, out of nowhere, Patty's sister's boyfriend, who had done some work for me in my last months with S/W, came to me with an offer. He was only twenty-one years old, but he had studied bookkeeping and some business. He was proficient on the typewriter and could administrate an office. His name was Greg, and he lived downtown with his mother and brother in a modest older house. It was quite nice, actually, if you like older-style buildings. Within the first month, I moved Patty and the boys to an upper apartment over a chiropractor's office located downtown about sixty seconds up the street from Greg's house, so the working arrangement would be very convenient. The most important ingredient of his offer came as a big surprise.

"I'll work with you if you market the clients. I'll do the work and administrate the office. You manage the clients, ongoing. I'll finance the business for fifty percent. I think we can start with $4,000," he said.

I sat there pleasantly surprised but cautious. Greg was a bit of an oddball. He was losing his hair at twenty-one, which made him very self-conscious about his appearance. On top of it, he had been dating Kim, Patty's sister, for the past four years, and he still had not gotten into her pants. Kim was still a virgin and held hard and fast to stay that way. She would respond to the MacGrandles' kidding that she hated cock, saying, "No, I don't like the thought of it inside me!" Then the lesbian jeers would begin from everyone. Kimmy had a habit of taking it out on Greg when this happened. She was very much a tomboy but had the girl next door cute thing happening. Kim was acknowledged as a potential leading softball pitcher. She competed all over Ontario in about every tournament there was to be played. I really liked her because there was a quiet, no-nonsense attitude about her. She would sit back and watch without giving any form of an opinion until it involved her or someone close to her. Don't cross her path, though! I found that out one night when Patty and I took Kim to see my old band, Copperfield, play in Hamilton. I gave Kim a kiss on the neck, and before I knew it, she hit me in the jaw. I thought a man had punched me, but no, it was Kim. You just didn't get too close, no matter how innocent the intent might be.

"Okay, Greg, let's do it," I responded. I really had no idea what could happen or would happen, but I was willing to try. Greg then announced the money was coming from his mother, and we had to make a presentation to her. She was a single mother and had a boyfriend who was the president of BASF paint factory in Brantford. She was his personal secretary. We, being the MacGrandles and I, when talking about her job and boyfriend would preface our sentence with, "And how convenient," and then finish our sentence.

The presentation was easy, but she wanted to test our skills as consultants. I took great value in her thoughts and advice. She stipulated her conditions, and we agreed without debate. Once we wrote and signed a one-page contract, she asked to talk to me alone. Greg left the room, and we walked to the living room window.

"I am doing this for a number of reasons, Frank. I know all about your rise and fall in the insurance business, and I felt very much for you. You worked so hard to succeed but, unfortunately, you did not see them coming. This hopefully is your big lesson in business. Always look out for the blindside attack. Your closest allies could be your worst enemies. The ones that say they will never hurt you will be the ones that take it all away. You have just experienced this move. Never forget how it hurt and how difficult it was to lose everything. I pray you will never have to experience this again. Finally, you were there for my son. You gave him a job in your firm, and he learned many skills while working for you. He experienced from a distance, but he saw what you went through. That was valuable for him. I hope he, too, will learn from all of that time and events. Good luck, my friend, and may you and Greg make it happen."

The next day Greg showed up with a cheque and we were off to the bank.

"Oh, right," I said to the bank manager, "we have to register the business." He had the necessary forms, so we filled them out. The bank manager was very kind and opened the account even though we were not yet properly papered as a company.

"We have to market," I said.

"What are we going to offer?" Greg responded.

"Let's make a list of what we can actually do for a company," I suggested. For about two hours, Greg and I actually started building our own business plan and, most importantly, we understood what we were actually doing. I had been involved in writing the business plans of the insurance agencies but really did not understand the importance or the structure. My accountant, Craig Keller, had done them for me, up to this point.

I had met and befriended a neighbour in my final days in Cambridge. He was a CA from the bankruptcy firm I recently used. He was very methodical and had taken a special interest in my situation. Ted agreed to advise us pro bono, which was not heard of in this neck of the woods, but he wanted to see me get out and get up from the hole I had dug for myself. I found that attitude admirable for a CA. Normally, professionals shut their doors the moment it starts to get too hot, or when their clients are under a whirlwind of trouble. Being CAs or lawyers, their rule of thumb is to guide you through the trouble, not help you avoid the attack from creditors or allegations or charges from opposing businesses. The moment you crash and burn, they write you off and avoid you like the plague.

This is where I began having my doubts about CAs and lawyers. Don't you think that after being paid thousands of dollars for so many years, they had a moral obligation to teach you how to avoid some of this business disparity? I discussed events with both my lawyer and accountant many times, looking for advice. I always left feeling very vulnerable. They protected themselves very well, I must say.

Ted, however, was interested in the actual operations of the setup stage of the business. He wanted to watch how far we could get with very little money. So, Ted offered a limited service to help us get started.

Greg showed up one morning with an automated phone telemarketing machine. You recorded a message, keyed in a series of telephone numbers, then plugged it into the phone line and set it on to start dialling for a pre-set period of time. The respondent had the option to disconnect or answer the questions, which in turn were recorded on a cassette tape. Greg wanted us to lease two of them and offer a polling or telemarketing service to businesses locally. Well, we got a few paying clients within the first week of our soliciting the service. One was the Municipality of Brantford and the other was Bata Shoes. We ran this service for two months, and we got paid a modest fee by both. I was able to generate a few consulting service contracts from small businesses. These were very small, work fee marketing services rendered and were short-lived.

I got a call from our bank one day from a business manager asking if we were interested in taking a look at a local recording studio that needed to raise some money for expansion. I almost jumped through the phone at the opportunity.

Shotgun Recording Studios was located on the east side of Brantford on the road to Hamilton. The building was an old two-storey house that looked like it was leaning left, but this was just an illusion due to the way it sat on the uneven landscape. To look at it from the road, one would never suspect that it housed about $150,000 worth of recording gear. The average person would never have known that this studio had recorded some respectable artists—local, mind you, and usually Canadian. But this studio could brag that these local artists had their music played on national radio, and some even had number one hits. In our case, the band that owned the studio, or should I say the owner of the studio, was the founder of the legendary Canadian country band called Whisky Hollow. His name, for this book's purpose, will be known as Len. His partner Steve's claim to fame was his membership in the band The Canadian Conspiracy. It was a high-energy, pop-rock band of the early to late seventies that landed an international recording deal with, I believe, Capitol Records out of Los Angeles.

Greg and I spent a lot of time studying the business and how it worked. We could not figure out at first how the studio was generating money. There seemed to be very little revenue coming in from any new contracts. We did experience a Canadian country recording act, the Danny Thompson Band, whose first album *Shotgun* had just been produced. Their first single release had hit number one on the Canadian charts. Greg and I visited the studio and watched the process of what was entailed in making a recording. I was obviously interested because of my love of performing music and my limited history in a band.

I also saw the need for the studio to have its services marketed more effectively because the owners were not interested in aggressively getting new acts to record. They believed that the new acts would come through word of mouth and reference. That might have been the case some five years before, but things were changing in the music business. The major labels were not talking to the small local studios. They were experiencing change internationally and were only interested in mergers with other majors and buyouts of publishing catalogues. They only signed well-established acts, and only rarely took on new faces that did not already have a fan base of at least a national level. New bands could only achieve this market position by performing all across the country seven days a week.

An example was a Kitchener-based band called Helix. They were a glamour hard rock band. Their first album was starting to get airplay on Canadian radio stations across the country. The only way they could support the album was to hit the road and play at every bar and rock hall they could, from Halifax to Vancouver. Their business manager, William Snypes, was very aggressive and committed. Billie, as he was known to very few acquaintances, also managed their money and made sure they were being interviewed live on every radio station in every city, cross-marketing their live performance with airplay exposure. Not long after Helix was launched, major labels came knocking on his door.

Lenny and Steve would consistently keep talking about the Helix plan and how they had to follow it to the letter, especially with the Danny Thompson Band. Lenny asked me one day to discuss with Danny the possibilities of me managing them on and off tour. Danny had his booking agents, and Lenny ran his record production. Danny needed business management. According to Len, Danny was a great player, performer, and writer, but he was out of control money management-wise. He always came home broke. I couldn't figure that one out at first because they were playing every night and recording during the daytime. When did they have time to spend? But I was definitely naïve about musicians and the live performance environment. I would soon learn firsthand what went on behind the curtain.

Danny and I met at the studio and quickly became almost inseparable. He agreed for me to take over his management "on and off the road," as the expression goes in the music business. We agreed to a fee structure for management services and a list of duties for us to perform. I immediately put Greg on the studio project while I concentrated on band management. The studio wanted us to write a business plan to attract investment money. Greg set out to complete the task. He spent weeks at the studio, asking a lot of questions, assembling financial statements, or writing financial statements that were not done. I was learning the recording and music business firsthand by spending every waking hour with the band and Danny.

My time with the band was more novelty at first because it seemed like one big party after every night of gigging. There was always an abundance of women and booze. I learned very quickly where the money went. I always assumed the party favours were supplied by the club or someone other than the band. That only happened for big-name bands that had a rider spelling out such additional requests. Bar bands hardly ever saw a rider on their performance contracts. They usually had to supply all sound and lighting, which was a very expensive part of live performance. The band had to be paid from the contract, and whatever was left over was the band leader's take. Sometimes there was nothing left due to travel costs and transportation, especially if the truck broke down somewhere in the middle of nowhere at about three o'clock in the morning. This was a regular occurrence with Danny. He always had truck problems.

One day Danny suggested that we buy a school bus from a musician in Hamilton who was coming off the road and wanted to dump the bus. It was supposedly in good shape and needed no repairs. I did the negotiations for Danny and got him the bus on a promise to pay note thirty days after Danny's run out West, playing four cities over four weeks. The gigs began in Thunder Bay and went to Alberta, then back again to Hamilton. Everyone seemed in sync and settled for the four-week tour. Danny left with the bus and his band. Also, we had gone to a sound company, Long

& McQuade, in Toronto and loaded up on new stage sound and light gear under a rental plan. Danny was feeling quite confident in my abilities to make things happen by then, and in return, he promised me my fees to be paid once a week by direct deposit.

The first week went by quietly with not much word from the band. Danny deposited $250 in the business account, like he was supposed to, and repeated the same at the end of the second week. On the Sunday of the third week, at about three o'clock in the morning, I got a call from Danny.

"We're in Saskatchewan, about halfway through it. The bus broke down. I think it was the transmission or drive shaft. We'll know soon enough. But we have to get to Saskatoon by seven tonight to play. We're about four hours away."

"Where are you now?" I asked.

"We're on Highway 1 at a Husky truck stop. The bus is about twenty miles east of the truck stop with all our gear. We have enough money to get a guy from the truck stop to tow us in, but I don't know about the repairs."

"Shit," I said in response to the situation. "Let's get the bus to the garage first and have them take a look and estimate the repairs. Then we'll figure out what to do," I suggested.

Danny agreed and so the band basically bunked up in the truck stop for the time being and waited for the mechanic to arrive in the morning.

At about six o'clock that morning, I got another call from Danny.

"It's not as bad as what we thought. The driveshaft needs new universal joints, and we could be out of here in about two hours."

"What's the damage?" I asked.

"He said he has a couple of joints from a wrecked bus in back that he can use, and it would be a labour thing. Maybe $200."

"Great," I said, "use the money from the business account, then replace it when you finish this week."

"Okay," Danny responded.

I heard very little to nothing for the next two weeks. One afternoon I got a call from Danny, advising they would be home the next Monday. We needed to have a meeting about the future of the band.

"Okay," I responded, "not really understanding why and what he meant." During the next week, Greg and I worked every day on the business plan for the studio. Greg was getting bored with the business by then, and I could hardly find him to get the work done. He was sleeping a lot and was becoming despondent.

One afternoon, after we had finally completed the business plan, Greg advised he was getting a job. I was somewhat shocked but understood. He also said I would need to get someone to invest so he could get his mother's money back. That one caused quite the argument between us because we had only been in business six months, and we had no real money or credibility to get a loan yet. I took offence to his demand. I advised him he would have to wait for the money. Then his mother started to put the pressure on for me to find the money. She threatened me, saying she would create some excuse to bring in the authorities and force me to pay her. She gave me thirty days.

The meeting with Danny and the band was held in the office I had rented from the owner of the building my family and I were living in, on the main floor. We lived on the second floor. The landlord was Dr. Shackleton, a local chiropractor. He also was a holistic specialist, naturopath, and reflexologist. The doctor was especially involved in the multi-level product sales of Herbalife, a health and weight loss program. He had already got me using the product. I was noticeably losing inches and body fat.

"Okay, boys, what's going on here?" I asked in my business tone.

Danny began. "The guys are getting tired of the road and want to play local more. Our drummer wants out because he can't take the problems on the road anymore."

The drummer, "Bill," stepped in. "I can't handle the mismanagement and how unprepared we are as a professional band."

"Are you getting paid, Bill?" I asked.

"Yes, I'm not complaining about the pay. I just think we should be better off by now. Danny's had two hit singles on the country charts, and we're still playing bars."

"Where do you think you should be playing by now?" I asked him.

"Fairs, special events, and we should be the opening act for someone like Michelle Wright by now. Hell, we've been playing before or after her in the same clubs for the past two years. She's a star now, and why can't we get her to get us booked as her opening act?"

I looked at Danny and asked him the same question.

"We aren't ready yet. We need a keyboard player, and we need to tighten up our show more. Actually, we need to have a show. We don't have any stage presence, just good music."

When I heard this, a light switch went off. "Let me audition to play keys, and I will manage and play for the same fee; that way, no extra cost." The band members looked at each other and agreed.

Bill reluctantly went along with it but said, "If we don't get things going here, I'm out by the end of the month."

We acknowledged his intent.

Danny and I went for a walk, and he stated, "Bill will be gone at the end of the month and I'll find a replacement. We'll start rehearsing at the labour hall downtown for the week, then try you out at the next gig in Toronto."

I agreed, and away we went to start rebuilding the band. I had no idea what I was getting myself into, but I was very excited because I was going to be playing with a real band—a band that had records on the radio and was well-known throughout the country. If ever I had a chance to do something I loved and still make some kind of a living, it was then or so I thought.

While my introduction to the music world was beginning, my marriage was ending. Patty was constantly off to bingo every night, and I was gone with the band. We shared raising the boys on a daily basis and tried to keep a semblance of consistency in their lives. The boys were not stupid about what was going on, but they did feel safe with both of us in the same house. Patty's family and my sisters filled in the gaps when they could. One thing I can say about Greg was that he continued to help us by babysitting the boys all the time. I think he partly wanted to help, but he was more interested in impressing Kim, Patty's sister. He was vigilant about his intentions with her. She wasn't biting. She was spending more time with her baseball friends than she was with Greg. I felt so sorry for him most of the time but, eventually I became sick of seeing him pine and dote over her.

The band was booked for a trip to Thunder Bay for one week, and Danny wanted me to go as a full member of the band. I thought this was great, but there were a couple of issues that needed to be cleaned up. Danny offered to invest in my consulting business to acquire fifty percent. I told him I would need $20,000 to make it work. He said he could find the money.

I said we would need a partnership agreement of sorts, written by a lawyer. I had no money, and Danny was pretty convincing on his part that he trusted my judgment and all he needed was an agreement between both of us. I went to a lawyer with him, but the lawyer wanted $10,000 to draft such an agreement. Both Danny and I were turned off over it. I felt confident to draft some kind of understanding between the two of us, so Danny and I sat down and wrote a one-page makeshift letter.

Danny then went and got his mother-in-law to loan him the money. I got a call from his mother-in-law the next day, and she wanted to meet with me. She was very positive about the loan and had some conditions of her own. She insisted that I co-sign the loan at the bank because she was borrowing the money against her house and wanted some protection. I was not thinking very detailed at the time because of my own financial stresses and agreed. Later this move would come back to haunt me. Danny should have been the one guaranteeing the loan, not me. If I could have afforded the lawyer, this would never have happened. Another thing that would not have happened was the letter between Danny and me. Somehow, I mistakenly wrote that the funds were an investment into my company and not a purchase of shares. I do not know to this day how that happened. Finally, Danny insisted on having his mother-in-law sign the agreement between him and me as witness to the deal. Why I didn't see what he was doing was beyond me.

You, see by having the whole deal set up as Danny insisted, it was an investment by both Danny and his mother-in-law, not a purchase of fifty percent. So, if anything went bad between Danny and me, then it was all on me. He was free and clear of any obligation of the loan between his mother-in-law, himself, and me. I had no clue I was a sitting duck to be baked at any time the two of them saw fit to do so.

I needed the money. Danny manipulated me to get some of that money. He was cunning like a fox and slippery like an eel.

By the end of the week, he'd convinced me to lease him and myself two new cars. He got a Camaro, and I got a Mustang GT Cobra, both 1986 versions. I paid off Greg's mother and felt relieved to complete that obligation.

Without warning, I was served with divorce papers from Patty. She was bound and bent to get her share of the remaining money. I could not believe what was happening all at once. I spent the next week calming everything down. We had spent the previous week playing a three-nighter in Pain Court outside of Chatham in a very small club out in the sticks. We actually camped at Rondeau Park near the beach. Danny had brought his girlfriend, who had been kept quite secret from us all and, obviously, his wife. I was a bit concerned that he had a mistress due to the loan we had entered into and especially the loan being with his mother-in-law. I started to have a lot of apprehension about the whole thing. Danny's mistress' name was Debbie, and she was young, naïve, and outstandingly attractive. I could tell Danny had her over a barrel, just like most people he indisposed. "Everyone has a purpose," Danny once told me. "The only way you survive today is to be the king of the jungle and control before they control you." How right he was . . . in his world. It was becoming quite a jungle.

Debbie and I caught each other's attention, and we spent a lot of time that weekend talking. I became very much enamoured and interested in her. I offered her a ride back to London, where she lived. Danny couldn't because he had to drive the van with the band members, and there was no room.

Debbie and I talked for hours about what she was going through, and I filled her in about my life. We became very comfortable with each other and agreed to meet later that week before the band headed out to Thunder Bay. After that weekend and what I saw as the real Danny, I knew I had to start to be careful of him. I was not going to let him use Debbie or myself. I decided to talk Danny out of having any relationship with Debbie. I felt this was an important move to protect this project and the financial relationship that existed between his mother-in-law and me.

The day we were leaving for Thunder Bay, I asked Danny, "How are we paying for the trip?"

"My mother-in-law gave me her credit card."

"Holy shit, Danny. We had better be careful."

"Don't worry, Frank. All is good."

I had ill feelings about the whole thing—using her card and letting Danny be in control. I had no choice. Away we went.

The week went as usual, as far as everyone getting along, and we played quite well as a band. The partying was at a minimum, and the band rehearsed regularly, as planned. The interesting and enlightening event for me was how the band could harmonize. We worked on the Eagles song "Seven Bridges Road," and we were able to capture the full sound and feel very easily. The crowd was growing each night, which created excitement for me in particular. I was addicted to the stage. I felt very much at home performing and ad-libbing with Danny. My presence was equivalent to my enthusiasm as a performer. Danny was noticing the crowd's acceptance of my voice. He was starting to show his apprehension. We weren't arguing over it, but he was a little unsettled by my abilities as a singer and musician.

On the way back home, there were rumblings amongst the members as to their future involvement. The bass player and the drummer, Bill, were totally disgruntled, to say the least, and swore by the time they got back, they were through. Danny talked the bass player into staying, but Bill had zero interest in staying and waiting. He was too strung out, and one could tell he had personal mental issues. His drug use was becoming out of control, and his behaviour was erratic. He would be yelling one moment, then crying another. His paranoia was alarming, to say the least. Danny would overcompensate the events as part of the gig and being in a band. He managed the players like he was babysitting. He said he had to constantly slap them on the wrist and tell them, "No, you can't do that."

As soon as we got back to Brantford, all hell broke loose. Patty had pushed for court custody hearings and threatened full custody. I was no longer allowed to live in the same house, so I had to find an apartment. Danny's mother-in-law offered the small room above her house, which I immediately took. I saw it as an escape, and being closer to her would save me trouble from her. Danny came back with very little money again, and we couldn't pay the loan payment. Tension was brewing between all the parties involved, and I knew the lid was going to blow off at any time.

I began seeing Debbie almost every other day, and she saw the trouble starting amongst everyone. We were playing in Sarnia the next week, and I decided to bring Debbie out for the last two nights. Danny had finally recognized Debbie and I were together and had accepted the situation. He said very little about the whole thing. All he had mentioned was that I owed him for the union of Debbie and me. We did, however, keep things jovial as much as we could.

The last day we were playing in Sarnia, Danny played a very dirty trick on Debbie and me. He slipped a wireless microphone into my room in between sets. On our last break, Debbie and I were in the room, and I was complaining about what was going on and how we were all screwed up in the band. I did not know that the mic was on, and the whole room full of people could hear our conversation. When we came back out, everyone was laughing at us. I couldn't figure out what was going on, then Danny told us what he had done. I could never forgive him for that, and neither could Debbie.

When I got back to Brantford, I had to make a decision about my existence with the band. The money issues were getting out of hand, my divorce was pending, and Danny was going off the wall with everything. He announced that CCMA's Country Music Week was coming up, and we were to play in Winnipeg for the seven days. I could not see myself going and pleaded with Danny for me not to go.

He just said, "Do whatever you have to. I got a band to run."

I took this as I could stay. I also saw this as my escape from this nightmare building in my life. My estranged wife was trying to ruin me and take my boys from me, and Danny was dissolving our relationship. My need to start earning money superseded everything else.

I told Danny's mother-in-law what was going on, and she agreed that I needed to look for a job or find a way to make money because she could not carry the loan herself. I reminded her that Danny had responsibility in the loan situation, and I was the guarantor.

She looked at me and said, "I do not expect Danny to pay a thing. I am counting on you."

I responded, "But that was not the deal."

She just looked at me like I had never seen before, and she said, "You had better not let me down because you will regret it."

That night, I called Debbie and told her of the conversations. I also called my friend, Norm Casseran, from my old band from the seventies, Copperfield, and told him everything. "What should I do, Norm? I'm lost here, and I don't know what to do."

"Get out of there, Frank. I see only bad things in the near future. You need to create distance from there. I think you're in over your head."

Danny had spent time in prison for armed robbery some five years previous, and I didn't know this until he confessed to me while on the road. He was trying to tell me why it was so important for him to show his family that he was on the road to success. But, in contrast, he admitted he struggled with lessons he had learned while in prison concerning how he dealt with people. I did not take this information to heart because I thought he could be bigger than his criminal nature. I was beginning to see he had set me up. In his own way, he even tried to warn me.

The bank account was empty. I again was penniless and about to be homeless. Debbie suggested I come live with her and look for a job in London. By ten o'clock that night, I made up my mind. I packed a very light bag of clothes and belongings and headed for the forest city.

I woke up the next day in Debbie's room, which she and her sister rented from a friend in his townhouse. The house was very nice and located on Wharncliffe Road, near the University of Western Ontario. I made a call to my old accountant, Craig Keller, and filled him in on the situation, and he suggested I come in and talk. I did that day. He recommended I drum up clients for him. He would pay me a commission and give me an office. I went to Waterloo that same day, and we set up our relationship. After the meeting, I visited my old watering hole in Kitchener, where my friend Cathy Stach danced. She listened attentively and suggested I should talk to a friend of hers, Brent Dehorner, the lead guitar player of Helix. He was sitting across the table from me. We met, and I told him my story and background. He had heard of me and suggested I should sell radio jingles. "You bring in the clients, and I'll write and record the songs," he said. I told him of my background in the music business and assured him I could write and perform as well. He agreed to participate.

I arrived back in London and stopped in at JB's Restaurant on Richmond Row, where Debbie was the head bartender. She bought me a couple of beers, and I told her about my day. She was very impressed that I could turn things around that fast. On the surface, I painted the face of total confidence, but deep inside I was scared to the bone. I had been through so much controversy already, and I was about to hit more turbulence. I also knew that I could not count on living off of Debbie, and nor should I, for she was just twenty and she had no clue what I was facing.

My next giant move was to go to Chatham and have a serious sit-down with my dad and mom. I was not looking forward to this because I knew they were totally beside themselves by now with my situation. They were aware of all that was going on and tried to stay distant from my life storm. But I had nowhere else to go. I had a plan of action by working with Craig, and I was committed to learning the radio and advertising business. I felt optimistic, and all I needed was cash flow to get me through the next month or so.

The conversation with my father was very business in nature, and he listened intently. When I was done, he sat and looked into my eyes and began talking.

"Your mother is totally against me helping you in any way. She represents your sisters, who demand I stay out of your life. They feel that you are a con and only want to take your mother's and my money. Frank, you have never asked for much from us until now. I need to know that you will repay every dime I give you."

"Yes, Dad. I will. I just can't tell you when right this minute."

"Okay, I will give you a credit card, my Bank of Montreal Mastercard. This way, we will know how and what you spend the money on, and you can pay at least the minimum every month."

"That's perfect, Dad. I just need to get through the next month or so," I said in relief.

"I don't think this is the end of it, Frank," Dad answered.

"It should be, Dad," I responded.

"You have a very serious problem brewing in Brantford, and you had better put a lid on it."

"You mean Patty?" I asked.

"Yes, Patty and your ex-partner. Danny. He's not out of the picture, son."

"I hope you're wrong, Dad, but I refuse to pay when he is truly responsible."

"He may be, son, but the old lady wants her money. She has already called here."

"I am sorry, Dad. I'll figure something out."

"Don't delay. She will make serious trouble for you."

The drive back to London was refreshing, knowing Dad had my back. I was disturbed to know that my sisters were very much against me. I thought they cared about me and would not disown me. They really showed their position, but I could not blame them, for they had to make their own way, and they certainly did not put the family through hell like I had with two divorces in twelve years. All I could do was focus on my situation and clean it up.

While Debbie and I started building our nest, we rented an apartment and set up my new business. I spent the first week travelling back and forth from Waterloo, spending at least two to four hours with Craig, learning the accounting business, then spending at least another two hours a day in the library, studying the advertising and radio jingle business. Brent and I spent that same week talking about operations and how we were going to handle the production of jingles. Helix was writing new material for an upcoming album, and Brent had access to the portable recording gear to put ideas down. I got him pre-writing samples for me to sell. Brent also gave me three leads, and with his samples, I sold all three. Right off the bat, we earned $5,000. You may think that wasn't much for Brent, but Billie Sipes had the boys in Helix on a very tight rein financially and gave them each a very modest allowance weekly. As Brent used to say, "a weakly allowance," so weak he couldn't eat half the time. In the long run, Brent changed his attitude about what Billie had done for them.

Over the next two months, I sold four more jingles, and we were off to the races. I took an office in London and worked with a group of advertising companies, all as small as I was, and they interacted openly.

Then the calls began from the mother-in-law. "Where is my money, Frank? You had better pay soon or else."

I did not want to alarm Debbie, and I was getting scared about the threats. One morning, I went out to my car and found a taped sledgehammer with nails sticking out of it. That weapon was very unnerving. I asked a cop friend what that meant, and he suggested I needed to file a complaint. He said I had a very bad enemy, and they were warning me that they were going to do damage to my car or me or both. I instinctively knew who it was—Danny and his mother-in-law—but I had no direct proof. I decided to let it all go and see if it blew over. The physical threats did, but the calls did not. She wanted her money, and I had not shown any attempt to pay. I got tired of the calls, so on the next call, I told her flat out, "I am not going to pay unless Danny pays half. He is the borrower, and it is up to him to pay. If he pays, I will pay."

The mother-in-law responded by threatening she would go to the police.

"Do it because I did not borrow the money. Danny did and I was no more than the guarantor."

She finalized the conversation by stating, "You will see who wins this, Frank, and you will burn for ripping me off."

I stated back her, "I am not ripping you off. All I want you to show me first is to get Danny to own up to his responsibility before I do anything."

She hung up the phone, and for some reason I thought this was over. How wrong I was, as I would find out not long after.

Debbie caught on very soon and questioned the situation. "Why is Danny's mother-in-law calling so much, and why is she threatening you?"

"She wants the money she lent Danny to buy in to the business," I answered.

"Why is it your responsibility, Frank?"

"She thinks I owe her the money and not Danny."

"You had better take care of this, Frank. I want no part of that creep, Danny."

"I'll talk to Craig and see if he can help me."

The next day I went to Waterloo and sat down with Craig and told him everything. He immediately called his lawyer and client and discussed the situation with him. The lawyer agreed to visit and talk with me. Later that day, he came to the office and said, "You had better go sit down with her and get an agreement and just pay her out, Frank."

"I don't have the money firstly, and secondly, why do I have to pay her when Danny borrowed the money?" I asked.

"You guaranteed the loan, and she is demanding the loan. She will make trouble for you, and I don't think you will win," the lawyer hastily replied.

"Will you talk to her and see if you can settle this with her?" I asked.

"No, I want nothing to do with this thing; you're on your own." Then he left.

"Damn," I said as Craig came into my office.

"Just talk to her, Frank."

"Okay," I said, so I picked up the phone and called her. "Look, I want this over with, and I do not want you to not get paid, but I really think Danny owes you this money," I pleaded with the mother-in-law.

"Danny left my daughter, and I can't find him. He is in the States," she said. "I have already gone to my lawyer, and I have started legal proceedings."

"Okay," I replied, thinking she was filing a civil suit. At least I would have my day in court.

"It's up to my lawyer now," she said.

"We will deal with this in court then, and I request that you do not call anymore."

She replied, "No problem. You're on your own now, Frank."

I told Craig, and he shrugged it off. "Well, it's going to court," he said, "so you can deal with it then."

I felt relieved that it was now controlled, or so I thought.

The jingles were becoming fun, and Brent was having a blast producing the songs. I was meeting the London radio stations. I found them very accommodating and willing to teach me what I needed to know about the business. I did find out that there were national companies that travelled annually to each city and blitzed the market, scooping up as much as they could. They pushed what we called "canned jingles", which were template songs, and they input synced the variations needed to make them individualized. I sold the uniqueness of our work and priced accordingly to be competitive. Brent thought that method was ingenious.

But as more work came in, Brent began demanding more money and started showing signs of disgruntled acceptance of the original deal. I then sold a very large multimedia deal with Sarnia Eaton Centre to not only do the jingle but to create their positioning statement for 1987. That included the mall boards. They did not want screen print but photo print. I did not realize the difference. When I began the project, I personally created the statement: "You'll find it all here." I also wrote the first draft of the jingle lyrics. Brent was totally reluctant to write the music, so I wrote it myself. By then, I had learned from Brent and the radio stations how to write a jingle and had written most of the lyrics and music for the seven we had previously done. Brent finally agreed to do the jingle based on what I had done. Helix, by then, was recording in Toronto with an international producer. Late one night, after Helix had finished a session, the producer and Brent sat down and cleaned up the jingle. Brent brought it back to Kitchener, and I had to sing the voiceover. We were actually very proud of the final results.

I then delivered the tape to the mall marketing manager, and she immediately was very impressed. She was so happy she played it for a party she was having that Friday night. Everyone loved it . . . then her friend commented that it sounded just like a Wang Chung song that was on the radio. She lost it! I got the call on the Monday, and she was livid. "Change it, or you have a real problem." Brent was frustrated, but he changed it enough to be different, and she accepted it.

The mall boards, however, were a big problem. I had to get one of the advertising Photoshop companies in the office in London to correct the mistake of the delivered mall boards, which were screen print and could not be used. I now owed that company half of the fee already paid. Brent was really upset and wanted his money immediately, which left me penniless on the deal. Brent got paid, but he refused to do any more work. The Sarnia Eaton Centre was finally okay and paid the rest of the fee.

Not long after, I sold the Italian Shoe Warehouse store chain their jingle. In order for me to complete the job, I had to get help from my cousin's husband, who was a recording musician and had a full studio in their basement. He and I completed the song. I played the keyboard, and he did the engineering and played guitar. I had met a singer-songwriter named Paul Langille at JB's one night, and he agreed to sing the song to record. He was well known for his work as a fill-in singer for Blood, Sweat & Tears, a very famous rock band of the sixties. He also sang the

Labatt Blue beer jingle, "All across the country," which aired regularly on all Canadian TV and radio stations. He was living off the royalties. I was really proud of the work we did on that one. Later, Paul had his own problems when a Labatt executive caught Paul drinking Molson's products. This breach was a contractual violation. Paul was immediately released and lost hundreds of thousands of residual dollars.

Debbie and I were becoming very close, and we decided to marry, but I had to complete my divorce. Patty and I had many arguments, and she had refused access to the boys for the past six months. I was very angry and weary about my situation. I found a London lawyer that agreed to help me by retaining him for very little. The fights and arguments went on between Patty and me to the point we ended up in front of a judge in Brantford. I did not want the case to be heard in Brantford because I knew Patty had court friends and the lawyers had a habit of protecting their own citizens, and I was considered an outcast.

The fight went on in court, and the judge awarded Patty the right to custody, and I had to pay her $400 to get the kids for two days. I was so angry that I called the court extortionists. That did not go over very well. As I left the room, I noticed, sitting at the front table, two men dressed in suits—not lawyers but, in fact, detectives. They turned and looked at me like they hated my guts as I walked past. I was definitely shaken by this event. *Who are they and what are they up to?*

I finally got the boys to come to London for the first time in six months. I was so excited and couldn't wait to see them. Debbie was reluctant, but I thought she understood. When I got back from picking them up in Brantford on the Friday night, I came home to find Debbie dressed up with plans to go out. She said she wanted to go shopping. I didn't think much of her plans and gave her the car. I wanted to spend time with the boys anyway.

By the time the boys and I had done our restaurant thing and got a movie, it was about 9:30 at night. I figured Debbie would be home soon. Eleven o'clock arrived and still no Debbie or phone call. I figured she had gone to her parents' place like she had done before, so I waited, but I was getting nervous. The boys had fallen asleep, and I really started to get concerned because it was midnight, and Debbie had not called. This was totally out of character, and I started to worry she had been in an accident. I called her family, and they hadn't seen her at all. I then called her uncle in St. Thomas and, finally, I got some news. She had met up with Joanne, her cousin, and went out to Birty Bob's, a local bar. I was relieved but a little upset she didn't call and tell me. Debbie finally arrived at about 2:30 in the morning.

"Why didn't you call?"

She said nothing but went directly to the bathroom. I knew something was wrong. She had never done this before now. When she came out, she went straight to bed. I slept in my chair with the boys until morning.

"What's going on?" I asked her as she opened her eyes.

"I don't want to get married anymore, and I don't want this relationship."

"What happened?" I asked her in shock.

"I just don't want it anymore; marriage and kids are not what I want."

We argued for an hour or so and, finally, she agreed to try to see if she could handle things now that my boys were in the picture for real. I told her it would take time, and I did not expect her to be a mom—just a friend to the boys. She calmed down enough to tell me she went to sit on the deck at Kelsey's, where we as a couple would go to meet friends from time to time. She said that she sat all night with Jim, an airline pilot we both knew, enjoying the stars and weather. I didn't push it because her uncle told me differently. I knew she was still lying about Friday night. I let it go for the weekend while my boys were there, even though the truth haunted me every minute.

The wedding went without a hitch; except that we had little money to take any kind of a honeymoon. Debbie was totally dejected when she was told we were going to have my parents' house to stay for the week and go to Erieau Beach each day. There was no passionate wedding night for me, only Debbie passing out in the bathtub with a bottle of Champagne in tow. I got the message.

Chapter 19

Jobs came and went for me. I was getting extremely frustrated and knew I had to go back to my roots as a life insurance agent. Debbie was getting impatient with my job status. She did not like the uncertainty of entrepreneurship. One day, I ran into an old Chatham acquaintance, Sam, who just so happened to be the London manager for Empire Life. He was very interested in having me join the team.

I spent three weeks doing all the preliminaries and passed the test with a 98%, one of the highest scores Empire ever had recorded. Sam was so excited and had me sign contract agreements and set me up in a very nice office. Then on my first day, Sam called me into his office.

"I got a letter back from head office after I submitted your contracts. It suggests that the Brantford police are investigating you and are alleging that you defrauded an elderly lady of some $20,000."

"That's bullshit, Sam," I replied in defence.

I then told Sam the whole story, and he sat back in thought for a few seconds that felt like minutes. "I want you to be a part of this company and team, Frank. Head office left it to my judgment whether to take a chance and hire you. I have decided to recommend that you straighten this situation out quickly, and then I'll hire you. It's the right thing to do, don't you think, Frank?" Sam asked.

I replied, "You're right. I'll deal with this crap, then we'll get started."

I was totally devastated and panicked to have been advised of this escalation in the Danny affair. I had no idea what to do either.

Later that week, I was called in to Acura West Car dealership by Paul Loach, the dealer principal. I had sold him advertising some weeks earlier, and he had liked my style and professionalism."

"I want you to bring your skills, and I'll teach you the car leasing business. You will manage the dealership leasing department, Frank . . . what do you think?" Paul pitched with confidence.

I was totally dumbfounded by his offer. One minute, I was being told I could be arrested for fraud and then the next minute, I was offered a leasing manager's position.

I took the offer.

The next few months were somewhat busy, learning my new craft and enjoying the weekends with Debbie and the boys when they came to London. Daren and Mike seemed to get along with Debbie for the most part, showing very little resistance. We would jog down a path along the river in the summer and fall months. Daren had a very hard time keeping up with the three of us. One time, he stopped and began crying in pain. I ran back, and he jumped into my arms and shook, as if he feared I was disappointed in him. I told him I loved him and to never think I was ever disappointed in him about anything. I hugged him until he was calmed down enough to get on with the run.

Later that month, Debbie and I moved to a different apartment, and Debbie started a new job with General Trust in the mortgage department. She needed a lot of pushing to apply for the job, but she finally did it. Now she needed to get her driver's licence. She had never gotten it before that time because she feared taking the test. I had discovered something in her by that time. She feared two things in her life: failure of any kind and being alone without a man. If she sensed I wasn't going to be able to support her, she would run off and meet discreetly with another man. I found out her pattern of activity as time went on.

Our daily ritual was for me to go pick up Debbie at five o'clock every day at her work, drive her home, then go back to the dealership until eight. Sometimes I'd find her home when I arrived, and sometimes I would not. When she wasn't there, I had a good suspicion of where she had gone.

One night, I went home after work and found she wasn't there. I had to go and pay a parking ticket, so I went to the parking lot and began opening my car door when from behind me, I heard a voice.

"Don't move. Put your hands behind your back, please. We can do this the hard way or the easy way. What way do you choose?"

I looked over my shoulder and immediately saw it was a very large police officer. He then placed my hands in cuffs and escorted me to the back seat of his cruiser.

On the way to the station, I assumed I had an outstanding ticket of some kind, so I asked, "What's the charge, sir? Did I have an outstanding fine or something?"

"There are some people waiting for you when we get to the station, and they will tell you what you are being charged with," the officer responded.

My mind was full of panic by this time, and all I could think of was the old lady. Danny had done it. He got me arrested. Payback for stealing his girlfriend, Debbie, was the answer running rampant through my mind as the cruiser pulled up to the station's loading door.

I was ushered up to the booking desk, and an officer began emptying my pockets. He took my belt and shoes off me and then escorted me to a cell.

"I need to call my wife and my lawyer, please," I requested from the officer.

"Not yet. There are a couple of detectives that want to talk to you first," he answered.

"I have the right to a telephone call, and I want it now," I demanded firmly.

"You want your call, you got it, buddy," the officer responded with authority.

He then took me from the cell to the phone in the next room by the booking desk, and I quickly chose my lawyer. They were kind enough to get his number for me.

"I've been arrested, and I'm in jail. I have no clue what the charges are, and I have not been read my rights," I blurted out to my lawyer. "Oh, and please call Debbie and let her know what has happened and please keep her informed."

My lawyer then asked to speak with the desk sergeant to get the details. After a few moments, they gave me the phone back.

"Frank," my lawyer said, "they're charging you with fraud and theft over $5,000 concerning a complaint from Danny's mother-in-law."

"Well, this is crazy. I didn't steal any money, and I didn't defraud her at all. I was a guarantor on a loan between her and her son-in-law," I answered directly.

"There's more, Frank. They are going to question you regarding a complaint from Paul Loach of Acura West regarding a lease transaction you were a party to at the dealership," the lawyer said with concern.

"I have no idea what that's about!"

"Also, you'll be transported to the Brantford jail for a bail hearing in the morning. Get a duty counsel and plead not guilty. Do not sign any statement. This is your first arrest, and you have no previous record, so you will be granted bail on your own recognizance, I suspect."

As my lawyer was about to hang up, I asked one big favour, "Please ask Debbie to find a way to come and get me in Brantford in the morning."

He responded, "I most definitely will, Frank."

As I hung up the phone, a very big detective entered the room and directed me to a questioning room.

He began asking me about a specific lease deal that I had sold to my own brother-in-law, married to Debbie's sister. He implied that I had forced the dealership to take his car as a trade at an unauthorized price and fudged the paperwork. I easily corrected his understanding and verbally proved the misrepresentation on the dealership's part. He quickly agreed with me and dropped the complaint, but did advise me that Paul Loach had filed the complaint, not the brother-in-law.

I couldn't believe what I had just heard. *How could Loach ever try such a thing? What did I ever do to him to make him do such a nasty thing to me? What a nice guy he is*, I thought. *When I get out of this mess, I'm going to give him a piece of my mind*, I kept telling myself.

As I left the detective's questioning office, there were two familiar faces anxiously awaiting my arrival by the booking desk. I immediately recognized them to be the same two officers that sat at the front of the courtroom in Brantford, when Patty and I had a hearing over child custody.

"Come with us, Frank. You're gonna take a little ride to Brantford," the two plainclothes detectives said with an arrogant tone and smug expressions on their faces. Police training must have classes on intimidation through expression. These two "one ball bobbies" had surely tried to scare me right from the get-go, but I, for some reason, did not buy into their attempt. Maybe because I kind of knew them, and they had never gained my respect. They both seemed to be the know-it-all types. I always had a disdain for these characters.

"Man, you have got this whole thing wrong. I didn't do anything that you are alleging," I stated firmly with some confidence.

"Yeah, that's what they all say when they are on their way to jail," the shorter, pudgier one responded coyly.

The ride to Brantford was swift and reflective for me. Thoughts of my marriage being over because of this event were sustained by thoughts of guilt for taking her away from Danny. Then anger for Danny setting me up like he did with his mother-in-law brought things back into perspective. I did not scheme to defraud anyone. If anything, Danny had planned this whole thing out using me to fleece his mother-in-law out of $20,000.

Why the hell did I get involved with that crook? Why did I let him convince me that he wanted to be my business partner and pay me the twenty grand as his?

More importantly, why did I not have a lawyer draft the partnership agreement like I had originally planned?

I couldn't afford the lawyer's fees! Now I'm facing serious charges for all these mistakes of judgment and a lack of money at the time.

When we arrived at the Brantford station, the detectives again tried to question me and ask me for a statement. I took the paper and wrote something to the effect of, "I did not steal any money, nor did I defraud this woman. I will make no further statement."

They then processed me and placed me in a cell for the remainder of the night.

The rest of the morning was a blur between eating a very dry egg sandwich, drinking coffee, and being placed in a holding cell at the courthouse.

The duty counsel did exactly what my London lawyer told me. At about 1:00 p.m., I was released on my own recognizance to face the outside of the system and a very cold day as I passed through the courthouse exit doors.

Waiting in her uncle's car on the curb in front of the courthouse was Debbie.

Chapter 20

The next six months were quite restrictive and filled with personal adjustments. I had to accept the fact that I had to fight for the first time to save my credibility in the eyes of the business community and in the mind and heart of my wife, Debbie.

The first thing I did was hire a lawyer I knew, Tom Brock, from Kitchener and a member of the Kinsmen club. Tom was a well-respected criminal lawyer, and he expressed to me a deep concern and understanding of my situation.

Everyone I knew had told me to retain a higher-profile Brantford lawyer instead of Tom. I would have a better chance to use the local inner circle than to bring in an outsider. At the time, I really didn't comprehend how the legal world really worked. On the surface, one thinks that lawyers are ruled rigidly by the law. The law is always at the basis and fundamental level of all cases, but what we do not know is that the outcome and your fate is decided between three parties huddled behind the courtroom walls—the judge, the defence attorney, and the Crown—unless you are subject to a jury trial.

Then there is a whole new set of rules. The decisions are predicated on how powerful the judge is. Does he like or dislike the case and defendant? Is the case a high-profile community case or is it a nagging pest that needs to be swept under the table? All cases are categorized, and as much as your defence attorney wants you to feel confident about their mysteriously chiselled credibility inside that courtroom, the following holds the trump card. The final demise or acquittal falls back on two key elements: Does the judge respect your defence attorney and has the judge worked together with them on a number of cases, and does the Crown fear and respect the historical win-loss record of the defence attorney? If there is a crack in any of those two prerequisites, then you are virtually doomed to the dungeons of the correctional system because you will lose every time.

Tom worked the system well, but admitted long into the case that he was like a duck out of the water dealing in Brantford. He had never tried a case there and knew no one on the Crown's side. All I could think while Tom explained his status was that I was screwed. The final nail in my coffin was at pretrial. Tom was embarrassing while questioning the witnesses. The judge was even laughing. Tom was so unprepared and so off base with some of his directive and leading deliberations . . . I could have defended myself better.

After pretrial, Tom sat me down and proposed I take a lesser charge offered by the Crown. One count of fraud and to be treated under the first-time young offender ruling, which would virtually bury my case and file. There was also the $20,000 debt to pay back and a fine in the amount of $4,000. I would only do one year of probation.

I took the deal.

Debbie said nothing to me about the charges and the outcome until the morning of sentencing. She had come to the courthouse with me that day and sat quietly in the back of the room. I was spoken to by the judge, and when the gavel was dropped, Debbie stood looking out of the window in the court while Tom and the Crown had their final words with me. I walked over to her and stood beside her. She just stared out the window.

"I am so sorry for all of this, Debbie," I said softly. "I had no choice but to take the deal. Do you understand what just went on today?" I asked, hoping for a comforting reaction from her.

There was no reply but silence as she continued to look out the window.

The weeks after were not easy for us. Debbie became more distant and elusive. She was spending a lot of time away from me, and I knew we were in trouble. I had long talks with my lawyer friend, Tim Jansen, who was assisting me in negotiating with my father to lend me the necessary funds to clear the debt.

"I think that if you ask Debbie to commit to six months of working on the marriage and not to leave or disrupt things by her disappearing acts, then you will have a chance to win her back, Frank," Tim suggested as a last-ditch effort to help me save the marriage.

I proposed the idea, and after a day of thinking about it, Debbie reluctantly agreed to hang in for no more than six months.

"I know life has not been easy for you, Frank, but I want to have a happy life, and up to now, things have not been good," she responded the next morning.

I retorted, "With all due respect, you have not made the past year and a half easy with your actions and goings-on behind my back either. But if we clear the decks and start over, we just might have a chance."

Debbie finally agreed to give it a try.

We had some extra money given to us by my father in an attempt to build a new beginning by buying a house with the hope that, after a few years, we could sell or refinance the house and return some equity to my father as repayment. He also paid off the court debt on my behalf.

I had finally got a job with Kitchener Nissan as a leasing manager and began stabilizing our income. We immediately moved from London to Kitchener and rented a house from a friend in a very nice neighbourhood.

Three months later, we bought a new house that would be built in Waterloo. I hoped Debbie would see hope and light. The house wouldn't be ready for at least six months, so I hoped that Debbie and I would have time to rebuild the marriage.

I came home one Thursday night to find a note on the fridge that read, "Went out with friends to a bar. Be home later."

I was somewhat startled at first because this was one of the many things we agreed not to do, but here we were again, right back to the beginning. I was very suspicious but thought maybe I should ride it out and not get too paranoid.

Ten o'clock came and went. Then twelve o'clock ticked by; one o'clock, two o'clock, three, four, five, and six o'clock struck, and that was it for me. I had been up all night, pacing the floor back and forth, worrying that she was not alright and, worse, that she was with another man.

I called her mother, her uncle, and her sister. No one had any idea where she was or could have gone. I knew that I had to wait another day before the police could get involved, but I still went down to the station and told the story. The desk sergeant was quite helpful and insightful.

"We see this type of thing almost daily, sir. The wife or the husband disappears for a few days, then they come home. Sometimes all is forgotten. Other times, it's the end of the marriage. I have to prepare you that we usually find these people shacked up with another person, and they do not want to get in touch with their spouse. All I'm saying," the sergeant summarized, "is be prepared for the worse scenario."

I thanked him and left the station feeling totally dejected and in despair.

I called my dad, and he hit me between the eyes. "Go to the bank and empty the bank accounts. Don't be surprised if she already has done that. Then go to Tim and change the title on the house. I think you should try to get out of the deal and save the money. Put it in trust with Tim if you can."

I immediately went to the bank and cleaned out the accounts. I then instructed her boss, the bank manager, about what was happening and asked that he have her call me or Tim when she got in or called.

I sat quietly in the house, getting angrier by the minute. Then finally, the next morning at about seven o'clock, I had waited long enough. I drove down to the bank where she worked and sat in the parking lot. Not five minutes went by, and there she was, walking right across in front of my car, rushing to work. I jumped out of the car and approached her. She wanted nothing to do with me, but I kept insisting that we meet at lunch and talk. She gave in and finally agreed to meet me.

I plotted out the conversation with a great deal of finesse. I was not going to waste time on who she was with or even argue about if she was with some other man. I felt that was a given. But what I was going to do was get her to stay put with me until the house was built. While I sat and waited for her to join me for lunch, I thought out all the ramifications if she left me for good, and I saw one major problem, closing the house deal. I needed her to co-sign the mortgage, forcing her to be equally legally responsible. I kept saying to myself, "Payback is a bitch, and she is not going to get away with this one. If this new guy wants her, he can have her, but she's going to him with a pile of debt.

"Be careful what you stick your dick in, buddy. You never know what you are going to get!" I chuckled to myself as Debbie arrived right on time.

"I am not going to question you and your whereabouts, Debbie. I know where you were and who you were with for the last three nights. You don't need to worry about me grilling you anymore. But I just want you to think about your commitment to me and the last one you gave me in front of my lawyer, Tim. Do you remember that one, and you signing the commitment for six months?

"You see, Debbie, it's one thing having an affair, but it is another going in front of a judge and facing infidelity and breach of a commitment of trust contract. I don't think any judge would look favourably or leniently on your plea or any reprieve of settlement. This is a tight place to be in, Debbie. You see . . . I am prepared to give you one more chance to make this marriage work. Only if you can honestly give it a shot . . . what do you think?" I finally asked.

Debbie sat through lunch, thinking about what I had said without speaking or answering my question. As we finished, she turned and looked at me for a few seconds and said, "I'll give you my answer tomorrow morning."

We slept in till about nine in the morning. Debbie decided to come home and stay the night. As we got dressed for a walk, she looked out the big bay window in the living room and then turned to me and said, "I'll stay and make this marriage work. No conditions or even promises. I'll stay and try, Frank."

Somehow, I wanted to believe her, but deep inside my gut, I knew better. My dad used to tell me about raising workhorses, and when you acquired them, the first thing you did was check their teeth, their gums, and then look in their eyes. If you see stars in their eyes, don't buy them because they are runaways by nature. Dad had said to me not long after I married Debbie that he looked into her eyes, and he saw stars.

"You got your work cut out for yourself, Frank," Dad had said.

He was right.

The house building got finished in late June 1989, and we began setting up like any new homeowner would. Family from both sides came over, and friends were always quite fun. I had bought into Beachwood Sun Tan and Tone Shop, located at the strip mall, as an additional business that would provide immediate cash flow. I agreed to do this in order to give Debbie something different to try and to change her environment, so she took a leave of absence from the bank and began her first venture as an entrepreneur. I owned the business on title and the bank account in order to protect Dad's investment. She didn't catch that one at first. It eventually became a very clear issue.

Christmas came, and we decided to go to London and spend the weekend with her parents. So, before we left, we went to the grocery store and got all sorts of food to assist in cooking the dinner. Debbie remembered she had forgotten something back at the house, so we returned and parked in the driveway. I left the lid of the trunk open where all the groceries were sitting and went inside to find what we had forgotten. I came out, shut the trunk, then proceeded to go to my sister's first, en route, and drop off a gift.

When we arrived, I popped open the lid of the trunk and found a big surprise. All of the groceries were gone. Debbie lost it! I couldn't believe she took it so hard, nor could I figure out where the groceries had gone. We began arguing over the missing groceries. I was convinced someone watched us scramble at the house and then ran up and took the groceries while we both went into the house. I had heard of this happening to other people in that neighbourhood. Debbie saw this as her spark to make my Christmas hell.

The rest of the trip was her yelling and screaming about how I never did anything for her family and that I was so insensitive about her family. It seemed after about an hour of this crazy stuff that she was enjoying giving me hell. I suspected something was up, and later in the week, the truth began to unravel.

The day after New Year's Eve, Debbie went to her uncle's in St. Thomas for the day on a Friday. By the Sunday morning, she hadn't returned again. I finally got a call from her on the Sunday afternoon, explaining she'd decided to stay at her uncle's for an extra couple of days. I'd finally had enough of her infidelity and lies, so I gave her a blasting over the phone and told her not to return again. If she wanted her belongings and clothes, she had better make an appointment.

The next morning, I got a call at about 7:30 a.m. from Debbie. "Hi . . . I called to say I'm sorry for everything. Uh, I'll be home in about three hours, okay?"

"No, it's not okay. I think we have trouble too big to fix right now." The phone was interrupted by a man on another extension, saying, "Talbot Plumbing, Talbot Plumbing."

"Who the hell are you?" I shouted.

"Who are you?" he shouted back.

"Debbie . . . who is this?" I screamed.

"That's just the other extension; it's something screwy with the line," Debbie said, trying lie her way out.

"Don't ever call me or come to my house again. Do you understand?" I shouted, and then hung up.

My dad had just arrived from Chatham to help me with the business accounting, and he'd heard the whole thing. He stood in the hallway and watched me crumble like I had just heard that someone had died. He came over to my side, put his hand on my shoulder, and tried to comfort me saying, "It's time to let her go, Frank. Stop the pain and bleeding now, before it's too late. She'll do more damage by you trying to get her back one more time. Let this new guy take over."

I knew he was right, and it was time . . . time to let go of all of her evil ways and usage of my good intentions. It was time to let go of her desire to gain other men's attention through sex. It was time for me to stand alone for a change and not rely on tradition, on having to have a wife to lean on in order to exist. It was time to be my own person as a man and take care of myself—something I had never done up to that point.

The rest of the week was a drunken blur for me. I couldn't stop hearing that guy's voice on the phone. I knew it was the person she was seeing. I couldn't stop imagining what he looked like or even what they would be doing in bed. I was haunted every time I tried to sleep.

My obsession got so bad I began drinking every day. I was focused on one thing and one thing only. I wanted to have sex with as many women as I could to try to get her out of my mind. I started hanging out with Tim, my lawyer, and Jerry Haufmyster, our friend. I began dating people I'd never thought I would be able to attract—real estate agents, social workers, accountants, and lawyers. They were all interested in one thing:

sex without consequence or conscience. They were all going through what I had experienced in some way or form, and concluded that open, free sex without commitment was the best drug of choice to suppress the pain and suffering our ex-partners had inflicted upon us.

One by one, my new girlfriends would be seen by my next-door neighbour. They would come up to my front door, walk in sometime in the evening, and leave in the same clothes in the early morning hours. My dad was told of my every move and of the flow of "Legs," as my dad sarcastically remarked in response to the suspicious neighbours' reports.

Debbie and I began to talk after a number of weeks of non-communication and my copious quantities of faceless fornication and wild orgies. We finally calmed down, and I allowed her access to get her things. We had our last talk, and she agreed to sign off the business and walk away from the house, asking for nothing in return. We met again at Tim's office, where she signed off for the last time and went her way to live in London, Ontario.

I sat that last day in the living room, and as I looked out the window, I committed to myself that I was never going to get married again. I had failed for the last time.

Chapter 21

I had perceived and accepted that my marriages had failed one way or the other as a result of my actions, reactions, state of mind, and of course, failures. I also accepted that these failures were ultimately a result of my infidelities and evil thoughts, words, and deeds as professed by my faith in Catholicism. I was an abomination in the eyes of the church and invariably in mine. I was useless to society; I had contributed nothing of any significance to this world except the birth of my two beautiful boys. They were my "candle in the window."

In the end, and up to this time, all that my ex-partners had done to me was immaterial. So, in essence, they all got away scot-free, got what they set out to get, and were standing in their glory in victory! One more man slaughtered and sent to hell! That's how I felt at that time, and nothing was going to change my state of mind.

The next disaster was when I tried to hook up with my business manager, who was running the Beachwood Sun Tan and Tone Shop. Beryl was a few years older than me, but she was a hot cougar! She was recently divorced and was as well a friend of my lawyer, Tim. We would sleep together, but she wouldn't let me have sex with her. I could touch her, but no penetration. When she would get the urge to go further with me, she would call Tim on the phone and ask him if he would give her permission, to which he always said, "No!"

Then one night, when all the shop's staff had gotten together for dinner out at our favourite restaurant, Beryl announced that due to her not being paid what was owed to her, she had taken legal action through my own lawyer, Tim. She said he had been her counsel before me, which gave her non-conflict rights to take over the shop in lieu of non-payment of monies due to her. By this time, my leasing business was flat, and I was relying on the cash flow from the shop to survive. It wasn't working. I then decided to go along with Beryl's action and let her have it for $1. I just couldn't fight anymore. She went after me to get the shop, and she got it. I'm sure my lawyer had something to do with her tactic because she couldn't have thought of how to corner me like that even if she had been fucking me all the while.

I knew I was in a spiral downward and where I was going to end up was far from reality. I wasn't able to sleep anymore. All I was thinking and focused on was carrying on as if my life was going great and I was financially independent. I kept telling myself to think as if I had endless access to money and to present myself to everyone in that light. The truth was I owed the bank $20,000, my credit lines were maxed out, my sources of income had dried up, and people were calling me daily for money. I had purchased a 1984 Porsche 944 sports car some weeks before through a bank loan, and I was unable to make the payments on time, but because my father had co-signed the loan, the bank was giving me time to get back on track. My sisters were beside themselves and began threatening me, telling me that I had to repay Dad all the money he had forked out on my behalf. The worst of it all was that I'd had my father guarantee the mortgages on my house. I was far behind in the payments and the taxes, not to mention the utilities.

I was left with no choice but to put the house up for sale. My timing was no help. Interest rates in 1990 were soaring through the roof, making the real estate market a distress seller's nightmare. No one wanted my house because the mortgage was over the fair market value, leaving me in a no-win position. I was totally tanked mentally and saw no light at the end of the tunnel for me. No one would hire me because of my lack of trade or profession. The job market was starting to fill nothing but with skilled labour opportunities. I had no construction background and no insight into starting something new.

My friend Stan Sherman started to drop by and check in on me. He began including me on some of his nights out to self-help meetings and men's therapy gatherings. He was going through a rough patch with his wife, and he found himself sourcing out extramarital encounters. What he really wanted from me was a wingman to justify his nightly escapes prowling the bars. I fell into the trap and began the walk into the abyss of self-destruction. Night after night, we would meet the same type of women, searching for distraction and the touch of a new adventure in the night as they tried to run from their own misery-riddled lives. Divorcees, disgruntled wives on the brink of separation, lonely widows, and of course, the black widows, preying on the men willing to give it all up to get into their beds at all costs.

Every encounter was a challenge where I felt superior and allowed the dark side of Frank to emerge. I went from forlorn to this imaginary person that had it all together and had all the right answers that these women actually wanted to hear. I learned fast, and I got really good at it. I was rarely shut out or rejected by my prospective bedmates. I asked for nothing but their time and sexual happenstance. They always ended up wanting more. They had no fear of me having a lack of discretion because they were confident that I would not disclose our affair, and they were safe from potential STDs. I was fortunate because at thirty-eight years old, I functioned and looked as if I were no older than twenty-eight, and I was very athletic and physically fit.

During all of this bohemian revelry, my children's mother was kicked out of her latest boyfriend's house along with my boys. I got a call from her late one Friday night, asking me to help them and come get them. She was calling from a phone booth in Brantford. He had thrown all their belongings out on the front lawn, locked the door, and refused them entry. Her family refused to help and let them have shelter. One thing I can say was no matter what was going on in my life, my boys always came first. I could not let them suffer for a second. I couldn't let my ex-wife suffer either. She was their mother, There was no question about it.

When I arrived at the gas station where the three of them were waiting, I realized I had let them down to be in this position. It was my fault that they were homeless. Even though Patty and I had been divorced for three years, and I had just gone through a recently collapsed third marriage, and now I was losing my house, I had no choice or even the thought of second-guessing what I was about to do. I had recently borrowed a couple of thousand dollars from a contact of mine and was going to pay down my mortgage arrears, but now planned a different approach. I needed to get Patty and the boys stable. We went to her boyfriend's house, picked up all of their belongings off the front yard, and put them in the back of the Porsche. I even strapped their bikes to my roof. What a sight that must have been, going down the road loaded up with all these belongings in and on a very expensive sports car. These were my kids I was taking care of; no one mattered but them. I drove to my soon-to-be foreclosed house, but I didn't care even though I knew I'd soon be evicted. The heat was on, and the hydro hadn't been cut yet. It was fully furnished, and they all would be safe.

The next day, Patty and I agreed to take the boys to a movie that would last for four hours. This would give us time to go to Brantford and look for an apartment for them to move into and settle.

We made application after application and were rejected at every turn. I could see no end to this pattern until we read in the paper about assisted housing for single mothers. We got an appointment, filled out the application, and had to wait for answers to be given by Monday. That worked because we needed to get the boys in school by Monday morning.

"Dad, are we going to have a house in Brantford, so we don't have to drive this far every day?" Daren asked.

Tears filled my eyes, and my heart clenched as I searched for an answer. "Yes, you can count on it, Daren!" I responded with confidence, hiding my own fears.

Patty just sat and looked out the window. She couldn't even try to say anything. She knew too that she'd let them down as much as I had. She knew that her being accepted into the housing program was a real gamble.

"Well, I have good news for you, Patty! You have been accepted, and you can move in this coming weekend. Frank, you will have to co-sign and provide a $100 security on the utilities."

"No problem," I responded.

When the boys heard the news, they were very excited and relieved. I saw something of great value in those two little guys during that whole affair. They had an unbelievable amount of inner strength and confidence in their mother and me. They counted on us pulling through, no matter what was confronting us. They stated that weekend that they knew I would be there for them because I'd promised them, and I had always been there in times of trouble. They understood their mother and I could not live together all the time and saw the importance of the way we were. They said many times since that event that every event, good or bad to them, was an adventure, not a struggle, because we never allowed them to feel the struggle even though they admitted they knew what it was doing to us. God blessed me through my boys!

Chapter 22

I decided to give Patty and the boys all my furniture to give them their duly deserved start to a new life. Patty was able to get mother's allowance benefits, which put the icing on the cake for them, and me as well, as they were totally relieved. Within days, I could see a whole new picture being created.

Now I had to rebuild.

I spent the next weekend helping them move in and set up their new home. Patty allowed me to stay with them as long as I wanted, with no prerequisites and conditions. She gave back by giving me a chance to do what I had to do to get my life in order.

While I was sitting in their place one morning, I began playing the keyboard that I had bought for them the previous Christmas. It was a good one I'd found at a music store. Roland had just released a basic version called Juno-2, which produced studio-quality sound. I spent most of that day fumbling around with it. I also had my acoustic guitar and fiddled with it. I found peace playing, and the boys enjoyed watching me put songs together.

"I think you should join a band again, Frank!" Patty stated between songs. "As long as I have known you, music has always been your favourite pastime. Remember when you played with Copperfield before Daren was born? You were really good! Maybe you should find a band and try out. At least you can make a few dollars, and you might enjoy the break from business for a while. Maybe something new may come of it."

Ironically, that night, while reading the local newspaper, I came across an article promoting a home-grown musician looking to put a professional band together. His name was Greg Zaluski. His telephone number was listed in the paper, so without pondering and procrastinating, I called.

"Greg, this is Frank Trousdell. I just read your article, and I would like to audition for your band."

"Frank who?" he answered with a chuckle.

"Trousdell, I used to play for the Danny Thompson Band and a few others," I responded.

Greg hesitated then with a loud, "Holy fuck . . . where have you been?" he blurted out. "I know you . . . you play keyboards and sing, right?"

"Yes, that's me," I joyfully responded.

"Man . . . yeah, I would be very interested in you playing with us. I have Harry Rich on lead, and my drummer comes from Tennessee. I'm playing second lead guitar, mandolin, and lead vocals. We'll be rehearsing in the Paris, Ontario fair grounds works building this Tuesday. Can you make it?" Greg asked

"I'll be there . . . see you then," I responded and hung up.

"Just like that," I said to Patty.

"You always find a way to get yourself going," she responded with confidence.

"What do you think of your dad playing in a band, guys?" I asked my boys with a big smile.

Mike, my youngest, jumped up and said, "Cool, Dad! Can we come and watch?"

"When you are allowed, son, but yes!"

By then, I had emptied as much as I could from the house in Waterloo. My mom and dad came down without my knowledge and had a garage sale, selling off the rest of my personal things. They then let the house go to power of sale. Another chapter was closed. I had to close my mind from the pain and embarrassment I was suffering, watching my mom and dad clean up the mess I had left. My dad was seventy-six, and he was not in good health. He was suffering from heart disease and was not doing well at all. But he was bound and bent to help me from falling any further. I learned later from my mother that he'd feared I would totally give up and consider suicide.

He wasn't far from the truth. Every day I fought with all the inner strength that I could muster to keep going and slough off the arrows of defeat. The band opportunity was all I had left to look forward to as I tried to re-mould my existence, self-worth, and confidence.

Greg welcomed me with great optimism, introducing me to the members of the band. I was a little overweight, had shorter hair than the other guys, and, of course, I was older. My dress was very much out of sync. They wore tight-fitting blue jeans with T-shirts. I was in dress slacks, a sweater, and a preppy-style shirt with Rebook running shoes. What a nightmarish first impression.

"Okay, let's start by playing something we all know," Greg announced. "How about Steve Earl's 'The Other Kind'," he directed and then stared right at me.

"What key are we doing this in?" I asked.

Everyone turned and looked at me as if to say, "You don't know this song?"

I immediately got the message. They were Steve Earl fanatics. We were going to play every Steve Earl song that he wrote. I was somewhat familiar with his style, but I had no idea how the songs went. So, I acted like nothing was out of the ordinary, and I would play it anyway.

The band kicked in, and I instantly found the sound needed and got the cord pattern down by the third verse.

I was away to the races.

After the second run-through, Greg looked at Harry and smiled, then turned to me and said, "If you can tighten up on the highs and lows, you got it, man!"

Harry then responded, "I remember you when you played with Danny Thompson. I thought you were great! That honky-tonk thing you did made that band. Do you remember how to do that riff again?"

I smiled and did a little bit of it, and Harry yelled, "That's what I was telling you guys about! He's the one!"

Shivers ran through my body upon hearing Harry accept me with such adulation. I could feel everyone else relax as if for them to say, "We have a band now."

"I'll give you a cassette with every song we're going to play, Frank. I want you to have down five songs for tomorrow night's practice. You okay with that?" he asked politely.

"I will have it, Greg. No problem," I answered with confidence, but deep inside, I had no clue whether I could do it.

Every night for the next two weeks, we rehearsed, and I must say we got really tight, and it did sound great. Greg possessed a vocal sound that imaged Steve Earl almost to the letter. Harry was the best lead guitar player I had ever played with, and I found his style easy to follow. Harry had a way to make everyone look and sound great!

The only downside was the bass player was not getting the songs right, and he was beginning to lose interest, so before we knew it, Greg brought in a new bass player named Craig McMillan.

Craig was a bit of a sore thumb at first because he weighed in at 300 pounds. It didn't bother me very much because through his shyness rose a phoenix in the form of outstanding skill, sound, and texture. He was college-trained and jazz was his love. That might seem odd for a southern rock band but, actually, it fit perfectly. He could fill in notes that anyone of us missed or played wrong.

Craig and I hit it off instantly, mainly because we both knew we were the odd men out when it came to the band's image. I was the old guy, and he was the fat guy.

Greg started to bring in his honeys to practice, trying to show off to them his new project. Harry was on the verge of getting married, so he was not into lady chasing. The drummer from the south was Greg's wingman, so they carried the magnet of sex appeal. My nature rose through very quickly and wanted a part of the women games. So, I started to let my hair grow and begged, borrowed, and bought a new style of dress. I was reinvented as a rock star bad boy. I wore the jeans, T-shirts, leather jackets, and infamous cowboy boots. I began losing the belly and got in better shape. I found playing was exercise enough to drop twenty-five pounds within the first month. Of course, my diet was limited. There was always beer and partying. Everywhere we went after practice, we were known as the new Greg Zaluski band. Not soon after, we agreed on a name, which Greg insisted on us wearing.

The Other Kind! Go figure . . . his mentor Steve Earl's favourite hit song.

Not long after, we were playing in front of Brantford crowds, and it became very apparent how well known Greg really was in that community. The first three gigs, we sold out to over 300 people each night. We all were very excited and looked to Greg as the true leader of the band. I felt that he really had it, and we were the next best thing since Honeymoon Suite had hit the scene some five years earlier. They were out of Niagara Falls, Ontario, and made it large worldwide.

Harry knew them well back in Honeymoon's fledgling beginnings. He had played for them with the full intention of being a long-term member. When they got the industry nod, Harry was removed and replaced by the current lead guitarist. The story goes that the new guy got his parents to fund their big first launch. "The money bought him a place in history," Harry would sneer.

"Frank, it's Greg. . . I need you to come to the house right now."

I could tell in Greg's voice there was a problem, and we needed to talk.

"I'll be right there," I responded with concern.

When I arrived at his parents' house, I found Greg sitting in a chair in his living room. There was a pillow under his right arm, which was bandaged up to his elbow. He just sat there, looking like his life was over.

"What the hell happened to you?" I asked in shock.

"I dropped a glass street light shade on the rig at work, and it sliced my wrist. It cut through the muscle, nerves, and scored the bone. I'm finished," he said with a very shaky voice.

"Is that what the doctor said, Greg?" I asked.

"No, not in those words, but I'm not to do anything that will move the nerves or muscles for eight weeks. Then we'll see if I can ever play guitar again."

I began telling him stories of sports people I knew who had gone through therapy and come back to play just as well as they had before. I tried everything in the book to motivate him and uplift his spirits. I learned very quickly that someone who has suffered trauma to that extent does not want to hear someone trying to convince them they will be okay and will get back to normal. I promised Greg that I would see him every day and if there was something he needed to get done or whatever he needed, I was his mule. He laughed and then joked.

"I might need you to take care of all my girlfriends for a while."

"I'm in," I chuckled, trying to imply I knew he was kidding. "You would, wouldn't you . . . you old dirt bag."

"Man, what are we going to do?" I asked him.

He replied, "You mean what are *you* going to do? This has been a long journey for you, and now I've just fucked it up. Harry's got his machine shop career, Craig can sub in with other bands, but you need to keep going."

Greg then asked, "Do you think you can do a solo gig, Frank? Have you got enough material?"

I thought for a moment and then responded, "I did solo back in the late seventies in Kitchener. I could put the material together and use my new keyboard I just got that has a drum track. Yeah . . . I can do it," I answered positively.

He smiled and said, "That's what you are going to do. I'll hook you up with all my solo gigs and get you in. Now get the fuck out of here and get to work. I want you ready by next weekend. I have a gig coming up at the Poor Folks Deli downtown, and you will be my replacement."

"Okay," I responded, and with great excitement, I left to go and practice.

With only seven days' breathing space, I worked my butt off, putting together forty songs that I could get away with playing by myself. Needless to say, I worked up all the songs we had in The Other Kind's setlist that came easily for me on the guitar. I was not a lead player, so everything had to be chord-related, and I had to express the song through my singing ability. My voice had to be my hook. I worked hard those seven days and found myself, ready or not, setting up that afternoon at the Deli.

The gig went very well, and the crowd was enthusiastic. I was reborn. *I am now a musician,* I thought as I went to sleep that night. The crowd liked me, I didn't make too many mistakes, and I got paid $200. *If I could do these three or four nights a week, I could be fine. This is the beginning of a very exciting life.*

The thought did become a reality. I was able to work at least three to four nights a week, and I was becoming well known throughout the area.

I needed a name to promote as my marquee. Frank Trousdell was not catchy, nor was the thought that there were still bill collectors out there looking for me. I could hide behind a pseudonym. Being I was paid in cash, no one would know any different.

That's when Franklyn Alexander was created. My real name is Franklyn John Alexander Trousdell, so I took my first and third name, trying to pattern Elton John style.

On the next billing, I arrived to find "Franklyn Alexander here tonight live." It felt good and somehow uncannily safe.

I performed for six months as a solo act. Harry would come out with Craig McMillan and sometimes Greg to see me play. Harry would get up and jam with me, which added even more of a show. I got really comfortable being the headline and singing forty songs a night. The money was gratefully appreciated.

"I've been rehearsing, Frank, and the arm is a little stiff, but it's working! My fingers are sore. They'll callus up quickly," Greg announced over the phone.

"Awesome," I replied. What's your plan?"

"We go to rehearsal next week," Greg directed as if to hear any hesitation in my response.

"No problem," I responded. I did have reservations, but I felt we would not be playing for a few weeks, so my solo gigs were safe for the time being.

Greg started soloing as well to get his chops back. He recovered extremely fast. Faster than I had thought, but I fell in line with the process. Within three weeks, we as a band were out knocking on doors and getting gigs. Greg lined up a rock promoter, Carlos DeBatista from Hamilton, who was also the leader of the horn band POWERHOUSE, a well-known band with a number of hit singles in the seventies. Carlos began booking us in a number of rock rooms throughout Southwestern Ontario but kept us somewhat close to home at first.

We picked up where we'd left off. Rooms got full every night. Owners loved us, and we got tighter. The fun got out of control somewhat, and the women and booze flowed like water. I slowly became not the old man anymore but the co-magnet. I found playing keyboard had intrigue to it in the crowd's eyes. I was getting as much attention as Greg. Overnight, he started to change his attitude toward me. He became a little challenging and stand-offish. I felt he thought I was stepping into his territory, and he felt threatened.

I began introducing original material that I had written. Harry loved the pieces and wanted to work them into our show. Greg was totally against it.

"We are a clone band, Steve Earl Band. We cannot play originals unless they are mine," Greg would respond in a resounding controlling voice.

"Okay . . . bring in your originals, and we will work them up. Isn't that what we are leading to anyway?" I would add.

Then I saw the problem. Greg would immediately show fear at the thought of producing his own originals. He showed a complete lack of confidence in his ability to write a song. I had found my home in writing. I wanted to be a songwriter and have the band play my songs. Greg would have nothing to do with this notion.

The tension continued about Greg not wanting to do originals. Then one night in a Brantford club, a guy walked up to me and asked if he could talk to me. I responded, "Yes."

"So, I've been watching for the last couple of nights, and you seem to have a great flare on the keys, and your voice is out of this world," he stated.

"With all due respect . . . who are you?" I asked.

"My name's Fraser Yates. I'm a producer, and I have a songwriter's studio in town. I'd like to work with you, if you are interested."

"Interested . . . when do you want to start?" I asked with excitement and enthusiasm.

"How much material have you got?" he asked.

"I've got about twenty songs, but I have four that Harry and I have been working on," I replied.

"Bring what you got to the studio Monday, okay?" he asked with a smile.

I felt something very positive about him, and I had to try this new thing called recording. I knew I would learn a lot just by being there, so there was nothing to lose.

The first session went really well, and I felt very much at home in the studio and working with Fraser. He had a way about him, making you feel relaxed and focused. His musicianship was exceptional, and he was acutely aware of his recording equipment, its functionality, and how to get the most out of all of his instruments. He taught me as we progressed what made things work and how to get more of what I was attempting to do with my guitar and voice. Fraser probed me to dig deep inside and express through my instrument what I was trying to play. His interpretation of the score was complementary to my version. I felt by the time we completed four songs that we had something. If anything, I was very pleased with the experience.

I presented my songwriter's tapes to the band, and to my expectations, everyone but Greg was very supportive. Greg was intimidated and felt I was breaching his expected loyalty by doing my own project. He blatantly refused to allow any of my tunes to be included in our setlist. I felt confused and disappointed. The drummer from Tennessee, named Craig, decided he'd had enough and wanted to go home. We talked one night, and he asked me what I thought he should do.

"When you know you have to break up with your girlfriend, but you don't know how to do it or what to say, it's very painful. I feel like I'm living a lie," Craig expressed to me as we stood outside of the practice hall, looking at the stars and clear sky.

"I want to stay for the sake of the band, and I feel like I'm letting you all down by wanting to go back home. I feel like a quitter, man. What would you do, Frank?" Ken asked like a little boy asking his dad for advice.

I took a big drag from my cigarette, looked up, and thought for a few seconds. "You know in your heart what you really want to do . . . see, I've learned that if you stop at a road crossing and you have to think about which way is the right way to go . . . your mind is saying turn left, and you feel your body pulling you to the left, but your heart keeps saying, 'Go straight' . . . then I say get off the road. Take some time to figure out what you really need to do. We, as humans, weigh in too much about the heart and the mind thing, Ken; we do not take time to look at the practical side of things. You're a very good drummer, but you and I know this band thing is a very big gamble, especially for a guy your age. You're twenty-five, right? Well, what are your options? What have you got going if this band folds one day? Do you have something to fall back on? You have to analyze these things. Do you have time to play out the band journey to its end, or do you need to make the change now?"

"I know the answer, Frank. You just helped me cement my decision. I have to go home. I've got to go back to college this coming fall and complete my teacher's degree. That's what I have to do. I just don't know how to tell Greg without hurting his feelings," Ken said. You could see his emotions swelling as he explained his concerns.

"Just take Greg aside, look him in the eye with honesty, and tell him what you just told me. He's a big boy, and he will understand. You won't lose any of our friendship. These are things that we will face for the rest of our lives," I said to Ken reassuringly.

So, the rest of the next two weeks was filled with working in our new drummer, Ron Lampky.

To our surprise, Ron was unbelievably amazing. You could close your eyes and hear John Cougar Mellencamp's drummer playing. It took us one practice to get him up to speed.

So away we went, gigging around Brantford and Southwestern Ontario.

I was asked to participate in a fireman's fundraising show in Paris, Ontario, one night in April 1991. The auction was designed around a male auction, with the crowd being women. I was to be sold to the highest bidder. My activity on stage was to sing for my supper, and then the women would bid. The highest bidder got to take me out on a date and have me do what they wanted of me. I was asked to participate by a girlfriend, who was a reporter for the local Paris newspaper. We had a deal that she was not to let anyone outbid her. In return, I would cook for her. Well, it didn't quite go our way. As the bidding got underway, the action was immediately a flurry of bids. Within seconds they were raising the price over $200. I kept looking at my friend, and she kept bidding until it hit $300. She raised her hands up, and she quit bidding, shaking her head as to say, "I'm done. I can't go any higher."

There were three more women spread out across the room, pushing the price, and then the auctioneer finally hammered down and announced the winner. From the back of the room, a sexy, long-legged, shapely, black-haired, olive-skinned lady appeared from the crowd to claim her prize. We were ushered to the side of the room, and then she was introduced to me as Janice O'Neil, a schoolteacher from Brantford.

"So, what grade do you teach?" I asked.

"I'm the librarian, but I teach grades two to grade eight at Greenbrier Public School." Janice spoke with a firm, pleasant, and confident tone, not too loud. Her smile was infectious, and she carried her presence with a pinch of superiority. If you were a student in her class, you would be feeling very much alive and wanting to gain her attention all the time. If you slacked off, her wrath would be immediately felt by every bone in your body.

"Well, you won me . . . now, what would you like me to do for you?" I coyly asked with a touch of male sexuality.

"She Hummed . . ." Janice replied with a big grin on her face. She hesitated for a moment, then she asked me if I would like to see a Collin James concert on Thursday night.

I replied quickly, accepting her invitation.

We made our arrangements to meet at the front door of the concert auditorium in Hamilton and parted company.

I look back, and I amaze myself as to how I survived this period. But I did. I lived my life as if I was sitting at a blackjack table with limited funds, thinking I would beat the house, yet I kept losing every time. Albert Einstein's theory of insanity, how alcoholics manage to exist, is they have an ego the size of an elephant and self-esteem the size of a flea while they sit on a barstool, watching their own personal movie, where they are the star, projecting in their own mind. This is how they deflect or hide their defects, by submerging into this deep-seated mind video of their brilliance and highly complicated intellect. I sit here today, writing about it all, and trying to make sense of it. The answer is . . . you can't. The good news is I am alive, and as Gary Clewely, one of my defence lawyers, once said to me, "Check for bullet holes," as he patted his chest. Great. There are none? There ya go, you'll live another day!"

But this unbelievable life only got crazier. Survival and desperation were each day's challenge, eventually on a world-class level. *The Adventures of Franky Fabs* continues in Volume Two, divulging my rise and the fall of the world business travel business that led to Canadian Secret Intelligence Service intervention, life and death confrontations, and survival of it all to new beginnings of hope and faith.

Get a copy and read more of my life and times in
The Adventures of Franky Fabs Volume 2!

CPSIA information can be obtained
at www.ICGtesting.com
Printed in the USA
BVHW080959071222
653410BV00006B/209/J